D1206718

THE POLITICS OF DEPRESSION

Samuel T. McSeveney

THE POLITICS OF DEPRESSION

Political Behavior in the Northeast, 1893–1896

NEW YORK OXFORD UNIVERSITY PRESS 1972

Library of Congress Catalogue Card Number: 72-85823

Printed in the United States of America

To

My Mother, my Father, and Sandy

Preface

> Even the most fleeting inspection of American elections suggests the existence of a category of elections in which voters are, at least from impressionistic evidence, unusually deeply concerned, in which the extent of electoral involvement is relatively quite high, and in which the decisive results of the voting reveal a sharp alteration of the pre-existing cleavage within the electorate. Moreover, and perhaps this is the truly differentiating characteristic of this sort of election, the realignment made manifest in the voting in such elections seems to persist for several succeeding elections. *All these characteristics cumulate to the conception of an election type in which the depth and intensity of electoral involvement are high, in which more or less profound readjustments occur in the relations of power within the community, and in which new and durable electoral groupings are formed.*[1]

Thus did the late V. O. Key, Jr., define "critical elections." Duncan MacRae, Jr., and James C. Meldrum subsequently modified Key's concept by suggesting the central importance of critical *periods* (i.e., series of elections) rather than critical elections.[2] In formulating his definition, Key studied the presidential elections of 1896 and 1928 in New England. For their part, MacRae and Meldrum analyzed a series of elections that included those of 1896 and 1928 in Illinois. By either definition, the 1890s emerge as a period of political realignment deserving of close analysis by historians.

Historians have written at length on the politics of the 1890s, but for the most part they have analyzed neither the pattern of political behavior before the critical period nor the dynamics of change that deeply and lastingly altered that pattern during the critical period. Rather, they have generally focused on the agrarian unrest that found expression first in the People's or Populist party and ultimately in the Democratic party, and on the climactic and most dramatic episode of the turbulent period, the presidential campaign and election of 1896. Such studies have captured the distress of staple-producing farmers in the South and on the Plains, the plight of silver mining interests in the Rocky Mountains, and the consequent coming together of the agrarian and free silver movements. Basically sympathetic to those vanquished rather than to those victorious in the presidential election of 1896, they have played up the handicaps of the Democratic-Populist coalition and William Jennings Bryan and played down the positive appeal of the Republican party and William McKinley.[3]

At the same time, considerable evidence exists to suggest that if we are to understand the lasting significance of the political upheaval of the 1890s, we must view the period from a different perspective. To begin with, political discontent was by no means confined to the South and West. On the contrary, fully two-thirds of the congressional districts that changed hands during the 1890s lay to the north and east of the regions of acute agrarian discontent.[4] Similarly, the decisive shifts toward the Democrats in the electoral vote in 1892 and toward the Republicans in that of 1896 occurred east of the Mississippi River and north of the Ohio River and Mason and Dixon's Line. Within this populous area where the fortunes of the major parties shifted so decisively, Democratic gains at the beginning of the decade were reversed with a vengeance by the Republicans following the onset of economic depression in 1893. Though the presidency changed party hands in 1892 and 1896, the congressional political pendulum swung to its furthest extremes in the midterm elections of 1890 and 1894, neither of which has received its due attention from historians.[5] (See Table 1.) Clearly, major shifts in political allegiances occurred before the presidential election year of

TABLE 1 *Representatives Elected to Congress, 1888–1896 (Fifty-first through Fifty-fifth Congresses), Selected Regions*

Region	1888 D	1888 R	1890 D	1890 R	1892 D	1892 R	1894 D	1894 R	1896 D	1896 R
New England[a]	3	23	12	14	8	19	1	26	1	26
Middle Atlantic[b]	25	44	39	30	36	36	6	66	8	64
East North Central[c]	26	48	55	19	44	34	2	76	18	60

Source: U.S., Congress, House, *Biographical Directory of the American Congress, 1774–1949 . . .*, 81st Cong., 2nd sess., House Doc. 607 (Washington, D.C.: Government Printing Office, 1950).

D=Democratic, R=Republican.

[a]Connecticut, Maine, Massachusetts, New Hampshire, Rhode Island, Vermont.

[b]New Jersey, New York, Pennsylvania.

[c]Illinois, Indiana, Michigan, Ohio, Wisconsin.

1896. The Republicans' repeated victories between the Panic of 1893 and Bryan's capture of the Democratic presidential nomination three years later suggest that we have been exaggerating the role played by the Nebraskan and his agrarian followers in the decline of the Democratic party. Further, without in the least disregarding the weaknesses of the Democratic party during the depression of 1893, we should seek a fuller understanding of the strengths of the Republican party, for in successive elections the Republicans triumphed over the disparate Democratic coalitions led by Grover Cleveland and William Jennings Bryan. Finally, the story of the Populist revolt should not be permitted to obscure the less dramatic but far more central political development of the 1890s—the forging of a durable national hegemony by the Republicans. The People's party lost its identity following fusion with the Democratic party in 1896. The Republican party emerged from the mid-1890s so powerful that except for elections from 1910 through 1916 it was to dominate American politics until the Great Depression of 1929.

The present study focuses on three contiguous urban-industrial states in the Northeast—Connecticut, New York, and New Jersey. A number of considerations underlie the choice of this bloc.

The geographical area within which the Republican party registered decisive gains during the 1890s is too large and varied to permit any intensive analysis of election returns and data relating to the socio-economic and cultural composition of the electorate, and such an analysis is essential if one is to measure continuities and discontinuities in voting behavior during a period of political flux. Concentration on Connecticut, New York, and New Jersey permits close study.[6] It further provides an opportunity to trace the disintegration of powerful Democratic coalitions that had battled the Republicans on better than even terms prior to 1893. (In all other New England and Middle Atlantic states, the Republican party had been dominant in the pre-depression period.) Finally, the study of three states permits one to deal with the interaction between national politics and grass-roots politics in a particular setting. Historians have too frequently dismissed state and local politics as unimportant or, at best, as national politics in microcosm.[7] But analysis of late-nineteenth-century popular voting behavior suggests that that behavior was rooted in the group experience of religious, ethnic, and racial communities, and that national issues (e.g., the currency, the tariff, governmental corruption, and civil service reform) neither shaped the original political identification of most voters nor, except under unusual circumstances, altered that identification. The depression of 1893 and the national issues arising out of that depression did contribute to major shifts among voters during 1893–96, but even during hard times, ethnic, religious, and racial factors continued to influence popular voting behavior and politics on the state and local levels. As a consequence, this work deals with cultural, as well as economic, factors in "the politics of depression."

Many individuals and institutions provided me with invaluable assistance and encouragement during the researching and writing of this book. I am pleased to have this opportunity to thank them for their contributions to my work.

I began my study of the 1890s under Samuel P. Hays at the University of Iowa. Christopher Lasch, who directed the writing of my doctoral dissertation, and the other members of my doctoral committee, were both kind and penetrating in their criticisms thereof; William O. Aydelotte was particularly helpful in this regard. I am profoundly grateful to Professor Hays, now at the University of Pittsburgh, both for his encouragement and for his suggestions that gave direction to my revision of the earlier manuscript.

I am deeply indebted to the Social Science Research Council, whose fellowships alone made possible my pre-doctoral research training program at Columbia University and my research in the Northeast. Subsequently, the Los Angeles State College Foundation and Hyman Kublin, then Associate Dean of Graduate Studies of the City University of New York, awarded me small grants that lightened the financial burden of research in various locations.

Among the scholars who generously shared their time, insights, and research with me at various points were Lee Benson, Thomas N. Brown, Howard E. Conklin, Elmer E. Cornwell, Jr., Michael Ebner, Fred M. Heath, John Higham, the late V. O. Key, Jr., Paul Kleppner, William E. Leuchtenburg, Father Robert F. McNamara, Edward M. Miles, Mary Cobb Nelson, Jiri Nehnevajsa, Dennis Palumbo, John W. Pratt, Ruth C. Silva, the late Festus P. Summers, and Albert E. Van Dusen. Richard Polenberg took time to comment on my manuscript, as did Joel Silbey, whose collaboration and friendship over the years have meant much to me. I bear full responsibility for all errors of commission and omission.

I am grateful to the Roman Catholic Archdiocese of New York, Diocese of Albany, and Diocese of Rochester for permission to cite their archives; to James Marshall for permission to cite the Louis Marshall Papers; to Jack I. Straus for permission to cite the Isidor Straus Papers; to the Columbia University Libraries for permission to quote from the [George] Frederick W. Holls Papers; to the Connecticut Historical Society for permission to quote from the O. Vincent Coffin Papers; to The Cooper Union for permission to cite the Abram S. Hewitt Papers; to the heirs of Whitelaw Reid and the Manuscript Division of the Library of Congress for permission to quote from the Whitelaw Reid Papers; to the Yale University Library for permission to quote from the Baldwin Family Papers and the Beer Family Papers; and to the *Journal of Politics* for permission to quote from V. O. Key, Jr., "A Theory of Critical Elections," XVII (February 1955), 3–4.

Librarians and archivists across the nation proved unfailingly courteous and helpful to me. In particular, I wish to thank those at the American Jewish Archives, Brooklyn College, the Brooklyn Public Library, Columbia University, the Library of Congress, the Connecticut Historical Society, Cornell University, the Henry E. Huntington Library, the California State College at Los Angeles, the Los Angeles Public Library, the Massachusetts Historical Society, the National Archives, the New Jersey State Library, the New-York Historical Society, the New York Public Library, the New York City Municipal Archives and Records Center, the New York State Library, the Rockport (Massachusetts) Public Library, and the University of Iowa.

I also wish to thank Jerome M. Clubb, Director, Historical Archive, and Janet Vavra, Supervisor, Servicing Section, Historical Archive, Inter-university Consortium for Political Research, University of Michigan, for their assistance.

At the Oxford University Press, Sheldon Meyer, Manuela Kruger, Caroline Taylor, and Marcia Erickson offered wise counsel in seeing my manuscript through to publication.

Finally, I am grateful to Paul Glad, Albert Goldberg, Frances and Edmund A. Moore, and my parents for their encouragement, and to my wife, Sandra McSeveney, who typed, edited, and calculated with equal skill, all the while sustaining my own efforts. We both know that this book is as much hers as mine.

S. McS.

Rockport, Mass.
June 1972

Table of contents

List of tables

THE POLITICS OF DEPRESSION

I

The Anatomy of Stalemate: Politics, 1874-1892

BETWEEN 1893 and 1896 the Republican party shattered a political stalemate of some twenty years' duration. Its success was all the more remarkable in view of Democratic gains between 1889 and 1892 that promised a tilting of the national political balance in favor of the Democrats. The era of political stalemate began in the midterm elections of 1874, in which the Democrats weakened the Republicans' hold on the national government by recapturing the House of Representatives. Between 1861 and 1875 the Republicans had controlled both houses of Congress, as well as the White House. For twenty years thereafter neither party was able to retain such control for long. During this period Democratic presidential candidates outpolled their Republican opponents in all but the election of 1880—when Winfield S. Hancock fell 7368 votes short of James A. Garfield—though neither Samuel J. Tilden's popular majority in 1876 nor Grover Cleveland's popular plurality twelve years later carried its recipient to victory. The Democrats organized the House of Representatives eight times in ten following biennial congressional elections, the Senate only twice. The Democrats controlled the presidency and had majorities in both houses of Congress only in 1893–95, the Republicans did so only in 1889–91. In 1881 the Republicans organized the Senate with the aid of William Mahone, a Virginia Readjuster, thereby gaining precarious legislative, as well as executive, control.[1]

The succession of closely contested presidential elections from 1876 through 1892 reflected a conflict between regional groupings which had approximately equal weight in the electoral college. (Within its own strongholds, each party held sway by varying popular margins.) For their part, the Democrats could generally rely on the states in which slavery had existed in 1860, the South and Border providing them with a solid bloc of electoral votes from 1880 through 1892. New Jersey alone of northern states never broke faith with the Democracy during the long stalemate. The Republicans depended on other regions to counterbalance these Democratic strongholds. New England, except for Connecticut, remained in the Republican camp throughout the period; Pennsylvania invariably contributed its large electoral vote to the Republican cause. From 1876 through 1888 every Republican national ticket carried eight East and West North Central states, as well as Colorado and Oregon. Each party's power base was disrupted once during the stalemate. In the disputed election of 1876 the Republicans were awarded the electoral votes of Florida, Louisiana, and South Carolina. Sixteen years later the Democrats captured a majority of the electoral vote in the Old Northwest, where the Republican coalition fell apart as ethnic groups protested Republican legislation they regarded as discriminatory, and denied the Republicans electoral votes in the wheat- and silver-producing regions, where discontent was mounting, by supporting Populist electors. (See Table 2.)

TABLE 2 *Electoral Vote, 1876–1892*

	1876		1880		1884		1888		1892		
	D	R	D	R	D	R	D	R	D	P	R
Normally Democratic Bloc	128	19	147	0	162	0	162	0	169	0	0
South[a]	76	19	95	0	107	0	107	0	112	0	0
Border[b]	43	0	43	0	46	0	46	0	47	0	0
New Jersey	9	0	9	0	9	0	9	0	10	0	0
Normally Republican Bloc	0	157	0	157	0	171	0	171	42	15	129
New England[c]	0	34	0	34	0	32	0	32	0	0	33

	1876		1880		1884		1888		1892		
	D	R	D	R	D	R	D	R	D	P	R
East North Central[d]	0	64	0	64	0	69	0	69	42	0	31
West North Central[e]	0	24	0	24	0	34	0	34	0	10	30
Pennsylvania	0	29	0	29	0	30	0	30	0	0	32
Colorado	0	3	0	3	0	3	0	3	0	4	0
Oregon	0	3	0	3	0	3	0	3	0	1	3
Doubtful States	56	9	8	57	57	11	6	62	65	3	1
New York	35	0	0	35	36	0	0	36	36	0	0
Indiana	15	0	0	15	15	0	0	15	15	0	0
Connecticut	6	0	0	6	6	0	6	0	6	0	0
California	0	6	5	1	0	8	0	8	8	0	1
Nevada	0	3	3	0	0	3	0	3	0	3	0
New States[f]									1	4	15
Majority Electoral Vote	185		185		201		201		223		
Democratic Electoral Vote	184		155		219		168		277		
Republican Electoral Vote	185		214		182		233		145		
Populist Electoral Vote	—		—		—		—		22		

Source: W. Dean Burnham, *Presidential Ballots, 1836–1892* (Baltimore: Johns Hopkins University Press, 1955), 888–89.

D=Democratic; R=Republican; P=People's party (Populist).

[a] Alabama, Arkansas, Florida, Georgia, Louisiana, Mississippi, North Carolina, South Carolina, Tennessee, Texas, Virginia.

[b] Delaware, Kentucky, Maryland, Missouri, West Virginia.

[c] Maine, Massachusetts, New Hampshire, Rhode Island, Vermont.

[d] Illinois, Michigan, Ohio, Wisconsin.

[e] Iowa, Kansas, Minnesota, Nebraska.

[f] Idaho, Montana, North Dakota, South Dakota, Washington, Wyoming.

The Republicans—spurred by the realization that theirs was clearly a sectional party, and probably the minority one as well —persisted in their efforts to weaken the Democrats' grip on the South during the stalemate. A succession of Republican leaders sought to restore competition to southern politics—by relying once more on the freedmen and a minority of southern whites, or by wooing erstwhile Whigs with internal improvements and tariffs, or by cooperating with Independents and Populists. Their every effort to achieve even limited objectives in the region frustrated, the Republicans lost interest in the entire troublesome Southern Question following the political realignment of 1893–96, which brought them national dominance without the support of any southern group.[2]

Since neither party controlled a bloc of electoral votes large enough to deliver the presidency without additional support and neither could depend on the success of forays into opposition bailiwicks, presidential campaigns resolved themselves into bitter battles fought out in a handful of swing states. Only five states—Connecticut, New York, Indiana, Nevada, and California—shifted camp once or more during the 1880s. (See Table 2.) Among these, New York and Indiana weighed most heavily in the electoral college. Indeed, New York alone provided the margins of victory in 1880, 1884, and 1888. Earlier, New York would have carried Tilden into the White House except for the Democrats' loss of three southern states in 1876; later, New York and Indiana contributed to the Democratic triumph in 1892, but Republican defections in the Middle West deprived the two states of their roles as President-makers. The creation of six western states in 1889–90 did not affect the outcome of the election of 1892. (See Table 2.)

Party managers recognized the importance of capturing the doubtful states, while retaining an often tenuous grip on adjoining ones. Rival campaign strategies reflected this understanding. The Democrats generally nominated New Yorkers for the presidency; they invariably tapped the Middle West, particularly wavering Indiana, to fill the second spot on national tickets. The Republicans also sought sectionally balanced slates; reversing Democratic priorities, they normally teamed midwestern presidential candidates with running mates from New York State. Between them, New York and Indiana provided thirteen of the two parties' twenty nominees for national office from 1876 through 1892. The rival parties also campaigned vigorously and spent lavishly in the swing states. The intensity with which partisans waged political war probably led some campaigners to overstep the bounds of propriety, and even legality; it certainly led to repeated charges, countercharges, and denials of corruption, coercion, bribery, and fraud—allegations that have been echoed by subsequent political biographers and historians. Taken at face value, these outcries would lead one to believe that the two parties alternated in cheating their opponents out of deserved victories.[3]

Subsequent generations have found little to commend in the strenuous efforts of the rival parties to break the deadlock in which they found themselves. Historians have generally scored the alleged sterility of political leadership, the low level of politics in general, and the absence of real issues during the stalemate. Referring to the "remarkable state of equilibrium" achieved by "the two great parties," Matthew Josephson went so far as to declare that, "During this phase, when Burning Issues and true class interests are dormant, *the veritable indifference of the public seems as marked as the excitement of the professionals seems feigned.*" [4]

As a matter of fact, the electorate was anything but indifferent to politics during the final third of the nineteenth century. Newspaper and other contemporary accounts suggest that there was widespread participation—and even wider interest—in political campaigns. Analyses of registration and voting data demonstrate that never in American history has voter turnout been higher. The electorate strongly identified with one or another party: straight ticket voting was the order of the day; voters customarily took the trouble to work their way down ballots to cast votes for candidates high and low; and midterm and off-year as well as presidential elections attracted large turnouts.[5]

Returns from New York, Connecticut, and New Jersey reveal the closeness of inter-party competition and the durability of partisan attachments during the stalemate. But the data also suggest that the Democratic party was slowly gaining the upper hand during this period. In New York State, Republican dominance in presidential elections before the mid-1870s (broken only in 1868) gave way to a marginal Democratic superiority during the subsequent national deadlock. Connecticut bestowed its electoral vote on the Republicans' first five presidential candidates, but on only one—in 1880—from 1876 through 1892. And the Democrats carried New Jersey in all presidential elections but that of 1872.[6]

An equally impressive record in gubernatorial elections, which were frequently held in off-years, indicates that the Democrats were not dependent upon their eastern presidential aspirants for success. After winning the governorship of New York six of nine times from 1856 through 1872, the Republicans won it only once in the next seven contests; New Jersey Republican gubernatorial candidates, twice successful before the Civil War, won but once in the following three decades. In Connecticut, on the other hand, the Democrats enjoyed considerable success during the Reconstruction period, but the Republicans insinuated themselves into the governorship in the election of 1878, and only in 1882 and 1892 did the Democrats subsequently dislodge them.[7] Actually, Democratic gubernatorial candidates often secured popular pluralities in Connecticut, but they were frustrated by that state's venerable constitution, which provided for legislative selection of the governor when no candidate received a majority of the popular vote. As Connecticut's system of town representation virtually guaranteed Republican control of the legislature, a series of minority Republican victors occupied the governor's office between 1885 and 1893.

Obviously, there were no widespread, lasting shifts in the political allegiances of voters during the stalemate.[8] But long-term population trends worked to the advantage of the Democrats during the late nineteenth century. In the Northeast these trends involved, first, a falling-off of the growth rate (or absolute population declines) in rural areas, and, second, the continued population growth of cities.[9] Within rural areas, population losses due to emigration to the West or to cities within the Northeast outweighed population gains due to births and immigration. Since a considerable proportion of the increasing tide of European immigrants settled in cities, urban population grew rapidly and generally surpassed that of rural areas during the second half of the nineteenth century.[10] The growth of small or medium-sized cities sometimes maintained the population level of counties in which the rural population was declining. But in many cases, no compensatory trend developed. As a consequence, several New York and New Jersey counties began losing population at some point between 1860 and 1890.[11] Although each of Connecticut's eight counties contained sufficient growing urban and suburban areas to prevent rural declines from registering on the county level, nearly half of the state's 168 towns were losing population.

Broadly speaking, units in which population began to decline between 1860 and 1890 were inhabited by religious and ethnic groups that gave them a Republican complexion. In New York State, for instance, there were twenty-four declining counties: fifteen voted Republican in every presidential election from 1860 through 1892; only one was consistently Democratic; the parties split the remaining eight which leaned one way or the other.[12] Connecticut's declining towns were generally Republican, and Tolland County, which suffered a net loss of population during the 1890s, was a party stronghold. In New Jersey, by way of contrast, the three declining counties were solidly Democratic.

On the other hand, the Democrats were strong—and generally maintained their strength—in counties undergoing rapid population growth. In New York State the Democrats held an edge in the twelve counties which exceeded the state's over-all rate of population growth between 1860 and 1890, while the Republicans clearly dominated the other forty-eight. Three Connecticut counties which exceeded that state's growth rate likewise leaned toward the Democracy; the Republicans exercised a near monopoly of control in the five other counties. The contrast between rapidly growing and lagging counties was not nearly as sharp in New Jersey.[13] The rate of population growth ran highest in the New York, New Jersey, and Connecticut counties that were already the most populous in their states by the time of the Civil War. These counties, which contained the great cities of the three states, grew rapidly during the late nineteenth century. Thus the political weight of cities, already considerable by 1860, increased markedly during ensuing decades. New York City and Brooklyn (an independent city until 1898) were not only by far the most populous cities in New York State, they also ranked first and fourth, respectively, among the nation's cities. Buffalo, which experienced vigorous growth during the post-Civil War period, was the country's eleventh most populous city by 1890. Newark and Jersey City, New Jersey, were also numbered among the twenty largest cities in the United States. New Haven, Hartford, and Bridgeport were not as populous, but together they contained a larger proportion of Connecticut's population than Newark and Jersey City did of New Jersey's population.[14]

Even as the Democrats generally carried races for national and state office in New York, New Jersey, and Connecticut, the Republicans dominated the legislatures of all three states. The Democratic position in the legislatures of New York and Connecticut was desperate.[15] Even in New Jersey, where the party sometimes captured the assembly, it rarely took the senate. Republican legislative dominance rested on apportionment formulas that over-represented areas normally carried by the G.O.P. and, in New York, at least, on the long-term contraction of Democratic areal strength, a development whose origins can be traced to the political realignment of 1854–60. Prior to that upheaval, the rival parties had shared the support of rural voters, but the anti-Catholic crusade of the 1850s permanently reduced the Democratic party to a minority position in most strongly Protestant rural counties.[16]

The Republicans reaped substantial rewards from their legislative strength. In Connecticut, Republican legislatures elected as governors Republicans whose Democratic opponents had failed to secure popular majorities. In all three states Republican legislatures frequently frustrated plans laid by Democratic governors. State legislatures directly influenced national politics: they redistricted their states' congressional seats and (until 1913) they elected U. S. senators. Where one or the other party won statewide elections and dominated the legislature, legislative election of senators had limited significance. But the legislatures of Connecticut and New York sent Republicans to the Senate during a period in which a plurality of the voters in both states was normally Democratic. So fine were senatorial margins during the 1880s that Republican control of the upper house depended on these delegations in no less than four congresses.[17]

The Democracy's loss of rural support and its increasing dependence on urban support affected the party's internal affairs as well as the balance of power between the major parties. In New York, upstate leaders dominated the party throughout the period, but they were forced to deal with a variety of problems arising out of or exacerbated by the shifts in the party's popular base. During the 1870s the state organization led by Daniel Manning of Albany and Samuel J. Tilden sought to advance Tilden's presidential ambitions while curbing the power of Tammany Hall in New York City. An anti-Tammany crusade dislodged "the Tweed Ring" from power, but "Honest" John Kelly led a Tammany comeback. Intra-party strife led Kelly to bolt in 1879. Running as an independent gubernatorial candidate, he cut into the Democratic vote sufficiently to defeat Lucius Robinson, the party's regular nominee.

In 1882 competing Democratic factions settled on Grover Cleveland of Buffalo to reunite the party and restore its fortunes in the Empire State. But Cleveland, who won the governorship in a landslide, and Manning, who retained control of the state organization, soon clashed with Tammany Hall. Upon Cleveland's elevation to the presidency, Lieutenant-Governor David B. Hill succeeded to the governorship, then won a term in his own right later in 1885. Hill forged a coalition that proved relatively effective in harmonizing divergent interests within the party. He worked hard to foster unity; his task was made easier by the deaths of Tilden and Kelly in 1886 and of Manning, who had followed Cleveland to Washington to serve as Secretary of the Treasury, a year later. Cleveland had never built up a personal organization in New York State; his position was further weakened when he failed of re-election in 1888, losing his native state even as Hill narrowly won again. Hill remained the most influential figure in New York State Democratic politics until the party's crushing defeat during the 1890s.[18]

In part, the Democratic struggle pitted ambitious urban politicians seeking to increase their power within state organizations and in state politics against entrenched outstate leaders who were reluctant to share power with newcomers. Tammany Hall, particularly under the leadership of Richard Croker, who succeeded John Kelly, moved to increase its state-wide influence, taking advantage of conflicts between Hill and Cleveland while cementing ties with upstate urban leaders such as Roswell P. Flower of Watertown, Edward Murphy, Jr., of Troy, and Anthony N. Brady of Albany.[19] In Connecticut, Democratic legislators representing small towns were reportedly opposed to the calling of a state constitutional convention which might weaken their constituencies' grip on the lower house of the legislature. Urban Democrats, on the other hand, demanded that their party incorporate in its state platform a plank calling for a constitutional convention. Other states experienced similar conflicts.[20]

The struggle also reflected a religious conflict—sometimes smoldering, at other times explosive—between Protestants (mostly rural) and Catholics (mostly urban) within the Democratic party. The first great tide of Catholic, particularly Irish Catholic, immigration had created resentment among important segments of the nation's overwhelmingly Protestant population during the 1830s and 1840s, a hostility that flared anew and with greater intensity during the following decade. As most Irish (and other) Catholics identified themselves with the Democratic party, anti-Catholicism—whether expressed through private organizations, independent political movements (e.g., the Know-Nothings), or the Whig and later Republican parties—generally involved attacks on the Democracy as a haven for Hibernians or worse still, as an instrument of papal power.[21] These recurring attacks upon the Democratic party, and distinct differences in the religious complexion of the two major parties, should not be permitted to obscure the strains produced within the Democracy by the entry into it of large numbers of Irish Catholics. In the extreme, many Protestant Democrats responded to the initial Irish Catholic invasion of their country and party by abandoning the party and joining others dedicated to the preservation of values they held dear.[22] The newcomers congregated in the cities of the Northeast, and there they more than compensated for Protestant defections from the Democratic party. But in rural areas, Irish

Catholics were not numerous enough to offset such defections: the rural Democracy entered into a decline from which it never recovered.

Still, the Democratic party did retain the loyalty of large numbers of Protestants. Accommodation between the old and new elements of the coalition was imperative if the party was to achieve success, but the process was difficult. Old-stock American party leaders resisted the efforts of Irish Catholics who sought success by climbing their way up the political ladder. Not until the eve of the Civil War did Irish names appear prominently on the party slate in New York City, and not until the 1870s did an Irish Catholic (John Kelly) lead Tammany Hall. William R. Grace became the city's first Irish Catholic mayor in 1880, but his narrow margin of victory suggests the continued sharpness of religious animosity.[23] In New Haven, Connecticut, old-stock Democrats established rules providing for equal ward representation in the party's city convention, thereby weakening the hand of politicians who represented heavily Democratic Irish Catholic districts. This arrangement, adopted in 1855 during the Know-Nothing excitement, was abandoned six years later in favor of weighted ward representation. But in 1869, native American leaders, anxious about the ambitions of Irish politicians, wholesale naturalizations, and a workingman's movement, employed their narrow majority to restore the earlier plan. An Irishman had been elected to New Haven's Board of Aldermen as early as 1857; by the 1880s, Irishmen represented over half of the city's wards. For a variety of reasons, however, city-wide political as well as economic power remained in the hands of old-stock businessmen.[24]

Irish Catholic politicians pressed their claims for advancement on reluctant old-stock Democratic leaders in other areas of the Northeast where their followers were numerous enough to give them political leverage. In Rhode Island they led a fight to liberalize the suffrage by amending the state constitution to eliminate property qualifications for naturalized citizens. Loath to accept an increase in the influence of immigrants, many old-stock Democrats opposed the proposal. The amendment ultimately passed; an expanded electorate swung Providence, long a Republican city, into the Democratic column in 1892, and within a decade the Irish dominated Democratic politics there. Boston's Irish politicians established themselves in lesser political positions during the 1870s; one attained the mayoralty in 1885. Benjamin F. Butler, who captured the governorship of Massachusetts in 1882, drove a number of old-stock Democrats into retirement; at the same time he advanced the careers of a number of young Irish politicians, thereby contributing to the emergence of the Irish in the Bay State.[25]

Pressures that had been building up within the Democracy for some time exploded during 1883–84, and they nearly cost the party the presidential election of 1884. Grover Cleveland, the Democrats' standard-bearer, had first attracted national attention by decisively winning the governorship of New York in 1882. Within a short time after assuming office, however, he had alienated important supporters. Cleveland frequently clashed with Tammany, securing the removal of its state legislative floor leader, repeatedly denying its patronage claims, and blocking the nomination of William R. Purcell, an Irish Catholic newspaper editor from Rochester, as New York Secretary of State in 1883. Such actions won the applause of upstate Democrats and anti-Tammany "respectables" in New York City. They did not sit well with organization Democrats, who retaliated by knifing Isaac Maynard, Cleveland's personal choice for Secretary of State.[26] Cleveland also angered antimonopolists, who opposed his appointments to the state railroad commission and his veto of a five-cent fare bill, and laborers, who resented his veto of a bill limiting the workday of streetcar conductors to twelve hours.[27]

During 1884, Tammany Hall, together with politicians such as Benjamin F. Butler and Patrick Collins of Massachusetts, attempted to block Cleveland's nomination for President. Feelings ran deep at the Democratic national convention, where Cleveland's supporters, who "love[d] him for the enemies he has made," triumphed. Meanwhile, the Mugwump revolt—i.e., the bolt of young Republicans who chafed under Old Guard domination of their party and opposed the nomination of James G. Blaine—strengthened the old-stock, "respectable" Democracy and added to the uneasiness of the Irish.[28] The party's internal wounds were slow to heal during the campaign. Collins reluctantly assumed leadership of the Massachusetts Democratic committee. After a widely publicized meeting with Cleveland, he proclaimed his satisfaction that Cleveland was not hostile toward Catholics, the Irish, or labor. Not until September, though, did John Kelly endorse Cleveland; even then, Tammany's campaign lacked spirit. And for some there was no reconciliation, however uneasy: Benjamin F. Butler ran for President as the candidate of the Greenback party.[29]

Most Irish Catholics voted in 1884 as they had in earlier elections—for the Democratic party. But Cleveland's nomination, which brought the party's internal tensions to the surface, appears to have reduced Democratic margins in Irish Catholic districts in New York City, Boston, and elsewhere in the Northeast. James G. Blaine, whose campaign was supposedly undone by the Reverend Dr. Samuel D. Burchard's alliterative but impolitic reference to the Democracy as the party of "rum, Romanism and rebellion," actually secured a higher percentage of the Irish Catholic vote than any other Republican presidential candidate from 1876 through 1892. Cleveland partially compensated for Irish defections by picking up votes in districts where Republican disaffection from Blaine ran high.[30]

In New York, Cleveland's home state, Democratic as well as Republican percentage strength declined between 1880 and 1884, albeit to a smaller degree. In New York City, a center of Mugwump protest against Blaine's moral unfitness for the presidency, the Democratic percentage loss was greater than that of the Republicans. Viewed from the perspective of Cleveland's resounding triumph in the gubernatorial election of 1882, the Democrat's decline in popularity in 1884 appears striking. Conversely, Blaine—facing an opponent whose majority only two years earlier had been the largest in state history, and running during hard times that had struck during a national Republican administration—appears to have been a strong rather than weak candidate. Nationally, popular shifts between the parties very nearly canceled one another; measured against the election of 1880, the election of 1884 "showed *less* arithmetic percentage change than any other in American history." [31]

Cleveland and his advisers learned some lessons from the near-disaster of 1884. The new national administration dispensed a share of the patronage to Tammany Hall and Irish politicians, lessening, though not eliminating, discontent. The effort seemed to pay off, for in 1888, Cleveland—allegedly weakened among Irish Catholics by the indiscreet suggestion of Sir Lionel Sackville-West, the British minister to the United States, to "Charles F. Murchison" (actually George Osgoodby, a Republican sympathizer), that British Americans vote for the Democratic candidate —ran stronger in Irish American districts than he had four years earlier. Just as preoccupation with Cleveland's victory and the speech of the Reverend Dr. Burchard has frequently obscured Blaine's comparatively strong showing in Irish Catholic districts in 1884, so emphasis on Cleveland's defeat and the "Murchison letter" has often led to a neglect of Cleveland's recovery in such districts in his second presidential race.[32]

David B. Hill, who succeeded Cleveland as governor and Democratic leader in New York, sought to blunt the discontents that had threatened the party under his predecessor. Sensitive to changing moods in segments of the electorate, Hill was concerned over the showing of Henry George as an independent labor candidate for mayor of New York City in 1886. Candidacies such as George's threatened the Democrats more than they did the Republicans, for a disproportionate share of the workers who might support them belonged to ethnic groups that normally voted Democratic.[33] Hill cultivated contacts with organized labor, making appointments and legislative proposals with this group in mind. He also voiced sympathy for the Irish nationalist cause and friendship for the naturalized citizen, while supporting legislation to permit the celebration of the mass in public institutions to which Roman Catholics had been committed. "Freedom of worship" bills, supported by the Roman Catholic Church, were repeatedly introduced, but not until 1892 did a modified version become law.[34]

Hill's political base lay in upstate New York, but he relied more upon contacts in the region's cities than in its rural towns, which could no longer turn out a strong Democratic vote. Further, just as Cleveland as President granted patronage to Tammany in part to restrain Hill's ambitions, so Hill cultivated Hugh McLaughlin, whose Brooklyn organization's patronage needs were not being met by the national administration, in order to provide himself with a powerful urban ally who was also interested in checking the growing power of the New York City Democratic organization. Within the metropolis itself, Hill initially worked with the County Democracy to retain the support of Democrats who opposed Tammany Hall. But Hill never broke with Tammany, and as the County Democracy, beset with scandal, declined while Tammany flourished under Richard Croker, he increasingly dealt with the regular organization.[35] Hill, an astute professional politician, capably led the Democratic party during the decade following Cleveland's initial election as President. Still, maintaining stability within a Democratic coalition was difficult, and nothing contributed more to Democratic tensions than the pressures for advancement applied by Irish Catholic political organizations and individuals who claimed the support of a growing and politically conscious Irish community.[36]

A number of Republican leaders, casting about for recruits for their party, sought to weaken the bonds between the Democratic party and Irish Catholics. In this they were following the course set by some earlier Whig politicians, most notably William H. Seward and Thurlow Weed, beginning in 1839.[37] The task before the Republicans was difficult. The Irish Catholic–Democratic party alliance had been forged in the fires of cultural conflict, and these never remained damped for long during the nineteenth century. Even for Irish Catholics who moved to areas relatively free of tensions, there were memories of past conflicts and accounts of contemporary ones elsewhere. Second-generation Irish Americans had shared the lot of their immigrant parents during youth; as adults, they were identified as members of the Irish community. The Democracy had originally beckoned to the Irish Catholics, and as Irishmen advanced within the party the interaction between politicians and ethnic community reinforced the group's identification with the party. Loyalty to the Democratic party had become part of the fabric of Irish Catholic life in the United States.

Republican professionals recognized the historic factors that made difficult any attempt to attract Irish Catholic support.[38] Still, given the close balance between the parties, the effort promised much, even if it were only moderately successful. During the 1880s and early 1890s, Republican politicians cooperated with a number of Irish American leaders, particularly some prominent in the Irish nationalist cause. Republicans contributed financially to Irish nationalist groups and newspapers. Irish nationalists praised the Republicans' willingness to stand up to Great Britain, damned the Democrats as Anglophiles, and called on Irish Americans to end their subservience to the Democratic party.[39]

Whitelaw Reid, the newspaper publisher, was long prominent in the efforts of Republicans to court favor among the Irish in the Northeast. His association with James G. Blaine brought him into contact with Irish leaders who were close to that politician. During his own campaign for the vice-presidency in 1892, Reid worked with state and national Republican leaders to improve party chances with the Irish. Reid's New York *Tribune* also labored to this end. Donald Nicholson, Managing Editor of the *Tribune,* specifically and pointedly instructed George W. Smalley, the newspaper's distinguished correspondent in Great Britain, to alter his positions on Prime Minister William E. Gladstone, the Liberal party, and Irish home rule to conform with political strategy for capturing the Irish Catholic vote. In fact, the *Tribune* censored at least one of Smalley's dispatches. Reid was aware of these matters; indeed, he had earlier suggested to Nicholson that Smalley be restrained.[40]

The Republican campaign failed for two reasons. First, Irish nationalists, though strong, were not powerful enough to capture leadership of the immigrant community from Irish politicians. Irish nationalism and politics were grounded in the trying experiences of the Irish in the United States as well as in their troubled homeland. In the final analysis, political activity was more attractive than nationalist agitation, for it resulted in tangible rewards in the United States rather than dreams of a free Ireland.[41] Second, voters who identified with the Republican party because they were hostile toward Catholics and toward the Democracy as the party of Catholics resented the efforts of Republican politicians to achieve a rapprochement with elements of the Irish Catholic community. Former Representative Samuel F. Barr of Pennsylvania recalled that during the 1884 presidential campaign daily references to Catholic support for James G. Blaine in the New York *Tribune* angered Republicans in western Pennsylvania, where the Scotch-Irish indicated that they might bolt the party if it were true that Blaine was the candidate of the Catholics. Disquieted by these reports, the Republican state committee finally sent Barr to inquire of Blaine whether Reid's campaign might be terminated.[42]

The hypersensitivity of anti-Catholics was demonstrated by an incident which involved the New York *Tribune,* even as that newspaper was ardently wooing Irish Catholics during the presidential campaign of 1892. A correspondent covering the New Jersey seashore sent in a story about a parade staged in Asbury Park by the Junior Order of United American Mechanics, a well-known anti-Catholic order. He candidly described the paraders and criticized their marching prowess. On the other hand, he favorably contrasted the character and dedication of the marchers with the qualities he perceived in the surrounding vacationers. Nowhere did he refer to, let alone criticize, the program or ideology of the order. Even so, members and friends of the J.O.U.A.M. denounced the "uncalled for and un-American" criticism of the parade in letters to the *Tribune* and Whitelaw Reid. The *Tribune* twice apologized for the publication of sentiments alien to the newspaper and once indicated acceptance of the order's principles. Whitelaw Reid was absolved of any responsibility for the article. Meanwhile, Reid personally explained his newspaper's indiscretion to indignant letter writers, suggesting to one that the article was "probably malicious" and promising that the correspondent would never again contribute to the *Tribune.*[43]

Episodes such as those of 1884 and 1892, though minor in themselves, reveal much about the emotional charge of late nineteenth-century ethnic politics and suggest that any major effort by Republican politicians to capture the Irish Catholic vote would have produced severe strains within the G.O.P. Under the circumstances, attempts based on contacts with Irish nationalists, if ineffectual, were probably less disruptive than tactics involving the absorption of Irish politicians and their followers by the party would have been.

Meanwhile, the Republican party suffered from its own internal stresses, especially those created by prohibitionism. Groups opposed to the consumption of alcoholic beverages—evangelical Protestants, in particular—had generally found their home in the Whig and Republican parties during the ante-bellum period.[44] Outside of the South, they continued to identify with the Republicans during the post-Civil War decades. But there was tension between prohibition workers and professional politicians, for the former viewed the Republican party as an instrument to effect moral reform while the latter, aware that prohibition was a divisive issue, sought to blur distinctions between drys and wets.

During the 1870s a number of states repealed or watered down their anti-liquor laws. The Republican party led or acquiesced in these retreats for political reasons. In Connecticut, years of Republican vacillation were brought to an end by the legislature's final rejection in 1871 of a bill providing for a state police to enforce prohibition, and by repeal one year later of the state's Maine law. Following the first legislative action, the prohibitionists organized a state party; following the second, they mounted aggressive political campaigns that contributed to Democratic successes between 1873 and 1876 by siphoning off Republican voters, particularly in the closely contested elections of sparsely populated rural towns. (Those towns exercised a disproportionate influence in the state legislature.) In New York, temperance forces ran an independent slate as early as 1870, stepping up their activity in 1873 in response to gubernatorial vetoes of two local option bills. New Jersey prohibitionists did not enter a state-wide campaign until 1877.[45] In neither New York nor New Jersey was the party as popular or influential as it was in Connecticut. (See Table 3.)

The Prohibition party, recovering from a decline that had begun in 1875, registered gains in the elections of 1882 and reached peak strength shortly after mid-decade. The impact of this second and more powerful wave of independent political activity varied from area to area according to local social and polit-

TABLE 3 *Prohibition Party Voting Strength, 1870–1892*

YEAR	CONNECTICUT OFFICE[a]	VOTE	(%)	NEW JERSEY OFFICE[a]	VOTE	(%)	NEW YORK OFFICE[a]	VOTE	(%)
1870	—	—	—	—	—	—	G	1459	0.2
1871	—	—	—	—	—	—	S	1820	0.2
1872	G	1549	1.7	—	—	—	G	177	0.02
	—	—	—	—	—	—	P	201	0.02
1873	G	2541	2.9	—	—	—	S	3272	0.5
1874	G	4960	5.4	—	—	—	G	11768	1.5
1875	G	2942	2.9	—	—	—	S	11103	1.4
1876	G	737	0.6	—	—	—	G	3412	0.3
	P	378	0.3	—	—	—	P	2359	0.2
1877	—	—	—	G	1438	0.8	S	7230	0.9
1878	G	1079	1.0	—	—	—	AJ	4294	0.5
1879	—	—	—	—	—	—	G	4437	0.5
1880	G	488	0.4	G	195	0.1	—	—	—
	P	409	0.3	P	191	0.1	P	1517	0.1
1881	—	—	—	—	—	—	S	4445	0.5
1882	G	1034	0.9	—	—	—	G	25783	2.8
1883	—	—	—	G	4153	2.0	S	18816	2.1
1884	G	2126[b]	1.5	—	—	—	AJ	23150	2.1
	P	2305[b]	1.7	P	6153[b]	2.4	P	25006[b]	2.2
1885	—	—	—	—	—	—	G	30867[b]	3.0
1886	G	4699[b]	3.8	G	19808[b]	8.6	AJ	36437[b]	3.8
1887	—	—	—	—	—	—	S	41850[b]	4.0
1888	G	4631[b]	3.0	—	—	—	G	30215[b]	2.3
	P	4231[b]	2.8	P	7904[b]	2.6	P	30231	2.3
1889	—	—	—	G	6853	2.6	S	26763[b]	2.6
1890	G	3413	2.5	—	—	—	—	—	—
1891	—	—	—	—	—	—	G	30353	2.6
1892	G	3926	2.4	G	7750[b]	2.3	CJ	38775	2.9
	P	3999	2.4	P	8134	2.4	P	38190	2.8

Sources: *Tribune Almanacs, 1871–1893.*

[a] P=President; G=Governor; S=Secretary of State; AJ=Associate Judge, Court of Appeals; CJ=Chief Judge, Court of Appeals.

[b] Prohibition vote exceeded Democratic plurality over Republicans.

ical circumstances. In Connecticut the Prohibition party never regained the popularity it had had in 1874. It did embarrass Republican presidential candidates in 1884 and 1888, but not gubernatorial candidates, for Democratic rural strength had so fallen off that prohibitionist defections no longer threatened Republican control of the legislature, which chose governors following plurality elections. On the other hand, in New Jersey and New York the dry party surpassed its earlier showing and played a politically significant role. In an electorate closely divided between the major parties, the Prohibition vote, drawn mainly from Republican ranks, exceeded Democratic pluralities in a number of elections. (See Table 3.)

After nearly a decade of campaigning, New Jersey prohibitionists scored dramatically in the gubernatorial election of 1886, when General Clayton B. Fisk polled 19,808 votes, 8.6 per cent of those cast in a three-way race. The Prohibition party actually received 21.4 per cent of the vote in Cumberland County; statewide, it held the balance of power in three Democratic and nine Republican counties.[46] Although the Prohibitionists attracted old-stock, rural Democrats in northwestern New Jersey, it was their success among old-stock, rural Republicans across southern and western New Jersey that gave G.O.P. leaders cause for concern. Southern New Jersey, in particular, was a Republican stronghold, as well as the political base of U.S. Senator William J. Sewell, a state party leader. The prohibitionist upsurge toppled the Republicans from control of the state assembly; a joint session of the legislature subsequently denied Sewell his senate seat. Republicans pondered the potential effect of the Prohibition party on the legislative elections of 1888, for the legislature elected that year would choose a successor to U.S. Senator John R. McPherson, a Democrat.

During 1888, the Republican party responded to the threat of the Prohibition party by securing enactment of a law that provided for county option and high license fees for taverns. The legislative vote clearly identified the Republicans as drys and the Democrats as wets.[47] That the Republicans had been caught on the horns of a dilemma was painfully revealed that autumn, when the Democrats took to the hustings to belabor their opponents as puritanical and opposed to individual liberty. The election returns suggested that the Republicans had succeeded in recapturing dry votes, for General Fisk, the third party's native-son presidential candidate, received only 7904 votes, or 2.6 per cent of those cast. The prohibitionist vote in legislative contests likewise declined. The price paid for these reconversions was high, for the Democrats won over sufficient wet Republicans to hold the state for Cleveland and to recapture both houses of the legislature, thereby safeguarding McPherson's senate seat. The Democrats gained one state senatorial seat in rural, pro-temperance, and traditionally Democratic Hunterdon County and a second in urban, anti-temperance, and normally Republican Passaic. The Republicans added two assemblymen in Cumberland County and one in Salem, but lost one each in Burlington, Mercer, Monmouth, and Somerset, and four each in Essex and Hudson.[48]

The Republicans' sharp reversal in northeastern New Jersey was particularly serious, for this urbanized area, already populous, was growing rapidly. No element within this region was more disaffected by Republican temperance legislation than the Germans, who were on the verge of becoming the state's largest foreign-born group. The Germans strongly resented puritanical attacks on the taverns and beer that were part of their culture. (Germans not only consumed beer; they were also intimately involved in its production and sale.) The issue of Sunday observance had divided Newark's Germans and old-stock Americans politically during the 1870s. The Democrats, recognizing their minority position, abandoned a stance unsympathetic to the Germans and captured the mayoralty of Newark in 1879 by championing personal liberty and nominating a candidate of German descent. Still tensions persisted, and they were fanned by the high license–county option controversy. The Democrats reinforced their appeal to German Americans as the party of personal liberty by nominating two Newark brewers of German birth for the assembly in 1888.[49]

In the meantime, prohibitionists, acting under the county option provision of the 1888 law, were drying up parts of New Jersey. As early as August 1888, Cumberland County opted for prohibition, and Salem and Warren counties followed suit the next month. Gloucester, Cape May, and Hunterdon counties later climbed aboard the water wagon. But a different spirit prevailed in the legislature of 1889; the Democratic majority translated its will into the Werts Liquor License Law, which specifically repealed the law of 1888, substituted local option for county option, and contained license fee and penalty provisions similar to those in the defunct measure. Despite the entreaties of the State Liquor Dealers' Association, the Democratic leadership was unwilling to go further in changing state policy. The prohibitionists subsequently condemned "license or compromise" in dealing with "the sin and crime of the liquor traffic" and repudiated an alliance with either major party. The Republicans roundly denounced the Werts Law, while the Democrats' state platform avoided the entire issue.[50] In the ensuing gubernatorial election, the Republicans held the Prohibition party vote at the level to which it had fallen the previous year; that vote was to remain remarkably stable for a number of years.

The political arm of the prohibition movement recovered its strength in New York State in 1882 and remained a disruptive force for some years thereafter. As elsewhere, dry sentiment generally flourished among staunchly Republican elements of the population. Since these were most heavily concentrated in strongly Republican rural counties, drys who voted the Prohibition ticket rarely turned over their towns and counties to the Democratic foe. Though such defections did not seriously threaten local Republican rule, their state-wide effect deeply concerned Republican managers.[51] As the Prohibition party registered small percentage gains during 1885–87, the Republicans sought to placate the drys without alienating the wets. The Crosby high license bills of 1887 and 1888 were efforts in this direction. Both fell before the vetoes of Governor Hill. Finally, in 1888, with the presidency and governorship at stake, Republican leaders sought to assuage prohibitionists who were not satisfied with high license bills and the party's state platforms. Accordingly, former U.S. Senator and Representative Warner Miller, who was close to the drys, was nominated for governor. The Prohibition party's share of the vote that year declined from its levels of 1885–87 and was smaller than it would be in subsequent elections. To this degree, Miller, though defeated for governor, contributed to Benjamin Harrison's success in New York State. The Prohibition party recovered somewhat in 1889, but never regained the strength it had attained in 1885–87. The Republicans, aware of the problem before them, straddled the temperance issue.[52]

The New Jersey and New York episodes illustrate the struggle between the prohibitionist and anti-prohibitionist forces during the 1880s and reveal the ways in which the major parties became involved in the conflict. Though politicians who were not deeply committed to one or the other side sought to minimize party involvement in the controversy, groups to which the issues were of transcendent importance would not permit those who wished to avoid taking a principled (and divisive) stand to get away with it. Professional politicians sought, unavailingly, to reduce these constituency cross-pressures by appealing to party loyalty, by denouncing the opposition party, and by stressing national issues. But the two major parties, responding to the pressures of strong and involved groups within their ranks, polarized as the cultural conflict intensified. The struggle between wets and drys raged in many other states during the 1880s. Legislatures passed on bills and constitutional amendments to restrain or prohibit the sale of alcoholic beverages; in some instances the electorate voted on these amendments. Elsewhere, the wets attempted to repeal or liberalize prohibitory or restrictive constitutional provisions and laws. Partisan lines were generally clearly drawn in these clashes.[53]

Other cultural issues produced controversy. In Illinois and Wisconsin, old-stock Americans, who viewed schools as instruments of Americanization, demanded legislation requiring that instruction be in English, while Germans, who hoped to preserve the cultural identity of their immigrant community, sought to continue instruction in their native language.[54] In Massachusetts, conflict over the schools pitted Protestants against Catholics. A number of states considered granting the vote to women—in all elections, or in alcoholic beverage license and local school board elections. Thus the issue of woman suffrage became intertwined with two of the major cultural conflicts of the period. Rhode Island debated liberalization of the suffrage to permit naturalized citizens to vote without property qualifications, and New Hampshire debated the elimination of sectarianism in the state bill of rights.[55]

These cultural conflicts contributed to a Democratic upsurge in the years before the depression of 1893. This resurgence has been variously ascribed: to a restless electorate expressing discontent over economic and social transformations—with which the political system seemed unable to cope—by voting no confidence in the party holding office; or to a popular reaction against the excesses of the Fifty-first Congress, in particular its passage of the highly protective McKinley Tariff.[56] Neither interpretation fully explains Democratic successes. To be sure, the winds of agrarian revolt blew hot across the plains, sweeping Populists to a number of victories in 1890 and 1892. But Democrats defeated Republicans in areas of the Middle West that were relatively sheltered from the blasts of Populism. Further, Democrats gained at the expense of Republicans in the Northeast, and if the Middle West was cool toward the agrarian revolt, the Northeast was cold. Indeed, more northeastern voters supported the Prohibition party than supported the People's and Socialist Labor parties combined. In short, the Democrats prospered not in a climate of acute economic distress but in one of comparative prosperity. In such an atmosphere the effects—real or imagined—of the McKinley Tariff Act on the cost of living may have prompted voters to turn to the Democracy. But this interpretation misses the point that the Democratic upsurge began in 1889, before the Fifty-first Congress even convened, let alone passed the McKinley bill.

The Democratic upswing coincided with the final round in the cultural conflicts that had raged in many states. In March 1889 the New Hampshire electorate rejected a prohibition amendment to the state constitution while approving an amendment that made the state bill of rights nonsectarian. Massachusetts and Pennsylvania voters subsequently voted down prohibition amendments to their state constitutions. Rhode Island repealed its three-year-old prohibition amendment; the vote gained added significance as it was the first under the amendment of 1888, which eliminated property qualifications for voting by naturalized citizens. Connecticut rounded out activity on the prohibition front, rejecting a dry amendment in October.[57] In the same year the Democrats rebounded from Cleveland's defeat in New York to win by a margin that exceeded expectations. The Democrats also gained percentage strength in New Jersey. Elsewhere in the Northeast, William E. Russell, running for the governorship of Massachusetts on the Democratic ticket, improved on his own showing of the previous year. Earlier in 1889, a Democratic gubernatorial candidate in Rhode Island had secured a popular plurality but failed of election in the legislature. To the west, the Democrats captured the governorships of Iowa and Ohio, and the Ohio legislature to boot.[58]

The Democratic tide reached flood stage in 1890. Early in the year—shortly before the passage of the McKinley Tariff bill—a Democrat won the governorship of Rhode Island. In the autumn midterm elections, the Democrats gained control of the U.S. House of Representatives by a wide margin, picked up seats in state legislatures across the country, and won governorships in Massachusetts, Pennsylvania, Michigan, and Wisconsin. The disruptive effect of cultural controversies on the Republican coalition was clearest in Wisconsin and Illinois, where German Lutherans, normally Republican, were angered by the Bennett and Edwards school laws, both of which required that schools teach key subjects in English. In Illinois, the Democrats ran Henry Raab, a German American, against Richard Edwards, whose name was attached to the controversial school law, for Superintendent of Public Instruction. Raab led his running-mate on the victorious state ticket by over 14,000 votes.[59] In the off-year elections of 1891, the Democrats lost governorships in Rhode Island (a legislative, rather than popular, defeat) and Ohio, but retained those in Massachusetts, Iowa, and New York. Roswell P. Flower, elected governor in New York, became the first candidate since 1882 to receive a majority of the state's vote.[60]

Democratic successes in normally Republican states influenced the planning of Grover Cleveland during the 1892 presidential campaign. Cleveland was obsessed by fears that Senator David B. Hill and Tammany Hall, having failed to block his renomination, would betray his candidacy. A vigorous campaign in Wisconsin and Illinois might force the recalcitrant New Yorkers into line by convincing them that they were powerless to destroy his chances; success in the two states would fully offset the possible loss of New York State's electoral vote. Enthusiastic eastern supporters dreamed of other midwestern conquests, but Cleveland wished to concentrate on the promising pair of states. William C.

Whitney, Cleveland's closest adviser, remained dubious about the venture; he finally convinced the obstinate candidate to reach an understanding with party regulars in New York. Meanwhile, personal supporters of Cleveland contributed money to the campaign among German Americans in the Midwest, an effort aided by the Illinois Democracy, which nominated German-born John Peter Altgeld for governor.[61] In the end, the Democrats combined a strong showing in their own bailiwicks with victories in doubtful and normally Republican states to win a decisive victory for the national ticket. (See Table 2.)

The Democrats gained less percentage strength between the presidential elections of 1888 and 1892 in New York, New Jersey, and Connecticut than they did in a number of normally Republican states in the Northeast and Middle West. Still, the small percentage shifts in the three states generally exceeded those of the 1880s. (See Table 4.) An analysis of county returns reveals a fairly consistent pattern of minute Democratic percentage gains and Republican losses in New Jersey and Connecticut, but in New York both parties lost percentage strength to minor parties in most counties.[62] Turnout increased moderately in New Jersey (10.8 per cent) and Connecticut (6.9 per cent), but the gain in New York State (1.3 per cent) was the smallest since 1868–72. Indeed, turnout declined in most counties, and this falling off clearly worked to the advantage of the Democrats: of the forty-

TABLE 4 *Net Changes in Percentage Strength, Presidential Elections, 1876–1892, Connecticut, New York, and New Jersey*

	CONNECTICUT		NEW YORK		NEW JERSEY	
ELECTIONS	D	R	D	R	D	R
1876–80	−2.2	+1.7	−3.0	+2.1	−2.9	+2.0
1880–84	+0.4	−2.4	−0.2	−2.2	−0.8	−1.7
1884–88	−0.3	+0.3	—	+1.2	+0.9	+0.2
1888–92	+1.4	−1.6	+0.8	−3.7	+1.0	−1.1

Source: W. Dean Burnham, *Presidential Ballots, 1836–1892* (Baltimore: Johns Hopkins University Press, 1955), 319, 629, 633.
D=Democrat; R=Republican.

five counties affected, all but seven were Republican. The decline was too much for the Republicans to overcome, for even under normal circumstances the party's upstate base cast a smaller and smaller share of the state's vote each year. Further, the Democrats benefited from both higher turnouts and increased percentage margins in a number of urbanized counties.[63] As a consequence, they carried the state by the largest plurality achieved by either party since 1872. Republican percentage strength sank to an all-time low.

As was to be expected, politicians' reactions to the election of 1892 divided along party lines. For the most part the comments were conventional. Nevertheless, statements of a number of politicians and laymen made clear the interrelationships many discerned between cultural conflicts and politics. Concern over "the foreign vote" had been voiced by Republican politicians during the campaign itself. Theodore Roosevelt identified the "Lutheran and Catholic Germans" of Wisconsin and Illinois as a threat to his party, whose only hope, a forlorn one at that, lay in awakening "the latent Americanism in native Democrats" to offset German defections. One campaigner, anxious about the outcome in New York, contrasted the decline in registration in Republican rural areas with the naturalization since 1888 of over 40,000 aliens, at least three-fourths of whom would vote Democratic. After the election, Benjamin S. Pardee of the New Haven *Palladium* lamented that even in Connecticut the Republicans had been forced to disseminate campaign literature in seven languages. Postmaster General John Wanamaker attributed the Republican defeat to the vote of New York City and Chicago, both "made up largely of a foreign element which has given the democratic party the preponderance of strength in the great cities of the country at large." [64]

Even before 1892, nativists and anti-Catholics had deplored the political situation east and west. During the campaign, the Reverend Madison C. Peters of the Bloomingdale Reformed Church in New York City, who later became the city's leading clerical spokesman for the American Protective Association, had charged that immigrants, whose quality he attacked, were concentrated in a handful of counties that controlled nearly one-half of the seats in the state legislature; New York's closely contested elections further magnified their political importance. Peters warned that "Home rule for America may yet become an issue in our politics." [65] Other strong statements followed the election. U.S. Senator William E. Chandler, Republican of New Hampshire, an avowed immigration restrictionist and the chairman of the newly created Senate Committee on Immigration, received considerable mail denouncing immigrants. Some correspondents were general in their denunciations; others condemned particular ethnic groups.[66] (On the other hand, one correspondent reminded Chandler that while the German American newspapers he represented were solidly Republican, the lessons of Wisconsin should not be forgotten. He concluded that legislation should seek to exclude undesirables while admitting good people.[67]) This is not to suggest that the election of 1892 or political developments in general lay at the root of the nativist and immigration restrictionist movements. The fears that motivated these movements were social, economic, and ideological, as well as political. But the tensions of the period did contribute to the series of political campaigns that reached its climax in 1892, and those who feared for their America were disheartened by the outcome of the election.[68]

In their fear and hostility, many nativists distorted reality. They exaggerated the magnitude of the "new" immigration from southern and eastern Europe, for northern and western Europe continued to contribute the bulk of newcomers. Indeed, in the 1880s British, German, and Scandinavian immigration reached new peaks, and Irish immigration still ran high. In fact, only during 1847–54 had Irish immigration been greater. Not until the depression of 1893 did the "old" immigration from northern and western Europe fall off; not until that depression lifted did the great inflow of "new" immigrants begin.[69] Nativists who related Republican setbacks to immigration *per se* misunderstood the political consequences of immigration. In fact, the steady stream of Scandinavian and British (English, Welsh, and Scottish) immigrants provided the Republicans with recruiting opportunities among ethnic groups that were traditionally hostile to the Democrats. Further, a shift among "old" immigrant voters (in this case the Germans), not the voting of "new" immigrants, contributed to Democratic gains in New Jersey, as well as in Wisconsin and Illinois. Finally, the "new" immigrants were not yet numerous enough to be a decisive variable in the political equation. Even in Chicago and New York City, the newcomers had not yet transformed the population, let alone the electorate. In 1892 and for some years thereafter, the "new" immigrants congregated in clearly defined areas of New York City; their votes could not have accounted for the Democrats' sweep of the city's thirty assembly districts.[70]

Fundamentally, then, politics during the pre-1893 period was cultural politics, involving old-stock American and "old" immigrant groups. These far outnumbered the "new" immigrants; they made up an even greater proportion of the electorate. The American-born offspring of "old" immigrants were often politically active adults; those of the "new" immigrants were still in their childhood. In this context, the emergence of the Irish Catholic and German communities was more important politically than the arrival of Roman Catholics and Jews from southern and eastern Europe.[71] The Democrats had capitalized on cultural conflicts that divided the Republican coalition, winning over sufficient Republicans—German Lutherans, in particular—to run off a series of election victories from 1889 through 1892. It remained to be seen what effect a severe economic depression would have on this political pattern.

II

1893: The First Shock

On March 4, 1893, Grover Cleveland took the presidential oath of office for the second time. For the portly New Yorker, the inaugural ceremonies provided a fitting climax to the vindication he had won at the polls the previous November. That victory was decisive by the standards of the late nineteenth century, for although Cleveland actually won a smaller percentage of the popular vote than he had received when he lost four years earlier, this reflected Populist inroads into the strength of both major parties; his popular plurality was the largest of any candidate since 1872, his margin in the electoral college the widest of any Democrat since 1852. Despite the loss of some seats won during the midterm landslide of 1890, the Democracy retained control of the House of Representatives by a comfortable margin, while continued successes in state legislative elections had enabled it to capture the Senate. Cleveland assumed the presidency with both houses of Congress in Democratic hands, support that he had been denied during his first administration. The Democratic party also rode high in New York, New Jersey, and Connecticut. Cleveland had carried all three states; New Jersey and Connecticut had elected Democratic governors, as well. The gubernatorial victory in Connecticut was the party's first there since 1882. (New York already had a Democratic governor; the party had won the most recent gubernatorial election there in 1891.) Democrats represented New York and New Jersey in the U.S. Senate and held a majority of the congressional districts in each of the three states. Only the state legislature of Connecticut remained in Republican hands.

The Democratic tide continued to flow during the early months of 1893. Late in March a Democrat crushed a Republican in a special state senatorial election in New York. Less than one month later, a Democrat won the Massachusetts congressional seat Henry Cabot Lodge had vacated to serve in the U.S. Senate. Meanwhile, the Democrats reversed the Republican plurality of 1892 in the Rhode Island gubernatorial election. No candidate polling a majority, the election was thrown into the state legislature; ultimately, the incumbent remained in office. The Democrats' strong showing in Rhode Island carried over into two runoff races for Congress, which they won after having trailed Republicans the previous fall.[1] The significance of these elections extended far beyond New York, Massachusetts, and Rhode Island. They clearly indicated that the Democratic upsurge, which had begun fully three years before the victory of Grover Cleveland, did not halt with his election. Thus, to understand the almost unbroken series of defeats suffered by the Democratic party from the fall elections of 1893 through the presidential election of 1896 one must analyze factors that emerged during that period to erase political patterns which had seemed clear enough through the spring of 1893.

Of greatest importance, a major economic depression struck the United States in 1893. The bankruptcy of the Philadelphia and Reading Railroad on February 26 signaled a financial panic. On May 4, the National Cordage Company collapsed for want of working capital. The New York stock market, which had been fluctuating wildly for some time, broke, and after a brief rally it sank steadily. In July, a paroxysm of distrust of banks swept the nation; many banks were forced to suspend cash payments. Though gold flowed back into the United States in August, the economy was clearly suffering from an illness deeper than a case of monetary nerves; in fact, the nation was sliding into a full-fledged industrial depression.[2] With factory closings and production cutbacks came wage reductions, shortened work weeks, and layoffs. Relief for the unemployed was a major problem in the Northeast as early as July and August, and the situation became more pressing as summer faded into fall and fall into winter. Voluntary organizations—some experienced, others formed to meet the emergency—offered assistance to the needy, most operating on the assumption that work in return for succor was a moral imperative.[3] A number of local governments took limited steps to alleviate want. In New York City, the Democratic administration established a relief committee to solicit funds for distribution among private relief organizations. Not surprisingly, municipal employees and businesses that maintained close connections with the Tammany regime were major contributors to the relief fund.[4]

Labor unions and workingmen's conferences called on city and state governments to launch public works programs. Governor Roswell P. Flower of New York, in responding to appeals to call the state legislature into special session for this purpose, sought to convey the impression that he had acted promptly and effectively by letting all possible contracts for work on the state canals while continuing construction on the state capitol. But privately and publicly he reiterated the Jeffersonian faith that "that government governs best which governs least," and he paraphrased Grover Cleveland to the effect that "in America the people support the government; it is not the province of the government to support the people." To call a special legislative session would set a dangerous precedent; to recognize government's responsibility for public works would inevitably lead to paternalism. Addressing upstate audiences, Governor Flower stressed the transitory nature of the depression; the essential prosperity of the state's agriculture; and the necessity for economy in government, since increased tax burdens would weigh most heavily on those least able to bear them.[5]

The deepening depression and mounting unemployment sharpened conflicts within the labor force and between job-holders and job-seekers. During a period in which the labor force in many localities and industries was recruited heavily from a single ethnic group while other groups sought to advance themselves by capturing such positions, the struggles frequently took on ethnic overtones. A major riot in Brooklyn pitted Irish laborers against

Italian laborers; disputes in other northeastern cities often involved attacks on or criticism of Italians or East European Jews. Animosity toward outsiders and foreigners sometimes led to restrictive governmental policies: the Newark Board of Works resolved that its engineer should negotiate contracts ensuring that the county's unemployed receive jobs before outside labor; the New York and Pennsylvania legislatures ultimately barred aliens from employment on state and local public works.[6]

Among East European Jews, particularly in the Lower East Side of New York City, where crowded tenements housed some 100,000 of the newcomers, deteriorating economic conditions combined with cultural alienation (a heritage of the Old World reinforced by experience in the New) to fan the flames of radicalism. Anarchist and socialist rallies, parades, demonstrations, and disturbances in the Lower East Side frightened the city's "respectables." The New York *Times* condemned the alien element as disruptive of law and order and called for a suspension of immigration for the remainder of 1893. Relations between the East European Jewish community and the police, already strained, worsened during the August unrest.[7]

The depression lent an urgency to political debates over the financial and tariff issues. These debates involved interest groups and their political allies, all seeking to attain economic objectives through governmental action. Though financial and tariff policies were important to various interest and sectional groups, the currency and tariff debates had even broader significance. To a considerable extent, the rival parties linked the functioning of the private economy to the working of governmental currency and tariff policies, each diagnosing the nation's economic malaise as a result of opposition policies and prescribing its own policies as economically restorative. The factors contributing to depression and those that would contribute to recovery were far more complex than the analysis of either party showed, but the leadership of each party clearly identified itself with particular economic policies and related these policies to the well-being of the nation as a whole, not merely of its own faction and the interest groups supporting it. As a consequence, each party staked its political future on the efficacy of specific economic programs in maintaining or restoring the conditions in which the private economy would flourish.

The first economic issue dealt with by the Cleveland administration in 1893 was the Sherman Silver Purchase Act of 1890. The Act—passed by a Republican Congress and signed into law by a Republican President—had been a political response to the demand for inflation by the debtor regions and to the demand for relief from the falling price of silver by the influential silver bloc in the U.S. Senate. The measure was the price paid by eastern Republicans to secure the votes of western Republicans for the McKinley Tariff bill. The Democratic national platform of 1892 had denounced the Sherman Silver Purchase Act, and President Cleveland agreed with this declaration. Cleveland felt that the Act threatened the treasury's gold reserve of $100,000,000, maintenance of which he deemed crucial to the financial integrity of the government.[8]

There was a consensus in New York, New Jersey, and Connecticut (indeed, in the whole Northeast) favoring repeal of the Silver Purchase Act. Businessmen, particularly financiers, many of whom were close to Cleveland, urged the President to call Congress into special session to effect repeal. Cleveland bided his time before doing so, partly because he feared that charges of catering to Wall Street would follow an early call and partly because he realized that the southern and western wings of the Democratic party opposed his policy. He hoped that time and worsening economic conditions might generate constituency pressures sufficient to force some opponents to submit to his will; the judicious dispensation of patronage might induce others—particularly Senator Daniel Voorhees of Indiana, an inflationist and the chairman of the Senate Finance Committee—to support him.[9]

Cleveland called Congress into special session on August 7. Three weeks later he won the first battle of his campaign, when the House of Representatives repealed the silver purchase clauses of the Sherman Act by a vote of 239 to 108. The battle in the Senate was more difficult, for the West was stronger there than in the House and Senate rules were conducive to obstructive tactics.

The President's patronage investment paid off early and handsomely: it was Senator Voorhees's vote that saved the repeal bill from being reported adversely to the Senate by the Finance Committee. As the fight dragged on, despairing Democrats counseled compromise. But Cleveland remained adamant, and on October 30 the Senate voted repeal, 43 to 32. The House concurred in a Senate amendment on November 1, and President Cleveland signed the measure into law the same day.[10]

Cleveland triumphed, but victory came dear. By demanding and securing unconditional repeal, he created in the South and West a reservoir of animosity toward his administration that would ultimately engulf it. To be sure, the northeastern business community, and the press that mirrored its views, applauded the President.[11] But not all of the region's politicians were as enthusiastic. Sound though they were on the financial issue, these politicians believed that politics was the art of compromise: they preferred party unity to a disruptive crusade in pursuit of a principle. Politicians understood that the platform of 1892 had been a compromise that denounced not only the Silver Purchase Act but the 10 per cent tax on state bank notes as well. Repeal of this tax would have been welcomed by the debtor regions as inflationary, and as a blow at the national banks, which they resented; it might have driven a wedge between the agrarians, who wished inflation, and the spokesmen for silver, who wished to bolster the price of that metal. Even some businessmen who favored repeal of the Sherman Silver Purchase Act were willing to recognize southern claims in this regard. But Cleveland did not move to redeem the platform pledge to repeal the tax nor did he forgive Senator Arthur Pue Gorman of Maryland, a conservative and an influential Democrat, for seeking a compromise during the October deadlock.[12]

Eastern Republicans strongly supported repeal of the Sherman Silver Purchase Act, even as their western colleagues opposed its revocation. (Western Republicans were not as numerous as southern Democrats. As a consequence, the G.O.P. congressional delegation was stronger for repeal of the Act, the handiwork of its own party only three years earlier, than was the Democratic congressional delegation.)[13] Thus, during the financial crisis of

1893, the northeastern Republicans appeared as sound as the Cleveland Democrats from the same area. Further, more was involved for the President than for other participants in the struggle. Cleveland clearly believed that the Sherman Silver Purchase Act was the principal factor depressing the economy; he had explicitly stated that belief when he called Congress into special session.[14] Having staked his reputation on this point, the President might have gained from the bitter fight, both in Congress and the nation, had recovery followed repeal. But recovery did not follow repeal; in fact, the depression deepened.

Public debate over the tariff issue did not cease during the financial controversy. Throughout the summer, Republicans charged that the mere promise—or threat—of the Democrats to reduce the protective rates of the McKinley Tariff Act had so undermined business confidence as to precipitate the sharp economic decline. Tactical considerations alone would have dictated such a campaign, for Republicans chafed under Democratic reminders that their party bore responsibility for the Sherman Silver Purchase Act.[15] But more than tactics was involved in the Republican counterattack. For years the party had been identified with the protective tariff. In effect, Grover Cleveland had thrown down the gauntlet in his tariff message of 1887, when he called for the reduction of import duties. One year later, during the presidential campaign, the two parties joined battle on the tariff question. Debate over the issue, sharpened even further by enactment of the McKinley Tariff in 1890, kept Grover Cleveland, who was then in private life, before the public. During the 1892 campaign Cleveland ran as the avowed champion of tariff reform, though he strongly disagreed with the Democratic national platform, which denied the constitutionality of tariffs save for the purpose of raising revenue.[16] Thus the Republicans were attacking the President on an issue on which his position was unequivocal.

Drafting a tariff bill during 1893 was not easy, for reformers were by no means agreed on the shape a reformed tariff should take. Generally speaking, the agricultural South and West opposed protection as a discriminatory levy on their regions. Contending that the tariff boosted the cost of manufactures imported from Europe and the North, their spokesmen argued that government should lower tariffs and raise revenue through an income tax that would tap the personal wealth of the Northeast. Producers of cotton, tobacco, meat, and grain did not usually fear foreign competition in the domestic market; they sought overseas markets for their surpluses. But even in the South and West some agriculturalists wished protection for their own specialties: e.g., sugar planters; citrus growers; and sheep raisers and cattlemen fearful of imported wool, leather, and hides. Producers of raw materials—coal, iron ore, forest products—also desired protection, as did such nascent industries as the iron industry of Alabama.[17]

Within New England, where protectionists still predominated, tariff reformers contended that the Republicans' policy of harmonizing the interests of the producers of industrial raw materials and manufacturers by protecting both worked to the disadvantage of the region. New England industries depended on outside sources for fuel and a wide range of raw materials. The industrial belt from New York through Illinois secured these at lower cost than New England could, and its more modern plants absorbed that cost with less difficulty. New England tariff reformers sought "free raw materials," so that the region might buy cheaply abroad where possible while benefiting from cheap transportation by sea. The demand for "free raw materials" did not lead the New Englanders to advocate the reduction of tariffs on manufactures, but the more sophisticated among them realized that such rates would have to be scaled down if their own program were to gain support elsewhere.[18]

Finally, the mercantile communities and shipowners of major Atlantic ports, particularly New York City, generally favored low tariffs, even free trade, rather than "free raw materials," for their interest lay in promoting international trade. Financial houses involved in international operations shared their view, as did wholesalers and retailers whose lines were produced abroad.[19] Although a few New England and New York City tariff reformers were willing to accept a federal income tax to compensate the national treasury for revenues lost through tariff reductions, most shared the general antipathy of articulate northeasterners toward such a levy.

The subject of the form that tariff revision should take was broached during the months following Cleveland's election. Even during these informal overtures, the differences between the needs of northeastern (particularly New England) industry and those of New York City commerce were obvious. Not until the bill repealing the Silver Purchase Act had cleared the House of Representatives did the Democrats begin to draft tariff legislation. In September, Representative William L. Wilson of West Virginia chaired open hearings of the Ways and Means Committee on the subject. Following the adjournment of Congress, the committee conferred with private groups interested in specific tariff schedules and with treasury officials concerned with the financial needs of the government. Wilson reported his bill to the House on December 19, and the proposal was taken up after the Christmas recess.[20]

The Democracy turned to tariff revision at a politically inopportune juncture. Even during economically brighter times, most Democratic politicians in the Northeast had shied away from the tariff-for-revenue-only position. In 1884 Cleveland's managers in the region were hostile toward tariff reform; prominent politicians advised against the tariff message of 1887; ex-Senator William H. Barnum of Connecticut, the party's national chairman in 1888, had been a protectionist; as late as 1892, Connecticut Democrats hedged on tariff reform in their state platform; throughout the period, Democratic congressmen from the Northeast displayed protectionist tendencies in their voting.[21] Now, in 1893, the economic crisis made tariff revision politically risky. As the depression grew worse, prudent Democrats warned against meddling with the tariff and politicians received advice to the same effect from their constituents. Manufacturers, workingmen, and farmers denounced revision, particularly during the open hearings of the House Ways and Means Committee. A minority of the witnesses recommended some rate reductions, especially on raw materials, but even among manufacturers in lines that supposedly would benefit from free raw materials there was general hostility toward revision of the McKinley Tariff. The public mood was clearly unfavorable toward experimentation.[22]

On November 6, 1893—less than one week after repeal of the Sherman Silver Purchase Act, even as the House Ways and Means Committee discussed tariff legislation and the nation struggled through its first autumn of depression—a number of states held off-year elections. Without exception, these elections reversed the political tide that had flowed Democratic from 1889 through the spring of 1893.[23] Across the nation, the Republicans had stressed the depression as a campaign issue, blaming the Democrats for having paralyzed the economy with irresponsible threats to reduce a tariff that protected businessmen, laborers, and farmers alike. In Iowa, at least, the Republicans had sought to reduce their own vulnerability on a cultural issue that had earlier embarrassed them: they made overtures toward local option, risking the loss of die-hard drys to win back German wets. To the east, Governor William McKinley of Ohio received more votes than any other candidate in the history of that state when he won re-election over Lawrence T. Neal, the ex-congressman who had introduced the plank asserting the unconstitutionality of the protective tariff at the Democratic national convention of 1892. In Pennsylvania, the Republicans equivocated on the currency issue, campaigned relentlessly on the tariff issue, and won their greatest victory since 1872. They also recaptured the governorship of Massachusetts, gaining their largest share of the gubernatorial vote there since 1885.[24] (See Appendix D.)

The Republicans also triumphed in New York and New Jersey: in New York they won all contested state offices and majorities in both houses of the legislature and in the state constitutional convention; in New Jersey they won majorities in both houses of the legislature. (New Jersey's governorship, that state's only elective office, was not at stake in 1893; Connecticut held no off-year state elections.) As elsewhere, the Republicans had taken heart as the depression deepened, and they hammered on economic issues as the political campaign developed.[25] All the same, analysis of the campaigns and elections in New York and New Jersey suggests that though the economic depression was already influencing political behavior across the nation, political conflicts with cultural overtones that flared within the two states accounted for the distinctive pattern of the vote in each.

A bitter fight within the Democratic party of New York State weakened it during the campaign and contributed directly to the Republicans' most decisive state-wide victory. The Democracy's nomination of Judge Isaac H. Maynard for a term on the New York State Court of Appeals touched off the conflict, which was, in reality, another round in the continuing struggle for control of the state party between the adherents of President Cleveland and those of Senator David B. Hill. Maynard's vulnerability to attack by Cleveland Democrats stemmed from his activities two years earlier, when as Deputy Attorney General he had participated in maneuvers to secure Democratic control of the closely divided state senate. Critics condemned Maynard's actions, but in 1892, Hill, by then a U.S. senator, secured for Maynard an appointment to the Court of Appeals by Governor Flower. Now, in 1893, Maynard and Flower sought to vindicate that appointment by winning for the former a full term on the bench. Hill privately suggested to Maynard that he withdraw from the race, but could do nothing except support him when he insisted on running.[26]

Maynard was nominated easily enough at the Democratic state convention, but his candidacy almost immediately drew heavy fire from a variety of sources, and the barrage did not let up until election day. The New York *Times,* a leading newspaper of the Cleveland Democracy, condemned the nomination as an affront to all decent citizens. Going so far as to praise the general level of Tammany Hall's ticket, the *Times* carefully disassociated Maynard from other Democratic candidates: to vote against Maynard alone would be to dramatize the personal nature of the deserved rebuke. Two organizations figured prominently in the anti-Maynard crusade. The German-American Reform Union—only recently created out of the German-American Cleveland Union, which had mobilized German support for Grover Cleveland in 1892—struck at Maynard with editorials, speeches, and rallies, climaxed by a mass meeting at Cooper Union at which Carl Schurz was the featured speaker. Major figures in the German American community led the organization; professionals and small businessmen were prominent in its ranks. The organized legal profession, acting through the Association of the Bar of the City of New York, also denounced Maynard.[27]

Attacks, by Democrats who generally supported Cleveland, upon party machines in the state's second and third cities added to the discomfort of Democratic regulars. In Brooklyn, the German Democratic Union, the Young Men's Democratic Club, the Brooklyn Democratic Club, Edward M. Shepard, and the Brooklyn *Daily Eagle* sided with a Committee of One Hundred, on which Democrats and Republicans were equally represented, in support of Charles A. Schieren, the Republican mayoralty candidate, against Mayor David Boody, the candidate of Boss Hugh McLaughlin's Democratic organization. In Buffalo a similar coalition attacked the machine of Lieutenant-Governor William F. ("Blue-eyed Billy") Sheehan, whose responsibilities in Albany were light enough to permit his continued dominance of Buffalo politics. Protestant ministers were vociferous critics of the municipal machines but they did not lead a state-wide crusade against Maynard.[28]

In the state campaign, Democrats did not counter the attack of the German-American Reform Union for fear of alienating the larger German community. Rather they relied on their traditional ties to sections of that community, which they hoped would be reinforced by the presence on the party ticket of a number of German candidates and by appeals to German fears of Republican sumptuary legislation. On the other hand, Democratic leaders did strike back at the New York City Bar Association. They sought intelligence regarding the identity and politics of its leaders; Senator Hill denounced the attorneys who attacked Maynard as "corporation lawyers who sell their opinions and their services to the great corporate interests" and ridiculed Mugwump lawyers as "a brainless set of namby-pambys" with "aristocratic pretensions and exclusive tendencies" who dressed as they did because "it's English, you know." [29]

Maynard fairly invited attack. He was vulnerable to a morality-in-government crusade, the type of campaign at which Cleveland's supporters excelled. Further, the time was ripe for such an assault. With their hero again in the White House, Cleveland

Democrats no longer had to fear jeopardizing Cleveland's career by condemning the state Democratic leadership. Relations between the camps of Hill and Cleveland had been strained a number of times during the 1880s. Hill's star had appeared to rise following his own victory and Cleveland's defeat in 1888, but Cleveland recovered to win his party's nomination and the presidency four years later. In the struggle for that nomination, Democratic financial and business leaders and their political allies in the Northeast supported Cleveland, who was sound on the money question and an advocate of judicious tariff reform. The selfsame men viewed Hill as an unreliable professional politician who was no friend of tariff reform and who might turn soft on the currency issue in order to mold a new political coalition. Throughout the Northeast, "the better element" worked for Cleveland against Hill.[30]

The presidential nomination won, Cleveland's managers moved to patch up intra-party differences during the 1892 campaign. The task was difficult: Hill had been hurt by his defeat, and Cleveland was not given to conciliating mere politicians. But William C. Whitney sternly lectured Cleveland on the necessity for unity in New York State; brought Cleveland together with Edward Murphy, Jr., William F. Sheehan, and Richard Croker; and secured Hill's endorsement of the national ticket. Whitney and Charles S. Fairchild, the prominent New York City lawyer who had organized Cleveland's pre-convention campaign in the state, discouraged the efforts of ardent but impolitic supporters of Cleveland who were working to capture the machinery of the state party. The New York City Democratic organization also had to be reassured, for during Cleveland's two earlier presidential races, anti-Tammany Democrats—many of whom were identified with Cleveland—contested with Tammany for the mayoralty. As recently as 1890 Fairchild had supported fusion with the Republicans against Tammany, but in 1892 he rejected any idea of opposing Tammany. The conciliatory effort was successful: the Democratic party waged a relatively united campaign in 1892.[31]

The uneasy alliance began to break up soon after Cleveland's election. Many of the President-elect's followers made it clear that they wished federal patronage in order to build up their faction's power at the expense of the state organization. Cleveland publicly opposed the election of Murphy to the U.S. Senate. Anti-Catholics, businessmen, and German leaders joined in this unsuccessful fight against Murphy. Indeed, uneasiness in the German American community, linked to Murphy's election, led men prominent in the German-American Cleveland Union to work for the creation of the German-American Reform Union.[32] Once in the White House, Cleveland angered the New York Democratic organization by nominating to the U.S. Supreme Court William B. Hornblower, who had served on the bar association committee that had condemned Maynard. Hill mobilized opposition to the nomination, and the Senate denied Hornblower confirmation in January 1894. (Cleveland next nominated Wheeler H. Peckham, an even more prominent foe of Hill and Tammany, to the high court. Once again the Senate rejected the nomination. Abandoning the fight, Cleveland sent the name of Senator Edward D. White of Louisiana to the Senate. White was confirmed. Subsequently, late in 1895, Cleveland cleared with Hill his plan to name Rufus W. Peckham, the brother of Wheeler H. Peckham, to the Supreme Court. Hill readily agreed; the Senate followed suit.) Meanwhile, the national administration held to a patronage policy that rewarded friends and passed over regulars. Within the state party, fighting between the Hill and Cleveland factions broke out in a number of county conventions.[33] As the struggle intensified, some Democrats warned that unity had to be restored if the party were to remain dominant. On the other hand, the New York *Times* maintained throughout the campaign that Maynard alone of the Democratic candidates would be punished at the polls. Organization Democrats remained outwardly confident, but the tone of a final letter of encouragement to Judge Maynard led him to reply that it was evident that his chances of election were problematical.[34]

Meanwhile, in New Jersey, a bitter conflict over state policy toward racetracks and gambling deeply influenced the partisan struggle for legislative control. In this debate the Democratic party could not very well claim itself to be the victim of economic forces it could not control or national policies it could not modify, for its own legislative majority had triggered the controversy in February 1893. For some years, important Democratic politicians in New Jersey had maintained lucrative connections with two racetracks. William J. Thompson, "The Duke of Gloucester," controlled one in Gloucester City, a suburb of Camden; Dennis McLaughlin directed another in Guttenberg, a town in Hudson County. Local opponents were thwarted by the racetrack operators' influence with local political groups and law enforcement agencies. An enactment of the state legislature, ostensibly aimed at the suspect tracks, succeeded only in injuring the Monmouth racetrack, a seaside resort operation. An effort by Assemblyman William T. Parker of Monmouth County to revive the track by lifting the strangling legislative restriction upon it failed in the face of a protest movement organized by the Reverend Dr. Everhard Kempshall, a Presbyterian minister who feared that the proposal would permit the opening of yet another track in Linden, near the minister's home in Elizabeth. Kempshall's followers formed an Anti-Race Track League and pressured Governor Leon Abbott, a Democrat, into denying the bill his signature. Protesters subsequently smothered a legislative proposal to grant the state a share of racetrack gate receipts.[35]

The climactic battle was joined in the legislature of 1893, where the racetracks were well represented. Assemblyman Parker introduced three bills favorable to gambling interests. The first granted to county boards of freeholders, city councils, and town committees the authority to license racetracks. (Existing courses were to be licensed by simple majority vote, new ones by two-thirds vote: the racetrack entrepreneurs did not wish to encourage new entries in the field.) The other bills legalized gambling at the tracks and permitted certain forms of off-track betting. Supporters rammed the bills through the legislature, denying opponents a public hearing before voting on them and promptly overriding the veto of Governor George T. Werts, a Democrat. Although Parker was a Republican, Democrats clearly favored and Republicans opposed passage of the bills.[36]

The actions of the legislature touched off an explosion among groups hostile to both the racetrack element and the leadership of the Democratic party. The Anti-Race Track League condemned the new laws and the legislature responsible for them.

Even Governor Werts did not escape attack, critics charging that his hasty veto of the bills had made impossible the mobilization of popular anti-racetrack sentiment before the legislature dealt with that veto. Across the state, ministers, church meetings, and public rallies in which clergymen figured prominently scourged the racetrack ring and its evil handiwork. In Trenton, delegations protested the laws in the statehouse itself. At a subsequent rally, they called for repeal of the measures and chose a committee to present their petition to the legislature and to organize a state law and order league. The anti-racetrack forces renewed and intensified their efforts during the autumnal political contest, and sermons by ministers and speeches by clergymen and laymen alike were heard throughout the state. Democratic as well as Republican newspapers supported the crusade.[37]

Newspaper reports indicated that the anti-racetrack movement was Protestant in leadership and following. Indeed, to a degree, the movement appeared to be denominational: Methodist and Presbyterian ministers and their congregations were more often identified as participants than Episcopalians, Congregationalists, and Baptists were. Roman Catholic and Jewish leaders seem to have been infrequently invited to join in the crusade; rarer still were the occasions on which spokesmen of these faiths actually appeared before rallies. Underlying these characteristics of the protest movement were differences regarding "moral" questions —in this case, gambling—among religions and among Protestant denominations.[38] The evangelical Protestant campaign against racetrack operators and their political allies, many of whom were Irish Catholics, contained overtones of cultural conflict. An incident during the Trenton rally clearly revealed this. Anthony Comstock denounced James E. Kelly as the state's leading gambler and, in response to a request from the audience, identified Kelly as an Irishman. An Irishman in the audience took exception to this exchange and to the crowd's hissing of the Irish, leading Comstock to backtrack.[39]

An abortive attempt by Roman Catholic priests to secure public support for parochial schools added to cultural tensions in New Jersey during 1893. Legislators, Catholic and Protestant alike, shied from risking political martyrdom for the Church in

1893: Democrats recalled their party's setback at the polls in 1875 after Democratic legislators had sought to aid a Catholic protectory and to gain access to state institutions for Catholic priests. One Democrat—from a safe district—finally consented to introduce the bill, but it was soon abandoned. The priests proselytized in the legislature at an inopportune time: the furor over the racetrack laws was at its very peak. The Reverend John L. Scudder of the Congregational Tabernacle of Jersey City, a leader of the anti-racetrack movement, denounced Roman Catholic designs on the public schools. Other clergymen did likewise. The Reverend James M. King, Secretary General of the National League for the Protection of American Institutions and a Methodist minister in New York City, went so far as to declare before a Newark audience that the school proposal was more dangerous than the racetrack measures. Sniping between Protestants and Catholics, particularly over school affairs, continued for some time in a number of communities. The parochial school controversy intensified tensions created by the conflict over racetracks.[40]

During the political campaign of 1893, anti-racetrack organizations sought to deny renomination to legislators favorable to the gambling interests and to secure from nominees pledges to vote for repeal of the controversial laws. These pressures led to a number of intra-party battles, particularly within the Democracy, a variety of "outs" challenging for leadership in local convenetions. In some instances, these clashes pitted pro-Cleveland elements against party regulars. Finally, the anti-racetrack groups endorsed major party candidates in some districts, secured the withdrawal of such candidates in favor of their own in others, and ran independent candidates in still others.[41]

From the foregoing, it becomes clear that the "reform" crusades in New York and New Jersey differed in important respects. That in New York reflected long-standing factional differences within the Democratic party; it involved attacks by anti-organization Democrats on one member of the party's state ticket and on party regulars in the cities of Brooklyn and Buffalo. That in New Jersey reflected the opposition of Protestant clergymen and laymen to racetrack and gambling laws they regarded as immoral; it involved attacks across the state on legislators (for the most part Democrats) who had supported such legislation. To be sure, clergymen were prominent among those who mobilized popular support for the municipal campaigns in Brooklyn and Buffalo, and Democratic factionalism played some role in the New Jersey struggle. Still, in New York the "reform" initiative lay essentially with urban, anti-organization political groups; in New Jersey it lay with church groups across the state.

Just as the "reform" campaigns in New York and New Jersey differed, so did voting patterns in the two states, and as a consequence each state deserves separate analysis. In New York, though the Republicans gained enough votes to capture all six contested state offices and control of the state legislature and constitutional convention, only in the race for Judge of the State Court of Appeals did percentage shifts match those in other urban-industrial states.[42] (See Appendix D.) The hapless Maynard actually showed worse relative to others on the Democratic state ticket than they did relative to Grover Cleveland's showing the previous year. (See Appendix E.) More Democrats and independents bolted to vote Republican for judge alone than they did to vote the straight Republican ticket. Even this formulation does not fully reveal the impact of Maynard's candidacy on Democratic fortunes, for opposition to Maynard led some protestors to vote the straight Republican ticket. At the same time, it is unlikely that many Democrats and independents protested the depression by voting against Maynard alone.

Historians have dramatized Maynard's defeat, but they have failed to analyze the pattern of the vote. In fact, Maynard did not fall victim to a moral crusade that moved voters equally in all quarters of the state. Only in the seven adjoining counties of the metropolitan New York City area—New York, Kings, Queens, Richmond, Suffolk, Westchester, and Rockland—did he suffer above-average losses. In those counties, Maynard fell 6.0 percentage points behind Cord Meyer, Jr., the Democratic candidate for Secretary of State; elsewhere in the state he trailed Meyer by only 1.7 points. Democrats who rejected Isaac Maynard in the name of "morality" thereby identified themselves as Cleveland Democrats. Such Democrats approved of their hero's stand on specific economic and political issues and agreed with his over-all view of the economic order, political life, and society. They found in him a Democrat whom they could support without endorsing "bosses," "machines," "the saloon," and the Irish Catholic politicians with whom they associated these pejoratives. The anti-Maynard crusade of 1893 was not to be the only revolt by Cleveland Democrats against their state party's duly nominated candidates. In the following year they supported a Democratic Party Reform Organization gubernatorial candidate against Senator David B. Hill, and in 1896 they supported the National Democratic party rather than William Jennings Bryan and the regular state ticket. Of necessity, protesting Cleveland Democrats voted Republican in 1893, but many chose to do likewise in 1894 and 1896, thereby directly strengthening the Republican opponents of their intra-party foes, rather than merely denying those foes their votes. In the later elections, as in 1893, voters in the seven metropolitan counties led the Cleveland Democratic revolt against party regulars.[43] This voting pattern probably reflected long-standing differences between organization and anti-organization Democrats in New York City and Brooklyn, running conflicts that had given rise to "reform" (i.e., anti-organization) groups capable of mobilizing voters (e.g., the German-American Reform Union and Brooklyn's Democratic Party Reform Organization) and exposed Democratic voters in the metropolitan area to extended press coverage and other reports, both generally hostile to party regulars, of intra-party strife. Standard accounts of the presidential campaign of 1896 treat the creation of the National Democratic party exclusively as a response to the nomination of Bryan by the Democratic party that year, but in New York State, at least, an identifiable Cleveland Democratic faction clearly antedated 1896.

In New York City (i.e., New York County), the depression appears to have had little effect on Democratic fortunes in 1893, the party actually losing less ground than the Republicans (0.3 vs. 1.5 percentage points) in the election for Secretary of State. At the same time, Isaac Maynard was severely punished in the city: he fell 7.3 points behind Cord Meyer, Jr.; Edward T. Bartlett, Maynard's opponent, ran 7.4 points ahead of John Palmer, Meyer's foe. Economic discontent was not completely absent: the Socialist Labor party increased its share of the city's vote from 2.1 to 3.3 per cent. Socialist Labor party strength lay primarily in the Lower East Side, where East European Jews were settling hitherto German districts, and secondarily in districts running up the East Side to the Bronx, where Germans, German Jews, and some East European Jews had settled or had climbed to from the poorer area to the south. In the Lower East Side, where economic conditions were almost certainly the worst in the city, Socialist Labor party gains did not come at the Democrats' expense. In that area the Democrats increased their margins over the Republicans in all but the Seventh Assembly District, where German Americans, led by Otto Kempner, a Democratic assemblyman, had been feuding with party regulars. Only in the 7th A.D. among those in the Lower East Side did Maynard fall badly behind Meyer. Democratic candidates, including Maynard, fared well in the 1st and 2nd A.D.s, Irish enclaves that lay to the south of the Lower East Side.[44]

To the north, along the East River, Meyer held his own, and defections from Maynard were kept within bounds in the 12th and 14th A.D.s, which contained considerable Irish populations. Farther uptown, where the Germans outnumbered the Irish, Democratic losses mounted and Maynard was badly cut. On the opposite side of Manhattan, along the Hudson River, the Democrats fared comparatively well in two Lower West Side A.D.s, the 8th, in which the Irish predominated over Italians and Negroes, and the 9th, in which old-stock Americans and the Irish were predominant. Five West Side A.D.s—13, 15, 17, 18, and 19—located between Nineteenth and Seventy-second streets, in all of which the Irish were numerous, also held firm for Meyer; Maynard suffered below-average losses.[45] If anything, the West Side contained more poor neighborhoods than the East Side: the Democrats' better showing there reflected the relatively light initial political impact of depression issues in New York City and the loyalty of Irish districts in the face of an anti-Maynard crusade that gained support in German and old-stock areas.

Elsewhere in the city the Democrats suffered serious setbacks. In central Manhattan, the 11th A.D., which contained a prestigious residential area as well as "the Tenderloin," a center of vice, turned more sharply against Maynard and Tammany's assembly candidate than it did against Meyer. To the immediate north, in the 21st A.D., the city's most famous silk-stocking district and home of the Union League Club, Meyer experienced his greatest percentage decline and Maynard fell farthest behind Meyer. (This district had been solidly Republican until Grover Cleveland sparked a Democratic upswing therein.) Congested tenement areas declined in number as one moved north through the 19th and 25th A.D.s: with local exceptions, the remainder of Manhattan and the Bronx (A.D.s 23, 26 to 30) afforded opportunities for decent living to their inhabitants, most of whom were old-stock Americans or the descendants of earlier German and Irish immigrants. In only two of these A.D.s did Meyer gain; in all, Maynard suffered sharp losses.[46]

The standoff in the election between Meyer and Palmer for Secretary of State indicates that no general shift toward the Republicans took place in New York City. On the assembly district level, percentage shifts toward Palmer were strongly and positively associated with the percentage margins by which Maynard trailed Meyer: the correlation between them was +.762. It would appear that Maynard weakened the entire Democratic ticket, particularly in districts that were silk-stocking or middle class rather than working class, and those that were old-stock American or German rather than Irish or East European Jewish.[47]

In the metropolitan counties of Queens, Richmond, Rockland, Suffolk, and Westchester, the entire Democratic slate suffered above-average losses. Still, in each, Maynard fell farther behind Meyer than Meyer fell behind Cleveland's 1892 vote.[48] In Kings County, where a revolt against the Brooklyn Democratic organization was a feature of the campaign, all Democratic candidates lost heavily. Boody, the Brooklyn regulars' mayoralty candidate, trailed even Maynard. There was no mistaking the decisiveness of the Democratic defeat: Meyer lost percentage strength in all of Brooklyn's twenty-eight wards; in nineteen, he fell by ten or more points. Maynard trailed him in every ward—by margins of 0.7 to 6.2 points. Boody, in turn, trailed Maynard in all but one ward, by margins of 0.6 to 3.5 points. Cleveland had received 56.0 per cent of the total vote in Brooklyn; Meyer, Maynard, and

Boody polled 44.9, 41.0, and 39.1 per cent, respectively. The Democrats' severe setback in Brooklyn contrasted sharply with their showing in New York City, where Maynard alone had been rebuffed. In another important respect, however, the Brooklyn election resembled that across the East River, for though the Democrats lost ground in their strongholds (Wards 2, 5, 6, 8, 9, 10, 12, 14, 17), which were, for the most part, tenement districts where the Irish predominated, they suffered their most serious reversals in districts where old-stock Americans, Germans, and other non-Irish immigrants predominated.[49] Silk-stocking and middle class wards contributed much to the Republican victory, but so did tenement districts whose working class inhabitants were German. To a certain degree, the increase in Republican strength in old-stock American districts indicated that the party had built on comparative strength: three such wards (20, 23, 25) had been the only ones to give majorities to Benjamin Harrison in 1892. But gains in German wards (16, 18, 21, 26, 27, 28) strengthened the G.O.P. in districts that had generally voted Democratic. These patterns combined to produce a rank-order correlation of +.566 between Republican ward strength in 1892 and percentage gains in 1893. (In New York City this correlation was +.613.) In Brooklyn, as in New York City, shifts in the election for Secretary of State were strongly and positively correlated (+.805) with those in the election for Judge of the Court of Appeals.

Outside of the New York City metropolitan area, moderate Democratic percentage declines, with Maynard falling slightly behind the ticket, were the rule in the election of 1893.[50] In many counties, one or more of the minor parties, as well as the Republicans, gained percentage strength. Increased support for the People's and Socialist Labor parties may have reflected an initial response to the depression by a small minority of voters, but the Prohibition party appears to have gained some support among anti-Maynard Democrats who could not bring themselves to vote Republican. A number of upstate counties departed from the general pattern of small Democratic losses and Republican gains, but Democratic factional politics, rather than factors related to hard times, seems to have accounted for these atypical cases. In

Clinton, an agricultural-lumbering county adjoining Canada and Lake Champlain in the northeastern corner of the state, Meyer lost 15.2 percentage points from Cleveland's 1892 mark, and Maynard lost an additional 2.3 points. Clinton had generally voted Republican during the late nineteenth century, but the Democrats had gained ground in 1890, 1891, and 1892. No economic catastrophe befell Clinton, alone of counties in northeastern New York State, and the Socialist Labor, People's, and Prohibition parties were weak there. Clinton was unique within this quarter of the state in that its Democratic organization was reported to be falling apart. As a matter of fact, Democratic defections cut across rural towns of varying prosperity as well as the city of Plattsburg. Those defections were greatest in towns carried by the Democrats in previous years—Clinton (−39.3 percentage points) Altona (−34.0), Plattsburg (−21.8), Ellenburgh (−19.5), and Champlain (−16.2), with Dannemora (−2.2) the exception. Of the eight other towns in Clinton County only Schuyler Falls (−15.9 points) showed a comparable Democratic decline. Elsewhere, the Democrats were decisively defeated in Monroe and Erie counties, which contained, respectively, Rochester and Buffalo. In Rochester, which had been Republican before 1893, the Democrats suffered heavy to disastrous losses in wards of diverse political persuasions, but in Buffalo, which Cleveland had narrowly carried in 1892, the anti-Sheehan revolt cost the Democrats heavily in all but the organization's strongholds, where the party held its own or gained slightly. The full impact of the Democratic disasters in Brooklyn and Buffalo on state-wide political patterns can best be understood by isolating their vote from that of the rest of the state. (See Table 5.) The two cities experienced unusually sharp Democratic percentage losses and unusually small declines in off-year election turnout. Voter shifts and turnout in Brooklyn and Buffalo were functions of the political interest generated by intense local conflicts.[51]

Six upstate counties, Chemung and Schuyler to the north of Pennsylvania, and Rensselaer, Albany, Greene, and Schoharie in the central Hudson River valley region, registered Democratic gains in 1893. In Albany and Rensselaer counties, the cities of Albany and Troy, in which the Irish were numerous, contributed

TABLE 5 *Shifts in Democratic Percentage Strength and Voter Turnout, 1892–1893, Brooklyn, Buffalo, and Other Areas of New York State*

	DEMOCRATIC %			
	1892 (Pres.)	1893 (Sec. of State)	1892–1893 Shift	Turnout 1892–1893
Brooklyn	56.0	44.9	−11.1	− 0.2%
Buffalo	48.2	39.7	− 8.5	− 4.6%
Rest of State	48.0	46.2	− 1.8	−17.6%
New York State	49.0	45.8	− 3.2	−14.9%

Sources: *Tribune Almanacs, 1893, 1894; Manuals of the Legislature of New York, 1893, 1894.*

disproportionately to the Democrats' success; in the others, gains were more evenly spread among urban and rural units of all descriptions.[52] Democratic successes in Albany and Troy and the stand-off in New York City in the election for Secretary of State indicate that no force set in motion by the depression was irresistibly shaping urban voting patterns about the state. Indeed, the Democrats' gains in six upstate counties support the hypothesis that factional conflicts within the Democracy underlay local differences in the outcome of the election of 1893 in New York State. During 1892, partisans of Grover Cleveland had voiced doubts regarding the loyalty of Democratic regulars in all of these upstate counties save Rensselaer; surprising percentage declines in some counties seemed to confirm their suspicions. Now, in 1893, organization Democrats, fighting for their political lives against a *de facto* coalition of Republicans and Cleveland Democrats, had every reason to get out the regular vote. Loyalty to the Democracy extended to Isaac Maynard, who trailed the ticket by narrow margins in all six counties.[53] The Democrats' showing in a half-dozen upstate counties and (to a lesser degree) New York City could not reverse the Republicans' decisive victories in Brooklyn and Buffalo and their varying successes across the state, but they did reduce the net G.O.P. state-wide gain.

Across the Hudson River, New Jersey Democrats suffered a resounding defeat, losing six of their seven contested state senatorial seats, while failing to unseat one G.O.P. state senator, and losing twenty-two assembly seats, while gaining only three at the expense of the opposition. They thus lost control of both legislative houses. (See Appendix E.) Analysis of shifts in the vote indicates that the anti-racetrack and anti-gambling crusade had the strongest impact on popular voting behavior in the state. The greatest shifts occurred not in urban-industrial regions, but in predominantly rural and small-town nonindustrial areas. Prohibitionist fires had burned brightly in the involved areas during the 1880s; the embers of that reform movement, still glowing in the early 1890s, were fanned into flames by the anti-racetrack crusaders. Methodists predominated in the affected counties, particularly in southern New Jersey; in the more northerly ones, Presbyterians were also numerous. Roman Catholics were distinctly in the minority in all of the counties.[54]

Changes in voting behavior were most marked in the state's three southernmost counties. Cape May County, a bastion of Methodism, registered the greatest percentage shift from the Democrats to the Republicans. In Sea Isle City, a Methodist town, the Democratic share of the two-party vote plummeted from 72.8 to 18.8 per cent; in Ocean City, which had been established "as a temperance and Methodist summer resort," it sank from 43.8 to 20.4 per cent. The Prohibitionists actually outpolled the Democrats in Ocean City. In West Cape May, the county's banner Prohibition town, the Democrats slid from 52.9 to 30.3 per cent of the two-party vote. On the other hand, in only one of four towns where Democratic losses were comparatively light was the Prohibition party strong. Cumberland County's demoralized Democrats abandoned one assembly district without a fight; their other assembly candidate lost 5.3 percentage points over-all, and 8.9 in Vineland, which had been "founded on the Prohibition idea." [55]

That southern New Jersey was swept by a moral revolt against racetrack legislators and not by an economic protest against the Democracy as the party in power during the first months of the depression was revealed in Atlantic County, where the state senator and the assemblyman, both Republicans, had voted for the condemned racetrack and gambling measures. Assemblyman Charles A. Baake ran for re-election against Frederick Schuchardt, a fellow resident of the German community of Egg Harbor City. Schuchardt unseated Baake, registering the Democrats' most impressive percentage gain in New Jersey. The Prohibitionists also gained as the Republicans suffered their worst defeat. The Democrats fared best in strong Prohibition towns: for example, they climbed from 50.9 to 91.4 per cent of the two-party vote in Buena Vista and from 59.6 to 90.1 per cent in Hammonton, in both of which the Prohibition candidate outpolled the Republican incumbent. Weymouth, where the Prohibition vote equaled the Republican vote, provided a minor exception to this generalization: there, the Democrats slipped from 72.7 to 71.2 per cent of the two-party vote. In Linwood, where the drys were weak, and in Egg Harbor City, among whose Germans they were virtually nonexistent, the Democrats gained 24.4 and 16.5 percentage points, respectively.[56] The evangelical Protestants' crusade against racetracks, unlike their attacks on beer drinking and "the continental Sunday," involved no challenge to the institutions and practices of Germans; voters in the two groups shifted in the same direction on this occasion.

Monmouth County, in east central New Jersey, was another center of anti-racetrack agitation. Assemblyman William T. Parker, a Republican, had introduced the racetrack bills; a Democratic senator and two assemblymen had supported them. None of the three assemblymen was renominated; Senator Henry S. Terhune failed of re-election. The Citizens' League endorsed the entire Republican slate; the Prohibitionists supported the G.O.P. in two races. Only in Parker's former district did the Democrats gain ground. This constituency had been considered Democratic until Parker's victories in 1891 and 1892. With Parker disgraced and removed from the running, the district reverted to the Democrats. Rascality was not always punished, however, for in Camden County William J. Thompson, "The Duke of Gloucester," survived the challenge of a Republican–Citizens' League–Independent Democratic coalition. Thompson lost ground in five districts but gained in the precinct in which his racetrack was located. Republican incumbents easily retained a senate and an assembly seat. In Camden County's remaining assembly district, the Citizens' League nominated and the Republicans endorsed a lifelong Democrat for the seat. The nominee resigned from his Democratic club and became a Republican. Though the Democrats did not renominate their racetrack assemblyman, they lost this normally Democratic district.

Three long-time Democratic counties in northwestern New Jersey—Warren, Sussex, and Hunterdon—were also involved in the moral revolt. The Republicans' failure to challenge an anti-racetrack Democrat in one of Warren's assembly districts—they defeated a racetrack Democrat in the other—permitted the Democrats to register a net percentage gain in the county's two assembly races. But in the state senatorial race, the Democrat running to succeed a racetrack Democrat who had resigned his seat in order to enter the U. S. House of Representatives (to which he had been elected before the anti-racetrack explosion), won by a margin much narrower than that of his predecessor. In Sussex, a racetrack Democrat failed of renomination; the Republicans captured his assembly seat. The issue was clearly operative in Hunterdon, where one racetrack Democrat ran and lost while a second was denied renomination, the Democrats salvaging his assembly seat. Northwestern New Jersey had been populated during the colonial era by Dutch, German, and Huguenot settlers from the Hudson River valley and by Welsh, Scotch-Irish, Quaker, and transplanted New England settlers from Pennsylvania. Irish and German immigration during the nineteenth century had altered the composition of some towns and cities, but the counties' stable populations basically reflected the earlier internal migrations. Democratic strength in the area had been widely diffused before 1893, but the party generally drew its greatest support from towns in which the old Dutch were strongest, and it more than held its own among other settlers from New York. Pennsylvania elements generally backed the Republicans. While towns in which the old Dutch lived gave the Democrats varying levels of support, the party's banner towns (Pahaquarry and Washington Township in Warren County; Walpack and Sandyston in Sussex; and Union in Hunterdon) were basically old Dutch settlements. Democratic percentage declines were the rule in these counties in 1893, but in a few old Dutch towns such losses were small, and in two (Sandyston and Montague) the party did better than it had in the 1892 assembly election. Old Dutch towns, whether Reformed Church or Presbyterian, were less moved by the moral crusade of 1893 than were old-stock, Methodist towns and towns whose Presbyterians were British rather than old Dutch in origin.[57]

Across sixteen New Jersey counties, the anti-racetrack explosion blasted the careers of pro-racetrack assemblymen, Democrats and Republicans alike, though the Democrats were more severely mauled. A solitary suspect Democrat was re-elected; three were defeated; eleven were denied renomination, the Democrats retaining only three of these districts. Two of three tarnished Republicans failed of renomination; the Democrats captured one of these districts and defeated the solitary incumbent who sought re-election. Six of ten Republican foes of the racetracks were renominated; the G.O.P. held all ten districts. Three of six such Democrats also survived, but the party lost both districts where anti-racetrack assemblymen were not renominated.

In the heavily populated, industrial northeastern quarter of New Jersey, which contained the state's three most populous counties (Hudson, Essex, and Passaic) and seven of its ten most populous cities (Newark, Jersey City, Paterson, Hoboken, Elizabeth, Bayonne, and Orange), repercussions of the moral revolt and the depression combined to produce Democratic defeats. Percentage shifts in the urban counties' vote were smaller than in the more disaffected rural counties, but solid, if unspectacular, Republican gains reaped a harvest in the large and preponderantly Democratic legislative delegations: the G.O.P. captured four assembly seats each in Essex and Hudson, two in Union, and one in Bergen, as well as senate seats in Essex and Union, while losing only a Hudson assembly seat.

In Essex County, the Republicans registered an average gain (3.3 percentage points) and the Democrats a below-average loss (4.1 points). The Prohibition party slipped slightly (from 1.3 to 1.2 per cent), while the Socialist Labor party, entering candidates in seven of eleven assembly races in its first effort, polled 0.9 per cent. The Republicans had carried three Essex assembly districts in 1892; they now increased their margin in each. Standing up to the racetrack interests did not guarantee political survival to Democrats: Senator Michael T. Barrett, who had been praised by anti-racetrack spokesmen, and two anti-racetrack assemblymen were defeated. One of these victims, Assemblyman Timothy Barrett, lost most heavily in the stronghold of native-born voters, though he suffered in Irish and German wards, as well. On the other hand, supporting the racetrack bills did not necessarily doom Democrats to defeat: four such assemblymen survived, three by increased margins, while a pair was defeated. In the latter two districts, the Socialist Labor party gained more percentage points than the Republicans; in one, it held the balance of power. The continued weakness of the Prohibition party in Essex (not even the moral revolt of 1893 could aid it there) and the emergence of the Socialist Labor party, which drew upon the area's German, German Jewish, and East European Jewish workers for support, suggest essential differences between politics in northeastern New Jersey and elsewhere in the state, as does the fact that the fate of Democrats in the election bore little relation to their stands on the racetrack issue. In this connection it is worth noting that the Democracy had won county and city elections in April, shortly after the legislature's controversial action but before the depression, and that the four Democratic assemblymen who survived the November election represented the districts that had ranked highest in party strength in 1892.[58] The election in Essex was hardly a landslide, but it did enable the Republicans to undo damage done them by their flirtation with prohibition during the previous decade.

The Democrats suffered a sharper setback in Hudson County, a party stronghold for forty years, losing 6.1 percentage points as the Republicans gained 3.5. The Prohibitionists remained below 1.0 per cent, but the Socialist Labor party climbed from 0.1 to 1.3 per cent. In Essex the Independent Citizens' Association endorsed Republicans; in Hudson the Association ran candidates in four of eleven districts, polling 1.6 per cent of the county-wide vote. The Democrats unseated one of three Republican assemblymen, their only success against a racetrack foe anywhere in the state. Three racetrack Democrats were re-elected; another district was carried by a replacement for a fourth such assemblyman. As in Essex, the salvaged districts had been the party's strongest in 1892, but in Hudson, the Democrats lost strength in all but one. The three Democratic survivors and the candidate who unseated a Republican were Irish; the Democrats appear to have been most successful among their most loyal bloc of supporters.[59] Four districts that had been represented by racetrack supporters fell to the Republicans. The only assemblyman among these Democrats to run for re-election suffered the worst defeat in Hudson County, losing 17.9 percentage points, but the Citizens' Association gained more (9.9) than the Republicans (7.2) in the district.

In Union County, where the Republicans defeated one racetrack Democrat and the legatee of another while retaining their own assembly seat, Elizabeth Democrats lost the most percentage strength in wards containing the highest percentage of native-born males (11, 12) and the least in the ranking Irish wards (1, 2, 4). The Democrats suffered moderate losses in two wards in which Germans were numerous, fairly held their own in a third, and gained slightly in a fourth (Wards 3, 5, 7, and 9, respectively). The Socialist Labor party showed best in the three most heavily German wards; Union ranked as the banner county of the party in New Jersey.[60]

No assembly seat changed hands in Passaic County, but percentage shifts there exceeded those in other northeastern New Jersey counties. In Paterson, the Democrats lost heavily in one German-Irish and three Irish wards that formed their bastion there.[61] Losses of this magnitude in organization districts suggest the operation of forces unrelated to the anti-racetrack crusade. Intra-party conflicts contributed to Democratic percentage losses in the party's two assembly districts, but these antedated the legislative controversy of 1893, for independent Democrats had polled 16.0 and 12.1 per cent in the 2nd and 3rd A.D.s the previous year. In the 2nd A.D., a new Democratic nominee gained 9.2 percentage points over his predecessor, but fell 6.8 points short of the combined regular and dissident Democratic vote of 1892; in the 3rd A.D., Thomas Flynn, a prominent racetrack supporter, fell 15.6 points behind the combined Democratic vote of 1892—and 3.5 points short of his own earlier mark.

The patterns of New Jersey voting behavior differed from those in New York State. Percentage point shifts were greatest in rural areas and small towns, rather than large cities. Racetrack Democrats were the prime victims of these shifts, but returns from Atlantic County revealed that Republican culprits also suffered the wrath of the electorate. Urban shifts were neither confined to particular cities nor concentrated in particular districts therein. The protest vote against Isaac Maynard in New York City and the metropolitan area and against regular Democratic candidates in Brooklyn foreshadowed similar anti-regular votes in New York during the following years, but the New Jersey crusade deeply affected voting behavior only in 1893, counties and towns returning to more normal voting patterns thereafter.[62]

Reactions to the elections in the two states varied. Republicans related their successes to the nation-wide political response to the depression, but they also stressed the factors unique to each state, particularly to New Jersey. Cleveland Democrats naturally attributed their party's defeats to the sins of the two state organizations, thereby scoring at the expense of intra-party rivals while avoiding embarrassment to the national administration, whose tariff policy was already under fire as the depression deepened. They failed to explain Republican successes in other states, where racetrack legislation or a suspect nomination was not an issue. Senator Hill blamed McLaughlin, Sheehan, and Croker for the defeat suffered by his New York State Democratic organization and, probing deeper, indicated that he regarded the success of any Democratic presidential candidate in 1896 to be unlikely. Finally, a number of Protestant clergymen viewed the elections, especially in New York, as a triumph of Protestant virtue over Catholic vice.[63] The Democrats were jarred by their defeats in the off-year elections, particularly in New York and New Jersey, where they had held the upper hand before 1893. But national power was still theirs, and, within New York and New Jersey, the governorships. It remained to be seen whether the elections of 1893 signified that the Democrats had passed through economic and political squalls, or whether they portended a major storm in 1894.

III

The Politics of Constitutional Revision: The New York State Constitution of 1894

AMONG the victories of New York State Republicans in the off-year canvass of 1893, none was more important to the future of the state than their election of a majority of the delegates to the state constitutional convention. The financial panic and depression of 1893 contributed to that year's upset Republican victory; hard times continued through the drafting of the revised constitution between May and September of 1894 and its ratification that November. Yet despite the depression, debate over the new state constitution centered on the partisan and cultural issues that had dominated politics before 1893.

The very timing of the constitutional convention was a consequence of the rival parties' maneuvering for advantage during the period before the depression, for as early as 1886 the electorate had called for such a convention by an overwhelming vote of 574,993 to 30,766. Governor Hill, a Democrat, and the state legislature, then under Republican control, disagreed over a number of issues relating to the convention, the most important of which involved the districts from which most delegates were to be elected. Hill proposed that delegates be elected from the state's congressional districts, which had been redistricted by the Democrats in 1883; he subsequently vetoed a bill providing for the election of delegates from assembly districts, the boundaries of which had been shaped by the Republicans in 1879. His veto was sustained, and, for the time being, the constitutional convention was relegated to limbo.[1]

With the Democrats' capture of both houses of the state legislature in 1891, the fortunes of the convention revived. Political and constitutional problems had to be ironed out, and not until January 27, 1893, was convention legislation enacted. The Democrats were confident that they would control the convention: their measure provided neither for the appointment of representatives of special interests (e.g., prohibition, license, woman suffrage, labor, antimonopoly) nor for minority party representation among delegates elected at large. The Republicans evidently discounted their own chances of winning control of the convention: they passed over party regulars, who would have clamored for recognition under more favorable circumstances, to nominate a distinguished slate of delegates-at-large led by Joseph H. Choate and Elihu Root.[2] The Democrats' plans went awry when the Republicans elected all fifteen delegates-at-large and eighty-three of the 160 district delegates. At the convention the Republicans increased their majority by unseating six Democrats and one labor organizer whose nomination by the Democrats had been suggested by the Central Labor Union of Buffalo.[3] Thus the convention, first discussed during an era of political stalemate and finally provided for during a period of Democratic supremacy, became an instrument firmly in the grip of its Republican majority.

Within the convention, partisan lines were clearly drawn over legislative reapportionment, by far the most important political issue before the body. The parties had repeatedly struggled over the issue in the legislature itself, and each was fully aware of the political consequences of specific reapportionment proposals. The Democrats, whose limited upstate areal base had made it difficult for them to control the legislature, wished to modify the State Constitution of 1846, which barred any major shift of seats from rural (Republican) areas to urban (Democratic) areas. The Republicans sought to safeguard their rural legislative base against the steady growth of urban population and, even more, the threatened consolidation of New York City and Brooklyn, with the emergence of a single and more powerful Democratic machine its frightening corollary.

The convention's Committee on Legislative Organization proposed a fifty-member state senate, each member of which would theoretically represent 2 per cent of the citizen population. Seats were first to be assigned to counties that contained 6 per cent or more of the citizen population—New York, Kings, and Erie.[4] The Republicans added three mandatory rules to the section dealing with apportioning senators to populous counties. These provided that: (1) no county was to be assigned four or more senators unless it had a full ratio for each senator; (2) no county was to have more than one-third of all the senators; and (3) "no two counties or the territory thereof as now organized, which are adjoining counties, or which are separated only by public waters, shall have more than one-half of all the senators." Speaking in behalf of the second rule, Elihu Root, vice-president of the convention, contended that New York City's representatives, "responsible to one political organization," would be more than a match for an equal number of representatives from geographically scattered, economically diverse, rural counties that lacked Tammany's centralized leadership. One upstate Republican argued that the third restriction, framed to limit the political impact of the creation of Greater New York, was desirable, but that it was too liberal as it would allow New York and Kings counties one-half of the senators. The first rule worked against New York and Kings counties in 1894; it was later to curb Erie, Bronx, and Queens counties. Neither the second nor third restriction has ever been invoked—because the situations they were designed to meet have never developed.[5]

By increasing the membership of the senate from thirty-two to fifty, the Republicans virtually restored rural areas to their original numerical strength under the State Constitution of 1846. This strength was effectively guaranteed by an amendment which provided that if any county assigned three or more senators were entitled to an additional senator or senators at a subsequent reapportionment, the senator or senators would be provided for by increasing the size of the senate rather than by reapportioning seats at the expense of sparsely populated areas.[6] Thus constitutional provisions pertaining to the state senate consistently discriminated against urban areas—and the Democratic party.

A new system for apportioning seats in a state assembly enlarged from 132 to 150 members also protected the Republicans' rural base and saved—for the time being, at least—a number of upstate counties from losing one of their two assemblymen. During convention debates, Republicans drew attention to other states that weighted representation to check the power of metropolitan areas, warned rural Democrats that without such a safeguard their legislators would be overwhelmed by urbanites in the party's legislative caucuses, and praised rural virtues. Democrats denounced the partisan scheme to represent acres rather than people, while defending the morality and praising the achievements of city dwellers. Though the Democrats also contended that the proposed amendment disadvantaged single-district rural counties, they were clearly less interested in wooing sufficient rural Republican delegates to block the proposal than they were in laying the groundwork for an appeal to urban voters to reject the reapportionment amendment in November.[7]

The final round in the apportionment struggle revealed the strength of party discipline on this particular issue. On September 7, the amendment was ordered to a third reading by a vote of 84 to 54, with only two Republicans, Benjamin S. Dean and Owen Cassidy, voting with the minority, whose ranks held firm. Six days later, Dean offered a substitute amendment that held the line against expansion of the legislature, ordered a census in 1895, and provided for a subsequent reapportionment on the basis of the rules established in 1826. The amendment failed, 53 to 94, Dean and Cassidy again voting with the Democrats, and Edwin Countryman, an Albany Democrat, siding with the Republicans. That evening the convention gave final approval to the Republicans' reapportionment plan by a vote of 96 to 60, with Dean the only delegate to stray across party lines.[8]

The convention retained the existing constitutional provision that "inhabitants, excluding aliens" serve as the population base for legislative apportionment. The Republicans could not countenance any other policy, for the state's alien population was concentrated in a few urban counties that the Democrats generally carried. Since aliens did not vote—and no delegate advocated granting them the suffrage—their inclusion in the population base would have increased the political weight of voters in districts where aliens were concentrated.[9] The Committee on Suffrage, acting on Republican allegations that the Democrats naturalized immigrants in large numbers immediately prior to election days, reported out an amendment requiring that naturalization precede voting by sixty days. On the floor, Edwin Countryman moved to recommit the amendment to lengthen the interval to six months. Recommittal carried, 72 to 53, but Elihu Root secured passage, 86 to 47, of a compromise recommittal motion that provided for a requirement of ninety days. The convention subsequently passed Root's version, 102 to 54. During the debate, one Republican chided his colleagues for supporting Countryman's extreme proposal while a Democrat from New York City arraigned "the Knownothingism of the Republican party."[10]

Concern with the political role played by immigrants was also displayed in resolutions introduced by upstate Republicans. The convention did not vote on proposals that the ability to read, or to read and write, English be made a requirement for voting. But Charles Z. Lincoln called on the convention to request Congress to propose an amendment to the Constitution of the United States requiring that all voters be citizens and prohibiting any state from granting the suffrage to aliens. A brief but sharp floor debate followed an adverse report on the resolution by the Committee on Suffrage. Indeed, the issue shattered Republican discipline and the party's leaders were forced to rely on Democratic votes to suppress the anti-alien suffrage revolt in their own ranks.[11]

The Republicans' concern for their rural base of power was apparent during the struggle over voter registration. They secured passage of an amendment stipulating that personal registration be mandatory only in cities and villages of over 5000 population. In 1892 and 1893, Democratic legislators had narrowly failed to extend the personal registration law to cover rural areas. Now, in 1894, Democratic delegates complained that the amendment drew invidious distinctions between the morality of rural and urban voters and would tie the hands of the legislature by imbedding the principle of non-personal registration in the constitution. Republicans stoutly defended the honesty of rural registration and voting practices.[12]

The Republicans were as loath to relax their grip on the legislative machinery that gave them political leverage in the cities of the state as they were to allow future legislatures any opportunity to harass their rural organizations. Accordingly, they killed a proposal to grant cities a measure of home rule.[13] Republican leaders did permit a provision for the separation of municipal from national and state elections to survive their emasculation of the home rule proposal. Proponents contended that the reform would free municipal government—which they claimed was a matter of administration, not politics—from the partisan influence of campaigns for national and state office. In reality, Republicans and anti-organization Democrats wished to reduce the political influence of Democratic urban organizations, particularly Tammany Hall, in one way or another. Elihu Root, identified with the businessmen's wing of the New York City Republican party that opposed both Tammany and Republican Boss Thomas C. Platt, went so far as to recommend (without success) that district representation on common councils of cities be abandoned in favor of some form of at-large elections with provision for minority representation. In effect, this reform would have weakened political organizations based on ethnic communities and strengthened businessmen and their associates whose city-wide influence did not depend on relationships with local organizations.[14] In the final analysis, Republicans supported the separate elections proposal less in the belief that it would weaken Tammany's grip on New York City than in the conviction that it would lessen the influence of New York City—and Tammany—on national and state elections. Since Tammany mobilized its forces most diligently for municipal campaigns, separation would deny this turnout to Democratic candidates in state-wide elections. Some urban Republicans feared that a decline in interest in municipal elections would ensue, but this mattered little to party leaders whose concerns lay elsewhere. Anti-Tammany Democrats supported the proposal because it would end Tammany's alleged bargains with G.O.P. leaders under which Tammany betrayed Democratic national or state candidates and the Republicans betrayed their own municipal candidates—while giving anti-Tammany Democrats freedom to challenge the organization in municipal elections without fear of Tammany retaliation in national or state elections. The amendment finally passed by the convention separated municipal elections from state-wide elections in cities of over 50,000 population by scheduling the former in odd-numbered years. The amendment's sponsors exempted smaller cities, which generally held their elections in the spring in any event, from its terms in order to win the support of convention delegates from such municipalities.[15]

The issue of public assistance to sectarian educational and charitable institutions confronted the Republican leadership with problems far more difficult than those they faced during the convention's handling of reapportionment and questions relating to registration and election. On the latter issues, the Republicans' objectives were clear and their attainment involved no great sacrifice by any element within the party. The religious issue was another matter: there were sharp differences of opinion among the public at large and among the delegates regarding public policy in this controversial area. Mounting pressures dictated a resolution of the conflict, but the question had to be dealt with delicately, if decisively, for it was fraught with political danger.

Friction between Protestants and Catholics was widespread during the nineteenth century, and clashes over schools were both frequent and important in this general conflict. To nationalists, the United States' expanding public school systems were not only educational facilities, providing youth with the basic skills necessary for advancement in a fluid society; they were also Americanizing agencies, bringing together children from diverse cultural and socio-economic backgrounds and inculcating in them a reverence for fundamental American institutions. To Roman Catholic communities, largely immigrant or second-generation, and of modest means if not poor, tuition-free public education provided opportunities for advancement in the United States. (Archbishop John Ireland estimated that, as of 1892, two-thirds of school-age Catholics attended public schools.) But conservative Catholics viewed the public schools as subversive of their faith. In effect, they condemned public schools for being either Protestant or irreligious. Conservatives argued that, given the State's commitment to compulsory education and the biases of public schools, Catholic schools should receive State support. Meanwhile, Catholics would struggle to maintain parochial schools while being taxed to support public ones. Prominent conservatives in the hierarchy, most notably Archbishop Michael Corrigan of New York City and Bishop Bernard McQuaid of Rochester, New York, were zealous defenders of parochial schools. Yet Catholics were by no means of one mind regarding the school question. Liberals, such as Archbishop John Ireland of St. Paul, Minnesota, combined praise of parochial schools and pronouncements of the justice of public assistance to such institutions with tolerance of the public schools. Realistically, liberals recognized that in the foreseeable future, Catholics could neither afford their own first-rate parochial school system nor expect public support except on a local, piecemeal basis. Still, factional differences can be exaggerated, for the conservatives were also pragmatic, and Archbishop John McCloskey of New York City and his successor, Archbishop Corrigan, supported an arrangement between the parish priest and school board of Poughkeepsie by which the church rented, for a nominal sum, its school building to the board during regular school hours, and a Roman Catholic teacher—certified and paid by the board—taught the standard public school subjects during the day, with freedom to give religious instruction before and after hours. Thus, a conservative archdiocese tolerated an agreement roughly comparable to that later entered into in Faribault, Minnesota, by a liberal archdiocese.[16]

Deepening Church-State conflicts frightened many Protestants and secularists and led, in 1889, to the founding of the National League for the Protection of American Institutions, which was dedicated to securing "constitutional and legislative safeguards for the protection of the common school system and other American institutions, to promote public instruction in harmony with such institutions, and to prevent all sectarian or denominational appropriations of public funds." Former President Rutherford B. Hayes, J. Pierpont Morgan, Cornelius Vanderbilt, and Levi P. Morton were among the more prominent members of the league, but a general secretary, the Reverend James M. King, pastor of the Union Methodist Church of New York City, and corresponding secretaries across the nation directed its activities. The N.L.P.A.I. sought an amendment to the Constitution of the United States to extend the religious protections of the First Amendment to cover state governmental actions and to prohibit state expenditures in support of sectarian or ecclesiastical activities, and was active in securing similar guarantees on the state and territorial levels. In New York State, the organization fought the Freedom of Worship bill; subsequently, it protested application of the law to the New York House of Refuge on Randall's Island.[17]

Fears regarding Catholic designs on the public schools of New York were seemingly given substance in September and November, 1893, when Dr. Michael Walsh, editor of two newspapers that circulated among Roman Catholics, twice broached the idea of state support of parochial schools. On the second occasion, Walsh indicated that a bill to this end had been drawn up by Dennis Spellissy and would be introduced in the next legislature. Protestant ministers, private organizations, government officials, and newspapers roundly denounced the proposal; the episode touched off bitter attacks on the influence of Catholics and Tammany Hall on the public schools of New York City. The Vicar-General of the Archdiocese of New York hastened to deny that the Church was involved in the Walsh-Spellissy plan. This statement did not satisfy the New York *Times,* which noted that the archdiocese had merely disclaimed responsibility for a particular proposal, while it had not disavowed all claims to assistance. Ultimately, the newspaper concluded, nothing less than a papal statement would satisfy Americans. Walsh, defiant, claimed that the hierarchy favored the measure but feared to speak out on a political issue. Walsh declared that he felt no such reticence; indeed, in a state in which Catholic voters held the balance of power, he looked forward to placing legislators on the record on this issue.[18]

The National League for the Protection of American Institutions vigorously opposed the Walsh-Spellissy proposal and moved to block any such plan. The N.L.P.A.I. asked a Republican assemblyman-elect to inform it of the introduction of any bill to divide common school funds along sectarian lines. It questioned prospective delegates to the state constitutional convention regarding their positions on sectarian appropriations; drafted for presentation before the convention an amendment to bar state and local governmental assistance to sectarian institutions; and advocated adoption of that amendment in an address to the people of New York State. The designation by convention leaders of Frederick W. Holls, a Republican delegate-at-large and a spokesman for the N.L.P.A.I., as chairman of the Committee on Education strengthened the hand of the forces supporting the anti-sectarian amendment. Holls, in turn, successfully championed Edward Lauterbach, a New York City Republican, as chairman of the Committee on Charities. Holls informed Joseph H. Choate, president of the convention, that Lauterbach strongly favored the amendment and suggested that the appointment of a Jew to the sensitive position "will tend to allay much of the hostility which the Hebrews might otherwise feel towards the Constitution." Shortly afterward, Holls introduced an amendment to prohibit all sectarian spending.[19]

Proponents and opponents of the proposed ban on sectarian appropriations argued their cases during joint hearings before the committees on Education, Charities, Taxation, and Legislative Powers. On June 6, seven witnesses, including the Reverend Dr. King and the Reverend William Croswell Doane, Bishop of the Protestant Episcopal Church of Albany, attacked sectarian spending. They stressed the school issue, but did not neglect the charities question. Bishop Doane, who prefaced his comments with an appeal to the delegates not to permit "questions of policy and expediency" to interfere with their duty, suggested that the Roman Catholic Church received appropriations large enough to support charitable institutions and "to have a sufficiently large surplus left behind to carry on a great deal of its own particular distinctive work." [20]

Two weeks later, witnesses hostile to the proposed ban testified before the committees. Myer Stern, representing Jewish charities in New York City, declared that the Jewish community wished no public support for religious or secular instruction, but that assistance in feeding and maintaining children confided to the care of Jewish institutions would be appreciated.[21] Frederic Coudert and Colonel George Bliss, Jr., spoke in behalf of Catholic interests. The Church prepared carefully for the occasion. Early in 1894 Archbishop Michael Corrigan called on the Committee on Catholic Interests of the Catholic Club, composed of seventeen prominent Catholic laymen and chaired by Justice Morgan J. O'Brien of the New York State Supreme Court, to defend Catholic charities against their enemies. Subcommittees were assigned the tasks of gaining support among non-Catholics, gathering data for use by counsel and delegates, and raising funds among threatened institutions to finance the costly effort. To avoid fomenting religious controversy, the Committee on Catholic Interests planned a quiet campaign among delegates to the convention, going so far as to admonish Archbishop Corrigan not to issue a pastoral letter on the sectarian issue before the convention opened.[22] Other Catholics contended that mounting attacks on the Church—those by the American Protective Association (A.P.A.) appeared to pose the most serious threat—should be countered with a lecture series on anti-Catholicism by a prominent Roman Catholic. John E. Robinson and George Parsons Lathrop questioned opposition within the Catholic Club to such a series. But Lathrop finally acknowledged that plans laid by men more experienced than he and approved by Corrigan had given him a better understanding of the situation. Though the Archbishop, Bourke Cockran, and Lathrop did counter the attack of the A.P.A. during the spring, the cautious strategy was generally followed.[23] Meanwhile, a representative of the Catholic Club in Albany prepared analyses of the membership of the committees before which Coudert and Bliss would appear and of the previous testimony of witnesses who had supported Holls's amendment.[24]

Coudert, prominent in legal, reform Democratic, and Catholic lay circles, and Bliss, descended from a venerable New England family but himself a convert to Catholicism, a legal adviser to

Archbishop Corrigan, and a leading Republican who numbered Joseph Choate and Elihu Root among his social and political contacts, were admirable choices for presenting the Church's case.[25] Coudert declared that while Catholics would not renounce the justice of their cause, neither Bliss nor he was "intrusted with the duty" of opposing a ban on public appropriations to parochial schools. Bliss read from a letter written to him "by one of the highest dignitaries in the Catholic Church in this state," which admitted that the current fight for assistance to parochial schools was lost and concluded that Catholics should avoid further conflict for the time being. Bliss then turned to a discussion of sectarian charities. He vigorously defended public assistance to them, warning that without continued governmental support, Catholic charities would have to close, thereby shifting the entire burden of those charities to the shoulders of taxpayers. He hoped that assistance to sectarian charities would not be prohibited. Both Bliss and Coudert reflected the thinking of the hierarchy on the school question: Bliss cited a letter from a high Church dignitary; Coudert had prepared his statement after conversations with Bishop McQuaid, and an intermediary had subsequently forwarded a draft of that statement to Archbishop Corrigan with Coudert's suggestion that Corrigan inform him if it coincided with his views.[26]

The Roman Catholic Church executed a brilliant tactical maneuver in abandoning the school fight and standing fast on the charities question. Whatever hopes Catholic leaders in New York State may have entertained regarding public assistance for parochial schools were shattered by the Republicans' capture of the state legislature and the constitutional convention in the elections of 1893. The intensity of Protestant and secularist feelings regarding the public schools had been revealed during the Walsh–Spellissy episode the previous fall, as it had been in the barrage of petitions and memorials demanding an end to sectarian appropriations that descended on the convention from religious and lay groups and prominent individuals. Faced with this opposition, the Church abandoned nothing attainable in temporarily renouncing its claim to aid for parochial schools.[27]

Still, no compromise was possible unless Republican leaders

abandoned the proposed blanket ban on sectarian spending in favor of one that barred aid only to schools. The Church's willingness to seek such an accommodation disarmed some erstwhile opponents while making it easier for sympathetic Republicans to support the Catholic position on the charities question. Even before the conciliatory speeches of Coudert and Bliss, the New York *Times* had reported that the delegates were united on protecting the common school fund but that there was no consensus on the issue of assistance to charities. Further, the extreme utterances of men such as the Reverend Dr. King and Bishop Doane enabled Catholics to tar their opponents with the brush of religious bigotry by equating the National League for the Protection of American Institutions with the American Protective Association. Republican politicians did not wish to contribute unnecessarily to a revival of religious strife that would strengthen traditional party loyalties in New York State. Their party had only recently won its first state-wide election in years; gubernatorial and congressional elections, as well as a vote on the revised constitution itself, were in the offing. An acceptable compromise would reduce the emotional charge of the religious issue, making possible a campaign based on depression issues. Joseph Choate—who later publicly alluded to his concern that bigotry had inspired extreme critics of Catholic charities—was personally sensitive to charges of prejudice; he had been accused of hostility toward Irish Catholics, and an Irish nationalist newspaper had opposed his election as a convention delegate.[28]

In seeking a *modus vivendi,* neither Republican nor Catholic leaders could have forgotten that earlier in 1894, Republican legislators had humiliated Archbishop Corrigan and Bishop McQuaid in their fight against liberals within the Church by electing Father Sylvester Malone of Brooklyn, a liberal, to succeed Bishop Francis McNeirney of Albany as a Regent of the University of the State of New York. Corrigan and McQuaid had used all their political influence to block the selection of Malone. Failing to win the post for McQuaid, they had even worked with Boss Platt in an attempt to insinuate a Protestant layman into the position, in preference to the liberal priest. In the end, the conservative prelates were reduced to seeking proof of their suspicion that the fine Italian hand of Archbishop Ireland had secured Malone's election.[29] The defeat had painfully demonstrated to Corrigan and McQuaid the hopelessness of their position on any educational issue on which the Republican party opposed them. The episode was also instructive for Republican politicians: George Bliss warned them that their choice of a priest who was "persona non grata just now" with his own superiors would hurt the party, for there were 70,000 Catholic Republicans in the state. He again referred to the sentiments of Catholic Republicans in his testimony of June 20.[30] Thus Republican leaders had to consider the possibility that a second humiliation—this time in the constitutional convention—would lead Archbishop Corrigan to campaign against the revised constitution and its Republican sponsors.

In fact, Republican and Catholic leaders did reach an accommodation. As late as July 23, Holls remained sanguine regarding the ultimate enactment of an absolute ban on state and local governmental assistance to sectarian charities. But the Reverend Dr. King, in public testimony and private correspondence, revealed his growing fear that a compromise was in the making.[31] On July 19 the Committee on Education approved the ban on aid to sectarian schools, but in later adopting the full education article, it exempted from this prohibition schools in institutions under the jurisdiction of the State Board of Charities. Meanwhile, following its hearings in Albany and its inspection of benevolent institutions about the state, the Committee on Charities unanimously reported out an article permitting a measure of assistance to sectarian charities. Two charities committee members made it clear that the draft article was based on an express understanding that no aid would be forthcoming under the education article, but that the education article as then worded violated this agreement.[32]

The convention took up the education article in Committee of the Whole on August 31. During the debate over the ban on aid to sectarian schools, President Choate moved to strike the clause exempting schools in institutions under the State Board of Charities, declaring that it violated "an implied understanding."[33] Owen Cassidy countered with an amendment substituting a ban on aid to institutions "not wholly owned and controlled by the State or a subdivision thereof" for that barring aid to schools "wholly or in part under the control or direction of any religious denomination, or in which any denominational tenet or doctrine is taught." [34] The bitter argument that ensued carried over into the next day. Matters were further complicated for the Republican leadership by an amendment proposed by Edward Lauterbach on August 31 and modified one day later by Louis Marshall, a Syracuse Republican. This amendment specified that secular instruction of inmates of orphanages or other institutions to which children were committed by court order and in which education was incidental was not to be prohibited by the education article. Elihu Root concluded the debate of September 1 with a sharp attack on those who sought to undermine the separation of Church and State, pointedly remarking that while "Hebrew and Catholic alike" were welcomed in the United States, the nation's Protestant founders and their descendants insisted on such separation. In referring to "Hebrew[s]," Root almost certainly had Lauterbach and Marshall in mind. The Reverend Dr. King was later to charge that Catholics and "a section of the Jews" had combined to prevent the prohibition of public assistance to sectarian charities. Despite the interest of Myer Stern, Lauterbach, and Marshall in the charities question, there is no evidence to support the contention that Jews played a significant role in the religious compromise.[35]

On September 4 the Lauterbach–Marshall amendment failed of passage, but only after Root rallied supporters of an absolute ban on aid to sectarian schools was Cassidy's proposal narrowly defeated. The education article was then advanced to a third reading, but final consideration was postponed until the charities article was dealt with in Committee of the Whole on September 14.[36] Lauterbach, Choate, and Root defended the charities proposal, as did Frederick Holls, whose speech (and vote) revealed that his commitment to the Republican party outweighed his loyalty to the N.L.P.A.I. The delegates overwhelmingly defeated John I. Gilbert's amendment to bar assistance to sectarian charities after January 1, 1905, and then agreed to the report of the Committee on Charities.[37] One day later, the convention voted final approval of the education and charities amendments. Friends and critics of compromise—even those who denied the existence of "an understanding or agreement or arrangement"—made clear the relationship between the two proposals.[38]

Reactions to the compromise varied widely. President Choate praised it at the convention and during the fall campaign; Senator Hill, the Democratic gubernatorial candidate, condemned it as anti-Catholic. Holls, acknowledging the thanks of the N.L.P.A.I., asserted to the Reverend Dr. King that they had accomplished much under difficult circumstances; the Law Committee of the N.L.P.A.I. urged endorsement of the revised constitution; and King subsequently expressed pride in the League's having achieved constitutional protection of the common schools and strict supervision of private charities. Protestant ministers endorsed the education proposal, but the Reverend Madison Peters, an A.P.A. spokesman, had harsh words for the charities article. A Protestant weekly, *The Independent,* complained that the charities article nullified the education article, even as *The Catholic World* termed the latter ". . . an important victory . . . for agnosticism." Father Alfred Young, in a campaign statement absolving the Republicans of charges of bigotry, pointed out that "accredited spokesmen of the Catholic Church" had offered the religious compromise adopted by the convention. But the Rochester *Cathedral Calendar* suggested that Catholics reject the constitution in protest against the education article, and priests in the Church of the Sacred Heart of Jesus in New York City condemned the revised constitution at each mass on the Sunday prior to election day.[39]

Even though Catholics in Rochester and New York City sniped at the revised constitution, there is no evidence that the hierarchy of the Roman Catholic Church worked to sabotage the convention compromise by defeating the constitution at the polls. The state's bishops reportedly considered publicly rebuking the Republican party for its failure to denounce the American Protective Association, but "prudence and expediency" dictated otherwise.[40] Church leaders displayed a similar discretion in regard to the revised constitution. Defeating the Republicans and/or the constitution would have been no easy task, nor—

given the temper of the Protestant majority—would doing so have guaranteed an acceptable program of public assistance to parochial schools. Further, political intervention by the hierarchy would assuredly have intensified anti-Catholicism. The action of Pope Leo XIII, who less than one year later personally made George Bliss, Jr., a Commander of the Order of St. Gregory the Great, indicated that the Church regarded the settlement of 1894 as the best attainable under the circumstances. In 1896, the Catholic Club of the City of New York presented silver loving cups to Bliss and Frederic Coudert for their services in behalf of Catholic charities at the constitutional convention. Archbishop Michael Corrigan, Elihu Root, and Edward Lauterbach were among the guests at the presentation.[41]

That the convention concentrated on political issues was understandable, for relatively few economic questions fell within its purview. By far the most important of these, economically and politically, involved the state canal system. The conflict was long-standing; it did not grow out of the depression of 1893. On one side were ranged spokesmen for commercial and related interests along the Erie Canal–Hudson River route from Buffalo to New York City. They wished to modernize the Erie Canal, thereby strengthening it as a check on the New York Central and Erie railroads, whose rate policies benefited ports in other states, and warding off the threat of alternative water routes from the Midwest to the Atlantic Ocean. On the other side stood spokesmen for a variety of upstate agricultural, processing, manufacturing, and mercantile interests. They felt that the canals, though supported by taxes levied throughout New York State, benefited only the areas adjacent to them and, increasingly, western competitors.[42]

Thwarted in the legislature, and with Governor Flower, who hailed from an anti-canals county, apparently unsympathetic to their cause, advocates of canals modernization turned to the constitutional convention for succor. A canals conference was organized in Albany; members testified before the convention and lobbied among the delegates. Interested labor organizations joined the campaign launched by business groups: the Canal Boatmen's Union sought the assistance of the Central Labor

Union in mobilizing support for an improvements amendment.[43] Farm organizations led the opposition, contending that a costly program of improvements would subsidize western agriculture at the expense of New York farmers, whose land—one-fourth of the wealth of the state—bore ten-elevenths of the tax burden. They proposed that the canals be turned over to the United States government, that *pro rata* freight rate regulation be employed to control exorbitant local railroad charges, and that personal as well as real property be taxed at full market value. On the other hand, they warned that rural voters would reject an amendment that provided tax support for the canals.[44]

On September 10 the convention, by a rising vote of 50 to 55, rejected a report of the Committee of the Whole containing three innocuous canals amendments. During the floor fight a bloc of delegates had occupied a middle position, opposing both transfer of the canals to federal ownership and improvement proposals involving bond issues and taxes. Some had feared that a far-reaching amendment might produce an upstate revolt sufficiently violent to plunge the revised constitution to defeat at the polls, or that a popular defeat for the canals amendment would doom the cause of the canals for years. Their spirit of compromise carried over into the Republican caucus and then into the convention, which returned the canals question to committee. Commercial interests made the most of this opportunity, and on September 20 the convention overrode diehard rural opposition to approve an amendment that for the first time granted the legislature specific authority to improve as well as to maintain and repair the canals. Improvements might be provided for by regular appropriations, an "equitable annual tax," or the issuance of bonds. Proposals to finance improvements with bond issues to be redeemed through the levying of a direct annual tax were to be subject to popular approval at a general election.[45] Thus the Republicans' adroit compromise held out the hope of relief to interests along the waterways without unduly jeopardizing the proposed constitution among voters in much of the state's interior.

Economic groups less influential than those interested in the canals did not fare as well at the constitutional convention. All but one amendment requested by organized labor or the Socialist

Labor party received short shrift. Only after some hesitation did the delegates approve an amendment prohibiting the competition of prison labor with free. This proposal, alone of those advanced by labor, had a measure of business support.[46] Other proposed amendments—protecting labor unions from anticonspiracy laws; broadening employers' liability for accidents; creating a court of labor-management arbitration; limiting working hours in nonagricultural jobs; barring the employment of women and children in "exhaustive occupations"; restricting the use of tenements for manufacturing; guaranteeing a free and non-sectarian education to all children (with free meals provided for children of destitute parents); and providing for municipal home rule, the initiative, and the referendum, as well as for public ownership of transportation facilities and utilities—were buried in committees.[47]

The convention submitted the revised constitution to the electorate in three parts, separating the sections relating to reapportionment and the canals from the body of the document. During the fall, the Republicans sought to cloak their handiwork in a mantle of statesmanship, but most Democrats charged that the proposed constitution, particularly the reapportionment article, had been cut of partisan cloth. Senator Hill attempted to rally Catholic and urban Democrats by attacking the education and reapportionment proposals. Still, many Protestant Democrats opposed sectarian spending and some Cleveland Democrats favored a reapportionment that would weaken Hill and Tammany Democrats. Further, a number of Protestant clergymen sermonized in behalf of reapportionment (as a curb on the corrupt cities), as well as the ban on sectarian spending. Meanwhile, commercial organizations and the New York Central Labor Union campaigned for adoption of the canals amendment.[48]

On November 6, 1894, New York State voters ratified the proposed state constitution and carried the Republican party to victory. Though the vote received by the Republican state ticket and the constitutional questions fell within a narrow percentage range, both state-wide and in many counties, sectional and local patterns were by no means obliterated in the voting.[49] The votes on the constitution were positively correlated with the Republican gubernatorial vote on the county level, that on reapportionment most strongly (+.647), followed by those on the main body of the constitution (+.437) and, very weakly, the canals (+.179). But the votes on the three constitutional questions were more strongly correlated: the main section with reapportionment, +.918; the main section with the canals, +.889; and reapportionment with the canals, +.702. Large numbers of voters appear to have regarded the three constitutional questions as one—and voted accordingly.

A comparative analysis of county returns sheds light on the areal strengths and weaknesses of the controversial amendments dealing with reapportionment and the canals. The reapportionment proposal ran behind both the main section of the constitution and the canals amendment in urban counties along the Buffalo–New York City water route. Still, it fared relatively well in these generally Democratic counties; the Republican tide and anti-Democratic machine sentiment actually carried New York and Kings for reapportionment—and that plan was specifically designed to discriminate against the two counties. A handful of upstate counties in which the Democrats had not yet been reduced to impotence—Chemung, Columbia, Greene, Montgomery, Otsego, Schoharie, Seneca, Sullivan, and Ulster—rejected the reapportionment amendment, as did Allegany, Tioga, and Warren, which were staunchly Republican. Allegany and Tioga, like most of the Democratic counties voting against reapportionment, opposed improvement of the canals. In these Republican counties, hostility toward the canals amendment apparently spilled over into opposition to the reapportionment proposal. Though Warren County was clearly an exception to this generalization, no other interpretation of the vote is as persuasive. (See Table 6.)

On the canals amendment, agricultural-lumbering counties benefiting from the Oswego (Oswego County) and Champlain (Clinton, Essex, Warren, and Washington counties) canals voted with counties containing commercial cities along the Erie Canal–Hudson River route (Erie, Monroe, Onondaga, Rensselaer, Albany, Westchester, New York, Kings, Queens, and Richmond) for improvements, while landlocked counties (e.g., Alle-

TABLE 6 *Popular Vote, Revised Constitution, and Governor (1894), Canals Proposal (1895), Selected New York State Counties*

COUNTY	REPUB. % OF TOTAL VOTE, GOVERNOR, 1894	VOTE ON REVISED CONSTITUTION, 1894: % FAVORING			% FAVORING CANALS PROPOSAL, 1895
		Main Section	Reapportionment	Canals	
Chemung	43.8	46.4	45.9	45.6	43.1
Columbia	51.5	48.1	48.9	46.5	41.9
Greene	49.3	39.8	39.9	40.9	36.6
Montgomery	54.0	50.3	49.9	53.8	65.3
Otsego	53.4	47.7	48.5	44.7	16.0
Schoharie	44.4	38.3	39.4	37.6	18.9
Seneca	50.8	44.1	44.7	46.9	48.7
Sullivan	52.8	42.5	43.8	40.9	24.0
Ulster	52.3	47.5	48.1	46.8	58.1
Allegany	58.9	44.7	48.4	37.7	21.8
Tioga	57.6	50.6	46.4	45.8	15.0
Warren	59.2	52.2	49.7	55.6	71.0
Clinton	63.6	54.3	55.0	57.1	57.7
Essex	68.0	70.0	69.1	72.0	66.7
Oswego	59.6	61.0	60.2	64.2	67.7
Washington	67.9	65.8	64.9	66.4	59.6
Albany	49.8	48.3	47.4	50.7	77.6
Erie	55.5	68.2	65.1	74.0	88.0
Kings	50.3	55.0	50.1	58.6	82.6
Monroe	56.9	58.8	57.5	58.9	63.8
New York	46.0	56.5	50.3	61.8	87.9
Onondaga	54.2	55.2	54.8	56.6	50.0[a]
Queens	52.9	58.1	54.7	61.0	72.0
Rensselaer	51.5	51.0	50.1	52.6	73.6
Richmond	50.4	56.0	54.9	57.6	59.9
Westchester	52.9	60.1	56.6	61.8	77.5
Franklin	66.4	47.5	53.2	39.4	13.6
St. Lawrence	68.5	57.8	62.9	51.4	10.2
Broome	57.6	56.0	58.1	53.7	34.4
Cattaraugus	58.1	56.3	57.3	57.7	33.7
Chautauqua	66.0	64.3	66.3	64.4	34.4
Delaware	59.5	52.9	54.0	49.3	30.1

TABLE 6 *Popular Vote, Revised Constitution, and Governor (1894), Canals Proposal (1895), Selected New York State Counties* (continued)

COUNTY	REPUB. % OF TOTAL VOTE, GOVERNOR, 1894	VOTE ON REVISED CONSTITUTION, 1894: % FAVORING			% FAVORING CANALS PROPOSAL, 1895
		Main Section	Reapportionment	Canals	
Jefferson	57.0	51.9	54.3	46.4	20.7
Schuyler	57.2	50.7	53.2	45.4	21.3
Steuben	56.1	57.5	58.6	55.4	27.9
Wyoming	61.4	61.0	61.1	56.9	20.2

Sources: for 1894, State of New York, *Manual for the Use of the Legislature, 1895,* 966–67, 973–74, 977–80; for 1895, State of New York, *Manual for the Use of the Legislature, 1896,* 969–70.

[a]The proposal failed to carry Onondaga County, receiving 49.98% of the vote there.

gany, Chemung, Franklin, and Tioga) and some adjacent to the Hudson (Columbia, Greene) and St. Lawrence (St. Lawrence) rivers opposed them. (See Table 6.) Though the positive correlation between the vote on reapportionment and that on the canals was the weakest of those on constitutional questions, it was quite strong (+.702), especially when one considers that spokesmen for rural, Republican counties in the interior had favored reapportionment and opposed the canals, while spokesmen for urban, Democratic counties along the waterways had opposed reapportionment and favored the canals. This surprisingly strong correlation probably reflected the widespread decision of voters to support or reject the three constitutional questions as one, and the dampening of the ardor of friends and foes of the canals alike by the compromise canals amendment. Analysis of returns from urban counties and from Brooklyn, the only city for which we possess the ward-by-ward vote on the constitution, suggests that opposition to the reapportionment section depressed the affirmative vote on the other proposals in these areas.[50] Conversely, the reapportionment section probably strengthened the other proposals elsewhere in the state.

That the conflict over the canals had indeed been blunted in 1894 became clear during a second confrontation the following year. Shortly after ratification of the revised constitution, businessmen interested in the canals renewed their campaign for improvements. Governor Levi P. Morton, who had won office in the Republican sweep of 1894, sympathized with them, but he appointed George W. Aldridge, the Republican mayor and boss of Rochester, instead of a businessman, as Superintendent of the State Department of Public Works, which was responsible for state construction projects—including the canals. Morton and Thomas C. Platt, who directed the Republican state organization, recognized the political potential of the department's budget and wished to have a professional politician hold the post.[51] The state legislature of 1895, dividing along lines similar to those in the constitutional convention the previous year, approved a bill to improve the Erie, Champlain, and Oswego canals through a bond issue not to exceed $9,000,000—subject, under the new constitution, to approval by the electorate.

This time, the issue was clear: proponents of the canals knew the improvements at stake, opponents the costs; no other questions would complicate matters.[52] Though turnout in state-wide elections declined by 8.1 per cent from 1894 to 1895, the vote on the canals increased by 19.7 per cent. (The canals vote was still 20.9 per cent smaller than the vote for state office, but it had been 39.3 per cent smaller one year earlier.) The vote on the canals also polarized sharply between 1894 and 1895. Over-all, support for the waterways rose from 57.5 to 65.0 per cent, but a heavy favorable shift in counties containing major cities accounted for this gain: pro-canals strength actually ebbed in 37 of 59 counties. Many counties that had swallowed or narrowly rejected the watered-down amendment strongly rejected the specific proposal. (See Table 6.) It was just such a rural rebellion that Republican strategists had feared—and avoided—in 1894. The polarization of the state's electorate on the canals question suggests that many voters believed they recognized their stake in the issue as defined in 1895 and voted accordingly. Within Brooklyn, where ward-level support for the canals had varied widely (in association with support for reapportionment) in 1894, a consensus overwhelmingly favorable to the canals revealed itself in the 1895 vote. The polarization of the 1895 canals vote contrasted with partisan elections, in which policy differences were often blurred and the strong party identification of voters generally militated against sweeping shifts in party preference.[53] The sharpness of divisions over the canals was all the more striking in view of the low-key campaign that had been waged on the issue. Apparently, voters did not need campaign stimuli to respond strongly one way or the other to the canals question.[54]

Republicans understandably rejoiced at the reception given the revised constitution by the electorate in November 1894. George Bliss acknowledged that Boss Platt had despaired of the document's chances at the polls; John W. O'Brien, a delegate to the constitutional convention, admitted that, had Republicans appreciated that a political landslide was in the making, they would have acted more radically in Albany.[55] At the time of the convention, of course, the Republicans could not have been aware of the strength of the tide setting in against the Democrats. Compromises effected to expedite passage of the constitution through the convention and election made political sense. But Republican leaders never lost sight of their primary objective—political dominance through control of the state legislature. To this end they compromised over sectarian spending and the state canals, maintaining party unity at the convention and retaining popular support about the state. The Republicans succeeded: in the very year that they won the governorship of New York for the first time since 1879, and fully two years before William McKinley's national victory over William Jennings Bryan, they well-nigh guaranteed their position in New York State politics into the second half of the twentieth century.

IV

The Midterm Upheaval of 1894

In a very real sense, the major political struggle of 1894 pitted a Republican campaign based on economic issues arising out of the depression against a Democratic campaign based on cultural issues that had defined politics before the depression. The stakes in this struggle were high, higher than they had been in 1893, for the fate of governors, state legislatures (and consequently, U.S. Senators), as well as the entire membership of the United States House of Representatives was to be decided in the midterm elections. In developing their case against the Democrats, the Republicans hammered at the tariff issue. They had done so in 1893, charging that the Democrats' declared intention to lower the tariff was sufficient to destroy business confidence, thereby bringing about a depression. Now they increased the intensity of these attacks, as first the House of Representatives and then the Senate dealt with the tariff bill, and they capped their assault during the fall political campaigns.

Republican leaders had for some time sought to maintain unity among various groups within the party's coalition by stressing the tariff as the bond that united Republicans. But the tariff debate of 1893–94, coming as it did during a deep depression, was of greater significance. The Republicans took this opportunity to argue that the protective tariff was a means by which government served a broad public—contributing to the high wages of American workers and to the maintenance of a rich domestic market for American farmers, as well as protecting the profits of

American manufacturers. Henry Clay's "American System" involved such a conception; the Whig and Republican parties repeatedly proclaimed this doctrine. Indeed, the protective tariff served as the cornerstone of successive governmental programs to foster economic development.[1] The economic nationalist argument gained in persuasiveness during the depression, for the Republicans were able to charge that the Democrats' disregard for the relationship between protection and prosperity had precipitated hard times, and now threatened to prolong them. To Republicans, the protective tariff was not only an instrument for stimulating economic growth; it was the major weapon in the government's limited anti-depression arsenal.

The Democrats, on the other hand, stood committed to an essentially negative program. Having gone so far in their national platform of 1892 as to declare unconstitutional the protective tariff, once in power they blamed the depression on positive governmental action—the Sherman Silver Purchase Act—and promised that recovery would follow repeal of the act and a downward revision of the tariff. Continued hard times gave the lie to the promise and undermined whatever shaky public support tariff reform may have had.

Republicans carried the fight to the Democrats on the tariff issue. Speaking in Indianapolis, ex-President Benjamin Harrison saw the broader implications of the growing acceptance of local governmental responsibility for providing public works jobs to the unemployed. He declared to an enthusiastic audience:

> The Republican theory has been all along that it was right to so legislate as to provide work, employment, comfort to the American workingman. We believe that the National Government has a duty in this respect, as well as the city council and the board of county commissioners. (Applause.) And that duty is best discharged by so legislating that American mills can keep their fires going. (Applause.)

During the Senate debate on the tariff bill, Henry Cabot Lodge vigorously attacked the Democratic position on government's responsibility for economic well-being. Noting that many free traders turned to the British experience for inspiration, he pointed out that the government of Great Britain intervened in the economy in a number of ways. In the United States, Lodge said, government excluded the Chinese laborer in order to protect the American worker; the exclusion of the products of cheap labor by protective tariffs was a logical corollary of this policy. Responses to such arguments underlined the differences between the contending views of governmental responsibility: the New York *Tribune* applauded Lodge ("He Vigorously Attacks the 'Laissez Faire' Doctrine"); *The Nation* condemned Harrison, asserting that "protection and socialism are one in principle." As their private correspondence reveals, men involved in the debate were not merely striking public poses on the tariff issue; they believed in what they were saying.[2]

One must not exaggerate the Republicans' willingness to employ the national power to cope with the depression. Certainly, they made no commitment comparable to that accepted by both major parties in mid-twentieth-century America, or even to that demanded by those protest groups of the 1890s that lacked the political leverage to move either major party. Still, the positive nationalism of the Republican party stood out against the negativism of the Cleveland Democrats. This contrast was of inestimable political advantage to the Republicans. Though the depression itself was severe enough to disrupt political loyalties to the disadvantage of the party in office, the tariff debate enabled the Republicans to focus popular discontent on Democratic policy, and to offer an analysis of the causes of the depression and a prescription for its alleviation that were calculated to gain public acceptance. That the causes of the depression were complex and the economic analysis of the Republicans simplistic did not detract from the potency of the tariff issue, particularly as the Republican party was free to criticize without fear of having to administer an alternative policy.

Constituency pressures against the Wilson bill reflected widespread opposition to tariff reform in the Northeast. Among those protesting the bill were the management, workers, and/or stockholders of the cutlery, brass and metal, hat, and woolen industries of Connecticut; the cutlery, pottery, hat, shoe, marble and bronze, spool cotton and fine yarns, oil cloth, knitting-machine needle, and parasol, umbrella, and walking-stick industries of New Jersey; and the paper, cut glass, optical gold, silver and metal leaf, shirt, knit goods, glove and mitten, collar and cuff, ready-made clothing, carpet, broom, manufactured rattan, steel spring, iron and steel, and drug industries of New York.[3]

Northeastern farmers, who generally produced for domestic urban markets, also feared foreign competition. Responding to this concern, the Republicans had increased a number of agricultural duties in the McKinley Tariff Act of 1890. Now fruit and vegetable growers clamored for continued protection from Canadian produce; New Jersey onion farmers expressed anxiety over Bermuda's production; Connecticut's broad-leaf tobacco farmers sought to maintain curbs on the importation of Sumatran wrapper tobacco; and New York wool growers were sensitive to overseas production in general. Though there were disagreements regarding particular tariff schedules, northeastern industrial and agricultural interests presented a common, protectionist front: the region's farmers would not join their fellow tillers of the soil in the South and West in a crusade against the protective tariff.[4] One misses the significance of the storm of protest that blew up over the tariff question if one dismisses it as merely a campaign waged by "big business" and its henchmen, with no objective other than the serving of self-interest. At a time when Andrew Carnegie, the personification of "big business," signified his willingness to accept lower duties on steel to end agitation regarding the tariff, myriad smaller businessmen and laborers, less secure than Carnegie, concluded that the Wilson bill was too high a price to pay for an end to the tariff controversy.[5]

Proponents of the Wilson bill alleged that manufacturers had coerced or deceived their employees into opposing the measure; sympathetic historians have echoed these allegations, for which supporting evidence is generally lacking. Such charges—even if accepted at but slight discount—simply cannot account for the outpouring of protests from the industrial Northeast, nor explain the opposition of agricultural groups. Fully as significant as the strength of constituency pressure against the Wilson bill was the weakness of the campaign in its behalf. To be sure, a number of tariff reform clubs reiterated their faith, but only a handful of businessmen declared in favor of specific tariff reductions. (These businessmen were no less parochial than those who favored higher duties on specific articles.) Even if one grants that opponents of the proposal were more likely to campaign than proponents, support for the measure was conspicuously lacking. As Simeon E. Baldwin lamented to a Democratic Congressman from Connecticut:

> I understand that the manufacturers' conventions are flooding Washington with petitions against the Wilson bill. It is unfortunate that we have, in Connecticut, and to some extent throughout the country, few great interests which the bill will directly benefit. Its good effects will be felt by the community at large, and their only organization for political effect is the House of Representatives.[6]

Basing a campaign for tariff reform on benefits for "the community at large" was risky at any time, but particularly so during a depression. Businessmen, laborers, and farmers did not think of themselves as consumers concerned with the over-all cost-of-living, but as producers desirous of protecting their own interests. Under these circumstances, the anti-tariff reform campaign touched, rather than manipulated, responsive chords in the Northeast. In fact, so sharp was the impact of the depression that New York City protectionists vetoed Wharton Barker's suggestion of a parade of 50,000 workers to protest the Wilson bill, for fear that such a march would attract an army of unemployed and produce bloodshed.[7]

Many Democrats revealed their opposition to tariff tinkering during the depression. In the House of Representatives, a bloc of about 40 Democrats secured a week's extension of floor debate on the Wilson bill; on February 1, seventeen congressmen (twelve of whom came from the Northeast, eight from New York alone) broke with their party to oppose the measure, which was passed, 204 to 140. Concern that tariff reform was politically unwise mounted within Tammany Hall, particularly after a Republican won election to Congress from New York City on January 30, the opposition's first victory in a straight two-party congressional race there since 1880. In the Senate, where the two parties were closely balanced, Senators Hill and Murphy of New York, Smith and McPherson of New Jersey, Gorman of Maryland, and Calvin S. Brice of Ohio fought to blunt the sharp edge of tariff reform. Not until July 3 did the Senate pass the heavily amended Wilson-Gorman Tariff bill. As the fight dragged on in a Senate–House conference committee, Representative Wilson read to the House President Cleveland's letter to him charging that abandonment of tariff reform would mean "party perfidy and party dishonor," to which Gorman replied in a Senate philippic against Cleveland and his tariff policy. The House finally capitulated, and on August 28 the Wilson-Gorman Tariff bill became law without the signature of President Cleveland. The House passed separate bills providing for free coal, iron ore, sugar, and barbed wire, but these were interred by the Senate Finance Committee.[8]

The Republicans' upset victory in New York City deserves attention, for it foreshadowed the political upheaval of 1894. The resignation of two Tammany congressmen, who had been elected to local office, forced special elections in the 14th and 15th Congressional Districts. Neither Democratic nominee—Colonel William L. Brown and Isidor Straus, respectively—was a Tammany regular; indeed, Straus was the personal choice of President Cleveland. Both campaigns resolved themselves into struggles over the tariff question; the rival parties spared nothing to score on this issue. At the same time, differences between the two Democratic candidates contributed to different outcomes in the two races. Straus was a strong candidate: a member of a prominent German Jewish family and a Cleveland Democrat, he ran in a congressional district that included numerous Germans, German Jews, and silk-stocking Democrats; his charity had received favorable publicity during the early stages of the depression. Brown was a less fortunate selection: his record as a state senator was vulnerable to attack by a workers' committee (whose members Brown denounced as "tramps and not citizens"); and he ran in a district that reputedly led the nation in manufactures and total volume of business.

Straus won, polling 55.3 per cent of the total vote to Frederick Sigrist's 38.5. Straus ran slightly better in the area than Meyer, who had suffered above-average to severe losses, and considerably better than Maynard, who had been cut to pieces the previous November. But Lemuel Ely Quigg defeated Brown, 49.1 to 45.5 per cent, in the other contest. Brown fared better than Maynard, though not as well as Meyer, in districts where the Democrats had been stung in 1893, but he fell below both in the 19th A.D., a congested workingman's district that had remained loyal to the ticket the previous year.[9] In analyzing the election, the New York *Times* refused to recognize Quigg's victory as a warning against tariff reform, contending that the district's voters had declared for tariff reform in 1890 and 1892 but had rejected the income tax, which southern and western representatives had attached to the Wilson bill.[10] The *Times* could not or would not admit that the depression was recasting the tariff issue; it would have its readers believe that many Democrats—allegedly favorable to tariff reform but opposed to the income tax—had deserted their party's nominee, who shared both sentiments, in favor of a Republican who shared the second but was pledged to block the first. The well-to-do did oppose the income tax, but there was no sign of an anti-income tax revolt in working class districts, where problems arising out of the depression, not those associated with paying a tax on an annual income of $4000 or more, were pressing.

Congressional struggles during 1894 did sometimes pit northeastern Democratic supporters of the President against Democrats from the South and West. Administration Democrats joined Republicans to sustain Cleveland's veto of the Bland bill, which authorized the Treasury to coin its silver seigniorage and other loose bullion, and (violating their party's national platform pledge of 1892) also worked with them to defeat a move to end the tax on state bank notes.[11] "Respectable" northeasterners were gratified that Congress had beaten back agrarian radicalism, but working class discontent, manifested in the marches of "industrial armies" of unemployed, particularly that led by Jacob Coxey, and in the great Pullman strike and railroad boycott, led by Eugene V. Debs of the American Railway Union, frightened many. Public figures and the press expressed this concern at the time, but it was not to become politically salient until the presidential campaign of 1896, when Republicans and conservative Democrats played on the fears of social conflict and anarchy created during 1894, attacking William Jennings Bryan through Debs and through Governor Altgeld of Illinois, who had opposed President Cleveland's intervention in the railroad boycott.[12]

The depression and the tariff controversy fairly assured that economic issues would predominate during the northeastern political campaigns of 1894, particularly insofar as the Republicans were concerned. Late in May, however, the New York *Times* informed its readers that "'A.P.A.' Reaches New-York," and launched an extended series on the American Protective Association, its growth, its anti-Catholic propaganda, and its alleged ties to the Republican party in New York. The *Times* also reported at length the views of friends and foes of A.P.A.[13] The controversy over the A.P.A. gave focus to the larger question of anti-Catholicism, and both became major political issues as the Democrats sought to counter the Republican campaign based on economic issues by raising cultural ones.

The American Protective Association was fully seven years old at the time of the *Times* exposé, having been founded in Clinton, Iowa, in March, 1887. The belief that Roman Catholicism poses a threat to American institutions has lain close to the surface throughout American history: specific developments, from the great Catholic immigration of the 1840s and 1850s to the presidential candidacies of Roman Catholics in 1928 and 1960, have caused such emotions to erupt. In this sense, the late 1880s and early 1890s were ripe for an explosion, for Roman Catholicism and Roman Catholics displayed great vigor during this period. Many Protestants reacted sharply to developments such as the meeting of the Third Plenary Council in Baltimore in 1884, the appointment of the first Apostolic Delegate to the United States, the founding of the Knights of Columbus and the Catholic University of America, the creation of twenty new dioceses, the expansion of parochial school systems and growing demands for public assistance thereto, and the increasing political importance of Irish Catholics, particularly in urban areas. The conflict also had an economic dimension, involving a cruel competition for jobs made all the sharper by hard times.[14]

Though the A.P.A. did reach the Northeast rather late, the sensational announcement of the *Times* was misleading in that newspapers (the *Times* among them) had already reported the association to be active in New York, Massachusetts, Connecticut, and New Jersey politics. Nor did A.P.A. fill an anti-Catholic organizational vacuum in the Northeast: foremost among established groups was the Junior Order of United American Mechanics, founded as an independent order in 1885 by men who felt that its parent organization, the Order of United American Mechanics, which dated from 1843, lacked militancy. The J.O.U.A.M. was particularly active in New Jersey, and it established itself in Connecticut in 1892, forming a state council there three years later. In Rhode Island, a local anti-Catholic organization, the United Order of Deputies, overran Republican caucuses and the Providence city convention, then campaigned against Democrats during 1893.[15]

The evidence is incomplete, but anti-Catholic organizations may have recruited more among immigrants than among old-stock Americans. In a nation that received a steady stream of immigrants, "nativism" ("intense opposition to an internal minority on the ground of its foreign [i.e., 'un-American'] connections") could and did flourish among immigrants. Protestant immigrants from England, Ireland, Scotland, Wales, Canada, Germany, and Scandinavia brought with them legacies of hostility toward Catholicism and particular Catholic groups, and they settled in a land whose institutions and traditions had been shaped by Protestants from the British Isles. Religious conflicts frequently flared anew in the United States as Protestant immigrants encountered Catholic newcomers from Ireland, Germany, Canada, and elsewhere. Thus British and British Canadian immigrants played leading roles in groups such as the American Protestant Association, the Loyal Orange Institution, the J.O.U.A.M., and the American Protective Association.[16] Immigrant groups, some of whose members joined anti-Catholic organizations, identified first with the Whig party and later with the Republican party—both of which opposed the Democracy, the party of Roman Catholics. As a consequence, the A.P.A. and other anti-Catholic groups recruited primarily from Republican ranks: an officer of the J.O.U.A.M. in Connecticut, inviting the governor to join the order, candidly acknowledged that while members of all parties belonged, Republicans predominated. Such relationships led Democrats to allege the existence of working agreements between Republican politicians and anti-Catholic leaders.[17]

Major economic and cultural disputes had been publicly aired through the spring and summer of 1894; inevitably they provided the issues on which the rival parties based their midterm political campaigns that fall. In the Northeast, Democratic state platforms and campaigners generally praised repeal of the Sherman Silver Purchase Act and passage of the Wilson-Gorman Tariff Act, sometimes pledging to adjust specific tariff schedules according to circumstances, more often denouncing Republican intentions to restore protectionism to the position it had occupied in the McKinley Tariff Act of 1890. The Democrats contended that they had translated into law their popular mandates of 1890 and 1892 and that prosperity was returning under the beneficent tariff enacted in 1894. They added that Republican talk of reversing that policy could only unsettle the economy, for no legislation sponsored by the Republicans stood a chance of enactment as long as Grover Cleveland remained president. Though Democratic spokesmen remained publicly sanguine regarding the outcome of the midterm elections, the last argument recognized that the Republicans might recapture Congress. As a matter of fact, a number of key Democrats realized that they were in a difficult political position. In Connecticut, Commodore E. C. Benedict, a wealthy businessman, close friend of President Cleveland, and the party's most likely gubernatorial nominee, decided to save his fortune for a more propitious year by withdrawing his name from consideration. Daniel Lamont, William C. Whitney, William J. Gaynor, Perry Belmont, and John Boyd Thacher declined the same sacrificial role in New York State; Tammany finally stampeded the party's convention into saddling Senator Hill with the nomination. John R. McPherson, aware that the Republicans would likely control the New Jersey legislature to be elected in November, did not seek a fourth term in the United States Senate.[18]

On the other hand, northeastern Republican politicians, confident of success against the Democrats, desired nomination in

1894: as early as February, O. Vincent Coffin, who subsequently won the Republican gubernatorial nomination in Connecticut, predicted that there would be "a car-load of candidates" in his state. Republicans campaigned aggressively on the tariff issue, arraigning the Democrats for having brought on the depression with their pledge to reform the tariff and for having drafted a tariff that benefited Great Britain and the South at the expense of the North. (During 1896, Bryanites would denounce the gold standard as benefiting Great Britain, while Republicans would go far beyond their tariff arguments of 1894 to condemn the Bryanite Democratic-Populist coalition as a southern threat to the North.) In pivotal states such as New York, national figures, among them Governor McKinley, ex-President Harrison, and Speaker Thomas B. Reed of the House of Representatives, reinforced local campaigners.[19] McKinley and Reed hoped not only to assist their party in 1894, but to advance their own claims to the presidential nomination two years later.

Though Democratic campaigners could not avoid discussing the depression and the tariff, they clearly sought victory by exploiting issues more familiar—and favorable—to them. Basically, they hoped to reconstitute the coalition that had enabled the Democracy first to hold its own and then to gain the upper hand against the Republicans from 1874 through 1892 by identifying their opponents with anti-Catholicism, prohibitionism, and animus toward cities. That the Democrats' tactics differed from state to state according to local circumstances does not obscure the central thrust of their strategy.

Connecticut Democrats concentrated on the old issue of constitutional reform and the new issue of Republican collaboration with the American Protective Association. The Democrats called for a constitutional convention that would amend the state charter to provide for plurality election of state officers and to reapportion the legislature. During 1893, Republicans in the House of Representatives had killed a bill providing for an amending convention. Contending that such a convention would be unconstitutional, the Republicans called for proposal of amendments by majority vote of the House of Representatives, approval by two-thirds vote of both houses in the following biennial legislature, and ratification by popular vote. To offset Democratic charges that this proposal was at best a delaying action, and that the support of two-thirds of the body that would be affected by reapportionment could never be mustered, the Republican House of Representatives passed plurality election and senatorial reapportionment amendments. Though the Republican state platform remained silent on the issue, the party press informed urbanities that the G.O.P. was committed to constitutional reform, and that its legislators would be able to block any Democratic proposal unacceptable to them.[20]

The Democrats condemned the American Protective Association and alleged that O. Vincent Coffin and Mayor George C. Corbin of New Britain had worked with the A.P.A. to secure the nominations of Coffin for governor and Nehemiah D. Sperry for congressman. Having denounced religious tests for office, the Democracy practiced what it preached by nominating Edward G. Kilduff, the Irish Catholic Mayor of Waterbury, for Secretary of the State. Democratic charges linking the Republican party with anti-Catholicism were not fabricated of whole cloth: as elsewhere, anti-Catholic groups appealed primarily to men who voted Republican; municipal politics in New Britain had involved intensive anti-Catholic activity; denying connections with the A.P.A., Nehemiah Sperry acknowledged that he had been a Know-Nothing. But the situation was more complex than the Democrats recognized. On the one hand, nativist maneuvers sometimes disturbed the Republican party. Anti-Catholics sought to capture Republican caucuses and conventions for candidates of their persuasion. Ambitious politicians sought to use nativist groups to promote themselves. In either case, interlopers threatened the position of regulars in local party organizations. Further, professional politicians wished to maintain broadly based coalitions: they feared single-issue groups, particularly those that proscribed entire religious or ethnic blocs. The Republican party of New Haven County nominated Charles R. Spiegel, a German American, for sheriff against the wishes of the A.P.A.; Coffin congratulated Spiegel, noting with pleasure the drift of German Democrats into Republican ranks. On the other hand, cultural issues cut two ways. Rural Democrats were cool toward reapportionment; some Protestant Democrats apparently resented both Representative James P. Pigott's repeated attacks on Nehemiah Sperry as an A.P.A.'er and the nomination by the Waterbury Democracy of an all-Catholic slate in a school board election. Other localities reported Protestant-Catholic splits within the Democratic party. And in New Haven, the A.P.A. sought to discredit Irish Democrats among the city's growing Jewish population by branding them as anti-Semites. For their part, Republicans accused the Democrats of raising a false issue in desperation, pointing to prominent Catholics who absolved the Republican party of being anti-Catholic.[21]

Matters were more complicated for the Democracy in New York State, where revolts disrupted the party both state-wide and in New York City. These developments colored every aspect of politics in the state: they deserve analysis along with the contest between Democrats and Republicans. The creation of the New York State Democracy and the declaration of the German-American Reform Union late in 1893 signified that that year's anti-Maynard campaign had been but a preliminary round in the renewed conflict within the Democratic party. Upstate, Cleveland Democrats sought federal patronage to facilitate their capture of Senator Hill's organization; in New York City, they hoped to weaken Tammany by denying it federal patronage.[22] But as long as the regulars controlled the state and city governments, they stood little danger of being broken by such pressure. Indeed, Senators Hill and Murphy were twice able to embarrass President Cleveland by blocking his nominations to the Supreme Court.

Darkening political skies led the New York *Times* and Senator Hill, who sought the President's ear through Secretary of War Lamont, to call for party harmony. Unity was more easily preached than achieved, however, and rival factions girded for the Democratic state convention. There, Hill delivered a conciliatory speech, calling for support of the national and state administrations; the platform praised Cleveland's currency and tariff policies. But the truce was shattered when Tammany and Boss McLaughlin, reportedly acting against the advice of Hill, blocked the seating of contesting delegations from New York,

Kings, and Erie counties. The New York City and Brooklyn regulars would not countenance the recognition of rival factions that had been disloyal in the past and that still threatened the machines. Anti-organization Democrats withdrew from the convention and subsequently nominated Everett P. Wheeler to run against David Hill as the Democratic Party Reform Organization candidate for governor, while endorsing others on the regular state ticket. The New York State Democracy endorsed the entire regular state slate, but repudiated Tammany's city ticket.[23] Hill attempted to gain the support of President Cleveland and those of his followers who were not irrevocably committed to Wheeler. He went out of his way to praise the national administration; his earlier tactic of opposing the tariff bill on the ground that it provided for an income tax now enabled him to praise the tariff schedules of the Wilson-Gorman Act. But ardent tariff revisionists condemned Hill, as well as Tammany, as hostile to true tariff reform, and the President, resisting pressure to declare one way or the other in the New York gubernatorial race, privately made clear his willingness to see Hill go down to defeat.[24]

The decision of the State Democracy to accept Hill while rejecting Tammany reflected the complexity of politics in New York City, where slowly, and not without difficulty, a powerful anti-Tammany coalition was forged. The Fusion forces ultimately included a number of overlapping groups within their ranks—Republicans, dissident Democrats, independents, businessmen, German Americans, moral reformers led by Protestant clergymen, and people hostile toward Catholics and the Irish.

Businessmen sought to reassert their direct influence in city politics while curbing the growing self-assertiveness of Tammany politicians. Twice during the 1880s, Tammany Hall had nominated important businessmen—William R. Grace in 1880, Franklin Edson in 1882—for mayor; it had accepted another, Abram S. Hewitt of the business-oriented County Democracy, to defeat Henry George in 1886. But Hugh Grant, a Tammany regular who had been defeated by Grace (running as an anti-Tammany Democrat) in 1884, won the mayoralty in 1888 against Hewitt and a Republican, then survived a Fusion campaign in 1890. Thomas Gilroy, another regular, succeeded to the mayoralty in the harmony election of 1892. During 1893–94, businessmen and professional politicians made it clear that they disagreed on who should run the affairs of New York City.[25]

Tammany frequently inveighed against the silk-stocking element, but its radicalism was rhetorical, not programmatic, and its relations with some business leaders (e.g., William C. Whitney) were mutually profitable. Still, many businessmen who did not receive comparable favors came to feel Tammany rule too costly to endure without protest. Democrats among them had been restrained in 1892 by the knowledge that intra-party strife had damaged Grover Cleveland in 1884 and 1888. Now they were free to resume hostilities. Businessmen were prominent among the founders of the State Democracy. The Chamber of Commerce of New York City called for a state senatorial investigation of police corruption and, when Governor Flower vetoed an appropriation to support the Lexow Committee, raised the money to sustain the inquiry. Leading members met—as "individuals," because the Chamber itself ostensibly did not mix in politics—to discuss mayoralty candidates. (Defending the Chamber against Tammany charges of politicking, the New York *Tribune* declared that the organization had always favored "honesty, efficiency, and non-partisanship.") Within the Republican party, businessmen who were at odds with Boss Platt called for a fusion ticket behind which "the better element" might unite to overthrow Tammany.[26]

Influential leaders of the German-American Reform Union also announced their opposition to Tammany: some members favored supporting an anti-Tammany Democrat, others fusion behind a suitable Republican. These men shared the hostility of businessmen and professionals toward Tammany. The attitude of such Germans seems to have been a reflection of their upward economic and social mobility. Most accounts agree that German immigrants, some of whom derived from urban, bourgeois origins, and their offspring climbed faster than Irish immigrants, wave after wave of whom came from impoverished peasant backgrounds, and their offspring. Such Germans viewed Tammany, which provided its Irish workers with political power and economic opportunities, with scorn. For Germans active in Democratic politics, Tammany seemed to offer more frustrations than opportunities. Tammany had become an Irish political machine: though by 1890 first- and second-generation Germans outnumbered the Irish in New York City, German politicians neither controlled the levers of power in Tammany nor received their share of nominations and patronage. Many German Lutherans had voted Democratic despite their antipathy toward Irish Catholics because of Republican involvement with prohibitionism. In 1894, at least, anti-Tammany leaders succeeded in playing down this divisive issue. German and Irish Catholics, who by no means saw eye to eye on all matters, drew together because of anti-Catholicism. But the primary thrust of anti-Catholic propaganda was directed at Irish Catholics, and this may have reduced the sensitivity of their German co-religionists. Thus a political coalition embracing old-stock Americans and German Americans came into existence in New York City.[27]

Various groups evinced displeasure with Tammany's pronounced Irish complexion. Polish and Italian Americans criticized Mayor Gilroy for failing to fly the flags of their homelands on national holidays. Others, including the A.P.A., took exception to acting Mayor George B. McClellan's flying the Irish flag over city offices on St. Patrick's Day; they applauded reform Mayor Schieren of Brooklyn for refusing to do so. A Republican-sponsored bill to restrict the flying of foreign flags over public buildings to visits by heads of state fell before Governor Flower's veto. Such episodes, minor in themselves, were symptomatic of important cultural tensions.[28]

Protestant clergymen joined the anti-Tammany crusade. The Reverend Dr. Charles H. Parkhurst of the Madison Square Presbyterian Church, the most notable of these critics, opened fire on the Tammany Tiger in 1892, but he did not draw blood until 1894, when Republican leaders, sensing the political potential of Parkhurst's sensational accounts of police connivance in gambling and prostitution, created a state senatorial committee to investigate corruption in New York City. The Lexow Committee was to keep Tammany on the defensive during 1894. To Parkhurst, Tammany was evil because it encouraged activities he regarded as immoral. But to other ministers, Tammany was immoral because it was Irish Catholic. Their denunciations added a clear note of bigotry to the rising anti-Tammany chorus.[29]

Boss Platt completed the encirclement of Tammany by bringing the Republican organization into the Fusion camp. Anti-Tammany leaders discussed fusion at length during 1894. Democrats among them hoped to run a Democrat for mayor, thereby symbolizing the opposition of righteous Democrats to Tammany and, more than incidentally, limiting Republican influence in the city. But Platt believed in partisan, not fusion, politics; he felt the political tide to be running Republican. He had seen Tammany defeat a fusion-backed Democrat in 1890; however important the support of Democrats and independents, Republicans would provide the bulk of anti-Tammany votes in November, 1894. He would support fusion only if a Republican ran for mayor. Platt finally endorsed Col. William L. Strong, a prominent dry goods merchant and banker and a Republican, who had been nominated for mayor by a Committee of Seventy, which represented various anti-Tammany groups. Platt distrusted Strong, a member of the businessmen's wing of the G.O.P., but he cooperated in the Fusion campaign in order to add to Democratic difficulties in New York City, thereby increasing Republican chances in New York State.[30]

Tammany sought to save itself by nominating Nathan Straus for mayor. The choice was calculated: Straus was a Cleveland Democrat, a businessman, and a German Jew. But Straus withdrew from the race following unsuccessful negotiations with President Cleveland and Senator Hill. Cleveland, unwilling to contribute to the rescue of Tammany (even by a friend), refused to endorse Straus. Hill refused Straus's request that he withdraw from the State Democratic ticket, which had endorsed the regular state ticket while opposing Tammany.[31] In this Hill was consistent, for he did not ask his running mates to reject nomination by the Democratic Party Reform Organization, which opposed him alone. Hill, a professional politician, was attempting to salvage as much as possible from the disaster he feared lay ahead. The Straus fiasco forced Tammany to call on Hugh Grant to head its ticket.

Though the Democrats were unable to run a Jewish candidate

for mayor, they sought to embarrass Col. William Strong among Jewish voters by identifying him with the Union League Club. In April 1893 the club had blackballed Theodore Seligman, son of Jesse Seligman, a long-time club member, banker, and financial contributor to the Republican party. It was the nation's most publicized anti-Semitic incident of the period. The affair had political overtones because the Union League Club played an important role in the Republican party: leading Republican businessmen were numbered among its members. Democratic politicians immediately criticized the club for its discriminatory act, Republicans quickly following suit. Later, Democrats sniped at the Union League Club during the campaign of 1893 and the New York State Constitutional Convention; Boss Platt's supporters, embroiled in a factional struggle with the businessmen's wing of the party, did likewise. Anti-Tammany leaders were particularly concerned over the issue, for they considered the support of the older, established German Jewish community important to their cause. Strong testified to his advocacy of Theodore Seligman in the Union League Club and to his long friendship with Jesse Seligman. Fusion speakers seconded Strong's personal defense and charged that Tammany exploited Jews and Italians in the Lower East Side. The Republican press even sought to plant the idea that anti-Semitism had figured in Nathan Straus's withdrawal from the mayoralty race. The depth of Republican concern over the issue was only revealed the following January, when Edwin Einstein resigned from the Union League Club. Einstein, a former Republican congressman and mayoralty candidate, was the only professed Jewish member of the club following the resignation of Jesse Seligman, who had withdrawn to protest the blackballing of his son. Einstein stated that he had delayed his own resignation on the advice of "some of the most prominent men in the Republican Party in New York City" to avoid jeopardizing the Republican and Fusion campaigns.[32]

Anti-Semitism figured as an issue only in the New York City mayoralty race; anti-Catholicism became an issue in both state and municipal campaigns, and it was even more heated. At the New York State Constitutional Convention Republican politicians had steered a cautious course between the demands of conflicting

Catholic and Protestant groups, but at the state party convention they took a different tack. The committee on resolutions revealed a healthy regard for the strength of anti-Catholic feeling by rejecting a proposed platform plank, which important Catholic Republicans had supported, denouncing the introduction of religious issues into politics. In his letter accepting the Republican gubernatorial nomination, Levi P. Morton advocated religious and civil equality, but some Catholics and politicians felt that the party itself should have taken such a stand.

The New York Democratic state platform, unlike others in the Northeast, denounced proscriptive societies in general, not specific, terms. But Senator Hill campaigned hard on the religious issue, charging the Republicans with being allies of the A.P.A. and with manifesting animus toward Catholics in the legislature and in the constitutional convention. Hill even drew attention to the "most extreme and illiberal" Republicanism of Vermont, from which Levi P. Morton, his opponent, hailed. Hill also condemned the prohibitionist views and reapportionment plans of the G.O.P.; he was clearly attempting to restore his party's urban coalition. (That Hill's addresses were well received by rural audiences, even Democratic ones, is open to doubt.) The campaign grew even more bitter following allegations by the New York *Times* that the Republican National Congressional Committee was disseminating a speech by Representative William S. Linton, a Michigan Republican, that took the A.P.A. position on sectarian appropriations, and that the speech was being mailed out of the New York State capitol. Republican politicians hastened to calm the fears of Catholic Republicans, but would not embarrass their party in New York by specifically denouncing the A.P.A. As elsewhere, Republicans accused Democrats of raising a false issue; in this they were joined by Catholic anti-Tammany Democrats such as John W. Goff, counsel to the Lexow Committee and Fusion candidate for city recorder, and former mayor William R. Grace.[33]

Roman Catholic clergymen took sides in the controversy. Endorsing the Republican state and Fusion municipal slates, Archbishop John Ireland of St. Paul, Fathers Thomas J. Ducey and Alfred Young of New York City, and Father Sylvester Malone of

Brooklyn absolved the G.O.P. of charges of anti-Catholicism and lamented the identification of their Church with the Democratic party. Only after the election did the New York hierarchy publicly reply to Ireland, Bishop McQuaid intemperately attacking Archbishop Ireland from the pulpit, charging him with meddling in the affairs of another diocese and accepting financial aid from wealthy Republicans. Though the bishops of New York State were angered by the Republicans' refusal to condemn religious proscription, they decided at a meeting early in October that "prudence and expediency" dictated silence during the campaign. This was a sound tactical appreciation of the political situation: any intervention would have increased anti-Catholic feeling and not even massive intervention could have turned the Republican tide. On the Sunday before Election Day, a handful of priests in New York City condemned at every mass the Republican and Fusion tickets and the proposed state constitution. This single Sunday of political preaching by priests, which shocked many, must be viewed against a background of weeks of political preaching by Protestant ministers in New York City.[34] Still, the Sunday activity did serve to bring the already acrimonious campaign in New York to an even more bitter conclusion.

In New Jersey, voters balloted for congressmen and state legislators; no state office was at stake in 1894. As a consequence, the campaign lacked the focus of those in Connecticut and New York. Cleveland Democrats pressed for a strong stand on the tariff issue: they envisaged the Democratic Society of New Jersey, which had opposed racetrack Democrats a year earlier, conducting a campaign of education on tariff reform; they denied renomination to Representative Cornelius A. Cadmus in the Fifth Congressional District (Bergen and Passaic counties) for his "treachery and unworthiness" in opposing the Wilson bill; and they condemned Democratic representatives (except Judson Cornish) and senators for their role in the tariff debate.[35]

Insofar as cultural issues were concerned, the Democrats denounced the Republicans for maintaining a friendly silence as the secret societies did their dirty work at the expense of Roman Catholics. Essex County Democrats condemned religious proscription and sumptuary legislation; they charged that the Republicans had exploited religious prejudices and had employed the pulpit as a political platform during the 1893 campaign. Concerned lest they go too far, the Democrats proclaimed their belief in the separation of Church and State. Shortly before the election, an outspoken Roman Catholic priest seconded Democratic accusations relating to the religious issue. After characterizing the A.P.A. as "whining, sneaking, canting, miserable, [and] pretentious," in an address before the Catholic Club in Newark, Father John J. Tighe charged that "the lying literature of this insane and treasonable association is being fully circulated by the connivance and assistance of the Republican party" and denied the existence of a Catholic vote in the Democratic party. Another priest, Father Martin Gessner, announced his withdrawal from the Republican party because of its identification with the American Protective Association. Meanwhile, the New York *Times* sought to convey the impression of differences between old-stock and German Republicans in various New Jersey localities.[36]

Republicans ridiculed the A.P.A. issue, one terming it a "jack-in-the-box, intended to frighten children." To reassure voters in politically sensitive Essex County, they declared that the G.O.P. favored "equal rights for every citizen under the law, without distinction of color, religious belief, birth, or property"—but they made it clear that A.P.A. or no A.P.A., patriotic voters would insist on the continued separation of Church and State. Republican legislators had already drawn the line between themselves and their Democratic counterparts. They secured legislation requiring that public schools fly the American flag. In criticizing the measure and its sponsors, Assemblyman William J. Thompson, "The Duke of Gloucester," pointed out that the Junior Order of United American Mechanics now requested the support of immigrants such as himself, yet regularly reviled the foreign-born. Other Democrats attacked the bill, but only one dared to vote against it. Charles B. Storrs, a Republican elected to the Assembly in 1893, sought to bar naturalizations within thirty days of elections. While some Republicans denied a Democrat's characterization of the bill as a throwback to the Know-Nothing era, Senator James A. Bradley, a moral reformer, "didn't hesitate to say that ignorant foreigners jeopardized true American citizenship." [37] Essentially, then, the New Jersey campaign resembled the campaigns in Connecticut and New York in its charges and countercharges over religious and other cultural issues.

On November 6, 1894, the Republicans triumphed in one of the great midterm election landslides of American history, sweeping to success in gubernatorial, congressional, and legislative contests across the nation. In New York, Connecticut, and New Jersey, they gained fifteen, three, and six congressional seats, respectively, while losing none of their own; strengthened their legislative majorities in all three states; and captured the governorships of Connecticut and New York. The Republican avalanche wiped out the Democratic congressional delegations from Connecticut and New Jersey and reduced the Democrats to four New York City congressional districts in the Empire State. Levi P. Morton emerged as the first Republican to win the governorship of New York since 1879—and the first Republican to receive majority support since 1872. In Connecticut, O. Vincent Coffin became the first Republican gubernatorial candidate to receive a majority of the total vote since 1880; his percentage of that vote was the highest since 1865.[38]

The midterm elections, involving as they did a range of contests in each of the states under study, indeed, in states throughout the country, provide an excellent opportunity for analyzing the politics of depression. Reference to the responses of contemporaries does not suffice in this connection, for the reactions of the politically involved to events of the magnitude of the elections of 1894 often shed more light on the perceptivity and commitments of the observers than on the events themselves. Analysis of voting patterns better enables us to assess both the elections and the judgment of politicians.

The Republicans' gains of 1894 exceeded by far the hopes of party leaders and even farther the modest advances conceded them by Democrats before the balloting. Some Democrats recognized the magnitude of their party's defeat, but many Clevelandites could not or would not comprehend its significance. Cleveland himself entertained mixed feelings regarding the outcome of the elections; to be sure, the Republicans had won firm control of Congress and the Populist vote had revealed the continued discontent of many in the West and South, but there was consolation in the thought that the Democracy had been defeated because it shied away from true tariff reform and flirted with silver. A close friend of Cleveland went so far as to assert that only in the unseating of Representative William L. Wilson had the Democrats suffered a defeat; that despite their temporary victory the Republicans were doomed; that the Republican vote was not large; and that Democratic defections were not numerous. The New York *Times* blamed senatorial obstructionists, who had unconscionably delayed and betrayed the cause of tariff reform, for the sharp Democratic defeat and, recovering its poise, asserted that the elections of 1894:

> . . . unlike those of 1890 and 1892, did not turn on the tariff. Everyone knew two years ago to-day that the McKinley tariff must be repealed. No one to-day expects that the new tariff will be repealed. It is physically impossible for three years, and when the next national election comes around it is more than probable that neither party will propose any radical change.

Insofar as particular elections were concerned, President Cleveland felt no pain at the defeat of Senator Hill in the New York gubernatorial race. The New York *Times* went further, celebrating the undoing of Hill, the organization politician, by "that intelligent, independent and prevailing multitude" which administers "the penalty of defeat for principles abandoned or policies ill chosen" and rejoicing in the defeat of Tammany Hall in New York City. Turning its attention to Connecticut, the *Times* claimed that one-fifth of the Republicans' gain had come from erstwhile Prohibitionists and that abstentions among Democrats had run twice as high as defections.[39]

Conjectures such as those of the New York *Times* suited the needs of Cleveland Democrats by minimizing everywhere the magnitude of the Republican victory and, in the case of New York, by claiming for Clevelandites a share of the credit in the defeat of Democrats whom the President opposed. Analysis of the New York State and New York City elections suggests the inadequacy of this interpretation of the Republican success in the gubernatorial canvass. In that election, David Hill suffered a sharper percentage decline than had Cord Meyer in the 1893 election for Secretary of State; Levi Morton gained more points than had John Palmer. Though percentage shifts were not as great as in the previous year's contest for Judge of the Court of Appeals, Hill fell short of Maynard's mark and Morton outran Maynard's foe. Daniel Lockwood, the Democratic lieutenant-gubernatorial candidate, benefited from not being opposed by the Reform Democrats, who polled 2.1 per cent in the gubernatorial election: he ran 2.2 percentage points ahead of Hill, his Republican opponent 0.1 points behind Morton.

TABLE 7 *Shifts in Percentage Strength, 1893–1894, All Parties, Selected New York Counties and Other Areas of the State*

	DEM.	REP.	PRO.	SLP	POP.	DPRO[b]
Four Counties[a]	−13.1	+12.2	−0.9	−0.4	−0.4	2.7
Rest of State	− 1.6	+ 2.4	−1.3	−0.5	−0.8	1.9
New York State	− 5.0	+ 5.2	−1.1	−0.5	−0.7	2.1

Sources: *Tribune Almanacs, 1894, 1895.*

[a] New York, Queens, Rensselaer, and Albany counties.

[b] The Democratic Party Reform Organization did not run a state ticket in 1893.

Major setbacks in New York, Queens, Rensselaer, and Albany counties contributed greatly to the Democratic debacle. (See Table 7.) Of the four, only Queens had begun to move toward the Republicans in 1893. The Democratic collapse in New York City was particularly damaging to the party, which depended on healthy pluralities there to offset upstate Republican pluralities. Hill carried the metropolis by an anemic margin—2780 votes. The Democrats' disappointing showing differed radically from the stand-off one year earlier, when they had gained or held their own in Lower East Side, lower Manhattan, and West Side strongholds, while losing in central Manhattan, uptown, and East Side districts. Hill lost percentage strength in every assembly district, suffering his sharpest declines in the Democratic bailiwicks of 1893. Republican gains in these districts attested to the success of the G.O.P. campaign based on depression issues; they contrasted sharply with those of the previous year, which had been associated with the campaign against Isaac Maynard. These differences produced a markedly negative correlation (−.762) between Republican percentage shifts in the successive elections for secretary of state and governor.

Republican gains and Democratic losses exceeded city-wide averages in all but two of ten assembly districts in the Lower East Side, lower Manhattan, and the Lower West Side. Reversing its decline in other parts of the city, the Socialist Labor party gained in three Lower East Side assembly districts (3, 4, 5) where East European Jews were concentrated, and in the 2nd A.D., into which they were moving. (Newcomers, rather than conversions among the older inhabitants of the 2nd A.D., almost certainly accounted for the Socialist Labor party's gains there.) Though Republicans and Socialist Laborites flourished in the Lower East Side, Cleveland Democrats did not, Everett Wheeler, the independent Democratic gubernatorial candidate, receiving above-average support only in the 7th and 10th A.D.s, where Germans were still numerous.[40]

Republican successes in lower Manhattan, particularly the 2nd A.D., led to renewed charges of Democratic election frauds there in 1893. Republicans had alleged such irregularities in testimony before the Lexow Committee. Now the majority of the Lexow Committee contended that an unusual decline in the vote of the 2nd A.D. testified both to a fraudulently large vote in 1893 and to the effectiveness of the committee in discouraging skulduggery in 1894. Republican allegations and Democratic denials can neither be proved nor disproved, but turnout did decline in A.D.s 1, 2, 3, and 4—especially in A.D.s 2 and 3—even as turnout rose in every other district.[41] This suspicious development may have reflected frauds consummated in 1893 but frustrated in 1894. At the same time, the Democrats had gained in 1893 in districts where fraud was not charged. Though the publicity generated by the Lexow Committee may have discouraged Tammany from committing frauds in 1894, the Democratic organization still controlled the city's political machinery. Despite the importance to it of the 1894 election, Tammany was unable to prevent its opponents from gaining in every district. In 1895 Tammany was to register impressive gains at a time when Fusion controlled the city, including its police, and the Republicans controlled the state government. Such fluctuations suggest that though fraud there may have been, flesh-and-blood voters contributed to shifts in political fortunes.

The Republicans' city-wide percentage gain was inflated by their landslide victories in lower Manhattan; elsewhere, only in the 29th A.D., in the southeastern Bronx, did they exceed their average gain. But gains throughout midtown and uptown New York City clearly established the strength of the Republican surge. Morton gained somewhat more in the East Side than in the West Side, but relative to the pattern of 1893, the Republicans' breakthrough in the West Side was more dramatic. The Reform Democrats fared somewhat better in East Side districts where Germans were numerous than in West Side ones where the Irish predominated.[42]

Democratic defections to the Democratic Party Reform Organization reached their peak in middle class and upper class districts. Indeed, Wheeler's percentage strength exceeded Morton's percentage gain in the silk-stocking 21st A.D., and matched it in the 23rd A.D. Unsurprisingly, the Socialist Labor party fared poorly in these districts.[43] The essential continuity between the Cleveland Democratic vote against Maynard in 1893 and that for Wheeler against Hill in 1894 was clear: they correlated at +.734. On the other hand, the pattern of Republican gains in 1894 was unlike the pattern of Democratic Reform strength: they correlated at −.199. (Republican percentage gains in the 1893 election for secretary of state had correlated with the anti-Maynard vote at +.762.)[44] The politics of depression, on which the Republicans capitalized in 1894, clearly differed from the Democratic factional politics on which the G.O.P. gains of 1893 and the Democratic Reform vote of 1894 were based.

The Fusion campaign against Tammany swayed more voters than the independent Democratic attack on Hill. Everett Wheeler polled 3.3 per cent of the city's gubernatorial vote, but Hugh Grant ran fully 7.0 percentage points behind Hill (and 10.3 points behind Hill and Wheeler together). William Strong ran 10.6 points ahead of Morton. Hill carried eighteen districts, eight by majorities; Grant carried five, three by majorities. Morton received majorities in six districts, Strong in twenty-three. Only two years earlier, Grover Cleveland and Tammany Hall had swept New York City's thirty assembly districts. Strong ran ahead of Morton in every district, achieving his widest leads in the 21st A.D., the home of the Union League Club, and the 25th A.D., an East Side German neighborhood. These A.D.s set the pattern for similar districts in Manhattan, in only two of which Strong's lead was below-average. In the Lower East Side, where charges of Union League Club anti-Semitism and countercharges of Tammany exploitation of the Jewish district had flown during the campaign, Strong showed better in the 7th and 10th A.D.s, where Germans were still numerous, than in A.D.s 3, 4, 5, and 6, where East European Jews were concentrated. The Democratic Reform and Fusion movements had resembled one another socio-economically and ethno-culturally. Their popular bases were also comparable, the Democratic Reform gubernatorial vote correlating at +.667 with Fusion's lead over the Republican state ticket.[45]

In New York City, the depression election of 1894 revealed the Democrats to be vulnerable to a Republican campaign based on economic issues, even in the Irish and East European Jewish working class districts where the Democratic organization was most powerful. At the same time, both the Democratic Reform gubernatorial and Fusion mayoralty votes, like the anti-Maynard vote of the previous year, revealed organization Democrats to be vulnerable to the very different campaigns of factional foes, particularly in middle class and upper class German and old-stock districts. Understandably, Cleveland Democrats preferred to view the events of 1894 in the latter terms. But a comparative analysis of the 1893 and 1894 elections suggests that one must deal with both voting patterns in order to understand the Democratic defeat of 1894 in the party's strongholds.[46]

Troy and Albany also moved toward the Republicans in 1894. Not even Senator Murphy's machine could save Hill from losing strength in all of Troy's thirteen wards, and receiving severe setbacks in organization strongholds. In Albany Hill held his own only in two Republican districts among the city's seventeen wards. The Democrats' losses more than wiped out their gains of 1893; they were now weaker than they had been in 1892, not a good Democratic year in either city. Gains in Troy and Albany paced Republican successes in Rensselaer and Albany counties.[47]

The results in Brooklyn, Buffalo, and Rochester differed from those in New York City, Troy, and Albany. Hill suffered a slightly above-average loss in Kings County, but Wheeler, rather than Morton, whose percentage declined slightly, was the beneficiary. Hill declined from Meyer's mark in the twenty-eight wards of old Brooklyn, but he did show better than had Maynard and Boody. (By way of contrast, Hill ran much worse than Maynard in New York City, where there had been no anti-Tammany revolt in 1893.) Percentage shifts were small: Morton gained from 0.1 to 3.7 points in ten wards, most of which were strongly Democratic districts that had experienced below-average Democratic losses in 1893; he lost from 1.1 to 6.0 points in eighteen wards, most of which were Republican or Democratic wards that had experienced above-average Democratic losses the previous year. Hill lost from 0.2 to 9.5 points in twenty-seven wards and gained 0.3 points in one ward. The limited shifts indicated that Brooklyn had undergone its political upheaval in 1893. Republican percentage gains at the expense of the Democrats in Irish tenement districts, and losses to the Reform Democrats in more comfortable old-stock districts, suggested that the depression was further cutting into traditional Democratic strength and that many "reform" Democrats who had had to vote Republican to register their disapproval of Democratic regulars in 1893 now did so by voting Democratic Reform. As in New York City, the patterns of Republican percentage shifts in 1893 and 1894 differed: they correlated at −.714.[48]

In a very real sense, Kings County was the operational base of the Democratic Party Reform Organization. Edward M. Shepard, whose "respectable" faction opposed Hugh McLaughlin's Brooklyn regulars, was a leader of the third party; his organization provided the nucleus around which Wheeler's campaign was built. Reform Democratic leaders had claimed 140,000 votes state-wide and 25,000 in Kings County, but Wheeler polled only 27,202 and 9707. At that, Kings was the ranking

Democratic Reform county—in votes and percentage strength. (Of the Reform Democrats' state-wide vote, 35.7 per cent was cast in Kings and another 33.2 per cent in New York County: together the two counties accounted for 35.2 per cent of the total state-wide vote for all parties.) Wheeler ran best in relatively prosperous old-stock American wards and better in German districts than Irish ones, though his showing in two German tenement wards (16, 18) was disappointing. Still the Reform Democrats were more broadly based in Kings County, where they received 5.0 per cent or above in nineteen of thirty-one wards and in Flatlands, than they were in New York County, where they did so in only three of thirty assembly districts. As in New York City, the socio-economic and ethno-cultural bases of Republican gains differed from those of the Democratic Reform movement; they correlated at −.443 in Brooklyn. The correlation between the anti-Maynard vote of 1893 and the Democratic Reform vote of 1894 (+.429) was lower in Brooklyn than in New York City. A growing disagreement between Germans and evangelical Protestants over the municipal reform administration's policy toward taverns seems to have contributed to this development.[49] In 1894 old-stock American wards ranked higher and German wards lower in the reform column than they had the previous year.

In Buffalo and Rochester the Democrats reversed the state-wide Republican tide of 1894 to recover some strength lost the previous year. Percentage point shifts were slight in Buffalo, the Democrats gaining from 0.1 to 7.5 points in twenty wards, including all of those that had contributed to the great Republican victory of 1893, and losing from 0.2 to 10.5 points in five wards, including some of those that had been comparatively immune to the Republican appeal of 1893. The Democratic revival was stronger in Rochester, the party regaining from 1.0 to 21.9 percentage points in all of the city's twenty wards. The factors contributing to these Democratic gains are unclear, but to a limited degree both involved recoveries in the districts hit hardest by the G.O.P. the previous fall. Democratic gains exceeded Republican losses in the two cities, the Prohibition, People's, and Socialist Labor parties all losing strength.[50]

The voting behavior of rural New York State is less easily categorized. As in 1893, the range of percentage point shifts was narrower in rural than urban areas. In fact, this range was narrower than it had been the previous year, Schoharie County's shifts (Dem. −6.1, Rep. +6.6) hardly matching those in Clinton (Dem. −15.2, Rep. +13.7). The Republicans gained in even more rural counties than in 1893; their losses in a few scattered counties were fractional. The Democrats again declined more often than they gained, but they did advance (albeit marginally) in more rural counties than in 1893. Both major parties advanced—the Republicans generally more than the Democrats—in a number of counties as minor parties fared badly. The Socialist Labor party, which had reached the 1.0 per cent mark in a number of rural counties in 1893, failed to do so in 1894. The People's party declined even more precipitously; the Prohibitionists fell to their lowest state-wide level since 1881. The Reform Democrats polled 1.0 per cent of the vote in only a few counties outside the metropolitan area.[51]

Allegany, the state's ranking Prohibitionist and Populist county in elections from 1892 through 1895, illustrates the pattern described above. Like other strongholds of the two parties, Allegany lay in western New York, much of which was settled during the nineteenth century by New Englanders and eastern New Yorkers who were themselves frequently of New England origin. (Smaller streams of settlement flowed northward from Pennsylvania and New Jersey.) The peculiar social and economic characteristics of western New York made it susceptible to religious revivalism—so often and deeply was the region seared by revivalistic fervor that it became known as "the Burned-Over District"—and related evangelical reform movements: antimasonry, anti-Catholicism, antislavery, prohibitionism, and Populism. Most of those who viewed politics as a means of achieving moral objectives identified with the Republican party: the Burned-Over District—except for Seneca County—was a bastion of Republicanism. In any event, the Democrats suffered an above-average loss in Allegany in 1893, but the Prohibitionists benefited more than the Republicans from this development. The Populists neither gained nor lost strength. The Republicans increased their percentage gain in 1894, but the Democrats gained slightly more to recoup most of their 1893 loss as both the Prohibitionists and Populists declined. In Allegany, where moral issues were important, the Democrats were able to recover partially from the Maynard campaign, but the Republicans, who stood for prosperity as well as probity and Protestantism, were the sole gainers between 1892 and 1894.[52]

Elsewhere, Republican rural gains were generally accompanied by Democratic losses, but even in counties where that occurred there was no clear connection between the economic and social characteristics of towns and the direction and intensity of voting shifts. Though the Republicans employed protectionist arguments among a variety of farm groups that faced Canadian and overseas competition, percentage point shifts in agricultural towns were smaller than those in most of the state's major cities, and if most such towns registered Republican gains, scattered ones moved the opposite way. Nor did cultural conflicts appear to have contributed appreciably to shifts among the rural electorate. This is not to argue that those conflicts were not politically salient. On the contrary, they lay at the very root of political behavior: towns in which one or another cultural group predominated were highly and consistently partisan in voting behavior during the pre-1893 decades. Towns settled by New Englanders and Protestants from Sweden, Holland, England, Ireland, Scotland, Wales, and Canada generally voted Republican. Old Dutch, Palatinate German, Irish Catholic, and French Canadian towns generally voted Democratic. Like the Irish and Canadians, Germans divided along religious lines, Lutherans and particularly Catholics voting Democratic, others Republican. During the 1850s, cultural conflicts had revealed their explosive power, contributing to major shifts in political behavior, particularly among those New Englanders who had voted Democratic during earlier decades.[53] By the 1890s, however, cultural-political lines were clearly drawn in rural New York: the activity, real and imagined, of the American Protective Association, and charges and countercharges regarding anti-Catholicism and temperance, did little to alter these alignments or to influence the depression-born shift of most towns of all descriptions toward the Republicans. In major cities, the Democrats suffered sharp defeats in either 1893 or 1894. A number of rural counties and towns broke toward the Republicans in one year or the other, but as a whole, rural New York slid rather than lurched toward the Republicans during 1893–94. The election of 1895 was to demonstrate that the slide had not yet run its course.

Unlike New York and New Jersey, Connecticut had neither held state-wide elections in 1893 nor experienced developments comparable to the Democratic factional conflicts or the anti-race-track revolt that had influenced politics in the respective states. Connecticut voters went to the polls in 1894 for the first time since the onset of hard times; their voting behavior in the gubernatorial election can be directly compared with that in the gubernatorial election of 1892. In 1894 Democratic campaigners sought to maintain pre-depression voting alignments by reinforcing their party's traditional appeal to Roman Catholics through denunciations of Republican involvement with the American Protective Association. Most Roman Catholics lived in cities, but the Democrats attempted to strengthen their position among urbanites in general by assailing Republican opposition to constitutional reforms that would increase the political power of Connecticut's cities. On the other hand, the Republicans sought to cut across Catholic-Protestant and urban-rural lines by stressing economic issues arising out of the depression and playing down older cultural and constitutional issues.

Election returns from towns containing Connecticut's eleven largest cities, which accounted for nearly one-half of the state's vote, must have sorely disappointed Democratic leaders. Their party fell by 8.1 percentage points in these towns, the Republicans gaining 7.5 points. The Democrats lost somewhat more heavily in New Haven, Bridgeport, and Waterbury, which with Hartford were the state's ranking cities.[54] In New Haven, Wards 3, 4, 5, 6, 7, and 12 formed the base of the Democracy. These wards contained the city's major Irish Catholic neighborhoods; some also contained smaller German elements. Wards 4, 7, and 12 experienced below-average, but marked, percentage shifts toward the G.O.P. in 1894. In Wards 3, 5, and 6, the Democrats suffered above-average losses. Italians were moving into Wards 5,

6, and 7, and East European Jews into Ward 3, during the 1890s, but the newcomers had not yet politically transformed these neighborhoods. Still, by 1894, the American Protective Association thought it worthwhile to allege that Irish Catholic Democrats were anti-Semitic, and Louis Ullman, of German Jewish extraction, had become a figure in the Republican organization in Ward 3. In the same year, the ward gave the Socialist Labor party 4.1 per cent of its total vote. (The ward ranked first in this respect; city-wide, the party received 1.7 per cent of the vote.) [55]

The Democrats' fortunes sank even lower in New Haven wards where their weak cultural appeal combined with economic discontent to undermine them. In elections to the New Haven Board of Education, held less than two months before the general election, candidates of the American Protective Association had outpolled Democrats in Wards 9, 10, and 15. Wards 9 and 10 had voted Republican in 1892; Ward 9 contained New Haven's largest Negro neighborhood and smaller English, Scottish, and Scandinavian settlements. Neither Ward 10 nor Ward 15 contained significant immigrant populations, but the former housed a second Negro area. Now, in November, the Democrats suffered severe losses in all three wards. City-wide, Democratic declines were positively correlated with earlier A.P.A. strength.[56]

New Haven's First Ward stood in clear contrast to other districts where the Irish were not numerous enough to provide the Democrats with a solid base. This centrally located ward contained banks, business and professional offices, and Yale University; the university community and the city's leading families contributed to its well-to-do, old-stock American population. (The ward ranked first in native-born whites of native parentage by a wide margin.) Ward 1, relatively secure, economically and socially, experienced percentage point shifts approximating those in Democratic strongholds, rather than those in other non-Irish wards. Comparable districts in New York City and Brooklyn were the scenes of Cleveland Democratic knifings of regular Democratic candidates, but there was no factional conflict to contribute to the Democratic decline in Connecticut in 1894. Neither depression nor Protestant-Catholic tensions affected voting behavior in Ward 1 as much as they did in a number of other New

Haven districts. Two years later, the silk-stocking ward was to react sharply in the Clevelandites' revolt against the Democrats' nomination of William Jennings Bryan.[57]

As in New Haven, Democratic percentage losses in Waterbury and Bridgeport were negatively associated with 1892 Democratic percentage strength, but the correlation was weak in Bridgeport and the party lost ground in every ward in the two cities. In Waterbury, Democratic losses were smaller in Ward 4, where Irish Americans were most numerous, than in Wards 1 and 3, where other immigrant groups had located, or in Ward 2, where native-born whites of native parentage were still in a slight majority. In Bridgeport, the Democrats suffered below-average declines in two strongholds, Wards 3 and 4, but had their worst setback in another bailiwick, Ward 6, where the Socialist Labor party received its greatest support (2.5 per cent). The Bridgeport Democracy was weakest in Ward 2, whose large Swedish population (Lutheran, Baptist, and Methodist) contributed to Republican strength.[58]

Only in Hartford did the Democrats escape crushing defeat in 1894. Percentage shifts there were small; the Democrats actually held their own in one district, Ward 3, where the Republicans lost a fraction (0.8 points) of their percentage strength. (This was the Democrats' best showing in thirty-three wards in Connecticut's four largest cities.) Sharp conflicts within their local organization probably contributed to the Republicans' relatively disappointing showing in Hartford. Certainly Hartford's voting pattern differed from that in other major cities, insofar as the Democrats suffered comparatively light losses in Republican districts.[59] The economic and political life of Hartford were influenced by its primacy in insurance and related financial activities. Hartford was to shift sharply toward the Republicans and give strong support to the National (Gold) Democrats in 1896, when Bryan's candidacy posed a threat to its dominant institutions, but the city obviously experienced no Clevelandite revolt in 1894.

The city of New Britain provided the most dramatic illustration of the political interaction between economic issues, which everywhere worked to the disadvantage of the Democrats during the depression, and cultural issues, which cut both ways. In April

1894 a Citizens' ticket captured municipal offices from the Democrats and elected councilmen and an alderman in two of four wards. Republicans supported the Citizens' movement, in which the American Protective Association was influential. Voter turnout set a record for a non-presidential election. The Citizens' ticket triumphed in Wards 1 and 2, which were normally Republican; the Democrats held Wards 3 and 4, party strongholds in which Irish Catholics were concentrated. Germans and Swedes, both numerous in New Britain—particularly in Wards 1 and 2—were identified as supporters of the A.P.A. campaign. At the time the new city administration took office, New Britain was dry, many Catholics (led by the Young Men's Total Abstinence Society) having joined Protestants to carry every ward for "no license" the previous fall. Now, in October 1894, many Catholics (members of the Abstinence Society among them) supported "license" to protest the involvement of Protestant prohibitionists in the A.P.A. and the Citizens' campaign. Germans, disillusioned with the operation of "no license," joined them. The wets swept the city, registering their greatest gains in Wards 3 and 4.[60] The wounds produced by these cultural confrontations were still open in November, as New Britons voted in the general election, but they had less influence on this canvass than on the vote on license the previous month. As might have been expected, the Republicans registered their greatest gains in Wards 1 and 2, but not even in Wards 3 and 4 could the Democrats stem the G.O.P. advance. For the second time in seven months turnout ran high, actually exceeding that in the presidential election of 1892. (In only nineteen other Connecticut towns was this the case.) Though all wards moved toward the Republicans, the polarization between Republican and Democratic wards actually exceeded that of 1892.[61]

The lines of cultural conflict were more sharply drawn in New Britain than in any other Connecticut city. These lines were neither etched nor obliterated by the depression of 1893, but the fact that cultural lines remained visible did not mean that they determined the outcome of the midterm elections in New Britain or any other Connecticut city. To be sure, the Democrats' losses were lighter in wards that contained religious groups strongly disposed to vote Democratic than they were in wards that did not, but in most such districts their losses ran unacceptably high and in some disastrously so. On the other hand, the Republicans gained considerable strength in Democratic urban bailiwicks and even more in districts where their own cultural appeal had been greatest before the depression. Long-standing cultural differences between the parties, reinforced by the Democrats' campaign appeals during 1894, accounted for these differences in voting patterns, but the politics of depression fairly guaranteed that urban districts of all descriptions would move toward the Republican party.

Connecticut's vote of no confidence in the Democracy was by no means confined to the larger cities, for the Democrats lost 7.1 percentage points and the Republicans gained 7.6 points in the remaining 157 towns, and they cast 52.3 per cent of the state's vote in 1894.[62] These towns cannot be categorized as easily as those containing major cities. They ranged widely in population: some contained bustling cities, boroughs, and villages; others were nearly deserted rural communities. Industry dominated the economy of numerous towns; agriculture remained the mainstay of many others. Prior to the depression, the Republicans predominated in most of the state's towns, particularly the rural ones whose populations were predominantly members of Protestant denominations that supported the G.O.P. Cultural differences and political loyalties dating from earlier periods, rather than the relative prosperity or agricultural emphasis of various towns, shaped voting behavior in rural Connecticut.

Agricultural towns did not respond as one to the campaign of 1894. During the 1890s, Republican spokesmen promised tariff protection to a wide range of farmers, but to none in Connecticut did they pledge more than tobacco growers. Tobacco, unlike other crops, was raised in geographically restricted areas of the state—the Connecticut and Housatonic river valleys. Tobacco was a commercial crop that faced foreign competition; its growers repeatedly and clearly expressed their opposition to the Wilson-Gorman Tariff bill. On election day the tobacco-growing towns all contributed to the Republican victory, but they did not lead the way. Though Suffield, the state's ranking tobacco-growing town, did record a sharp Democratic percentage loss, other important tobacco towns in Hartford County did not shift to the same degree.[63] Neither did rural towns in which dairying, mixed farming, or specialty crops predominated, the Democrats losing badly in some, declining moderately in many, and gaining in a few.[64]

The Democrats lost more heavily and consistently in towns of varying size in which non-agricultural activities were significant than they did in essentially agricultural towns. Manchester, an important manufacturing town, ranked first in Democratic percentage decline in Hartford County. In Litchfield County, to be sure, the Democrats' worst setback occurred in the agricultural town of Warren, but losses in other such towns ranged downward from well below average to the lowest in the county. At the same time, the Democrats lost more sharply in Litchfield's ranking manufacturing towns and in towns where quarrying or the mining and smelting of iron, as well as agriculture, were conducted.[65] In Windham and Tolland counties, a number of towns contained important textile manufacturing cities, boroughs, and villages. As elsewhere in the Northeast, textiles, Connecticut's leading industry, had been sharply hit by the depression of 1893. Indeed, hard times exposed weaknesses in the industry in Windham and Tolland; it was not to revive fully during the general economic recovery toward the end of the decade. Many textile firms would relocate or abandon mills in northeastern Connecticut as they moved their operations to large cities or closer to major markets. Related firms followed suit. With the decline of Windham and Tolland counties' prime industry, other businesses began to suffer.[66] The two counties contained seven of the state's major industrial towns. The Democrats suffered severe percentage declines in three of these towns and above-average losses in all but one. Several lesser towns in which manufacturing was also important fell into the same pattern. As in other counties, agricultural towns displayed no such consistency in their political behavior.[67]

The Democrats actually gained percentage strength in ten towns—in three of which the Republicans also gained—scattered through five counties of the state.[68] In general, these towns were agricultural and not populous: among them only Griswold (41st) and Newtown (49th) ranked among Connecticut's 61 leading manufacturing towns and cities in 1900; these towns ranked 46th and 52nd in population, respectively. Irish Catholics were numerous in some of these towns, but too much should not be made of the point, for if in Lisbon and Griswold Irish immigrants and their children had accounted for 28.6 and 22.0 per cent of the population in 1880, in nearby Salem—where the Democrats fared even better in 1894—they had contributed only 5.4 per cent of the population. Three contiguous towns in Fairfield County offer another striking case in point. Newtown was regarded as an Irish Catholic town: 45.1 per cent of its 1880 population had been first- or second-generation Irish; no immigrant group that identified with the Republican party had constituted more than a fraction of the population. In 1892, Newtown had been the county's banner Democratic town (72.8 per cent). Two years later, the Democrats gained 2.2 percentage points there, even as they lost 8.3 points county-wide. At the same time, the Democracy gained 2.6 points in Brookfield and 11.1 points in New Fairfield, neighboring towns that had been one-fifth and one-tenth Irish, respectively. Elsewhere, in Hartland, whose very small Irish population was outnumbered by a handful of English settlers, the Democrats gained 10.5 points. In Windham, the Democrats registered their only gain in Pomfret, the county's second-ranking Prohibition town. At the same time they suffered their worst setback in Chaplin, a culturally homogeneous town in which "temperance," "good order," and "sobriety" were prized.[69] Again, no discernable cultural differences separated rural towns where the Democrats gained from those where they lost.

A note of caution is in order. The unavailability of local election returns within the more populous industrial towns may conceal the political manifestations of cultural conflicts within them. Certainly the situation within the textile towns of Windham and Tolland counties was combustible even before the depression intensified the competition for jobs. Irish, English, Swedish, and French Canadian immigrants had followed New Englanders into the textile mills. County histories refer to the existence of nativist groups during this period; they further reveal the shock felt by their old-stock American authors as cultural homogeneity gave way to heterogeneity. Anti-Catholics were active in Willimantic, the textile borough that dominated the town of Windham. As the campaign of 1894 drew to a close there, a priest exhorted Catholics to vote against the Republican-American Protective Association alliance.

Interestingly, Windham town recorded the only below-average Democratic decline (−2.3 points) among the major textile towns in Windham County. The Democrats' comparatively good showing may have reflected the fact that the Irish still outnumbered the French Canadians by a fair margin there. In Killingly, Putnam, and Thompson, the county's other textile towns, French Canadians heavily outnumbered the Irish. Voters of both Catholic nationalities identified with the Democratic party; immigrants (e.g., the English and Swedes) and old-stock Americans hostile to Catholics identified with the Republican party. But French Canadian immigrants did not become citizens or voters as quickly as their Irish counterparts. They had not yet become a political force in their own right. As a consequence, the Democrats lacked a broad political base in towns where the Catholic population was predominantly French Canadian, rather than Irish.[70] These circumstances may have contributed to the Democrats' disastrous showing in such towns in 1894.

Clevelandites' explanations of the Democrats' defeats in Connecticut simply do not hold water. There was obvious evidence of a widespread shift of popular support from the Democratic party to the Republican party, but none of an uprising of voters against the Senate's tardiness in reducing tariff protection. Connecticut's congressmen had felt constituency pressure to oppose, not to expedite, tariff reform. Districts that were to give marked support to the National (Gold) Democratic ticket in 1896 during the revolt of Cleveland Democrats against William Jennings Bryan—e.g., the silk-stocking First Ward of New Haven; the city of Hartford; and many rural towns—did not lead the shift toward the Republicans in 1894. Support for the Prohibition party did decline between 1892 and 1894, as the New York *Times* pointed out, but even if one assumes a shift of these 1617 voters to the Republican party—by no means a certainty, for some drys may have contributed to the midterm decline in turnout—77.6 per cent of the Republicans' net gain in votes would remain unaccounted for. The Republicans' gain (7230 votes) over their 1892 gubernatorial tally takes on added significance in view of the over-all declines in turnout (9582 votes) and Democratic support (16,500 votes) between 1892 and 1894. Not only did the Republicans' share of the vote in 1894 exceed that of the Democrats in 1892, their vote was actually larger—despite the smaller turnout. Democratic claims regarding abstentions to the contrary notwithstanding, voter interest ran high in 1894: turnout declined less markedly and a higher percentage of registered voters balloted than in other midterm elections during the period.[71]

Some Cleveland Democrats, ignoring the losses suffered by their party throughout Connecticut, attributed its setback in the Second Congressional District to the candidacy of Representative James P. Pigott. Pigott was disliked by some of the older and more "respectable" elements within the party; his dispensation of patronage left the unrewarded disgruntled; he had favored the income tax amendment to the Wilson Tariff bill; he was of Irish descent; and, to some, he had been too vigorous in his attacks on the A.P.A. But Pigott had been erroneously deemed a fatal handicap to the ticket in 1892, and if he ran slightly (1.6 points) behind the state ticket in 1894, so did the other Democratic congressional incumbents. Edward Kilduff, the only Irish Catholic candidate for state-wide office, fell even more slightly (0.2 points) behind his running mates. This is not to discount the possibility that some Democrats cast straight Republican ballots to protest Kilduff's presence on the ticket. In Massachusetts, by comparison, the G.O.P. Lieutenant gubernatorial candidate fell 3.2 points behind his ticket after the American Protective Association had called on supporters to cut him by voting for the candidate of the Prohibition party.[72] Ironically, such an appeal would naturally have been more effective against a Republican than a Democrat, for most supporters of the A.P.A. were Republicans. In short, neither Democratic factionalism nor the characteristics of particular Democratic candidates could account for the decisive shift of Connecticut voters toward Republican candidates for state-wide office, Congress, and the state legislature, a shift that reduced the Democracy to the position of the minority party within the state.

Voting shifts in the New Jersey congressional elections of 1894 are best viewed against the background of voting patterns in the legislative elections of the previous year. The anti-racetrack campaign of 1893 had been charged with emotion: it had produced particularly violent shifts in voting behavior in southern and western parts of the state. These shifts had been greater than shifts in underlying partisan identifications, for when the uproar over the racetrack and gambling questions subsided many voters returned to their traditional party folds. As a consequence, in 1894 the Democrats regained lost ground in counties where they had been trounced in 1893. But so strongly did the Republican tide run in the depression elections of 1894 that nowhere could the Democrats fully recover. Thus in Cape May County, where they had lost 14.4 percentage points in 1893, the Democrats gained 4.7 points at the expense of the Republicans and Prohibitionists, who lost 4.2 and 3.4 points, respectively. In Sussex County, the Democrats gained 5.3 points and the Prohibitionists 0.4, the Republicans losing 5.8 points. Sussex, unlike Cape May, contained pockets of industry—iron mills that worked local minerals. Towns associated with this declining, depressed industry did not contribute proportionally to the Democratic revival: the party registered below-average gains in Andover, Byram, and Hardyston but lost ground in Vernon, where it suffered its worst setback in the county, and Sparta. Reversing 1893 shifts in Hunterdon County, both major parties picked up the pieces as the Prohibition party fell apart after its earlier strong showing. Comparison of 1892 and 1894 returns reveals that the Republicans scored net gains there while the other two parties declined.[73] The Prohibitionist decline in Hunterdon was unusually sharp, but it reflected as well as exaggerated the party's state-wide loss of strength as the protest temper of 1893 faded.

On the other hand, the Democrats suffered severely in Atlantic and Warren counties, where they had earlier been the beneficiaries of the anti-racetrack revolt in assembly races. The Republican party not only regained voters lost in 1893, it won over Democrats disgruntled over hard times in 1894. The counties ranked first and third in Democratic percentage losses. Atlantic's normally Republican electorate reversed its upset verdict of 1893 with a vengeance, the G.O.P. gaining 18.9 percentage points, the Democrats and Prohibitionists losing 18.5 and 2.5 points, respectively. These shifts were particularly striking in four towns where the Republicans' racetrack legislator had been trounced the previous year.[74] In Warren, the Republicans gained 17.1 percentage points, the Democrats losing 13.4 points and the Prohibitionists 4.3, moving this Democratic stronghold into the Republican column.

Anti-Catholicism did not appear to figure in the outcome in southern New Jersey, which was widely regarded as the stronghold of the Junior Order of United American Mechanics. (U.S. Representative Henry C. Loudenslager and State Senator Maurice Rogers, both Republicans, were identified with the order in this area.) The Republicans scored an above-average gain in only one rural/small-town county (Atlantic); in Cape May they lost strength. These counties, Republican to begin with, had reacted sharply to the conflicts of 1893; by 1894, Republican ranks already included virtually all of those who opposed the Democracy as the party of Irish Catholics, racetracks, gambling, liquor, and aid to parochial schools. There were simply few Democrats sensitive to these issues left to recruit.

The Republicans showed well in Camden and Trenton, the two largest cities in southern and western New Jersey. Camden offered no religious or ethnic barriers to Republican success: native-born whites and Negroes accounted for over four-fifths of the population in all nine wards; neither Germans nor Irishmen were numerous in any ward. Camden had contributed little to the anti-racetrack revolt, the Republicans gaining but 2.8 points in the two-party percentage shift. In 1894, they gained 19.2 points, increasing their share of the two-party vote in every ward. The Democrats also lost strength in Camden County's outlying towns and in Gloucester City, where the closing of the racetrack scattered its employees, reducing turnout as well as the Democratic percentage of the vote. Trenton moved more sharply toward the Republicans in 1894 than 1893, even as passions subsided in surrounding towns.[75] The Republicans' share of the two-party vote fluctuated slightly one way or the other in wards where the party had run well in 1893, but rose markedly in wards controlled by the Democrats the previous year.

In pivotal northeastern New Jersey, the Democrats declined and the Republicans gained in three or four major urban-industrial counties.[76] Passaic County provided an unusual illustration of the politics of depression, the Socialist Labor party outgaining the Republicans, 9.3 percentage points to 2.6, to poll 11.5 per cent of the total vote, compared with 55.3 per cent for the Republicans, 31.2 per cent for the Democrats, and 2.0 per cent for the Prohibitionists. The Socialist Labor party showed to particular advantage in Paterson, a textiles center, outgaining the Republicans 12.3 to 1.2 percentage points and capturing 14.5 per cent of the three-party vote. Socialist Labor clearly undercut the Democrats, who lost 13.4 percentage points, its gains correlating at +.905 with Democratic losses. The correlation between Republican shifts and Democratic losses was not as strong— +.476. (Earlier in 1894, Matthew Maguire of the S.L.P. had won election to Paterson's Board of Aldermen.)[77] In Passaic the Democrats lost 10.1 percentage points, and the G.O.P. outgained the Socialist Labor party 9.3 to 0.9 percentage points. Only in two outlying towns did the Democrats escape disaster in Passaic County. Thus percentage shifts in the cities of Paterson and Passaic, as well as Camden and Trenton, exceeded those of 1893. The reverse was true in Elizabeth, in Union County, but though the Democrats regained some ground in the predominantly native-born and Republican wards where they had lost heavily the previous year, they generally lost ground in wards where Germans and Irishmen were most numerous, districts where they had not fared so badly in 1893.[78]

The state's two largest cities shifted in opposite directions in 1894, Newark accelerating its movement toward the G.O.P., Jersey City partially reversing its 1893 drift toward the Republicans. One cannot compare the Newark units reporting in 1894 with those of 1893, but the erosion of Democratic support since 1892, when Grover Cleveland had polled over 55 per cent of the vote in six of nine wards, is clear. In 1893 the Democracy had remained above this mark in four of the original six wards, but in 1894, it carried only four of fifteen wards, receiving majorities in two and barely reaching 55 per cent in one. The Republicans won over 60 per cent of the vote in seven wards, compared with two in 1892 and 1893. The parties split Jersey City's six aldermanic districts, the Democrats carrying poor to modest areas where the Irish were most numerous, the Republicans modest and better neighborhoods where old-stock Americans and Germans predominated.[79] A unique feature of the campaign in Hudson County was the uniting of the Socialist Labor and People's parties behind a single candidate in the Seventh Congressional District, which included Jersey City and outlying areas. A comparison of returns from the congressional election and legislative elections in which the two parties did not fuse suggests that over three-fourths of the coalition vote came from Socialist Laborities (who were most numerous in German localities). Elsewhere, the protest parties competed against one another, as well as against the major parties.[80]

Less is known about relations among Populists, socialists, and labor in the East than in the Midwest.[81] It should be understood that there were cultural as well as doctrinal differences between socialists and Populists. Contemporaries agreed on the essentially German and East European Jewish composition of the Socialist Labor party; conversions among Americans were evidently rare enough to be noteworthy. (Some immigrant groups were indifferent to or hostile toward the party.) On the other hand, in the Northeast the People's party recruited primarily among native Americans. More to the point, Prohibitionists and Populists frequently shared evangelical reform beliefs that were anathema to most Germans, let alone to secularists and socialists. Thus Miss Frances E. Willard, President of the World's Woman's Christian Temperance Union, could express to Henry Demarest Lloyd her hope that a wisely framed platform plank might bridge the narrow gap between Prohibitionists and Populists. Within the conventions of both parties, groups sought to construct such a bridge of cultural as well as economic planks. The position of the two parties on cultural issues was clearly "American," rather than "foreign." In 1895, the New York State People's and Prohibition parties ran a single candidate for Attorney-General; the following year, many Prohibitionists turned to William Jennings Bryan, the presidential candidate of the Democratic and People's parties. On the local level, during 1894, the Essex County People's party held its convention in the meeting hall of the Woman's Christian Temperance Union. At the same time, the Central Labor Union of New York City refused to cast its lot with the Socialist Labor party because it was "German." Some socialists recognized the cultural limitations of their movement: Friedrich Engels lamented that German immigrant socialists did not inform themselves of conditions in America; Joseph B. Keim, the Socialist Labor party's gubernatorial candidate in New Jersey in 1892 and 1895, resigned from the party in 1896 to support Bryan for President, on the ground that the party's inability to broaden its ethnic base was frustrating the socialist cause in America. On the other hand, some German socialists viewed the Socialist Labor party as a German party, and they resented the recruiting of Americans; Florence Kelley asserted that so badly had the party treated its English-speaking members that it was essentially composed of greenhorns.[82] Small wonder that unified Populist-Socialist Labor action was the exception, rather than the rule.

In sweeping to midterm election victories in New York, Connecticut, New Jersey, and elsewhere in the nation, the Republicans capitalized on depression discontent by offering positive alternatives to the economic policies of the Cleveland administration while minimizing their own involvement in the cultural conflicts that had weakened them in the past. The Democratic attempt to stem the Republican tide by campaigning on cultural issues proved unsuccessful, even in districts that can be assumed to have been most sensitive to such a campaign. Democratic attacks on Republican links with the American Protective Association certainly did not prevent Roman Catholic districts from increasing their support for the Republican party. Nor did Democratic criticism of Republican involvement with prohibitionism prevent German districts from doing likewise. The Democratic campaign was not without its risks: German Lutheran and old-stock American Democrats were not necessarily favorably disposed toward Roman Catholics; old-stock American Democrats were not necessarily hostile toward temperance. But whether the Democratic campaign decreased party losses in Catholic and German districts, increased them elsewhere, or both, nowhere did the Democrats succeed in reversing the flow of voters toward the G.O.P.

The Republican party benefited from the continued operation of a strong two-party system that led voters who were discontented with one major party to vote for its primary opponent. The People's and Socialist Labor parties did offer other alternatives to the electorate, but though the two protest parties did gain percentage strength nationally in 1894, the Populists failed to score breakthroughs in northeastern rural-agricultural districts, let alone urban-industrial ones, and the Socialist Laborites generally remained a narrowly based party even within urban-industrial constituencies. These parties lacked the local organization, press, and financial resources of the major parties; they advanced programs of limited appeal; the identification of the Populists with evangelical reform and the Socialists with Germans and East European Jews further handicapped their potential for growth. The Republicans gained in 1893 in New York and New Jersey and in 1894 in these states and Connecticut. On the other hand, the share of the vote received by minor parties rose in both years only in New Jersey, where the Socialist Labor and People's parties fared better than the Prohibition party, which lost its gains of 1893 the following year. In Connecticut, the Socialists and Populists gained ground between 1892 and 1894, but failed to match Prohibitionist losses. In New York, the three minor parties lost as much or more strength in 1894 than they had added in 1893. Clearly, the minor parties played unimportant roles in the Northeast, neither attracting many voters with their programs nor serving as rallying points for discontented Democrats who could not bring themselves to vote Republican, even during the depression.

The Cleveland Democrats played a different role in New York, where they contributed to, but did not account for, the defeat of Senator Hill in the gubernatorial election. Analysis makes it clear that in New York the popular bases of Cleveland Democratic support and Republican gains differed one from the other.

Elsewhere in the Northeast, where Democratic factionalism was not a significant political factor, rank-and-file Democratic discontent born of hard times rather than the defection of articulate Cleveland Democrats over the alleged betrayal of tariff reform by their party contributed to sweeping Republican successes.[83] As was to be expected in a midterm election, voter turnout ran lower in Connecticut, New York, and New Jersey in 1894 than in the presidential election of 1892. Under these circumstances, increased Republican percentage strength in the midterm elections could have reflected the failure of more Democrats than Republicans among 1892 voters to vote in 1894. Even this would have suggested that in 1894 the Republicans appealed more to their supporters of 1892 than the Democrats did to theirs.[84] But turnout ran high for a midterm election and so strong was the Republican surge that the G.O.P. vote of 1894 actually exceeded the winning Democratic presidential vote of 1892 in both Connecticut and New York. In New Jersey, the Republicans surpassed their own showing of 1892, but not that of the Democrats. Earlier in 1894, Edward Atkinson had claimed that with the passage of the Wilson-Gorman bill, tariff protection would be "intellectually dead." [85] With the midterm elections that November, it might better have been argued that the Democracy of Grover Cleveland was politically dead.

V

1895: Off-year Political Patterns

INSOFAR as students of the 1890s devote attention to the events of 1895, a political off-year, they generally focus upon the preliminaries to the presidential nominating and election campaigns of 1896. All the same, there are compelling reasons for viewing politics during 1895 as the consequence of the political upheaval of 1893–94, as well as the prelude to the campaigns of 1896. Certainly this holds true for the Northeast, whether one examines the region's role in national politics or whether one concentrates on grass-roots developments within the area.

Confidence born of party victories during 1893–94 led to a scramble for the Republican presidential nomination among Thomas B. Reed of Maine, Speaker of the U.S. House of Representatives; United States senators Matthew Quay of Pennsylvania, Shelby M. Cullom of Illinois, and William B. Allison of Iowa; and governors Levi Morton of New York and William McKinley of Ohio. Of these aspirants, William McKinley was the front runner. Retired from Congress following his narrow defeat in the Democratic landslide of 1890—in a district that had been gerrymandered by the Democrats—McKinley secured a broader political base by winning the governorship of Ohio one year later. The onset of hard times and Democratic efforts to revise the McKinley Tariff Act placed the Ohioan in the political limelight. McKinley made the most of his opportunity, winning reelection in 1893 and campaigning about the nation the following year on the issues of the depression and the protective tariff. During 1895 McKinley aggressively sought to capture delegates to the Republican national convention of 1896. Though he had to maneuver skillfully to win nomination, McKinley led from strength: more than any other presidential hopeful, he was popularly identified with the protective tariff, the issue that enabled the Republicans to focus the public's depression discontent on the Democrats while playing down embarrassing cultural issues. McKinley planned to march to victory as "the advance agent of prosperity." [1]

The Republican victories of 1893–94 altered the balance of power within, as well as between, the major parties. In the Northeast, Republicans hostile to free silver now occupied political positions once held by Democrats of the same persuasion. These Republicans reinforced the sound money forces within their own party. The full implications of this development would become clear at the Republican national convention of 1896, where party managers would make no attempt to placate spokesmen for the silver-producing states of the West. During 1895, however, Republicans continued to stress the tariff issue on which they had been victorious and stood united. Even in the East they avoided inflexibility on the currency question, leaving the Democrats to tear themselves apart on the issue.[2]

Tear themselves apart the Democrats did. From the beginning of the Fifty-fourth Congress, which convened in December 1895, southern Democrats made clear their animus toward the Cleveland administration. In February 1896 a majority of Democrats in both houses voted for free coinage of silver, but Republican votes carried the day for the administration. President Cleveland had been hard pressed by southern and western Democrats before the elections of 1894—it was Republican votes that had assured repeal of the Sherman Silver Purchase Act, and Cleveland's own veto had killed the Bland Silver Seigniorage bill—but the midterm elections reduced him to virtual dependence on Republican congressmen in the intensifying sectional struggle over the currency question, for as the Republican base of power moved eastward as a consequence of those elections, so the Democratic base of power moved southward. Where forty-four Democratic representatives from New England and the Middle Atlantic states had sat in the Fifty-third Congress, only seven answered the roll call in the Fifty-fourth. The Democrats' rebellious western congressional contingent was also all but wiped out in 1894, but only an occasional southerner was unseated: representatives from the eleven former Confederate states had made up two-fifths of the Democratic House delegation in the Fifty-third Congress; they contributed three-fourths of its members in the Fifty-fourth. (Southerners accounted for one-half of the Senate's Democratic membership in 1893 and a bare majority in 1895.)

As a consequence of these shifts, during 1895 the South became the key battleground in the factional conflict within the Democratic party, the President and a number of his associates (particularly southerners serving in the cabinet) seeking to curb the free silver movement there. Northeastern businessmen and bankers supported the effort. Their task was difficult, for the free silver issue had become a rallying point not only for Democrats who favored inflation, but for opponents of the administration's policy during the Pullman strike and railroad boycott; critics of decisions of the Supreme Court that upheld the injunction issued by a lower court against Eugene V. Debs and the American Railway Union during the railroad crisis, emasculated the Sherman Antitrust Act, and nullified the income tax provisions of the Wilson-Gorman Tariff Act; politicians who resented Cleveland's use of the patronage to whip into line or destroy dissenting Democrats; and many conservative southern Democrats, who viewed free silver as the issue with which to undermine the appeal of the Populists, whose radical program threatened Democratic hegemony in the South.[3] Northeastern Democratic politicians hardly figured in this struggle: the thinning of their ranks had deprived them of political leverage.

Just as national politics during 1895 reflected developments during 1893–94, so did politics within the Northeast. Though the Republicans had ridden economic discontent into power, 1895 was uneventful insofar as debate over major economic problems was concerned—except for action on the state canals in New York. In general, the state parties merely echoed their national parties' stands on the tariff and currency questions. At the same time, Republicans and Democrats did deal with important cultural issues, for on the state and local levels, these still lay at the heart of politics. For one, Republican politicians who had been equivocal toward the American Protective Association and other anti-Catholic groups during 1894 gradually took a stiffer position toward them during 1895 and early 1896. This shift was rarely marked by dramatic confrontations, but it was nonetheless important for all that. During 1894 Republican leaders probably overestimated the political potential of the anti-Catholic movement. (To what degree Democratic and press exaggerations of the threat of the A.P.A. contributed to this overestimate cannot be determined.) In any event, the Republicans refused to be drawn into an extended debate on the subject in 1894, confining themselves to periodic denials of an official liaison between the A.P.A. and the Republican party. The American Protective Association subsequently crowed that its anti-Catholic crusade had carried the G.O.P. to victory in 1894.[4] Republican politicians were hardly naïve enough to believe this interpretation of the elections. On the contrary, they realized that Republican victories had made possible the boasts of the A.P.A., rather than the A.P.A. having made possible those Republican triumphs.

Various Republican politicians came to appreciate that their party could only benefit by repudiation of anti-Catholic organizations: Catholics who were discontented with the Democratic party would find it easier to vote Republican; anti-Catholics would continue to vote Republican in any event. In 1894, Catholic Republicans had argued to no avail that their party's repudiation of the A.P.A. would lead their coreligionists to vote Republican on economic grounds. Within a year, Senator George Frisbie Hoar of Massachusetts, a prominent Republican, revealed a keen understanding of political and demographic realities, publicly attacking the A.P.A. as "driving and compacting together, in solid mass, persons who will soon number nearly or quite fifty per cent. of the voting population in Massachusetts." Blanket attacks on Roman Catholics by organizations such as the American Protective Association led Catholics of various nationalities to draw together in self-defense and rendered difficult Republican efforts to exploit conflicts among Catholics to their partisan advantage. There was friction among Catholics of diverse national origins: Irish workers felt threatened by Italian and French Canadian competitors; French Canadians, Italians, and Poles resented Irish domination of the Church hierarchy and the presence of Irish priests in their own parishes; anti-clerical Italian Catholics sniped at the religious subservience of the Irish Catholics who dominated Tammany Hall; the unwillingness of the Irish to share political power with other Catholic immigrant groups angered some. In a few instances, discontents found expression in political action: French Canadian and Italian Republican clubs were organized in New York, Connecticut, and other northeastern states during this period. Only a few years earlier, Republicans had sought to win Irish Catholics away from the Democrats; now they assigned first priority to winning over Catholics other than the Irish.[5]

The politically disruptive activity of nativists angered Republican professional politicians. In Bridgeport, for example, the American Protective Association dominated the Republican primary in March 1895, and at the subsequent party convention it denied renomination to two Protestants on the board of education for having voted for a Catholic as board chairman. The Democrats then defeated a supposedly united Republican-A.P.A. ticket in municipal elections and outpolled A.P.A. (Republican) and independent Republican slates in board of education elections. The following March, Republican regulars soundly trounced A.P.A. candidates in the party primary. The influence of the American Protective Association in Republican politics in New Britain also declined during this period. By the fall of 1896 a newspaper correspondent could report that in Connecticut, the A.P.A. "is a thing of the past." [6]

New Jersey Republicans repeatedly rebuffed State Senator Maurice Rogers of Camden County, who in 1895 based his campaign for the party's gubernatorial nomination on nativist and prohibitionist groups. (In that year, Rogers served as chief marshal of the annual parade of the Junior Order of United American Mechanics in Asbury Park.) Republican state senators killed Rogers's bill that would have prohibited public school teachers from wearing religious garb, insignia, emblems, or markings; they smothered his borough liquor licensing proposal. The Republican state convention, over one-half of whose delegates represented northeastern counties where Catholics and immigrants were numerous, subsequently passed him over in choosing a gubernatorial nominee.[7]

In the Northeast the Republican party curbed the political activity of anti-Catholic societies before the national political conventions of 1896. The idea that the bitter Bryan-McKinley campaign drained the emotions that had gone into the A.P.A. does not hold true for this region: the fate of the organization was sealed in the year and a half following the elections of 1894. At the same time, the decline of anti-Catholicism as a political force did not mean its disappearance as a social phenomenon. While the rout of the Democracy in the Northeast in 1894 probably reassured many who feared Catholic domination of their land, newspapers reported continued A.P.A. and J.O.U.A.M. meetings, rallies, and campaigns; anti-Catholic speeches; and one bloody religious riot—in Boston.[8] The emotions that had gone into the creation of the American Protective Association clearly survived its decline and demise.

The containment of the A.P.A. and other anti-Catholic groups by the Republican party reflected the politicians' tactical appreciation of the political situation in the Northeast: these societies sought the proscription of a religious group of considerable size in the area and frequently disrupted local party organizations. But too much can be read into this rejection of the nativist societies. The cultural roots of the Republican party ran deep, and its leaders were not about to abandon traditionally Republican religious and ethnic groups in order to embrace normally Democratic blocs that had given the G.O.P. increased support because of the depression. On the contrary, the Republican party remained faithful to its traditional supporters and their values.

Information regarding Republican patronage policy in Connecticut and New York, where the party came into power in 1895, is lacking, but such evidence as we do possess points to a reluctance to dispense patronage to Irish recruits of the class of 1894. Republican leaders were aware that Irish Catholic Republicans had proselytized among their fellow Irish Catholics during 1894, but a Connecticut Republican worker lamented the failure of his party to reward either the missionaries or the converts, while Governor Morton of New York admitted that the appointment of John T. McDonough as Commissioner of Statistics of Labor would please Irish Catholic Republicans, who felt that they had received little or no patronage. McDonough, whose qualifications were strong, did not receive the appointment.[9]

In 1894 New York State Republican leaders had been willing to compromise party principles by framing an amendment to the state constitution that permitted a measure of public support for sectarian charities. The hierarchy of the Roman Catholic Church was still anxious lest its charities be strangled by the state legislature, now controlled by the Republicans, but these fears were exaggerated. On the other hand, the Republicans had stood firm against government aid to parochial schools in 1894, and Charles R. Skinner, the new State Superintendent of Public Instruction, following the terms of the revised constitution, moved to terminate local arrangements between school boards and Roman Catholic churches under which public funds or facilities supported parochial education.[10] Many Protestants wished not only to eliminate public assistance to the parochial schools they feared, but to protect from Catholic and other "alien" influences the public schools they cherished. In order to achieve the latter objective in New York City, the state legislature passed and Mayor William Strong approved legislation whose objectives included reducing the influence of Tammany Hall, Roman Catholics, and immigrant groups on public education in the metropolis. Among other provisions, the law of 1896 created a new and more powerful board of education, whose members were to be appointed by the mayor, and abolished the ward trustee system that had lodged power over school appointments, promotions, purchases, and construction with laymen in each of the city's wards. The measure was passed only after a bitter, protracted fight: during 1895, Boss Platt, angered by Strong's patronage policy, opposed this proposal, which would empower the mayor to make additional appointments; Democrats charged that abolition of the ward trustees would deny to communities within the city local control of their schools and reminded New Yorkers that support for the proposal came from well-to-do Protestants. In the end,

Boss Platt relented and upstate Republican legislators won the day for a school bill. The law sought to destroy the influence of ethnic (i.e., Irish and German) and religious (i.e., Catholic) communities upon local schools, transferring responsibility for the city's common schools from twenty-four ward boards of trustees to the central board of education, and to nullify Tammany's grass-roots strength, lodging authority to choose the now-powerful board of education with the mayor, rather than the electorate. The conflict revealed the extent to which New York City "reformers" depended on a Republican state legislature and a Fusion mayor to achieve their objectives, and also the degree to which the means necessary to these ends did violence to the "reformers'" rhetoric regarding "home rule," "popular control," and "taking the schools out of politics."[11]

States enacted legislation embodying the Republican position on other cultural issues. The New Jersey legislature passed for the second consecutive year the Storrs Naturalization bill, which prohibited naturalization during the thirty days before general elections; this time the Republican majority overrode Governor Werts's veto. In Connecticut the legislature proposed an amendment to the state constitution requiring prospective voters to be able to read in English any article of the state constitution or any section of the statutes of the state. This modified an amendment ratified in 1855, during the Know-Nothing era, by specifying that the reading requirement had to be met "in the English language." Approved a second time by the succeeding legislature, the amendment was popularly ratified in the town elections of 1897. On the other hand, in New York the Republicans supported and the Democrats opposed legislation to secure for Negroes equal treatment in public accommodations. Republican reforms were symbolic as well as substantive: the Connecticut, New York, and New Jersey legislatures, as well as those of Rhode Island and Pennsylvania, outlawed the flying of foreign flags over public buildings, except during visits by heads of state—which precluded the hoisting of Ireland's colors. Governor Flower of New York had vetoed a similar measure in 1894; Governor Morton promptly signed this one into law.[12]

Though the Republicans gained in northeastern cities during

the depression, their traditional base in the area was rural. Republican leaders consequently rejected constitutional reforms that would threaten the party's rural bastions. For their part, rural Republican leaders were loath to increase the representation of cities that had until recently been Democratic and the power of urban Republican leaders at their own expense. In New Jersey the Republicans avoided a state constitutional convention, at which the issue of legislative reapportionment could hardly have been sidetracked, by resorting to piecemeal revision of the constitution. In New York, on the other hand, the Republicans translated their upset victory of 1893 into a revised state constitution that safeguarded rural Republicans against anything but a Democratic landslide. Connecticut Republicans followed a more tortuous course. To counter Democratic propaganda, during 1893 Republican legislators proposed constitutional amendments providing for the plurality election of state officers and a limited reapportionment of the state senate. The party neither endorsed nor repudiated these reforms during the midterm campaign. Once safely past the hurdle of the elections of 1894, however, Republican legislators balked at constitutional revision. They opposed the creation of a constitutional commission to draft amendments; both houses of the General Assembly rejected the plurality elections amendment; the State House of Representatives was willing to reapportion the State Senate, but the Senate was not, and it killed that plan. Democrats predicted that the Republicans would pay dearly for their perfidy, but until such a reckoning, the G.O.P. stood to gain from its action. Republican unwillingness to tamper with the political balance in Connecticut extended to the party's state convention. In 1896 Isaac Ullman, a rising Republican leader in New Haven, called for a reconsideration of the apportionment of delegates to that convention. He pointed out that Republican convention seating, based on representation in the lower house of the General Assembly, discriminated against cities and populous towns, and that the Democrats weighted representation at their convention to reflect party voting strength in cities and towns. Party leaders smothered Ullman's request for a discussion of this inequity.[13]

The Republicans' strong identification with a particular set of cultural values, and the continued political importance of cultural issues, even during a depression, were most clearly revealed in New York during 1895. Indeed, cultural conflict gave the state and New York City campaigns a unique cast. The conflict was touched off in New York City, where the Fusion coalition fell apart over excise policy. This controversy pitted elements of the old-stock Protestant community and their ministerial leaders against elements of the German community and their organizational spokesmen. These forces had fought side by side in the anti-Tammany crusade, but while they agreed that Tammany was evil, they disagreed over the direction "reform" should take. Evangelical Protestant reformers sought to smash the saloon as well as Tammany Hall. They fully expected that the Fusion administration would put a halt to the illegal Sunday sale of alcoholic beverages. Such sales had long since been prohibited by state statute, but Tammany—taking advantage of the law's unpopularity in New York City—had permitted taverns operated by friends of and contributors to the organization to slake the thirst of New Yorkers on Sundays, while harassing other establishments. (Breweries, as well as taverns, had an obvious stake in this matter.) German reformers opposed Tammany's tapping of the trade in beer, but hoped that the Fusion administration would adopt a tolerant and graft-free policy toward the "continental Sunday" while persuading the state legislature, which was under Republican control, to succor New York City drinkers by liberalizing the excise law. Thus the issue was drawn: to evangelical Protestants, "reform" meant the Sunday closing of taverns; to most Germans, "reform" meant freeing the Sunday flow of beer from corrupt and "puritanical" influences.[14]

The administration of Mayor William Strong soon found itself under pressure from both sides over the Sunday closing law. The controversy intensified as Theodore Roosevelt, President of the New York City Board of Police Commissioners, ordered strict enforcement of the law. Roosevelt, who was not a prohibitionist, appreciated the difficulty of enforcing the Sunday law, but he recognized that the existing relationship between the police and saloon-keepers bred bribery and extortion. (Ironically, Roosevelt's campaign against police corruption did not satisfy a few zealots who had hoped that he would do no less than purge the force of its Irish Catholic officers.) Having taken his stand for law and order, Roosevelt was immovable: cross-pressures within the German community mounted as would-be drinkers experienced their driest summer in years. To Carl Schurz's suggestion that those opposed to the law should seek its modification by the state legislature, the *Staats-Zeitung* countered that there was no chance of relief from that quarter. The German-American Reform Union condemned Strong and Roosevelt and indicated that it would send representatives to the Republican and Democratic state conventions to scout the positions of the rival parties relative to the Sunday closing issue. Dissidents within the union charged that its leaders were allying with Tammany in the expectation of political rewards. Receiving no satisfaction from Roosevelt, the United Societies for Liberal Sunday Laws, an organization in which German groups were prominent, announced that it would campaign for the election of a sympathetic legislature. Roosevelt remained calm under fire, but Mayor Strong began to view his energetic subordinate as a political liability.[15]

The Sunday closing issue spilled over into the state political arena when Senator David Hill hit upon it as the stick with which to beat the Republicans in state-wide and legislative campaigns. In two public letters and an address before the Chemung County Democratic convention, Hill charged that "the Puritans" were in the saddle in Albany and New York City and asserted that only the Democrats could be trusted to enact a liberal excise law. Returning to his theme of 1894, Hill denounced Levi Morton as a narrow and prejudiced Vermonter; then he argued that the Sunday closing law denied the poor their beer and humble meals in taverns while permitting Theodore Roosevelt his champagne dinners at the Union League Club. Hill's barbs touched sensitive nerves, if one can judge from the outcry among Protestant ministers and Republican politicians and newspapers.[16]

Hill obviously sought to draw the line between a Republican party committed to forcing the moral values of evangelical Protestants upon diverse cultural groups and a Democracy committed to cultural pluralism. He could not have been unmindful of Democratic losses among German voters during 1893–94, or of the sensitivity of many Germans to questions involving "personal liberty." Hill's strategy created concern in both political camps. Republican politicians in New York City feared continued agitation over Sunday closings. So did Boss Platt. Indeed, Platt planned to have the Republican state convention ignore the disruptive issue. Platt's clique failed to gauge the temper of upstate rural Republicans, among whom prohibitionist sentiment was widespread. (Upstate legislators had shaped the state's excise policy; earlier in 1895 they had secured legislation requiring temperance instruction in public schools.) To the drys, Hill had issued a moral challenge; to avoid the duel would be to dishonor the party. George E. Green, President of the New York State League of Republican Clubs, took up the gauntlet at his organization's convention, declaring that "a very large majority of the Republicans outside of New York City are unalterably opposed to any modification of the existing laws in the direction of Sunday opening." Over the objections of delegates from New York City and Brooklyn, the league's convention endorsed those laws. At the Republican state convention, the committee on resolutions carried out Boss Platt's strategy, rejecting one plank that endorsed local option and another that supported police enforcement of the Sunday closing law in favor of a platform that ignored the issue. But Warner Miller, long identified with the party's dry wing, touched off a floor rebellion of rural delegates by demanding "maintenance of the Sunday laws in the interest of labor and morality." Platt bowed before the storm: Miller's words were added to the Republican platform.[17]

On the other hand, some Democrats—even as they congratulated Hill for having maneuvered the Republicans into a vulnerable position—warned that their party risked alienating rural and urban supporters, particularly Baptists and Methodists, who preferred the "American Sabbath" to the "continental Sunday." Upstate delegates to the Democratic state convention blocked resolutions endorsing the Sunday sale of alcoholic beverages and attacking Theodore Roosevelt. Instead, the Democrats denounced the "hypocrisy" of "prominent Republican politicians in the large cities" in repudiating their own platform, and they declared for:

> Equal and honest enforcement of all the laws; a proper observance of a day of rest and an orderly Sunday; modification or repeal of laws unsupported by public opinion; no unjust sumptuary laws; no blue laws; recognition of the fundamental American principle of freedom of conscience; home rule in excise as well as in other matters within reasonable limitations established to protect the interest of temperance and morality and an amendment of the excise and other laws by the Legislature of the State which shall permit each municipality expressing its sentiments by a popular vote of a majority of its citizens to determine within such proper legislative restrictions as shall be required by the interests of the entire State what may best meet its special necessities and conditions.[18]

Though Boss Platt had been unable to prevent his party from taking a stand on the Sunday closing issue, he hoped that Republicans would run on the plank upstate while ignoring it in New York City. Platt reckoned without Warner Miller and Theodore Roosevelt. Miller, speaking upstate and in the city, declared the campaign "more of a moral battle" than any in the past, proclaimed that a majority of voters opposed "the unlimited desecration of the Sabbath," and exhorted immigrants to become "Americans and Americanized." (Ministers also stressed the moral aspect of the campaign.) Roosevelt stood his ground despite pressure from Mayor Strong and Edward Lauterbach, chairman of the New York County Republican committee and Platt's lieutenant. Roosevelt, not invited to speak before Republican rallies, addressed temperance groups; he delighted in carrying his fight into the hostile East Side. Lauterbach actually absolved the Republican party of responsibility for Roosevelt; the county Republican convention nearly resolved to repudiate Roosevelt. In the county platform the Republicans praised the Republican state platform, but they adopted the excise plank of the New York State Democracy, which called for local option. This concession was insufficient to prevent the German-American Reform Union, which was pleased with Tammany's excise plank and was given places on its local ticket, from declaring for the Democrats. Warner Miller emotionally defended the state platform (and the "American Sabbath") while denouncing the evasions of New York City Republicans; regular Republicans and reform Democrats condemned the German-American Reform Union, the New York *Tribune* referring bitterly to a Tammany rally at which "all the speeches were in a foreign tongue" and all the arguments were addressed "to citizens of a single nationality." [19]

The Sunday closing controversy merited the attention it received from contemporaries. At the same time, the dispute was widely publicized because it involved articulate, well-organized groups. Sunday closings affected more than brewers, tavern keepers, and their patrons. The Jews of the Lower East Side were, by and large, poor customers for the area's saloons, but the pushcart and sidewalk retailers among them felt the law's enforcement. Under Tammany, peddlers had paid for the privilege of plying their trade on Sundays; by curbing Sunday business as well as bribery and coercion, Mayor Strong earned for himself the title of "Czar" Strong. In another policy matter, Colonel George E. Waring, Jr., the street cleaning commissioner, reputedly kept the city clean, but his businessman's view of efficiency, which was applauded by the New York *Times* and the Good Government clubs, angered the Knights of Labor, the Central Labor Union, the Grand Army of the Republic, and many street cleaners.[20] Such disputes were revealing: before 1895 ran out, perceptive and disillusioned veterans of the Fusion campaign of 1894 admitted that the essentially unrepresentative nature of the reform movement underlay its failure to generate continuing support among the masses. Recruiting its key personnel from the city's business and social elites, which were overwhelmingly old-stock and Protestant, the Strong administration lacked an understanding of many of the human problems involved in governing New York City.[21]

To round out the difficulties facing anti-Tammany coalition leaders, the Good Government clubs, which had supported fusion in 1894, nominated an independent municipal slate in 1895, charging that the Republicans and State Democrats were more interested in dividing local nominations between them than in drawing up a non-partisan slate. But the Chamber of Commerce, through its Committee of Fifty, and the Board of Trade and Transportation endorsed the Republican–State Democratic coalition, various members of which joined dissenting members of the

Good Government clubs in attacking club leaders for having abandoned fusion.[22]

On the other hand, the Democrats campaigned in New York State less burdened by factionalism than in any other contest from 1893 through 1896. Partisan and personal considerations led Senator Hill, who directed the state organization, and Secretary of War Daniel Lamont, a Cleveland Democrat who was not fanatically anti-Hill, to cooperate in efforts to restore a measure of unity to their party: anti-organization Democrats were to be represented in the Erie, Monroe, Queens, Kings, and New York county delegations to the state convention; a ticket acceptable to the Clevelandites was to be nominated. And the state convention did applaud the name of President Cleveland, avoid the delicate issue of a third presidential term, praise the national administration in its platform, and nominate a representative slate. But Hill was unable to resolve a dispute between the New York State Democracy and Tammany Hall over factional representation and Tammany's demand for assurances that the State Democrats would not again combine with the Republicans in local elections. The State Democrats stalked from the convention, John Jeroloman, their spokesman (and President of the New York City Board of Aldermen), declaring that they were returning to the city "to pulverize Tammany Hall." In the end, the State Democracy fought Tammany Hall candidates but reluctantly endorsed the Democratic state ticket, as did President Cleveland, who was finally prevailed on to do so by Lamont. The Democratic Party Reform Organization opposed the regular Democratic municipal slate in Brooklyn, but not the state ticket. For the only time during the political upheaval of 1893–96, no Democratic candidate for state-wide office faced opposition by Cleveland Democrats.[23]

The New Jersey gubernatorial campaign, that state's first state-wide contest held during the depression, lacked the controversy that marked the New York campaign, for in effect both major parties played down, rather than stressed, the cultural issues that divided them. Each of the rival gubernatorial candidates was vulnerable on one cultural issue, but neither party aggressively exploited its opponent's weakness. John W. Griggs, the

Republican nominee, had voted for the high license–county option bill of 1888. Major Carl Lentz, chairman of the Essex County Republican Committee and a spokesman for the large German community of Newark, warned that Griggs's candidacy would jeopardize the party in Newark. Democratic newspapers carefully noted Republican attacks on Griggs, but, significantly, Democratic platform framers deliberately remained silent on the high license–county option issue and Democratic campaigners did not stress Griggs's vote in their speeches. The Democrats may have hoped to pick up a silent protest vote among Germans in northeastern New Jersey, but they undoubtedly feared that a vigorous campaign on the issue would expose them to reverses in the state's prohibitionist areas, some of which were normally Democratic. For his part, Griggs contended that he personally had favored only high license in 1888, and had supported the controversial county option proviso solely because a party caucus demanded it. Republican legislative leaders saved their party potential embarrassment during 1895 by killing a bill, introduced by Senator Maurice Rogers of Camden County and supported by Senator James Bradley of Monmouth, that would have transferred licensing authority in the state's eighty-six boroughs from county courts to locally elected boards of commissioners, thereby increasing prohibitionist chances in such localities. Democratic legislators had hoped to force the Republicans to pass on the Rogers bill, but the Republicans killed it without a vote. It is unlikely that New Jersey Republicans, any more than New York Republicans, would have compromised on the Sunday closing issue—but they avoided agitation on this controversial matter. At the same time, Griggs and the platform on which he ran did appeal to evangelical voters by recalling the corruption that had characterized Democratic rule in New Jersey.[24]

Seeking to undo the damage done them by the racetrack controversy, New Jersey Democrats held a representative convention, whose platform "denounce[d] as maliciously false" Republican allegations regarding Democratic wrongdoing, reminded voters that the Republican legislature of 1880 bore responsibility for legalizing gambling on horse races, and endorsed a constitutional amendment barring "any law for the legalization of gambling in any form." Further, the convention nominated for governor Alexander T. McGill, Chancellor of the Court of Chancery, who had voted against pardons for Democratic gamblers and corrupters of the ballot box. (McGill was to carry his judicial role too far for some party workers, spending the campaign on the bench rather than on the stump.) McGill's strength within the Democracy lay in the urbanized, northeastern counties of the state. Augustus W. Cutler, a former congressman and state senator who contended with McGill for the nomination, drew support from the normally Democratic rural counties of northwestern New Jersey. Subsequent reports had it that the patriotic societies, which flourished in northwestern as well as southern New Jersey, were determined to destroy McGill in Warren County, and that local Democrats, resentful of the victory of McGill and the urban Democracy over Cutler and the rural Democracy, were likely to respond to the nativists' campaign. McGill's alleged vulnerability stemmed from his favorable vote twenty years earlier on the New Jersey Catholic Protectory bill, a measure favored by the Roman Catholic Church. Just as no outcry was made over Griggs's support of high license–county option in 1888, no full-blown controversy developed over McGill's support of the Protectory bill. The Republican state platform did pledge opposition to "any attempt to impair or divert from its proper use the fund for the support of the free public schools," but the party launched no crusade on the issue. The Democrats, who had denounced Republican sponsorship of measures inspired by the American Protective Association during the legislative sessions of 1894 and 1895, avoided the matter in their platform and campaign.[25]

In the final analysis, only in their exchange over questions that had been central to the anti-racetrack crusade of 1893 did New Jersey Republicans and Democrats deal in issues potentially as explosive as those in New York. Even then, the emotions that had influenced the New Jersey election of 1893 had had no comparable effect in 1894 and there was little reason to believe that they would in 1895. The Republicans' rejection of Senator Maurice Rogers, who was closely identified with nativistic and evangelical causes, in favor of John W. Griggs, revealed the caution of that state party insofar as cultural issues were concerned; the

Democrats' selection of Chancellor Alexander McGill did likewise. The parties' platforms and campaigns were generally consistent with their gubernatorial nominations.

The Democrats gained and the Republicans lost percentage strength in both the New York and New Jersey state-wide elections. (See Appendix E.) Analysis of returns from the two states reveals differences between patterns in their vote consistent with differences between their campaigns. In New York, marked Democratic gains in the New York City–Brooklyn metropolitan region outweighed smaller upstate Republican gains. (See Table 8.) No such situation obtained in New Jersey, where the Democrats gained in urban and non-urban counties alike. (See Table 9.)

TABLE 8 *Shifts in Percentage Strength, 1894–1895, All Parties, Selected New York Counties and Other Areas of the State*

	DEM.	REP.	PRO.	SLP	POP.	DPRO[c]
Greater New York City[a]	+9.0	−6.0	—	+1.4	−0.2	−4.1
Metropolitan Area[b]	+2.9	−1.1	+0.1	+0.6	−0.4	−2.0
Rest of State	−1.1	+1.7	+0.6	—	−0.3	−0.9
New York State	+3.0	−1.5	+0.3	+0.5	−0.3	−2.1

Sources: *Tribune Almanacs, 1895, 1896.*

[a] New York, Kings, Queens, and Richmond counties.

[b] Rockland, Suffolk, and Westchester counties.

[c] The Democratic Party Reform Organization did not run a state ticket in 1895.

The redrawing of New York County's assembly and election district boundary lines in 1895 precludes a district-by-district comparison of 1894 and 1895 election returns, but it cannot obscure voting shifts in New York City, where the Democrats gained 9.2 percentage points and the Republicans lost 7.2. David

TABLE 9 *Shifts in Percentage Strength, 1894–1895, All Parties, Six Urban New Jersey Counties and Other Areas of the State*

	REP.	DEM.	PRO.	POP.	SLP	POP.-SLP[b]
Six Counties[a]	−4.2	+5.8	−0.1	−0.5	−0.3	−0.7
Rest of State	−1.4	+3.2	−0.6	−1.2	—	—
New Jersey	−3.0	+4.7	−0.3	−0.8	−0.2	−0.4

Sources: *Manuals of the Legislature of New Jersey, 1895, 1896.*
[a]Camden, Essex, Hudson, Mercer, Passaic, and Union counties.
[b]The People's and Socialist Labor parties did not fuse in 1895.

B. Hill had carried eighteen of thirty assembly districts in his unsuccessful gubernatorial race, receiving majorities in only eight; Horatio King, the Democratic candidate for Secretary of State in 1895, won twenty-eight of thirty-five newly created districts, all but one by majorities. Essentially, the Republicans found themselves reduced to five A.D.s (5, 25, 27, 29, 31) that ran northward through the heart of Manhattan, including Negro and Italian enclaves as well as middle and upper class, old-stock neighborhoods that had given a Republican complexion to old A.D.s 11 and 12, and to two A.D.s (19, 21) that contained comfortable residential areas in the Upper West Side. Despite an impressive showing by the Socialist Labor party, which polled 10 per cent or more of the total vote in six A.D.s, the Democrats fared well in Lower and Upper East Side districts.[26] (City-wide, the Socialist Labor party received 4.4 per cent of the total vote, a gain of 1.6 percentage points over 1894 and its best showing during the depression.) Tammany Hall's recovery was even more remarkable. Given up for dead in 1894, the Tiger gained 11.1 percentage points in 1895 as Fusion declined by 14.9 points. Tammany had carried five A.D.s, three by majorities, the previous year; it now won twenty-seven, receiving majorities in twenty-five. The margins by which Tammany trailed the Democratic state ticket and Fusion led the Republican state ticket were smaller in 1895 than they had been the previous year.[27] Significantly, Tammany candidates no longer fell behind the Democratic state ticket by above-average margins in predominantly German districts. At the same time, the Democratic municipal slate again trailed the state ticket by above-average margins in old-stock American, middle and upper class districts where "the better element" continued to knife Tammany candidates. Contemporaries related the victories of the Democrats' state and local tickets to the return to the Democratic fold of Germans who had opposed Tammany Hall in 1894 but now rejected a Fusion administration that strictly enforced the Sunday closing law in New York City and a state Republican party that endorsed this policy "in the interest of labor and morality." Against the advice of an important German Republican, the New York *Tribune* criticized those Germans "whose business interests, or stupidity, or prejudice, or hatred of decent order has put them into a class which might be called the Beerites." The Reverend Madison Peters of the American Protective Association, who before the election had denounced Democratic appeals to Irish Know-Nothings in 1894 and to German Know-Nothings in 1895 and warned that such appeals gave rise to American Know-Nothingism, now asserted that Americans would have to choose between "German or Irish Sabbaths or the Lord's Day." [28]

The Democrats regained the upper hand in Kings County, where their state ticket picked up 9.1 percentage points as the Republicans lost 4.2. The Democratic Party Reform Organization, whose banner county (5.6 per cent) Kings had been in 1894, did not contest for state offices. Hill had received majorities in eight and pluralities in three of thirty-two wards and towns; King won majorities in sixteen and pluralities in three such units. At the same time, the Republicans, benefiting from the continued schism between regular and anti-organization Democrats on the municipal level, managed to retain the mayoralty of Brooklyn, though by a smaller margin than in 1893, when they had received 58.2 per cent of the vote to the Democrats' 39.1. Now, Frederick W. Wurster won 46.1 per cent of the vote to 44.8 per cent cast for Edward M. Grout, the candidate of the Democratic organization, and 5.7 per cent for Edward M. Shepard, who carried the banners of his own Democratic reform faction. (Shepard showed well for an independent, but his 9510 votes fell far short of the 57,000 hoped for by his enthusiastic supporters.) Analysis of the campaign and election in Brooklyn suggests that the recurring struggle over taverns, similar to (and perhaps reinforced by) the Sunday closing controversy in nearby New York City, contributed to the revival of Democratic party fortunes and produced shifts within the reform Democratic coalition beyond those of 1894. Seeking to avoid a repetition of the disastrous campaign of 1893, organization Democrats had included some reform Democrats on their city ticket, Grout, the mayoralty candidate, among them. Reflecting on this development, one reform Democrat testified to the old-stock versus Irish Catholic dimension of Democratic factionalism in his assertion that "but for our insistence that fit candidates should be nominated for office, the entire regular ticket would have been composed of Coffeys and McCarrens." As in 1893, the Republicans had turned to the German community, which was regarded as a crucial variable in Brooklyn's political equation, for their mayoralty candidate. Once again they won, but their narrow victory in the three-way municipal race and their defeat in the state-wide election revealed the erosion of Republican support in Brooklyn. Exchanges between Germans and evangelical Protestants had punctuated the campaign in the "city of churches"; outgoing Mayor Charles Schieren attributed the Democratic revival to "Puritanical Sunday laws." [29]

Election returns from Brooklyn revealed shifts of sentiment in the German community. German wards not only ranked lower in the Democratic Reform mayoralty column than they had in the Democratic Reform gubernatorial column the previous year, they showed absolute percentage declines—even as old-stock American wards generally held firm or increased their support for the Reform Democrats. Though the ward-level correlation between the Democratic Reform votes of 1894 and 1895 was strong and positive (+.706), successive shifts in the Reform Democratic vote in 1894 and 1895 had combined to alter markedly the popular base of the anti-organization coalition. Indeed, the correlation between the vote against Isaac Maynard in 1893 and that for Shepard in 1895 was −.013. In Brooklyn, as in New York City, the Republican state ticket also lost support in the wake of a controversy over municipal policy regarding the alcohol question. Though the Republicans' percentage strength ebbed in every Brooklyn ward, their losses were negatively associated with Reform Democratic strength. Republican losses ran highest in German districts and below average in old-stock American, middle and upper class wards, where Democratic gains were less the consequence of Republican defections than of the return to the party fold of Reform Democrats. In German districts, Republican percentage losses exceeded the 1894 percentage strength of the Reform Democrats and approached Democratic percentage gains. In old-stock American districts, Republican percentage losses were smaller than the 1894 percentage strength of the Reform Democrats and far smaller than Democratic percentage gains.[30] Fundamentally, then, voter shifts toward the Democrats in the state-wide election in Brooklyn were primarily at the expense of the Republicans in German wards and essentially the consequence of the return to the Democrats of Reform Democrats in old-stock American wards. Differences between these patterns produced a remarkably low correlation (+.224) between ward-level Democratic percentage gains and Republican percentage losses.

Outside of New York and Kings counties, the Democrats gained the most percentage strength in the adjoining counties that rounded out the metropolitan area—Queens, Richmond, Rockland, Suffolk, and Westchester—and in Niagara County, located in the far northwestern corner of the state. The seven metropolitan counties may very well have felt the shock of the temperance controversies in New York City and Brooklyn, but only one characteristic linked them with distant Niagara County: those counties ranking highest in Democratic gains in 1895 had ranked highest in Democratic Reform strength in the gubernatorial election the year before and in Democratic defections from the candidacy of Isaac Maynard in 1893. The Democracy's recovery in counties where it regained the support of Cleveland Democrats revealed the importance to the state party of at least partial unity in the face of a powerful, indeed, now dominant, Republican opposition.

Still, essential though such unity was to the Democracy, it

could not restore the party to a competitive position unless large numbers of Democrats who had defected to the Republicans during 1893–94 over depression issues also returned to their traditional political ways. This they did not do in 1895. To be sure, among the eight aforementioned counties the Republicans lost percentage strength in all but Suffolk, where they gained fractionally (0.2 percentage points). But elsewhere in New York State, the Republicans gained and the Democrats lost percentage strength in thirty-seven counties; the Republicans gained in two counties where Democratic strength held firm and held their own in one county where Democratic strength ebbed; both parties gained strength in six counties (each party outgaining the other in three); and the Democrats gained and the Republicans lost percentage strength in only five counties. As Table 8 reveals, within the counties that were to compose Greater New York City, Republican percentage losses exceeded 1894 independent Democratic percentage strength; within the metropolitan area counties, the reverse held true. At the same time, upstate New York Republican gains reduced the G.O.P.'s state-wide percentage loss to a level lower than the state-wide percentage mark of the Reform Democrats the previous year.

The pattern of New York State's 1895 vote differed in important respects from the voting patterns of 1893 and 1894. In the earlier elections, the Democrats had generally suffered their most severe setbacks in counties containing major cities (e.g., Erie, Kings, and Monroe in 1893; Albany, New York, and Rensselaer in 1894), but net shifts in upstate rural areas had been in the same direction as net shifts in the state's major cities. Now the Democratic Party Reform Organization (−0.7) abandoned the field. The Democrats showed to slightly better advancan gains in most upstate counties outweighed small Democratic gains in a few such counties to produce a net Republican gain outside of the New York City–Brooklyn metropolitan area. For the first time during the political realignment that had begun in 1893, metropolitan area counties and upstate counties shifted in opposite directions. (See Table 8.)

Within upstate New York, one can discern slight but consistent differences between voting patterns in the Hudson River valley region and other areas. In the Hudson River valley region, the return to the Democratic column of independent Democratic voters of 1894 barely offset Democratic defections to the Republican and Prohibition parties. The Democrats (+0.1), Republicans (+0.7), and Prohibitionists (+0.5) all gained percentage points. At the same time, the People's party continued to lose strength (−0.4 points); the Socialist Labor party fell off slightly (−0.1 points), even as it gained strength elsewhere in the state; and the Democratic Party Reform Organization (−0.7) abandoned the field. The Democrats showed to slightly better advantage in their former strongholds, Troy and Albany, than in outlying towns in Rensselaer and Albany counties, but in neither city did the party stage a comeback remotely comparable to those in New York City and Brooklyn.[31]

To the north and west of the Hudson River valley, the Democrats fared worse. Despite the absence of an independent Democratic opposition that had drawn off 0.9 per cent of the total vote the year before, the Democrats declined 1.5 percentage points, the Republicans gaining 2.0 points and the Prohibitionists 0.6 points. Socialist Labor gained 0.1 percentage points; the Populists declined 0.3 points. Shortly before the election, the New York *Times* reported that Democratic efforts to arouse Buffalo's large German population over the exise question were proving unsuccessful because local authorities had not vigorously enforced the Sunday closing law there. Election returns from Buffalo were consistent with this analysis: the Republicans gained 3.3 percentage points and the Democrats lost 2.2 points. Percentage shifts favored the Republicans in all but four (three of them strongly Republican) of twenty-five wards. Except in three Democratic, predominantly Irish districts, where the Republicans scored impressively, percentage shifts within Buffalo's wards were small. Erie County's outlying towns, including those that contained concentrations of Germans, shifted much as did Buffalo, the Republicans gaining 2.9 percentage points, the Democrats losing 2.1 points. Popular shifts in Rochester, another upstate city with a large German population, paralleled those in Buffalo, and Monroe County's outlying towns behaved as did those in Erie County. The Prohibition party gained fractionally in both counties.[32]

Election returns from rural towns across upstate New York revealed a continued, general Democratic decline. A number of towns resisted the trend, but far too few to reverse it. Towns populated by New Englanders and their descendants, and those settled during the nineteenth century by Protestant immigrants from the British Isles, Canada, Sweden, and Holland, constituted the backbone of upstate Republican strength. The Republicans generally increased their share of the vote in such towns in 1895. Towns settled during the nineteenth century by Germans of various religions were almost always more Democratic than the counties in which they were located. Interestingly enough, such towns generally shifted in 1895 as other towns in their counties did, whether toward the Republicans or the Democrats.[33] Clearly, the Democrats had been unable to generate a drive among upstate Germans, whether in cities such as Buffalo and Rochester or in rural areas. In short, the Democrats may have regained important lost ground in districts of all descriptions, particularly those of German complexion, within the New York City–Brooklyn metropolitan area, but they did so by waging a polarizing campaign on cultural issues that appears to have contributed to Republican and Prohibitionist gains across much of upstate New York. The Democracy's upstate losses markedly cut into its gains in the metropolitan area.

In New Jersey, on the other hand, the Democratic party gained percentage strength as all other parties declined, actually advancing in all but one of twenty-one counties as the Republicans retreated in sixteen.[34] Still, percentage shifts between the major parties were generally small on both the county and local levels. Indeed, the Democrats registered their greatest county-level gains—in Cumberland and Passaic—more at the expense of minor parties than of the Republicans. Though the Democrats recovered percentage strength in all areas of the state, they did not do so to the same degree in all voting units. The narrow range within which most shifts occurred suggests that caution should be exercised in generalizing about these movements, but certain tendencies can be identified.

In southern New Jersey, a Republican bastion, the Democrats benefited primarily from the decline of minor parties in Cumberland and Gloucester counties, while they recaptured some of the support they had lost to the Republicans in Camden city and county the previous year.[35] In Cape May County, where the Republicans gained slightly more percentage strength than the Democrats in 1895, the continued Democratic revival in Methodist strongholds, in which the party had lost grievously in 1893, almost overcame small Republican gains in most towns. Sea Isle City best illustrates the continuing, partial recovery of the Democracy in Methodist towns that had been Democratic in 1892 but had moved sharply toward the Republicans in the anti-racetrack election the following year. As the emotions of 1893 faded, many erstwhile Democratic voters in Sea Isle City returned to their former ways—some as early as 1894, others in 1895.[36] The Democrats were less successful in regaining former adherents in dry towns where their party had been weak before 1893. In such towns the dominant Republican political culture apparently stifled any serious Democratic recovery. Egg Harbor City, a German community in which Prohibitionist voters were virtually non-existent, led the incomplete Democratic comeback in Atlantic County, where (uniquely) the Democrats had capitalized on anti-racetrack sentiment in 1893, but lost disastrously in 1894. Old-stock American towns in which the Democrats had also lost badly in 1894 did not necessarily follow suit, Buena Vista and Hammonton registering slightly above-average Democratic gains, Linwood a Republican gain.[37]

In western and northwestern New Jersey, the Democrats fared best in Mercer and Warren counties. Their recovery in Mercer involved percentage gains in all of Trenton's eleven wards and in eleven of thirteen outlying towns. Within Trenton, the Democrats generally gained more ground in wards where the party had been strong before the debacle of 1894 than in those where the Republicans had predominated before the depression, but no such relationship obtained in the rural towns. The Democrats' gains in Warren were great enough to swing that county back into their column. The strong showing of the Democrats in Warren should have sobered Republicans who had predicted that the nativist societies would fan the resentment of local Democrats over the selection of Alexander McGill rather than Augustus Cutler as the party's gubernatorial nominee, and that they would lead the G.O.P. to a second successive victory in this normally Democratic county. At the same time, the Democrats did not show to particularly good advantage in their other rural bailiwicks, gaining marginally in Hunterdon County and losing slightly less percentage strength than the Republicans in Sussex County.[38] On the whole, Democratic rural counties contributed only slightly more than Republican rural counties to the Democrats' comeback.

The Democratic party registered above-average percentage gains in northeastern New Jersey's four most populous urban counties, wresting one of them—Hudson—from the Republicans.[39] Indeed, Hudson became the Democrats' banner county, as their recovery in that traditional party stronghold was not matched by their recovery in the rural counties (Hunterdon, Sussex, and Warren) that had rivaled it in this respect before 1893. Unfortunately, Jersey City reported election returns from six aldermanic districts in 1894 and from twelve wards, unrelated to the aldermanic districts, one year later; as a consequence, comparison of the two sets of returns from the key city in Hudson County is impossible. In Essex County, the Democrats gained and the Republicans lost percentage strength in all of Newark's fifteen wards. In Newark, as elsewhere, German districts, which were crucial swing districts throughout the period, moved toward the Democrats in 1895, Wards 12, 13, and 14 leading the way. The Democrats' success in German districts in Ward 12 clearly revealed this development. Irish districts (2, 3, 4) had provided the Democrats with their margin of victory in Ward 12 in 1894. They continued to rank highest in Democratic percentage strength in 1895, but German districts (1, 5) registered the Democrats' largest percentage gains in the ward. (Working class districts in which Germans and East European Jews were numerous also recorded the largest vote for the Socialist Labor party.)[40] The Democrats did not stage a comparable recovery in old-stock American districts: the three wards recording the smallest Democratic percentage gains in Newark fell into this category, and all remained staunchly Republican.[41] During the campaign, one Republican newspaper had dismissed as a useless maneuver the Democrats' nomination of four German American assembly candidates in Essex County; another had earlier reported the Republicans' elimination of thousands of fraudulent Democratic registrations from the elections rolls in Essex and Hudson counties.[42] Democratic gains suggest that their campaign maneuver in Essex was by no means useless and that the Democrats did not depend on fraudulent registrations to advance in the two counties.

The return of German voters to the Democracy above and beyond the general shift toward that party in 1895 could also be observed in Elizabeth, where two German districts (Wards 5 and 7) led the Democratic recovery. That the Democrats were reclaiming former adherents rather than converting Republicans is suggested by their disappointing gain in Ward 3, a German district where they had not declined sharply the previous year. Meanwhile, the Democrats continued the revival that had begun in 1894 in Wards 10, 11, and 12, old-stock American districts where their supporters had broken badly in the anti-racetrack election of 1893. In Passaic County, the Democrats gained more at the expense of the Socialist Labor party than of the Republican party. The Socialist Labor party, which had received an impressive 14.5 per cent of the three-party vote in Paterson the previous year, sank to 5.9 per cent, while the G.O.P. slipped only from 53.4 to 51.5 per cent as the Democrats climbed from 32.2 to 42.6 per cent there. In the city of Passaic, both the Democrats and Socialist Labor gained while the Republicans lost percentage strength. Only in Ward 3, their old-stock American stronghold, did the Republicans barely reverse this trend.[43]

New Jersey Democrats came close to recovering in 1895 the ground they had lost the previous year. But they had suffered a worse defeat in 1893 than in 1894; their party was still well below its 1892 strength. At the same time, New York Democrats fell far short of undoing the damage of 1894, let alone that of 1893. In both states, the Democrats appeared to have gained ground by winning back voters who had deserted them in 1893 or 1894, rather than by winning over voters who had traditionally identified with the Republicans. The Democrats' limited success reflected the partial cooling off of the heated nation-wide economic and cultural controversies of 1893–94 over the depression, the tariff, and anti-Catholicism, and the easing of conflicts peculiar to one or the other state—i.e., the anti-racetrack crusade in New Jersey, Democratic factionalism in New York State. Two points bear emphasis. First, though the Democratic party registered its most important gains in urban areas in both states, the culturally divisive campaign in New York State reduced the Democrats' net gain there by producing percentage shifts toward the Republican party across major upstate areas. These partially offset Democratic gains in the New York City–Brooklyn metropolitan area. No such cleavage marked the New Jersey vote, for if Democratic gains across the state did not match those in counties containing the state's major cities, neither were there Republican gains across the state to reduce the impact of those urban gains. (For a clear view of these divergent patterns, compare Table 8 with Table 9.) In New York, Democratic gains in counties where the party had been relatively strong the previous year, and losses where it had been weak, widened the dispersion of Democratic and Republican county-level percentage strength. In New Jersey, widespread Democratic gains of varying sizes reduced the dispersion of both parties' county-level percentage strength.[44] Second, though the patterns of Democratic recoveries in New York and New Jersey differed, they shared one politically important characteristic: as noted earlier, they were only partial. Nor was the Democrats' failure to recoup party fortunes in November 1895 confined to these two states. State elections in Iowa, Ohio, Pennsylvania, and Massachusetts produced percentage shifts no more encouraging to the Democrats than those in New York State and New Jersey.[45] There was no escaping the fact: the Democratic party remained the minority party throughout the North.

VI

"The Enemy's Country": The Presidential Campaign and Election of 1896

THE PRESIDENTIAL campaign and election of 1896 climaxed the Republican upswing that had begun in 1893. Though other regions decided the outcome of the presidential race, the contest in the Northeast was important in that it pitted sharply conflicting political coalitions against one another in the heart of urban-industrial America. Within the Northeast, the campaign so disrupted Democratic organization and the election so reduced Democratic support that the Republican party was able to establish its regional dominance beyond question.

Neither major party chose a northeasterner as its presidential candidate in 1896. That the Republicans, whose national convention met first, did not do so was not surprising, for only once in forty years had they failed to nominate a midwesterner. The choice of William McKinley of Ohio reflected in part their continuing appreciation of the strategic importance of the Midwest in the piecing together of a successful Republican coalition in national elections. The selection of McKinley also reflected their recognition of him as a candidate who could bring many strengths to the presidential campaign. To be sure, some northeastern Republicans had sought to block McKinley's drive for the presidential nomination by portraying him as vacillating on the currency question and inflexible on the tariff issue. And McKinley, as an astute Ohio congressman, had voted for the Bland Free Coinage bill and the Bland-Allison Silver Purchase bill, and had voted to override President Hayes's veto of the latter; he had also championed the Sherman Silver Purchase bill. But even in the Northeast, many Republicans felt that McKinley had demonstrated his popularity in the Ohio gubernatorial elections of 1891 and 1893, and that the protective tariff, with which he was identified, would again provide their party with an effective issue around which all could rally, just as they had in 1894.

McKinley and Marcus A. Hanna, his manager, dominated the Republican national convention in St. Louis, McKinley easily winning nomination on the first ballot. The platform's currency plank, drafted by midwestern supporters of McKinley, declared for "the existing gold standard" and pledged the party to "promote" an "international agreement" to permit the safe remonetization of silver. Though McKinley would have omitted specific reference to "gold" in the plank, he favored opposing the free coinage of silver except by international agreement. Following adoption of the currency plank, delegates from silver mining states, whose free coinage plank had been voted down in committee and on the floor, bolted the convention. McKinley and Hanna had hoped to avoid such a split, but the mere omission of "gold" from the currency plank would hardly have placated western advocates of free silver. Republican leaders were willing to abandon the Rocky Mountains region in order to strengthen their party's position in the more populous Midwest and East.[1]

That the Democracy turned away from the Northeast for its presidential candidate for the first time since 1860 did not reflect any change of strategy on the part of the party's northeastern leaders, but rather gave evidence of the humiliation of those leaders by southern and western politicians at the Democratic national convention in Chicago. Girding for that convention, the New York State Democratic party, the most important in the Northeast, had buried most of its factional differences in the face of the agrarian-free silver threat from the South and West. Its platform, shaped by Senator David B. Hill and William C. Whitney, endorsed the Cleveland administration and a tariff for revenue only, appealed for party unity in 1896, declared for gold and silver at parity and against gold or silver monometallism, and called on the government to retire United States and Treasury notes and to maintain the gold standard "until international co-operation for bimetallism can be secured." This appeal for international bimetallism pleased neither advocates of free silver nor die-hard gold monometallists. The New Yorkers were criticized for acting less than two weeks before their party's national convention, but there is no reason to believe that an earlier stand for gold would have turned the tide of battle in the Midwest and Upper South, where the issue was decided. Whitney, at least, hoped that he had laid the groundwork for compromise on a moderate nominee and a moderate currency plank at the national convention.

Whatever the hopes of sound money Democrats, they were quickly dashed in Chicago. The convention chose silverites from the South and West as temporary and permanent chairmen and seated silver delegations in contested cases, thereby assuring the agrarian-silver forces of the two-thirds majority necessary to name a candidate. After defeating a substitute platform proposed by the minority of the resolutions committee, Senator Hill's motion to commend the Cleveland administration, and Hill's two amendments to the currency plank drafted by the majority of the resolutions committee, the convention adopted the committee's platform, which embodied the program of the agrarian-silverite Democracy. The platform condemned the Cleveland administration's bond issues, "arbitrary interference by Federal authorities in local affairs," and "government by injunction." (The last two of these were reactions to governmental moves during the Pullman strike and railroad boycott.) The platform also criticized the Supreme Court for declaring unconstitutional the federal income tax. In its most dramatic challenge to the Cleveland administration, the document demanded the free and unlimited coinage of silver and gold at 16 to 1 without international agreement.

Following their defeat in the platform fight, the New York delegates caucused. Many wished to bolt, but Whitney cautioned against hasty action and, at a second caucus, he and Hill prevailed on the delegation to accept a compromise: it would remain in the convention but not participate in the choosing of a nominee and would later issue a statement explaining why the group could not support the national platform and ticket. Other sound money delegations assumed passive roles at the convention. As a consequence, only one easterner, former Governor Robert E. Pattison of Pennsylvania, was placed in nomination, and sound money delegates either voted for him or abstained during the balloting. William Jennings Bryan of Nebraska won nomination on the fifth roll call. The convention then chose Arthur Sewall of Maine for Vice-President. Sewall, a shipbuilder, banker, and railroad man, had earlier been removed as a national committeeman by his state's conservative delegation for having voted against Hill as temporary chairman.[2] Throughout the convention the South and West defeated the Northeast: as the elections of 1894 had signified the repudiation of the Cleveland administration by the electorate, so the Democratic national convention of 1896 marked its repudiation by the American Democracy. Bryan's subsequent nomination by the People's and National Silver parties deepened the southern and western complexion of the coalition that supported him.[3]

The Republican and Democratic national conventions had widely differing impacts on the northeastern wings of the respective parties. Republican politicians, united as they were behind a strong and acceptable national ticket, mindful of the fruits of victory, and fearful of the Bryanite Democracy, faced no serious problems. To be sure, factionalism existed among the New York Republicans. Appreciating this, McKinley and Hanna turned to New Jersey, from which they chose Garret A. Hobart to run for Vice-President, thereby providing the national ticket with its traditional sectional balance while avoiding involvement in the strife between friends and foes of Boss Platt in the Empire State. Afterward, Hanna worked with and through Platt in New York. Anti-Platt Republicans were disappointed, but they were unable to undo the arrangement.[4]

Northeastern Democratic leaders faced difficult problems in the wake of their party's national convention. Precious few sympathized with the program of the agrarian-silverite coalition that now dominated the national Democratic party. Some, motivated by loyalty to party or ambition or both, were willing to support the national ticket and platform. Others, recognizing the unpopularity of the Bryanites in the region and seeking above all to protect their personal and organizational interests, gave little support to or dissociated themselves from the national party. Still others, irrevocably opposed to the southern-western leadership of the Bryanite Democracy, sought some means of defeating their party's national ticket. The interaction among these groups formed an important chapter in the presidential campaign in the Northeast.

In considering alternatives open to them, many Cleveland Democrats refused either to swallow the Democracy of Bryan or to support the Republican party, which would have involved abandoning both their identity as Democrats and their opposition to Republican tariff doctrine. Clevelandites from the Midwest and Border took the lead in launching a third party. Gathering in Chicago on July 23, they scheduled an organizational meeting for Indianapolis on August 7. The Indianapolis group issued a call for a national nominating convention, which met on September 2 and 3 in the same city. The self-styled National Democratic party nominated Senator John M. Palmer of Illinois for President and Simon B. Buckner of Kentucky for Vice-President; its platform praised President Cleveland, while denouncing the Democratic national platform.[5] Palmer had commanded in the Union army, Buckner in the Confederate. In choosing them the National Democrats sought to symbolize national unity and to weaken Bryan in closely contested midwestern and border states.

It has been argued that impetus for third party action came from conservative Democrats in the Midwest and Border because they were directly threatened by the agrarian Democrats' capture of their state organizations, that their northeastern counterparts were less anxious to wage such a campaign because they remained in firm control of their state parties, and that the easterners largely confined themselves to financing the National Democratic effort in swing states. Exception to these generalizations must be taken on two counts. First, some northeasterners shied away from leading the third party not because they retained control of their own state parties but because they felt that midwesterners should lead the way lest the party be written off as a front for Wall Street. (B. B. Smalley, Democratic national committeeman from Vermont, refused even to join because he felt he could better serve various corporations, his friends, and himself by not doing so.) [6] Second, examination of state Democratic party politics in Connecticut, New York, and New Jersey suggests that such generalizations oversimplify, indeed, distort, a complex political situation within the Northeast.

In Connecticut, Clevelandites dominated the Democracy during the spring of 1896, the state party platform declaring against both free silver and any "general revision" of the Wilson-Gorman Tariff. The editor of the New Haven *Register* predicted that if the Democratic national convention declared for free silver, the state party would call a second convention to reaffirm its platform and nominate candidates for Congress and state offices. He concluded that the designation of electors might be construed as a bolt, but that if a slate were named, it would be pledged to sound money. Following the Chicago convention, conservatives denounced the course taken by the national party, but by and large they sought to retain control of the Connecticut party rather than bolt. If successful, they would reduce Bryan to running as a Populist in Connecticut. Though silverite activity in the Connecticut Democracy had been reported for some time, only in the New Haven town committee could the Bryanites claim a share of power during this period. To the clamor of some businessmen and professionals for a third national ticket, the New Haven *Register* replied (without criticism) that it was unnecessary, since conservatives remained firmly entrenched in the Democratic party.[7]

During August, the Bryanites, their demand for control of the party machinery rebuffed by the Democratic state committee, appointed a provisional state committee and set out to capture the state party convention, which was to meet early the next month. They quickly won primaries and caucuses, securing a majority of delegates even in Hartford, a sound money citadel. A number of factors contributed to their success. Some sound money men, Commodore E. C. Benedict among them, were sitting out the campaign in disgust at the Chicago convention or, having decided to abandon the Democracy, felt it improper to participate in the struggle; others, used to having their own way in national party affairs but unused to the ways of local party politics, were of little use in the infighting. On the other hand, party workers, who appreciated the rewards of regularity, supported the Bryanites. The second Connecticut Democratic convention, safely in Bryanite hands, endorsed the Chicago ticket and platform. Conservatives now deserted the party in large numbers. In October they held their own convention, reaffirmed the original Democratic state platform, nominated candidates for state office, and chose electors pledged to the National Democratic ticket. Former Governor Thomas Waller assured anti-Bryan Democrats that they were free to vote for McKinley or Palmer, but suggested that they vote for the National Democratic state ticket in order to bury silver sentiment in Connecticut.[8]

In New York, by way of contrast, a number of prominent Democrats broke with the national party soon after its convention, and Clevelandites ultimately formed a third party because the state Democratic party, which they had never controlled and had often fought, again took a course unacceptable to them. Senator David Hill, who led the state party, opposed the Chicago ticket and platform out of conviction, but also because he judged them to be political liabilities in the Empire State. Concerned with the survival of his organization, Hill planned to keep the state party noncommittal toward the presidential campaign until its mid-September convention in Buffalo. There it would ritually endorse the national ticket—but not the national platform—and launch an all-out gubernatorial campaign behind a candidate acceptable to gold and silver factions running on a platform confined to state issues. Though Tammany Hall's executive committee endorsed Bryan and Sewall on July 31, the Democratic state committee adopted Hill's strategy. Resisting pressures from friends and foes of Bryan, Hill refrained from public comment on the explosive issues of endorsing the national ticket and platform. Not even Bryan's tailoring of an Albany speech to make it easier for Hill to endorse him could draw out the state leader.[9]

Developments on both flanks of the Democratic party soon deprived Hill of maneuvering room. Cleveland Democrats did not wait for the Democratic state convention before acting. Operating through the Democratic Party Reform Organization and the New York State Democracy, during late July they laid the groundwork for a third party campaign in New York and chose delegates to the organizational meeting of the National Democrats in Indianapolis. At their state convention, held in Syracuse on August 31, they denounced the Democratic national ticket and platform (particularly the currency plank), chose delegates to the national nominating convention of the National Democratic party, and designated at-large electors. They postponed naming electors from congressional districts and candidates for state office until a second state convention, which they scheduled to take place in Brooklyn following the regular Democratic state convention. Some Clevelandites favored campaigning solely on the national level but others wished to challenge old organization foes within New York State as well as new Bryanite foes in the nation. Cleveland Democrats made it clear that they would take independent action in New York State unless regular Democrats assumed their position regarding national candidates and platforms; they also indicated they realized this was not likely to happen. Their unequivocal declaration for gold, echoed within the week by the National Democrats in Indianapolis, disappointed Senator Hill, who viewed the New York State Democratic party's June endorsement of international bimetallism as a wiser sound money statement.[10] That pronouncement had served as the basis of the conservative Democrats' currency plank at the Democratic national convention. There international bimetallism had been rejected by silver Democrats. Now, two months later, it stood repudiated by gold Democrats as well.

Meanwhile, Hill learned from trusted local politicians whom he had asked to report on political sentiment in their districts, and from other correspondents, that Bryan and free silver were firing the imagination of rural and small-town voters in upstate New York.[11] On another front, U.S. Senator Edward Murphy, who dreamed of controlling patronage in New York should Bryan become president, pressed for endorsement of the national ticket and platform. A correspondent informed Hill of the same pressure (and motive) on the local level; another reported an ambitious politician riding the wave of Bryan's popularity to victory over Hill's local organization.[12]

In the end, Senator Hill and Secretary of War Daniel Lamont, the only member of President Cleveland's cabinet to cooperate with the New York leader, failed to steer the state party clear of national issues. Their workers managed to control a number of upstate county conventions, but others endorsed Bryan and his platform. Supporters decided against nominating Hill as a delegate to the state convention from his home county for fear of precipitating a fight with silverites in the Chemung County convention; Hill declined to represent an Albany County district whose convention had instructed him to endorse the Chicago ticket and platform.[13] Downstate, the powerful New York and Kings county delegations were in line behind Bryan. The surge toward the position of the national party led more sound money Democrats to bolt the Democratic party. But to Hill, bolting was unthinkable. Such an act, he explained to Lamont, would open the door for adventurers and scoundrels to capture the Democratic organization.[14]

The September Democratic state convention stood on far different ground from the June state party convention. Its platform "unreservedly" endorsed the Democratic national platform and "cordially" approved the nomination of Bryan and Sewall, to whom it pledged "hearty and active support," before turning to state issues. As planned, Hill's lieutenants secured the gubernatorial nomination for John Boyd Thacher, a sound money man whose willingness to run on the Chicago platform was vouched for by supporters. Despite the convention's endorsement of Bryan and free silver, Hill still hoped that former Governor Flower could persuade the National Democrats, who were to meet in Brooklyn on September 24, to accept Thacher as their candidate. To this end, the Albany *Argus,* an organization newspaper, called for unity in the state despite differences over national issues because in New York the "issue is Plattism, not Bryanism" and Thacher released a letter reiterating his opposition to free silver but stating that he would vote for Bryan and Sewall.[15]

Thacher's letter unleashed a storm within the Democracy. Rural politicians, whether converts to free silver or representatives of districts where inflationist sentiment was marked, and Tammany leaders, who demanded regularity of party nominees, cried betrayal and called for Thacher's immediate withdrawal from the race. Hill fought back, gaining time for Thacher, but both were undercut by the National Democrats' nomination of an independent state ticket. Shortly thereafter, Thacher withdrew from the race.[16] The National Democrats acted as they did because the regular state Democrats had endorsed the Chicago ticket and platform while Thacher had indicated support for that ticket and for international bimetallism, rather than gold monometallism. On the other hand, Thacher's nomination by the National Democrats would not have assured the success of Hill's plan: it would only have increased the resolve of Bryanites and regular Democrats to scratch Thacher for having repudiated his party's national and state platforms.[17] Though Bryan and his campaign manager, U.S. Senator James K. Jones of Arkansas, expressed concern over the situation in New York, they did not have sufficient leverage in the state party to influence decisions relating to Thacher's withdrawal from the race.[18] From beginning to end, New York politicians made these decisions. Following the collapse of Hill's plan, the Democratic state committee designated Wilbur F. Porter, the party's nominee for lieutenant-governor, to replace Thacher. Porter dutifully endorsed Bryan and the national and state Democratic platforms, but the demoralized New York party mounted only a token campaign for the national and state tickets.

Despite its actions during and after the Democratic state convention, Tammany Hall's commitment to Bryan was quite limited. It had opposed his nomination, after which a number of members, prominent politicians among them, bolted the party. Tammany's executive committee endorsed Bryan and Sewall on July 31, but not until the Thacher crisis did it endorse the national platform. Tammany, like the state organization, would have liked to avoid serious involvement in the national campaign, and for good reason. The Cleveland administration had denied it patronage; the loss of the mayoralty and governorship in 1894 had further weakened its position; now the defection of businessmen was depriving it of financial contributions. Local success in 1895 had held out hope of winning the mayoralty of Greater New York City in 1897; essentially, Tammany leaders sought to preserve organizational unity during 1896 in preparation for that campaign. The leadership's problem was compounded by factionalism within the organization. Early in 1896, dissidents led by County Clerk Henry D. Purroy had challenged John C. Sheehan, who was guiding Tammany during Richard Croker's extended leave of absence. This local clash was unrelated to national issues, but during the presidential campaign the Purroy faction sought to score with party regulars by vocally supporting Bryan and criticizing state and city leaders for not doing so; in October, Purroy organized the Central Bryan and Sewall Association. Congressman William Sulzer, who appears to have admired Bryan as well as opposed Sheehan, had earlier formed the first Bryan and Sewall Club in New York City. Sheehan countered by nominally supporting Bryan while avoiding a break with those hostile to Bryan and free silver.[19] Tammany threatened to deny standing to members who bolted—but cooperated with the National Democrats to minimize Democratic disruption within the city. Thus Croker, Charles F. Murphy, and Daniel Lamont secured for U.S. Representative George B. McClellan, Jr., renomination by Tammany and nomination by the National Democrats. Under the arrangement, McClellan maintained silence on the currency question. This drew fire from the Purroy faction of Tammany; from the Populists, who ran a candidate against McClellan; and from the Republicans, who sought unsuccessfully to draw him out on the issue.[20] In the end, Tammany managed to weather the storm of 1896 in reasonably good shape.

Across the Hudson River, the New Jersey Democracy reeled under the impact of Bryan's nomination. Organization leaders, though not Clevelandites, were conservative and fearful that a campaign in behalf of a national ticket and platform that gave every evidence of being unpopular in New Jersey would further weaken a state party sapped by defeats during 1893–95. Still, as professional politicians they normally placed a premium on party regularity. Under the circumstances, U.S. Senator James Smith, Jr., chairman of the state committee and the state delegation to the party's recent national convention, decided to summer in Europe. Before leaving, Smith declared that an effort would be made to carry New Jersey in November but stressed regaining control of the House of Representatives to check McKinley should he win. Smith remained evasive regarding the national ticket and platform, matters—he concluded—to be referred to the state convention in September.[21]

During the summer, various Democratic local and county committees and, finally, the state committee endorsed Bryan and Sewall. Some members resigned various committees in protest; others were expelled by the victorious Bryanites. The coalition that assumed control of the New Jersey campaign consisted of silverites and mavericks, who had easily been held in check by conservatives before Bryan's nomination, and regular party workers, whose loyalty and ambitions led them to back Bryan. The new leadership dominated the state convention, which enthusiastically endorsed Bryan and the platform on which he ran. Returning from Europe afterward, Senator Smith resigned as chairman of the state committee, stating that he could best serve his party in another capacity. The committee first rejected, then accepted Smith's resignation and handed to Colonel E. L. Price, Chairman of the Essex County Democratic Committee, the difficult task of managing Bryan's New Jersey campaign.[22]

Bryan's nomination quickly touched off a wave of defections from the New Jersey party by Cleveland Democrats. Some three weeks after the Democratic national convention, William J. Curtis, who even before the Chicago convention had considered bolting, invited conservative Democrats to organize a party dedicated to maintenance of the "single gold standard." The New Jersey National Democrats drafted a platform, sent delegates to the Indianapolis convention of the National Democratic party, and chose a slate of electors. They also entered candidates in many congressional and legislative races, hoping thereby to establish their position in state Democratic affairs. In the Seventh Congressional District they did so only after plans to unite with regular Democrats behind Allan McDermott of Jersey City fell through.

In the Fourth Congressional District, however, the National Democrats backed Representative Mahlon Pitney, a Republican, against the serious challenge of Augustus Cutler, a Bryan Democrat.[23]

The foregoing makes clear that Clevelandites, far from retaining power in the state Democratic parties of Connecticut, New York, and New Jersey during the campaign, lost control in Connecticut and never exercised it in the other two states. Further, northeastern National Democrats not only supported their national party to defeat Bryan and free silver in the Midwest and Border, but also campaigned in the Northeast, both to weaken Bryanite candidates and to strengthen their own position within state Democratic parties. Internal conflicts weakened the Democracy during 1896 and produced or accelerated shifts of power within state and local parties. Though Bryan's candidacy created opportunities for political outsiders such as James Martine in New Jersey and veterans of assorted reform causes such as Alexander Troup in Connecticut, Bryanism failed to sink any roots into the inhospitable soil of the Northeast: Democratic politicians who loyally or nominally supported Bryan benefited more than radicals and reformers from the defection of party "respectables." [24] Some organization politicians bolted Bryan in New York, but National Democratic leaders were generally veterans of anti-Hill and anti-Tammany campaigns. The Clevelandites' failure to sway or topple Democratic regulars enabled Elliot Danforth to console David Hill after the election with the thought that though the Democrats had lost the election, Democratic regulars would soon be able to rebuild the party machinery without interference from anti-organization Democrats.[25] At the same time, the political upheaval of 1893–96 further weakened popular support for the Democratic party in upstate New York. As a consequence, Tammany Hall, which broadened its base by capturing Greater New York City in 1897, soon eclipsed Hill's upstate organization in the state party.[26]

Democratic factionalism had long had an ethnic-religious dimension. The defection during 1896 of Cleveland Democrats, who were for the most part old-stock Protestants, worked to the advantage of Irish Catholic politicians in localities where the two groups were rivals for control of the Democratic party. In Connecticut, Lynde Harrison reported that two Irishmen alone of all Democratic state candidates of the past twenty years were supporting Bryan. Two other Irishmen alone of that state's delegates to the Democratic national convention did not boycott the nominating balloting; though both had voted against Bryan in Chicago, they loyally supported him in Connecticut as their party's nominee. Old-stock American names predominated on membership lists of National Democratic groups and committees; Irish names were common on lists of regulars. (The prominence of the Irish was also noted in Massachusetts.)[27] In New Haven the Democratic split carried over into 1897, a Republican defeating his divided opposition in a three-way mayoralty race. Two years later, the Democrats rallied behind Cornelius R. Driscoll to win the office. Driscoll's victory ushered in a new era in New Haven politics. Before 1899, every mayor had been of old-stock American origin; those before the 1840s were generally patricians, those afterward usually entrepreneurs. Driscoll was an Irish Catholic. All his Democratic successors have been Irish Catholics, too; most have sprung from working class or lower middle class families. Irish politicians profited from struggles within the Democracy in other northeastern cities during 1896, among them Albany, Boston, and Providence.[28] The widespread support of Irish politicians for Bryan's candidacy reflected their deep loyalty to the Democratic party, reinforced by long rivalry with Democrats prominent among those bolting in 1896, rather than any commitment to Bryan or free silver. That loyalty benefited the Irish politicians more than it did Bryan.

The analysis of the state of the Republican and Democratic parties in the Northeast following the national party conventions provides a background against which the campaigns of the rival national parties can better be understood. To begin with, if the Democrats' repudiation of Cleveland and nomination of Bryan threw northeastern Democrats into disarray, they also temporarily threw the Republicans' national leadership off stride. Before the Democratic national convention, McKinley and Hanna had planned to campaign on the tariff issue, which had served them and their party so effectively against the Cleveland Democrats.

Bryan's nomination forced upon them the realization that the currency issue would figure prominently in the campaign. Without playing down the tariff issue, they sought thereafter to turn the currency issue to their own advantage. Second, neither party considered the Northeast an area of primary concern. From the beginning both parties assigned the northeastern states to the Republican column and concentrated their efforts in the Midwest, where they assumed the election would be decided, and the adjoining Border and Plains regions. Rival headquarters were established in Chicago, the nerve center of the Midwest. Bryan, short of money and denied the support of many Democratic politicians and newspapers, carried his case to the electorate by railroad. Of 249 major stops on his campaign swings, he made 160 in eight midwestern states. McKinley made no whistle stop tour, campaigning instead from his front porch in Canton, Ohio, to which the railroads carried delegations. Hanna did set up offices in New York City, the wealth of whose major businesses he tapped to finance his costly "campaign of education" in closely contested areas. Hanna did not immediately strike gold in the Northeast, but contributions were finally forthcoming and if the Republicans did not have unlimited funds at their disposal, their campaign treasury exceeded earlier ones and dwarfed that of the Democrats.[29]

Though neither party viewed the Northeast as a contested area, both campaigned there, Bryan himself twice touring the region to add his voice to the Democratic effort. Republican spokesmen, in developing their economic appeal to the northeastern electorate, particularly to laborers, argued that free silver would destroy business confidence, plunge the nation into another depression, increase unemployment, and injure those who retained their jobs by reducing the purchasing power of the dollar. Free silver might benefit selfish silver barons in the Far West and impecunious agrarians in the West and South, but it could only wreak havoc among workers in the East. Further, the Republicans reminded voters that the low tariff policy of the Democrats had precipitated a depression, and they promised that their own protective tariff policy would restore prosperity. Thus they combined the sound money and protective tariff arguments into a single appeal for votes. McKinley set the tone of this campaign in his letter of acceptance; Republicans followed his lead throughout the campaign in the Northeast. (One of McKinley's sentences gained particularly widespread currency: "Not open mints for the unlimited coinage of the silver of the world, but open mills for the full and unrestricted labor of American workingmen.") [30] The Republicans' stress on the tariff issue angered Cleveland Democrats who wished to campaign against Bryan solely on the currency issue. Republicans took note of the remonstrances of conservative Democrats—Whitelaw Reid instructed his New York *Tribune* staff to treat National Democrats "with the utmost consideration"—but they refused to permit them to define the issues of the 1896 campaign. Republicans were not about to abandon the issue on which they had triumphed over the Cleveland Democrats two years earlier, particularly as they felt that it retained its mass appeal and that under no circumstances would sound money Democrats support Bryan.[31]

Bryan was vulnerable to both prongs of the Republican attack on Democratic economic policies. His party's platform had declared for a tariff for revenue only and denounced "the Republican threat to restore the McKinley law, which has been twice condemned by the people." Within the Northeast, Republicans linked Bryan to the tariff positions of both the Cleveland administration and spokesmen for the South and West. Bryan's obsession with free silver also hurt him in the Northeast. Upper and middle class hostility toward free silver is well documented, and such evidence as we possess suggests that workers were either confused and unconvinced by the complex arguments advanced by opposing sides in the currency debate or increasingly uneasy regarding free silver, the inflationary effect of which was more likely to benefit debtor farmers than underpaid or unemployed laborers. Attacks on free silver as inimical to working class interests were by no means confined to Republicans; the Socialist Labor party repeatedly struck at this point during 1896.

By harping on free silver, Bryan lost precious opportunities to discuss an issue of potentially greater interest to workers—federal intervention in labor disputes, particularly "government by injunction." Eugene V. Debs contended that employers were stressing the currency issue to divert laborers from the injunction issue, but Bryan bore no less responsibility for this emphasis. (Mark Hanna's observation that Bryan is "talking silver all the time, and that's where we've got him" assumes its full significance when viewed in this context.) Indeed, Bryan appeared ill at ease discussing matters of interest to workers as workers. During an address on free silver in Lynn, Massachusetts, he was called on by a worker in the audience to discuss the injunction in labor disputes. Bryan replied that in time arbitration would replace the injunction as a means of settling such conflicts. On Labor Day, he declared that the claims of society were superior to those of employers or employees and that "the best interests of society demand" the settlement of labor disputes "by courts of arbitration rather than by trials of strength." Elsewhere, notably in his Chicago "Cross of Gold" and New York City notification speeches, Bryan spoke in Jacksonian terms of the worker as producer.[32] He failed to appreciate the irrelevancy of such rhetoric to the industrial wage earner of the 1890s.

In addressing voters in the rural Northeast, Republicans again argued that since the region's farmers produced for domestic consumption, the protective tariff would safeguard them against foreign competition and assure them of their urban market by contributing to industrial prosperity. They also attacked as unjust the requests of western farmers for governmental assistance, while eastern farmers, who faced problems of their own, made no such claims on government.[33] The G.O.P. tailored its arguments to the assumed needs of northeastern farmers; Bryan did not. As he did everywhere else, Bryan emphasized free silver while campaigning in the rural Northeast. He subsequently recalled that in upstate New York, at least, he had noted support for free silver among farmers. Bryan's encounters occurred during the same period in which Senator Hill received reports of free silver sentiment from various upstate quarters. All the same, the carrying power of the free silver issue in the rural Northeast was open to question. The rural population was disproportionately composed of ethnic and religious groups predisposed to vote Republican; during 1893–95, the G.O.P. had strengthened its powerful position among ruralites. In order to score, Bryan would have to win over large numbers of voters who were accustomed to voting Republican.

To be sure, times were difficult for northeastern farmers, and had been for two decades, but this did not necessarily make them allies of hard-pressed southern and western agrarians. The northeasterners were acutely aware that cheap western meats and grains had contributed to their own plight. New York farmers had generally opposed state improvement of the Erie Canal as of benefit to the West. Now Bryan's supporters called for effective regulation or nationalization of the railroads to reduce through rates from the Midwest to the East Coast. Eastern farmers felt such rates were already too low and favored rate structures that benefited producers close to their markets. They also opposed the liberalization of laws pertaining to the acquisition of federal lands by farmers and the invasion of eastern markets by western oleomargarine and "filled cheese." [34] Other issues divided northeastern farmers, militating against the growth of a farmers' movement within the area. Dairy farmers close to major urban markets and those farther removed disagreed regarding railroad rates on milk. The shift of farmers into various specialties further fragmented agriculturalists. Finally, diversification contributed to the success of many farmers. Such farmers, along with agricultural societies and farm editors, preached that scientific farming and efficient management and marketing would bring prosperity to eastern agriculture. This emphasis on individual responsibility for success or failure in farming hardly encouraged the growth of a radical agrarian movement.[35] In short, Bryan no more understood the peculiar needs of northeastern farmers than he did those of urban laborers.

The Republicans attacked more than Bryanite financial and tariff policies in their northeastern campaign. That campaign involved nothing less than an assault on the Democracy of Bryan as a southern threat to the Northeast, a radical menace to the social order and prosperity, and a front for the Populist party. A variety of groups supported the G.O.P. in this attack. The Republicans skillfully played on fears of Bryan and his supporters by stressing the theme of patriotism in their own campaign. In New

York and other major cities, October 31 was observed as a flag day in honor of McKinley: flags, banners, and buttons were displayed; patriotic parades were staged. A trainload of Union army heroes carried the patriotic message through the Midwest during the campaign. Through their use of patriotic symbols, particularly those associated with the Civil War, the Republicans sought to identify Bryan as the candidate of the South and their own party as the nation's defender against secession in 1861 and sectionalism in 1896.[36]

Republicans and conservative Democrats vilified Bryan and his followers. The New York *Tribune* thought Bryan's "Cross of Gold" speech at the Democratic national convention blasphemous and the behavior of the "half-drunken, howling mob" that paraded with a cross and a crown of thorns at the Populist national convention sacrilegious. The Hartford *Courant* seconded Theodore Roosevelt's indictment of free silver advocates as thieves—and consequently violators of the Eighth Commandment. Governor Altgeld of Illinois, who had pardoned the survivors among those convicted of the Haymarket bombing and defied President Cleveland during the Pullman strike and railroad boycott, inspired particular fear and hatred; he was frequently viewed as Bryan's gray eminence. During the campaign months, northeasterners frequently expressed their concern over "anarchy," "revolution," "Jacobinism," and "conspiracy." Agrarian radicals' denunciations of "the money power" were no more exaggerated than urban conservatives' condemnation of the Bryanites. Though public attacks on the Bryan Democratic-Populist coalition were obviously intended to influence the electorate to vote for the Republicans, they also reflected genuine fears on the part of many, as private correspondence from 1896 reveals. Thus William C. Beer called on his wife to pray for Bryan's defeat and to fly an American flag outside their home until election day. Republicans and conservative Democrats alike shared these anxieties, anxieties deep enough in the case of John Hay that not even McKinley's victory over Bryan could fully restore his confidence in the future of the Republic.[37]

The campaign against Bryan took on the overtones of a religious crusade as Protestant ministers, some of whom had earlier figured in attacks on organization Democrats, Roman Catholics, and the Roman Catholic Church, repeatedly condemned Bryan, his supporters, and his platform from the pulpit and in public statements. Some could scarcely contain themselves: one denounced Bryan as a "mouthing, slobbering demagogue, whose patriotism was all in his jaw-bone"; a second declared that the Chicago platform had been "made in hell." Still another spoke of a struggle between "Christian patriotism" and a Democratic platform "traitorous" in its sectional appeal. Only "a coward or a traitor" would not oppose the Democratic ticket, one clergyman claimed. Again and again ministers returned to the currency question, which they claimed was a moral issue ("Thou shalt not steal"), not a partisan issue. The ministry's commitment to sound money was nothing new; the preachers' fervor reflected the social tensions generated by the depression and unleashed by Bryan's candidacy.[38] The conservatism of the clergy had been denounced by Eugene V. Debs even before the onslaught against Bryan began. Now Mrs. Mary Elizabeth Lease, Kansas Populism's female orator, and Bryan himself criticized clergymen for their political activity. Many of Bryan's faithful followers were shocked by clergymen's betrayal of their just cause; correspondents vented their bitterness in letters to Bryan following his defeat.[39]

German American organizations also joined the struggle against Bryan and free silver. A German-American Sound-Money League, founded in New York City in May 1896, first sought to influence both major parties, then campaigned against the Bryanite Democracy. Businessmen, professionals, and others active in the German-American Cleveland Union and German-American Reform Union were among the league's founders. Opposition to free silver among Germans was by no means confined to leaders long identified with the Cleveland wing of the Democratic party. Tammany proclaimed the loyalty of Germans, particularly laborers, to Bryan, but others reported widespread defections. The Democrats were anxious enough to assign Governor Altgeld of Illinois to address his co-nationals in New York City; Representative William Sulzer did likewise in his district. Newspaper surveys of German communities in New Jersey claimed them to be "almost wholly on the side of sound money."[40] Reports from the closely contested Midwest placed most Germans in the Republican camp.[41]

Businessmen participated in and contributed financially to political organizations that opposed the Democratic national ticket. But Bryan and others charged that many businessmen went further, coercing voters into supporting the Republican ticket. The issue gained widespread publicity late in October when Senator James K. Jones, Chairman of the Democratic National Committee, alleged and Mark Hanna denied that coercion was being employed as a campaign tactic. Following the election, some of Bryan's supporters publicly charged that coercion had contributed to his defeat; individuals privately echoed the allegation in letters to Bryan. To this accusation were added charges of vote-buying and election fraud.[42] Reports of Republican coercion are now firmly imbedded in the historical literature. Most such accounts rely heavily and uncritically on Bryanite sources in analyzing the nature and significance of campaign pressure tactics.[43] This reliance is unfortunate, for sources sympathetic to McKinley point to the pressuring of laborers and farmers by businessmen to oppose Bryan.

Such pressure did not account for the outcome of the election, but it was applied. Some employers were reported merely to have instructed employees to wear McKinley emblems or to participate in McKinley demonstrations. But a number of firms announced production cutbacks, even factory closings, as a response to free silver agitation and others placed orders contingent upon McKinley's victory. Businessmen polled their employees and arranged for or permitted sound money advocates to propagandize their workers during lunch hours—the latter a campaign tactic to which laborers, especially union members, occasionally objected. Railroad companies in particular seem to have campaigned among their employees.[44] The Connecticut School Fund Commission publicly announced that it was refusing loan requests from farmers in Ohio and Indiana and that it would foreclose mortgages in the two states if Bryan won the election. (Not surprisingly, a disproportionate share of charges regarding coercion, vote-buying, and fraud involved closely contested midwestern states, even when northeasterners were allegedly the corruptors.)

The president of the Connecticut Mutual Life Insurance Company warned 65,000 policy holders that free silver would reduce the value of their insurance.[45] Newspapers opposing Bryan denied charges of intimidation—even as they reported that factories were shutting down in anticipation of Bryan's victory, that mortgages would be foreclosed if Bryan won, and that industry would expand operations if McKinley won.

Naturally, Republican politicians argued forcefully that Bryan's election would be a national calamity. Bryan and his followers were free to rebut this argument, though their effort was hampered by a lack of party organizational, financial, and newspaper support, but they did not possess effective means of countering the campaign directed at workers, farmers, and others by businessmen. Still, though the presidential campaign of 1896 was the most bitter to that point, one should not exaggerate the impact of coercion, corruption, and fraud on the election. National campaigns from 1876 through 1888 had featured charges of such irregularities, but neither party had been able to gain the upper hand during those years. On the other hand, the Republicans had not needed coercion, corruption, or fraud to win decisive victories over the Cleveland Democrats, who held important political positions and were supported by wealthy financial contributors and a powerful partisan press, during 1893–95. Nor would the Republicans rely on such tactics to maintain their dominance during the years following 1896.[46]

During 1896, Republicans, aided by conservative Democrats, sought to persuade Democratic voters that Bryan and his supporters were not true Democrats, but Populists. In so doing, they were attempting to make it easier for Democrats to vote against their party's national ticket, no easy act during an era marked by widespread party loyalty. In the Northeast, at least, Bryan played into the hands of his foes by insisting that opposition to the gold standard was the "overshadowing issue" in defining political commitments during the campaign. This argument suited his needs in areas where he could hope to win over Republicans sympathetic to free silver (i.e., the West and the Far West), but not in the Northeast, where he had to retain the support of Democrats hostile to free silver. The Republicans' emphasis on nationalistic and patriotic themes fit in with their strategy; so did the national party leadership's effort to submerge the cultural issues that had led diverse groups to identify with the Democratic party over the years. William McKinley was an excellent standard-bearer in such a campaign. On the one hand, he had served in the Union army during the Civil War and he was identified with the protective tariff, which symbolized the Republicans' commitment to contribute to national prosperity through positive governmental action. On the other hand, McKinley was free of involvement in anti-Catholic, temperance, and anti-foreign language crusades.[47]

Republican leaders revealed their desire to dampen religious controversy at their party's national convention. They chose a rabbi to open the convention with a prayer, not to please Jews but to avoid offending either Protestants or Catholics. Further, they avoided taking a public stand on a divisive religious issue by refusing to reaffirm in the national platform the 1876 Republican platform plank condemning both public expenditures for sectarian purposes and any union of Church and State. Archbishop John Ireland opposed adoption of this plank, while the exclusion of it from both the Republican and Democratic national platforms angered the Reverend James M. King of the National League for the Protection of American Institutions.[48] Before the Republican national convention, many members of the American Protective Association had revealed their displeasure with McKinley's record. That record and the attacks of A.P.A.'ers on it could only have stood McKinley in good stead as he labored to broaden the appeal of his party. During the presidential campaign, Bryan was forced to meet contradictory charges leveled against him in whispering campaigns in the Midwest. He denied any connection with anti-Catholic societies and reaffirmed his belief in the public schools.[49]

The efforts of McKinley and Republican national leaders to play down divisive cultural issues during the presidential campaign were noteworthy, but all the same the continued involvement of other Republicans with some of the causes that were central to cultural conflicts should not be overlooked. Certainly the Republican national platform of 1896 echoed past party documents in expressing sympathy with "all wise and legitimate efforts to lessen and prevent the evils of intemperance and promote morality." To be sure, the Populists' endorsement of Bryan and the support given him by many Prohibitionists created an unusual situation in that it added evangelical reformers to a Democratic coalition that had long appealed to Catholics and German Lutherans because it opposed evangelical reform, but on the state and local levels in the Northeast, at least, the Republican party clearly remained the party of temperance.[50] In New York, passage of the Raines Excise Act of 1896, coming on top of the temperance instruction law and Sunday closing controversy of 1895, confirmed that.[51] By the same token, though some leaders of the declining American Protective Association endorsed McKinley and others Bryan, there is no reason to doubt that most anti-Catholics continued to identify with the Republican party.

If Protestant-Catholic conflict played a diminished role in the political campaign of 1896, anti-Semitism appeared on the national political stage for the first time and played a minor part in the contest.[52] Some Populists were rhetorical anti-Semites who identified Jews with the international gold standard and banking structure that, agrarian radicals contended, lay at the root of the farmers' plight. The People's party had failed to become an independent force in the Northeast, but its endorsement of Bryan lent political significance to Populist ideology in the metropolitan New York City area, which contained a comparatively large Jewish population. The anti-Semitic overtones of the campaign did not escape contemporaries. General circulation newspapers and English-language Jewish periodicals reported the anti-Semitic atmosphere of the conventions of the National Silver and People's parties in St. Louis; Mrs. Mary Elizabeth Lease's explicit attack on Jews during a speech in New York City; and an anti-Semitic remark of B. F. Shively, the Democratic-Populist gubernatorial candidate in Indiana. Late in the campaign, Bryan felt the need to reassure a group of Jewish Democrats in Chicago: he said that in denouncing "the financial policy advocated by the Rothschilds . . . we are not attacking a race; we are attacking greed and avarice, which know neither race nor religion." A letter of thanks to Bryan from a Jewish supporter in New Jersey suggested that others perceived the situation differently.[53]

A faint trace of Europe's virulent anti-Semitic strain appeared in the United States during the political campaign. Herman Ahlwardt, a leading German anti-Semite who had been disseminating his doctrines in the United States since the previous December, endorsed Bryan and the Democratic national platform for promising to diminish the value of gold, which would aid "the farmer, the laborer, the artisan" against "the gold clique with that European Jew Rothschild and his puller-in Belmont as leaders." Ahlwardt alleged that "the Jews have made Mr. McKinley their tool." Of course, neither Bryan nor the Democratic platform earned Ahlwardt's praise by attacking Jews; their championing of free silver alone won them that. But the bizarre episode does suggest a point of contact between European and American political movements during the period.[54]

Still, the anti-Semitic content of Populism and the 1896 campaign should not be overestimated, for though anti-Semitism was present in both, it was central to neither. Bryanites sometimes struck at bankers in general or at Wall Street, the House of Morgan, England, or Lombard Street, rather than the Rothschilds or Jews. Individuals brought their own fears and hatreds to the campaign: some supporters of Bryan feared or hated Jews; others similarly regarded Catholics, Protestant clergymen, Negroes, or various nationalities. Moreover, northeastern conservatives as well as southern and western radicals exaggerated the importance of the financial question and sometimes irrationally attacked Jews for playing a pernicious role in American economic life. Sigourney Butler blamed the Jews for fomenting panics in the New York and London exchanges during the Venezuelan crisis; Joseph Pulitzer's New York *World* condemned the syndicate handling the third loan of the Cleveland administration as being "composed of bloodsucking Jews and aliens." Even a newspaper editorial critical of Russian anti-Semitism referred to the international power of Jewish bankers. Brooks Adams, an anti-Semite, opposed McKinley as the candidate of the "bankers" against the "producing classes." Theodore Roosevelt, an ardent foe of Bryan and no anti-Semite, could reflect on one of "several Capuan entertainments" he had attended following McKinley's victory:

> One was a huge lunch by the Seligmans, where at least half the guests were Jew bankers; I felt as if I was personally realizing all of Brooks Adams' gloomiest anticipations of our gold-ridden, capitalist-bestridden, usurer-mastered future.[55]

Such expressions reveal the acceptance by diverse individuals of wild tales regarding the financial prowess of the Jews. Finally, whatever the long-term threat of ideological anti-Semitism, during the 1890s Jews in the Northeast were more directly affected by the acts of anti-Semites within the region than by the rhetoric of anti-Semites elsewhere in the nation. By 1896, social discrimination against Jews could no longer be ignored. Indeed, the blackballing of Theodore Seligman by the Union League Club had already embarrassed the Republican party in New York City. Within northeastern cities, conflicts over jobs and street altercations sometimes involved Jews. Neither social discrimination nor urban conflicts could be attributed to the Populists or the free silver movement.[56]

On November 3, 1896, William McKinley led the Republican party to its greatest presidential victory in twenty-four years. William Jennings Bryan suffered a resounding defeat in the Northeast, but his chances for victory were dashed in other sections. Basically, Bryan's hopes had lain in combining areas of traditional Democratic strength—the South and the Border—with distressed silver mining and agricultural regions—the Rocky Mountains, Pacific Coast, and Great Plains (as well as the South)—and one or more states in the Midwest to win a narrow majority in the electoral college. This strategy involved shifting the Democratic party's base in the electoral college, in that it abandoned New Jersey, which had consistently voted Democratic during 1876–92, and New York and Connecticut, which had leaned toward the Democrats during that period. Only in Indiana did the Bryanites wage an all-out campaign to capture a swing state of the period of stalemate. In the end, Bryan went down to defeat because he failed to hold traditionally Democratic states, fell short of sweeping the West, and captured not a single state in the Midwest. Bryan did sweep the Solid South, but he fared badly in the Border, carrying Missouri alone. On the Pacific Coast he won only Washington. He carried all of the mountain states, but on the plains he lost North Dakota. In the Midwest, Bryan pressed McKinley only in Indiana.[57]

Nowhere did Bryan's candidacy affect Democratic fortunes more adversely than in the Northeast, where the party's support fell precipitously from the low levels of 1894–95 in every state except Maine and Pennsylvania. This decline contrasted with the Democrats' showing in the Midwest, where Bryan recovered some of the ground lost by the party duing 1893–95, and the Rocky Mountains region, where he carried the party to victories even more one-sided than those of the G.O.P. in New England. (See Table 10.) The Gold Democrats as well as the Republicans benefited from Democratic defections in the Northeast, receiving below-average support only in Pennsylvania. Paradoxically, though the Gold Democrats concentrated their national campaign efforts in the Midwest, they ran most strongly in the Northeast and

TABLE 10 *Shifts in Democratic and Republican Percentage Strength, 1894 or 1895 to 1896, Northeastern and Selected Midwestern and Rocky Mountains States*

STATE	DEM.	REP.	STATE	DEM.	REP.
Maine	+ 0.9 (− 4.0)[b]	+ 3.6	Ohio[a]	+ 6.9 (+ 0.6)[b]	+ 0.9
New Hampshire	−15.0 (−16.0)	+12.7	Indiana	+ 5.6 (+ 0.3)	+ 0.5
Vermont	− 7.7 (− 9.0)	+ 6.5	Illinois	+ 5.1 (− 1.9)	+ 2.6
Massachusetts[a]	−10.8 (−13.2)	+12.7	Wisconsin	− 0.9 (− 7.7)	+ 7.5
Rhode Island[a]	− 5.5 (− 6.5)	+10.9	Iowa[a]	+ 4.8 (− 3.4)	+ 2.2
Connecticut	−10.3 (−11.3)	+ 9.0	Kansas	+42.2 (+ 3.2)	− 2.4
New York[a]	− 5.1 (− 5.7)	+ 6.0	Nebraska[a]	+41.6 (+ 0.2)	+ 2.7
New Jersey[a]	− 7.6 (− 8.3)	+ 7.4	Colorado	+79.8 (+38.4)	−38.4
Pennsylvania[a]	− 0.4 (− 1.4)	+ 1.6	Montana	+58.9 (+28.9)	−27.3

Sources: *Tribune Almanacs, 1895–1897*. Elections to highest state office, 1894, 1895; presidential election, 1896.

[a]Elections of 1895. Other states, elections of 1894.

[b]Democratic percentage shift, 1894 or 1895 to 1896, when percentage strength, People's party, is added to percentage strength, Democratic party, in elections of 1894 or 1895.

South.[58] This distribution of the National Democratic vote appears to have been a function of anti-Bryan Democrats' perception of the political situation in various sections. During the campaign a number of their spokesmen had stressed the importance of defeating Bryan, even if that meant voting Republican. In the Midwest, where the outcome of the campaign was held to be crucial and in doubt, many anti-Bryan Democrats did just that. In the Northeast, which was deemed safe for McKinley, and the South, which was conceded to Bryan, Gold Democrats felt freer to vote for Palmer. For conservative Democrats, voting National Democratic rather than Republican minimized their break with tradition, particularly in the South, where the specter of Republican-Negro rule haunted many. Still, though there was no danger of Bryan winning the Northeast, many Gold Democrats so opposed him that they voted for McKinley, and then for their own state candidates. As a consequence of this ticket splitting, the National Democrats' state tickets ran ahead of their national ticket in a number of states, Connecticut and New York among them.

Connecticut, New York, and New Jersey fit into the Northeast's voting pattern, but factors unique to each suggest the value of separate state analyses. The Democrats entered the campaign of 1896 with slightly more popular strength in New York and New Jersey than Connecticut, thanks to their having regained in 1895 some of the support lost duing 1893–94 in the first two states. Connecticut had held no off-year elections in 1895; there the most recent voting alignments were those created in the Republican landslide victory of 1894. Percentage shifts in Connecticut between 1894 and 1896 exceeded those in New York and New Jersey, whether the latter are measured in terms of 1894–96 net shifts or 1895–96 shifts. During 1892–96, the period of realignment, the Republicans gained and the Democrats lost more percentage strength in Connecticut than in New York or New Jersey. In this, the three states contributed to and reflected overall differences between New England and the Middle Atlantic region.[59]

The election of 1896 was an unmitigated disaster for Connecticut Democrats, whose state, congressional, and legislative tickets suffered defeat along with Bryan. Not only did the Democracy lose more and receive less percentage support in Connecticut than in New York or New Jersey, it suffered an even sharper setback than it had two years earlier, its defection ratio jumping from 14.9 to 24.1. The percentage shifts of 1896 differed from, as well as exceeded, those of 1894. In the midterm election, Democratic percentage losses in towns containing the state's eleven most populous cities were comparable to those in other towns. Now the Democrats lost much more lightly in the population centers than the lesser towns. The National Democrats did not fare well in the populous towns; not unexpectedly, Socialist Labor exceeded and Prohibition fell below their state-wide averages in these units. (See Table 11.)

New Haven, which alone among the state's five major cities did not redistrict between 1894 and 1896, lends itself to analysis. McKinley and Lorrin Cooke, the Republican gubernatorial can-

TABLE 11 *Shifts in Percentage Strength, 1892–1894 and 1894–1896, and Percentage Strength, All Parties, 1896, Eleven Populous Towns and Other Connecticut Towns*

UNITS	REP.	DEM.	ND	PRO.	POP.	SLP
Towns, 11 Major Cities						
1892–1894[a]	+ 7.5	− 8.1 (15.1)[b]	X	−0.7	+0.7	+0.6
1894–1896[a]	+ 6.0	− 6.1 (13.4)[b]	X	−0.4	−1.2	+0.2
1896 %	57.3	39.5	1.6	0.5	X	1.1
Other Towns						
1892–1894[a]	+ 7.6	− 7.1 (15.0)[b]	X	−1.0	+0.4	+0.1
1894–1896[a]	+12.7	−15.0 (37.3)[b]	X	−0.4	−0.8	+0.1
1896 %	69.5	25.2	3.5	1.6	X	0.3
Connecticut						
1892–1894[a]	+ 7.6	− 7.5 (14.9)[b]	X	−0.9	+0.5	+0.3
1894–1896[a]	+ 9.0	−10.3 (24.1)[b]	X	−0.5	−1.0	+0.2
1896 %	63.2	32.5	2.5	1.0	X	0.7

Sources: *Connecticut Registers and Manuals, 1893–1897.*
[a] Gubernatorial elections, 1892, 1894; presidential election, 1896.
[b] Democratic defection ratio.

didate, carried the city by 54.3 to 42.1 per cent and 52.9 to 41.3 per cent, respectively, gaining only 3.1 and 1.7 percentage points over their party's 1894 showing as Bryan lost 3.7 and Joseph Sargent, the Democratic gubernatorial candidate, lost 4.5 percentage points. The National Democrats polled 1.3 per cent of the presidential vote and 3.4 per cent of the gubernatorial vote. The returns make it clear that New Haven voters shifted decisively toward the G.O.P. in 1894, not 1896. The Democrats experienced slightly below-average losses in their Irish bailiwicks (Wards 3, 4, 5, 6, 7, 12) and in two of the three districts (Wards 9, 10) where the A.P.A. had been strongest two years earlier. In Wards 3, 9, and 10, the Republicans actually lost fractionally.[60] The Democrats suffered serious percentage losses in Wards 8, 13, and 15, outlying wards whose old-stock American, German, and Swedish voters were already giving them below-average support. (Ward 15 had been an A.P.A. district in 1894.) Finally, Ward 1, which housed the city's elite and the Yale community, clearly revealed the intense opposition to Bryan in predominantly old-stock American, well-to-do urban districts in the Northeast. In a widely publicized campaign incident, Yale students had roundly heckled Bryan. Now Ward 1 ranked first in percentage shifts between the major parties and in Gold Democratic voting strength, Palmer receiving 3.6 per cent and the party's gubernatorial candidate 9.9 per cent there.[61]

Democratic ward-level losses in New Haven were correlated positively (+.465) with native-born whites of native parentage, and negatively (−.335) with first- and second-generation Americans; Republican gains correlated very weakly (+.071, +.074) with both. Though the G.O.P. did not depend on old-stock communities for its 1896 gains, Republican and National Democratic percentage strengths were strongly associated (+.910 and +.804, respectively) with such communities. On the other hand, Democratic strength was strongly correlated (+.968) with immigrant communities.[62] This association was stronger than that between the Socialist Labor party and such communities (+.579), for most of New Haven's first- and second-generation immigrants belonged to groups that leaned toward the Democrats, while the Socialist Labor party had limited appeal to the Irish, the largest of these groups. The importance in the electorate of Irish Catholic voters, who remained relatively loyal to the Democracy, and the regularity of many politicians, Irishmen in particular, contributed to Bryan's avoidance of a rout in New Haven. But Democrats could derive small comfort from their showing, for they had entered the campaign as the minority party and then lost additional ground.

The Democrats fared even worse in other Connecticut cities. Percentage shifts in Waterbury fell short of those of 1894; shifts in Bridgeport nearly equalled the previous ones. Bryan carried two Waterbury districts that contained concentrations of Irish voters, one of them—Ward 5—by 69.8 to 28.2 per cent, but lost the other three wards by decisive margins. He showed to worst advantage in Ward 2, which contained the city's largest old-stock population, polling only 23.6 per cent of the vote to McKinley's 73.7. Of twelve wards in Bridgeport, Bryan carried only two, in both of which the Irish predominated. (The Democrats had won four of six wards in 1892 and three in 1894.) As in New Haven, Democratic (even more than Socialist Labor) strength was positively associated with the immigrant population, while Republican (and even more so, National Democratic) support was negatively associated with the same population.[63]

McKinley routed Bryan in Hartford and New Britain. Throughout 1896 Hartford's business leaders had made clear their opposition to Bryanism, free silver, and the income tax. Businessmen had called for sound money; the insurance industry had enlisted in McKinley's campaign. Bryan's nomination had been received coldly (even by Connecticut standards) by local Democrats; the Democratic state senator had run for re-election as a National Democrat. (Bryan had actually campaigned in Hartford—but offered his audience little save a denunciation of the insurance industry.) McKinley received 65.2 per cent of Hartford's vote to Bryan's 29.9, gaining 16.1 percentage points as his foe lost 18.5. Bryan narrowly carried one ward; in only two of nine others did he receive one-third of the vote.[64] Two years earlier, the Democrats had held four of eight wards and received at least 40 per cent of the vote in all eight. The hypothesis that factionalism had limited the Republicans' gain in 1894 is credible, but their victory of 1896 cannot be written off as merely a delayed triumph. Every report from Hartford during the campaign, and the magnitude of the G.O.P. victory, pointed to a city-wide rejection of the Bryanite Democracy. So did the showing of the National Democrats, whose average ward strength in Hartford—3.3 per cent—exceeded their performance in all but one of thirty-eight wards in New Haven, Waterbury, Bridgeport, and New Britain. In New Britain, the Republicans scored heavily for the second consecutive time, adding 13.7 percentage points to their earlier gain of 9.6 to poll 65.0 per cent of the vote to 31.0 per cent for the Democrats, who lost 12.8 points on top of the 10.1 they lost in 1894. Redistricting had created four Republican wards in place of two and left the Democrats with a pair; McKinley's margins in the former were far greater than Bryan's in the latter.[65]

Severe though Bryan's setback in Connecticut's major cities was, it paled by comparison with his defeat in the state's smaller towns, especially its rural ones. (See Table 11.) Indeed, it was this voting pattern that most dramatically distinguished Connecticut from New York and New Jersey in 1896. [66] Bryan carried 10 of 48 wards in Connecticut's five major cities; he won only three of its 168 towns—Naugatuck and Newtown, industrial towns, and New Fairfield, an agricultural town—in each of which the Democrats declined from their 1894 mark. In some manufacturing towns where the Democrats had been routed in 1894, Bryan suffered smaller losses or held his own. At the same time, he was mauled in other manufacturing towns where the Democrats had experienced a wide range of percentage losses two years earlier.[67] We cannot identify the precise origin of Democratic losses within these industrial towns, but in Newtown and Windham Irish Catholic voters, who had held firm for their party in 1894, may very well have broken ranks in 1896.

During the campaign, a prominent Gold Democrat had reported to Senator David Hill that anti-Bryan feeling ran high among traditional Democrats in the rural towns of Connecticut. The election returns bore him out, for it was in such towns that Bryan suffered his sharpest rebuff. To be sure, Bryan gained over 1894 in scattered rural towns. This modest recovery occurred in towns where the Republicans were traditionally strong and/or had scored heavily two years earlier. But nowhere in rural Connecticut did the Democrats come close to pre-1894 levels, and in most towns that resembled the handful where Bryan registered small gains he led his party to disastrous defeat.[68]

Republican gains in rural towns were generally striking, but to some traditional Democrats voting for McKinley was nearly as unthinkable as voting for Bryan. These Democrats, old-stock Protestants for the most part, had remained loyal to their party through cultural conflicts and political wars. Now they rejected Bryan and his cause as alien to the Democracy to which they paid allegiance. Such men voted National Democratic, thereby keeping the faith in the face of the Bryanites' seizure of the Democratic party. National Democratic percentage strength ran over twice as high in Connecticut's lesser towns as in its more populous ones. In fifteen of the former, Palmer received over 10 per cent of the vote and/or outpolled Bryan.[69]

Towns where Palmer cut deeply into Bryan's support resembled towns where he did not, socio-economically and ethno-culturally. Political factors alone accounted for differences among towns in this regard, Bryan faring worst in towns where conservatives dominated the local Democratic party. In some towns, conservatives were influential enough to secure the nomination of National Democrats to provide the sole Democratic opposition to Republican legislative candidates. These National Democratic legislative candidates ran ahead of Bryan and Palmer combined in the presidential race; their relatively strong showing attested to conservative Democratic strength in such towns.[70] (Connecticut's towns appear to have been more deeply affected by strife within the Democratic party during 1896 than were comparable units in New York and New Jersey. The important political role of towns in Connecticut—they were the districts from which members of the State House of Representatives were elected—almost certainly contributed to this local turmoil.) The anti-Bryan Democrats' control of local party machinery did not extend beyond rural towns. In the cities, Democratic organizations generally remained regular. Only in a Hartford assembly race and in one senatorial district (composed of Stamford and five other towns) did the rival Democratic factions unite behind a single candidate; in no instance were the National Democrats free to run without a Democrat in the field.

Even as many Democrats actively opposed Bryan by voting for McKinley or Palmer, some passively opposed him by abstaining from voting. Though the national campaign was bitterly contested and widely publicized, a slightly smaller proportion of Connecticut's registered voters cast ballots in 1896 than in 1892 (after a reputedly dull campaign) or in 1900. Abstainers, like Democratic bolters to McKinley or Palmer, were more common in rural towns than urban. As a consequence, towns containing the eleven most populous cities increased their share of the state's vote from 46.8 per cent in 1892 and 47.7 per cent in 1894 to 51.3 per cent in 1896. By way of contrast, in the Midwest, where the race had appeared close and decisive to the outcome of the presidential election, turnout was generally high and National Democratic strength low as the campaign mobilized supporters of Bryan and McKinley and frightened anti-Bryan Democrats into voting Republican rather than voting National Democratic or abstaining. Still, Connecticut turnout was impressive, as it had been from 1876 through 1892. With a high percentage of the potential electorate regularly voting, the Republicans were able to gain markedly between 1892 and 1896 only by winning over Democratic voters. This distinguished the realignment of the 1890s from the "critical" election of 1928 between Herbert Hoover and Al Smith, when—in New England, at least—the activation of non-voters was central to the outcome.[71]

The Republican national and state tickets also won decisive victories in New York State. No congressional seats shifted party hands, but the G.O.P. increased its margin in the State Assembly. Still, the Democrats did not go down to a defeat as total as that in Connecticut. New York's voting patterns also differed from those of Connecticut. The Republicans gained heavily over 1895 in the New York City–Brooklyn metropolitan area. Upstate shifts were not as great, the G.O.P. showing to better advantage in eastern and some central counties, the Democrats in western, northern, and other central ones. (See Table 12.) These voter movements reversed those of the previous election, both Republi-

TABLE 12 *Shifts in Percentage Strength, 1895–1896, and Percentage Strength, 1896, All Parties, Selected New York State Regions*

	REP. Shift (%)	DEM.[e] Shift (%)	NAT. DEM. (%)	POP.[e] Shift	PRO. Shift (%)	SLP Shift (%)
Metropolitan Area[a]	+11.1 (54.0)	−11.3 (41.3)	X (1.9)	−0.3 (X)	−0.3 (0.4)	−1.0 (2.5)
Eastern and Central Areas[b]	+ 4.8 (59.7)	− 4.1 (37.4)	X (1.0)	−0.3 (X)	−1.2 (1.4)	−0.1 (0.5)
Western and Northern Areas[c]	+ 0.2 (60.6)	+ 2.5 (36.5)	X (0.9)	−1.3 (X)	−2.0 (1.8)	−0.3 (0.3)
Upstate New York[d]	+ 2.2 (60.2)	− 0.4 (36.9)	X (0.9)	−0.8 (X)	−1.6 (1.7)	−0.3 (0.3)
New York State	+ 6.0 (57.6)	− 5.1 (38.7)	X (1.3)	−0.6 (X)	−1.1 (1.1)	−0.6 (1.2)

Sources: *Tribune Almanacs, 1896, 1897.*

[a] Metropolitan Area: New York, Kings, Queens, Richmond, Rockland, Suffolk, and Westchester counties.

[b] Eastern and Central Areas: Albany, Columbia, Dutchess, Essex, Fulton and Hamilton, Greene, Herkimer, Madison, Montgomery, Oneida, Onondaga, Orange, Putnam, Rensselaer, Saratoga, Schenectady, Schoharie, Sullivan, Ulster, Warren, and Washington counties.

[c] Western and Northern Areas: All other counties.

[d] Upstate New York: All counties outside of the Metropolitan Area.

[e] In 1896, the Populist vote was included in the Democratic total.

can and Democratic percentage shifts correlating negatively (−.702, −.692) with the respective earlier shifts. These correlations were stronger than the comparable pairs in Connecticut (R −.149, D +.024) and New Jersey (R −.339, D −.139). Indeed, the correlation between successive Democratic percentage shifts in Connecticut was not only weak, it was positive.

The politically decisive shift in New York State occurred in the metropolitan area, which cast over two-fifths of the state's vote in 1896. Bryan lost both New York and Kings counties; he was the first Democratic presidential candidate to lose either since 1848. McKinley polled 50.7 per cent of the vote in New York City, a gain of 11.5 percentage points over 1895; Bryan received 44.0 per cent, a loss of 12.2 points. Palmer captured 1.8 per cent and Charles H. Matchett 3.3 per cent, a loss of 1.1 points for Socialist Labor. Bryan carried twenty of thirty-six districts, but lost at least 5.6 percentage points—a defection ratio of 9.7—in every district. City-wide, the Democratic defection ratio was 21.7. The Democratic standard-bearer fared best in Tammany's strongholds in lower, lower west side, and west side Manhattan. The party loyalty of Irish Catholic voters, rather than any particular appeal of Bryan, accounted for the Democrat's escape from disaster in these areas.[72] Bryan failed to do as well in A.D.s 34 and 35, in the Upper East Side and the Bronx, where Henry Purroy had conducted a widely publicized and supposedly effective campaign in behalf of the national ticket. Regularity, even when energetic rather than nominal, was not enough to carry the day for Bryan in New York City.

In the Lower East Side, where campaign reports had it that Bryan would be badly cut by East European Jews and Germans impressed by the economic arguments of the Republicans, the Democrat lost more ground than in Irish quarters but suffered above-average losses in only two of six districts. Irish and native American holdovers from the period before the Jewish influx may have bolstered Bryan in the area, but the returns yield no evidence of unusually heavy Jewish or German defections to McKinley. The Lower East Side had been hard hit by depression; if its Jewish population responded to any particular threat in Bryan's program, that threat was economic, rather than religious. As elsewhere in the urban Northeast, many Germans and Jews voted Socialist Labor; though the party lost strength in 1896, it remained an important force in the Lower East Side.[73] Bryan suffered more serious setbacks in eight assembly districts extending northward through the Upper East Side into the Bronx, but his losses were above average in only one district. This area contained tenement districts better off than those in the Lower East Side as well as more substantial neighborhoods; its East European Jewish population was smaller than that in the Lower East Side. Its core districts, which contained a large German population, gave above-average support to Socialist Labor.[74] (Outside of these two groups of contiguous assembly districts, the Socialist Labor party reached its city-wide average only in the 35th A.D., an area of the Bronx that contained a German colony.) Over-all, the socio-economic and ethno-cultural bases of Socialist Labor strength and Republican gains were unrelated; they correlated at only +.024 (Kendall's tau).

Bryan suffered his worst defeats in assembly districts that ran up Manhattan's spine, and those that formed the Upper West Side, areas containing the highest proportion of middle and upper class, old-stock American neighborhoods in the city. His percentage declines ranged from 11.9 to 30.7 points; Democratic defection ratios ran from 23.7 to 64.6 in these districts.[75] The Republicans scored well everywhere in the city, but National Democratic strength was largely confined to the aforementioned districts, just as anti-Tammany support had been in 1895: these eight A.D.s ranked among the top ten in both columns. (City-wide, the successive votes correlated at +.585.) Boundary shifts preclude correlations with the anti-Maynard vote of 1893 and the anti-Hill vote of 1894, but these neighborhoods clearly contributed to both. The Republicans' broad appeal produced a modest correlation (+.335) between G.O.P. gains and National Democratic strength. Still, the association was positive, unlike that between Republican gains in the depression election of 1894 and that year's anti-Hill independent Democratic vote (−.199), if less strong than that between 1893 Republican shifts and the anti-Maynard vote (+.762). Thus the data make clear that in New York (as in other northeastern cities) Bryan lost most heavily in middle and upper class, old-stock American neighborhoods, but also that this shift away from the Democracy failed to polarize the electorate because other groups moved in the same direction, if not as sharply.[76]

In Kings County, McKinley received 53.6 per cent of the vote, a gain of 10.2 percentage points, and Bryan 39.7 per cent, a loss of 10.5 points. Palmer polled 1.9 per cent, and Matchett 1.8 per cent, a decline of 1.1 points. Bryan received a smaller share of the vote in Brooklyn than in New York City, carrying only eight of thirty-two wards, but his percentage loss was slightly smaller in Brooklyn. He lost 2.8 percentage points—a defection ratio of 5.0—or more in every ward; the city-wide defection ratio was 20.9. Brooklyn's voting pattern differed somewhat from New York City's in that some Democratic strongholds reported unusually heavy percentage losses. Other Irish wards remained loyal to their political faith.[77] This cleavage helped reduce the correlation between 1895 Democratic percentage strength and 1896 resistance to Republican gains to an insignificant +.078. (In New York City, this correlation was +.500.) Bryan's losses were only slightly heavier in predominantly German wards. Relatively light Republican gains in German wards that ranked highest in Socialist Labor strength accounted for a correlation between the two phenomena that was negative (−.612) and stronger than New York City's (+.024).[78] As in New York City, the Republicans and National Democrats both scored in relatively well-to-do, old-stock American neighborhoods (e.g., Brooklyn Heights and Fort Greene): Republican gains and Gold Democratic support correlated at +.767.[79] The National Democratic vote revealed the continuity of support for Cleveland Democratic crusades against Maynard, Hill, McLaughlin, and Bryan: correlations between the votes of 1893, 1894, and 1895 and the vote of 1896 were +.566, +.835, and +.645, respectively.

Democratic routs in New York and Kings counties were by no means without precedent during the period. In New York, Governor Hill had suffered a somewhat more serious setback in 1894; in Kings, the Democratic defeat of 1893 had been only slightly less decisive—and had been followed by a further decline one year later. But in no single election had the Democrats suffered defeats in both New York and Kings counties comparable to those of 1896. Further, since the Democrats' 1895 recovery had been only partial, they stood in a weaker position after 1896 than after 1894. The defeat of 1894 had reduced the share of the statewide Democratic vote cast in New York and Kings from 42.1 per cent in 1892 and 44.1 per cent in 1893 to 38.3 per cent; the defeat of 1896 comparably reduced that share from 44.2 per cent in 1895 to 38.5 per cent. The five metropolitan area counties that had swung with New York and Kings in earlier elections did so again in 1896, the Republicans scoring their heaviest gains in Richmond and Queens. The metropolitan counties also appeared at the head of the National Democratic column, just as they had in the factional campaigns of Cleveland Democrats in 1893 and 1894.[80] In both respects, the seven metropolitan counties again revealed that they formed a political sub-region of New York State. The concentration of Republican gains and Gold Democratic strength in the metropolitan area differentiated the New York vote from that of Connecticut. (In only two upstate rural towns did the National Democrats poll 5.0 per cent of the three-party presidential vote, a far cry from their showing in rural Connecticut.)

The Republican tide swept up the Hudson River to cover eastern New York and westward to form a salient into central New York as far as Onondaga County. (See Table 12.) Within this region a number of counties along the Hudson and to the north and west of Albany had been closely contested by the major parties during 1860–92. In these counties and others, the Democrats had derived considerable support from most of the towns where descendants of Dutch and Palatine German immigrants of the colonial period were still numerous. German and Irish Catholic immigrants who settled in cities along the Hudson River during the nineteenth century had provided the Democracy with fresh recruits, even as some of the party's older supporters deserted in reaction against the newcomers. The Republicans had held the upper hand in most towns whose inhabitants were of New England origin.[81] Neither the Prohibition party nor People's party had flourished in the region. During 1893–94, Democratic support had declined; in the latter year only Schoharie County voted for David B. Hill. The minor popular shifts of 1895 had not changed the situation. Now William McKinley gained percentage strength in all of the area's twenty-one counties, Bryan losing strength in all but Essex, Madison, and Schenectady counties, where he gained less than McKinley. Bryan did poll 51.0 per cent of the vote in Schoharie, the only county he carried in New York State and New England.

Within the area under analysis, Bryan received a higher percentage of the vote in the ranking cities of Albany, Syracuse, and Troy than in the outlying towns of their respective counties, but then Democratic candidates had traditionally done so. Of greater significance, Bryan fared worse relative to the Democrats' previous showing in two of the three cities than he did in those cities' hinterlands: he lost strength in Albany even as he gained in the county's towns and lost more ground in Syracuse than elsewhere in Onondaga County. His vote declined slightly less sharply in Troy than in surrounding Rensselaer.[82] In Albany the Democrats lost ground in seventeen of nineteen wards, reversing this trend only in one of their own strongholds and in one Republican district. Bryan lost strength in all of Syracuse's nineteen wards, but the Democratic state ticket escaped with a percentage loss less than one-half as great. Onondaga ranked second among New York counties in the percentage margin by which the Democrats' state ticket led their national ticket; this lead was largely built up in Syracuse.[83] Bryan showed to better advantage in Troy, which emerged as the largest city in the Northeast not to fall to McKinley. Senator Edward Murphy, Troy's Democratic boss, had wholeheartedly supported Bryan; the city's large Irish Catholic population provided a relatively loyal Democratic rank-and-file. Even then, the Democrats gained in only two of their strongholds, though in most of the other wards their losses were light. Syracuse alone among the three upstate cities shifted toward McKinley as heavily as New York City and Brooklyn did, but Bryan's showing in each revealed his weakness among urban voters.

Bryan's percentage gain in the hinterland of Albany County was exceptional, for elsewhere in the region he lost strength in rural towns. In general, towns of diverse socio-economic, ethno-cultural, and partisan characteristics experienced comparable shifts toward McKinley. In some counties, however, a number of towns where the Democrats had been traditionally strong broke more sharply away from Bryan than did towns where they had been weak. It bears emphasizing that by no means did all such towns witness unusually heavy desertions from Bryan: e.g., in Schoharie, long the Democrats' most loyal rural county, he lost only 1.0 percentage points, McKinley gaining 2.0 points. Still, the exceptions were numerous enough to suggest that rural communities that had traditionally identified with the Democratic party may have had relatively greater difficulty in accepting the new Democratic party of William Jennings Bryan than those that had never so identified. (This contrasted with the cities, where Bryan suffered least heavily, though heavily still, in strongly Democratic Irish districts.) In a few instances, Bryan actually gained percentage strength in towns that had habitually supported the Republican party. To illustrate: in Columbia County, Bryan suffered above-average losses in one old German town (Clermont) and two old Dutch towns (Kinderhook and Stuyvesant) that had been strongly Democratic, while he registered his only gain in an old German town (Germantown) that had been strongly Republican.[84] But Bryan's appeal was not strong enough in the region to move many G.O.P. bailiwicks in this way, the great majority of such towns increasing their Republican support in 1896. In some towns, Bryan gained as the Prohibitionists declined and the weaker Populists fused with the Democrats, but neither of the minor parties had many voters to lose in eastern New York. Further, though Bryan's appeal to drys had been noted during the campaign, the Republicans fared better than the Democrats in most eastern New York towns where the Prohibition party had been strong.[85]

These patterns suggest that shifts took place within a regional framework favorable to the Republicans. Though a number of counties contained large populations of New England origin, eastern New York had not contributed as much to nineteenth-century evangelical reform movements as western New York had. Prohibitionism and Populism were comparatively weak in the area, even in counties populated by the likes of those who supported one or the other in areas to the west. Eastern New York farmers had already been forced to adjust to the competition of cheap western grains and meats; they had shifted toward dairying and mixed farming. So protective of their locational advantage (i.e., proximity to urban markets) were eastern New York farmers that they opposed the demands of farmers in western and northern New York, let alone those in the West, for cheaper transportation to the metropolitan area. Thus social and economic factors worked against Bryan in this area and contributed to a broad-based shift toward McKinley.[86]

Elsewhere in New York State, Bryan actually gained percentage strength over the Democrats' 1895 showing. (See Table 12.) In doing so, he picked up points in twenty-seven counties, seventeen of which recorded Republican declines. In one county Bryan gained while Republican strength did not fluctuate. Of the nine other counties, McKinley gained more than Bryan in one, as much as Bryan in another, and less than Bryan in seven. Finally, McKinley gained and Bryan lost ground in four counties. Bryan's showing in western, parts of central, and northern New York must be placed in perspective if it is to be understood. Bryan did improve the Democrats' position over 1895 in a large area, in sharp contrast to his over-all impact on Democratic fortunes in Connecticut, New York, and New Jersey. But McKinley gained fractionally over the Republicans' 1895 mark in the same area. Percentage losses suffered by the Prohibition, People's, and Socialist Labor parties made possible the advances of both major parties. Though Republican strength did ebb in seventeen counties, such losses were generally small. Even in his area of greatest gains, Bryan slightly trailed the Democratic state ticket in most counties.

As noted earlier, the Prohibition party had flourished in upstate rural areas, particularly the Burned-Over District, during the 1880s; as late as 1892 it received over 5.0 per cent of the vote in sixteen counties. Agrarian discontent had given birth to the People's party, which first contested for office in New York in 1892. The Prohibitionists and Populists recruited from among the same groups, but the former generated wider and greater support in upstate New York. Populist strength was largely confined to western counties that lay south of the Erie Canal, an agricultural region whose location and dependence on railroad transportation placed it at a disadvantage in competition with the Midwest, areas adjacent to the state canal system, and eastern New York. The Populists received over 5.0 per cent of the vote and/or outpolled the Prohibitionists in only three counties in 1892. The fortunes of the two minor parties fluctuated during 1893–95. Along with the Republicans, they gained at the expense of the Democrats in 1893. Along with the Democrats, they lost ground to the Republicans in 1894, mustering less support than they had in 1892. In 1895, the Prohibitionists regained some of their lost strength and the Populists continued to decline statewide while gaining in some western counties.[87] Meanwhile, the Republicans gained and the Democrats lost strength. Thus the G.O.P., long dominant in western and central New York, alone benefited from voter shifts during 1893–95. But though Prohibition and Populist strength had declined, both parties remained relatively stronger in the Burned-Over District than elsewhere in the state. This difference assumed considerable significance in 1896.

William Jennings Bryan increased Democratic percentage strength in the Burned-Over District more by gaining Populist and Prohibitionist voters than by capturing Republican voters. The two minor parties' percentage losses exceeded those of the Republicans in the counties ranking highest in Democratic percentage gains—in one of which McKinley actually gained percentage points.[88] Historically, the largely evangelical Protestant electorate of the Burned-Over District—descended from Methodist, Baptist, and Congregational migrants from New England and eastern New York and, in some towns, from Dutch, Swedish, and Scottish immigrants—had been strongly hostile to the Democrats. Now Bryan's crusade increased Democratic support among these very groups. Never had a Democrat sought their votes with arguments and rhetoric such as Bryan's. (Opponents' charges that Bryan was not an authentic Democrat could only have increased his appeal among voters suspicious of Democrats.)

Analysis of town-level returns sheds light on the dynamics of voting shifts within the area. Bryan was most successful in increasing Democratic percentage strength in towns where the People's party had commanded considerable support, rank-and-file Populists overwhelmingly following their leaders into fusion with the Bryanite Democracy.[89] On the other hand, the voting behavior of Prohibitionists suggested that they had been severely cross-pressured by the political campaign. Many moved into the Democratic camp, but some swung into the Republican, and still others remained loyal to the Prohibition party, which retained its identity and nearly one-half of its 1895 percentage strength. Over-all, the Democrats fared better in ranking Prohibition towns in western New York than in those in eastern New York. Both major parties gained in some towns as Prohibitionist and Populist strength declined.[90] The Democrats advanced to varying degrees at Republican expense in some towns. In others, the Republicans gained as the Democrats (and sometimes other parties) declined.[91] There was no apparent relationship between the relative economic position of towns and the direction and intensity of voting shifts therein. But there was a relationship between the prior partisan balance within towns and these shifts. Populists responded strongly to Bryan's appeal; many Prohibitionists held firm, but most of those who broke ranks voted for Bryan; the overwhelming majority of Republicans voted for McKinley.[92]

Bryan's success in western and central New York was a limited one: Democratic gains, achieved more at the expense of minor parties than of the G.O.P., were no match for the Republican gains, achieved directly at the expense of the Democrats, in eastern and southeastern New York. Democratic percentage gains fell far short of disrupting Republican hegemony in the very counties where those gains were registered. The mean share of the vote received by Bryan in such counties was 35.7 per cent. In only five counties did Bryan lift the Democracy to a percentage higher than that it received in 1892—and in four of these the net Republican percentage gain, 1892–96, was greater.[93] In no county did Bryan's percentage strength (increased as it was by Populist recruits) exceed the combined Democratic and Populist percentages of 1892. Further, except in a limited number of counties, Bryan's percentage gains were small; they were accompanied by smaller Republican losses or (in a few cases) gains. In eleven counties, Bryan failed to recoup 1895 Democratic losses, let alone those of 1893 and/or 1894. This was the case even in western and central areas, but more so in northern New York. This region, populated largely by New Englanders, had been strongly Republican since the realignment of the 1850s. Despite the evangelism of its population and the transportation and other economic difficulties faced by farmers and lumbermen, neither the Prohibition nor People's party had won support comparable to that each received in the Burned-Over District. Thus there were few Prohibitionists and still fewer Populists to increase the magnitude of the generally minor shifts between the Republicans and Democrats in these counties.[94]

Bryan did not gain in all counties within the areas where he was strongest as McKinley did within his, the Democrat's failure in these counties further revealing the limitations of his upswing in parts of New York. As elsewhere in the state and Northeast, Bryan ran into difficulty in urban areas. Thus in traditionally Republican Broome and Jefferson counties, he gained slightly over 1895 in the rural towns, but lost sufficient support in the cities of Binghamton and Watertown to increase Republican margins in the presidental race in both counties. (The Democratic state ticket ran far enough ahead of Bryan in Jefferson County to gain percentage points over 1895.) In Chemung, a county that had leaned toward the Republicans, the Democrats lost ground in rural towns, but lost even more in the city of Elmira.[95] Bryan actually gained percentage strength in Erie and Monroe counties, but fared better in the outlying towns than in Buffalo and Rochester. Ticket-splitting at Bryan's expense was marked in Erie and Monroe, which ranked first and sixth among New York counties in the percentage margin by which the Democratic national ticket trailed the state ticket. (The success of the state ticket in Buffalo was particularly striking.) The Gold Democrats ran well in Buffalo, especially in old-stock American, upper class wards.[96] At the same time, Buffalo and Rochester, western New York's largest cities, did not move away from the Democrats as sharply as Syracuse, Albany, and Troy, to say nothing of New York City and Brooklyn. Sectional differences in the state's vote were discernible in urban as well as rural units.

Democratic reversals in western and central New York were by no means confined to cities. Shifts in rural towns contributed to Bryan's setback in Chemung County; they accounted for McKinley's gain (3.5 percentage points) and Bryan's loss (2.9 points) in Seneca. Alone of counties in the Burned-Over District, Seneca had voted Democratic in presidential elections from 1876 through 1892, but a narrowing Democratic margin there gave way to a Republican majority in 1894–95. Now that majority was strengthened.[97] As already noted, even in those counties where Bryan showed to best advantage, the Republicans gained and/or the Democrats lost percentage strength in a number of rural towns that economically and culturally resembled those contributing to the Bryanite upswing. In other counties, the weakness of the People's party, the three-way split of the Prohibitionist vote, and an undercurrent of Democratic defections to the G.O.P. reduced both net county-level Democratic percentage gains and Republican losses—or made possible Republican gains.

Rural towns that leaned toward the Democracy had been few and far between in western, central, and northern New York before the depression. Republican strength increased and Democratic strength decreased in most, though by no means all, of these towns during 1893–95, a number moving into the G.O.P. column. (At no time were more than a handful of the rural towns strongly Democratic; only five gave the Democrats over 60 per cent of their vote in 1892 and only three did so in 1895. By way of contrast, the number of counties giving the Republicans over 60 per cent of their vote rose from two in 1892 to fifteen three years later.) Now Democratic towns offered varied responses to the Bryan-McKinley campaign. The Democrats fared best in heavily Catholic towns, where deep party loyalty worked to their advantage. In High Market (Lewis County), an Irish town where their ranks had held firm during 1893–95, they gained markedly, scoring a victory more decisive than that of 1892. There Bryan trailed the state ticket by only one vote. In Clinton, which French Canadian and Irish voters had made the ranking Democratic town in Clinton County, the Democrats registered a small gain, Bryan actually running two votes ahead of the state ticket.

In Cape Vincent, a town containing Catholics of various nationalities which was the highest ranking Democratic unit in Jefferson County, the Democrats held their own while the Republicans declined fractionally. Indeed, in E.D. 3, their stronghold, the Democrats gained strength. Still, in neither Clinton nor Cape Vincent did the Democrats approach their pre-depression vote.[98]

Returns from three towns in Lewis County revealed the range of voting behavior in German towns that had been Democratic in 1892. Lewis, a town where the Democrats had retained a commanding lead despite depression setbacks, recorded an above-average Democratic percentage increase. In Croghan and New Bremen, where the Republicans had captured narrow leads during 1893–95, Democratic strength increased and decreased slightly, respectively. The Democratic state ticket surpassed the party's 1892 showing in the town of Lewis. Though Bryan trailed the state ticket in all three towns, he matched Cleveland's 1892 showing in Lewis. Lewis was also unique in that many anti-Bryan Democrats simply abstained from voting in the presidential election, for though Bryan trailed his state ticket by fifty-nine votes, McKinley led his by only one vote and Palmer received no votes. The Democrats gained markedly in Wayland (Steuben County), where they had surrendered their lead to the G.O.P. only the previous year, particularly in E.D. 2, the more heavily German of the town's two districts. Bryan fell behind the state ticket, but he too reclaimed Wayland from the Republicans. By way of contrast, in Wheatfield—a Niagara County town whose Germans had voted Whig during the 1840s, Democratic from the 1860s through 1892, and Republican during 1893–95—the Republican state ticket gained 3.7 percentage points and the Democratic state ticket lost 0.4 points. McKinley's vote was unusually larger (12.2 per cent) and Bryan's unusually smaller (11.8 per cent) than that of the respective gubernatorial candidates.[99] Such ticket-splitting at Bryan's expense revealed his weakness in German towns that had voted Democratic at least through 1892. Still, considering the nearly unanimous opposition of articulate German Americans to Bryan and free silver, and the likely concern of German Americans (who viewed the Democratic party as the defender of their "personal liberty") over the support given Bryan by Prohibitionists and Populists, Bryan lost less support in such towns than might have been expected and the Democratic state ticket fared even better. The pattern of the vote suggests that in New York, at least, the state Republican party's identification with temperance, which remained strong through the political campaign of 1895 and the enactment of the Raines Excise Law of 1896, reduced G.O.P. gains among German Democrats.

Democratic support declined in most of the small number of old-stock American towns where the party had held the advantage through 1895. A few of these towns were exceptional in that they had been settled by New Englanders, most of whose towns were Republican; others had received old German and old Dutch migrants from Pennsylvania and New Jersey, and those groups leaned toward the Democrats. (This northward flow from Pennsylvania and New Jersey contributed to the Democratic complexion of Seneca County and to the reduction of the Republican coloration of other counties.) Towns that were narrowly Democratic and/or in which Democratic strength had sagged during 1893–95 generally experienced small Republican gains, though in a few such localities the Democrats registered minor gains. The Republicans scored in a few towns that were more strongly Democratic and/or in which the Democrats had gained during 1893–95.[100] Thus Bryan again demonstrated his weakness in old-stock American Democratic towns. Still, his losses were not as great as in eastern New York, and Democratic towns were too few in number in western and northern New York to influence the election markedly one way or the other. Bryan succeeded in winning over sufficient Populists, Prohibitionists, and Republicans in Republican towns to increase Democratic percentage strength. But he failed both to win over enough Republicans and to retain the support of enough Democrats, particularly in the cities, to register decisive Democratic gains and to reduce Republican percentages.

Limited shifts favorable to the Democrats in upstate areas that cast 33.7 per cent of New York's vote reduced, but could not overcome, the impact of stronger shifts favorable to the Republicans in upstate areas that cast 24.2 per cent of the state's vote. (See Table 12.) In this situation, the Republicans' strong showing in the New York City–Brooklyn metropolitan area, which accounted for 42.1 per cent of New York's vote, made possible their decisive victory in the Empire State. The political consequences of these shifts were clear. The continued decline of Democratic voting strength in eastern New York further weakened the position of Democratic politicians (e.g., David B. Hill) whose base lay in this upstate area. Meanwhile, local Democrats as well as Bryan fell far short of victory in western New York. No politicians representing rural evangelicals were to join the leadership of the state Democratic party. Instead, Tammany Democrats, who survived Bryan's defeat in New York City, were to exercise a preponderant influence in the post-1896 state party.

New Jersey fell between Connecticut and New York insofar as the size of the Republicans' percentage gain and percentage margin in the presidential election was concerned. New Jersey's governorship was not at stake in 1896, but the G.O.P. maintained its dominance in the state's congressional delegation and in the state senate, while it tightened its grip on the state assembly. McKinley scored impressively in New Jersey's major cities; these urban gains fell within a narrower range than they did in Connecticut and New York State. At the same time, percentage shifts in counties containing the state's most populous cities were paralleled, if not matched, by shifts in other counties. (See Table 13.) The Republicans registered above-average gains in all but one of the highly urbanized counties in the northeastern quarter of the state.[101] Hudson County, which had voted Democratic in 1895 after going Republican in 1893–94, fell to the G.O.P. for the first

TABLE 13 *Shifts in Percentage Strength, 1895–1896, All Parties, Six Urban New Jersey Counties and Other Areas of the State*

	REP.	DEM.	NAT. DEM.	POP.	PRO.	SLP
Six Counties[a]	+8.8	−9.3	+1.6	−0.3	−0.5	−0.4
Rest of State	+5.5	−5.4	+1.9	−1.0	−0.8	−0.2
New Jersey	+7.4	−7.6	+1.7	−0.6	−0.6	−0.2

Sources: *Manuals of the Legislature of New Jersey, 1896, 1897.*
[a]Camden, Essex, Hudson, Mercer, Passaic, and Union counties.

time in any presidential election since 1848, Bryan losing all the ground regained by his party the previous year and more. Jersey City shifted decisively into the Republican column. Bryan gained slightly in one Irish-German ward and suffered below-average, but marked, losses in two Irish wards; these were the only districts he carried. (McGill had won eight of twelve wards in 1895.) Bryan suffered particularly heavy losses in Wards 7 and 12, German districts, the latter of which had voted Democratic in 1895, and Ward 8, a native-born district that was the city's ranking Republican ward in 1895 and 1896.[102] The Hudson County Democratic organization had ignored Bryan, confining its efforts to local contests. But the magnitude of Bryan's defeat and the at-large system of electing state assemblymen combined to strike the organization a painful blow—the loss of all eleven Hudson County assembly seats to the Republicans. (Only two seats changed hands elsewhere in the state.)

In Essex County, which had voted Republican during 1893–95 after having supported Grover Cleveland in 1892, McKinley led the hapless Bryan by better than two to one; percentage shifts were comparable to those in Hudson County. McKinley gained even more ground in Newark than in Jersey City, capturing three wards from the Democrats to carry fourteen of fifteen in the city. Ward 12, the only district won by Bryan, had been referred to as a "hotbed of Democracy" during the campaign, but the election painfully revealed the limitations of Democratic strength therein. The ward ranked fourth in Democratic percentage point loss, though much better—twelfth—in Democratic defection ratio. Within the ward, Bryan polled a larger share of the vote and lost fewer percentage points in Irish districts than in German districts.[103] This pattern was repeated on the ward level elsewhere in Newark, but Bryan clearly suffered intolerable losses in every ward, Irish ones included. In no ward did Bryan escape with a loss of less than 8.7 percentage points—a defection ratio of 15.4. As elsewhere, McKinley fared best and Bryan worst in well-to-do, old-stock American districts, the former capturing 83.5 and 85.5 per cent of the two-party vote and the latter suffering defection ratios of 40.9 and 37.5 in Wards 8 and 9.

The pattern of percentage shifts in the city of Elizabeth

(Union County) resembled those in Jersey City and Newark, Bryan suffering heavier losses in German wards than in Irish, and most heavily in old-stock American districts, in two of which (Wards 10, 11) he lost some two-fifths of 1895 Democratic percentage strength and polled less than one-fifth of the vote. Two observations are in order at this point. First, the rejection of Bryan by "the better element" of Democrats in New Jersey (and elsewhere) was not confined to the middle class and silk-stocking wards of cities; it could be observed in the voting behavior of outlying residential communities that housed businessmen and professionals who worked in cities. Essex and Bergen counties provided illustrations of this phenomenon.[104] Second, the fact that Democratic percentage losses were negatively correlated with the percentage of Irishmen in the male populations of wards in Jersey City, Newark, and Elizabeth (and other New Jersey cities) did not mean that Bryan gained or even held his own in Irish wards, only that his not inconsiderable losses therein were lighter than losses in German and old-stock American wards.[105]

The Republicans won handily in other New Jersey cities. McKinley crushed Bryan in Trenton, gaining 11.5 percentage points and polling 68.1 per cent of the two-party vote in the state capital. His gain of 6.2 percentage points in Camden was less impressive, but he did receive a remarkable 74.2 per cent of the two-party vote there. The most salient feature of the Republican vote in Camden's nine wards was its narrow range—from 71.1 to 78.4 per cent. None of Camden's wards contained many Irish Catholics or other strongly Democratic groups. Democratic strength had begun to decline in Camden in 1893; by 1896 the cultural homogeneity of the city was fully reflected in the uniformity of its ward-level Republican majorities. McKinley also registered below-average gains in two Passaic County cities, Paterson and Passaic, but picked up strength in every ward of both cities as both Democratic and Socialist Labor support declined.[106]

Taken together, New Jersey's rural counties did not experience Republican percentage gains and Democratic percentage losses comparable to those in the state's urban counties. Percentage shifts in the agricultural towns and small cities of most such counties were generally small; the counties in which they occurred resumed the movement into the Republican column that had been interrupted in 1895. Analysis of returns from towns in counties that experienced shifts diverging from this pattern sheds light on differences between voting patterns in New York and New Jersey as well as on the election in New Jersey itself. In southern New Jersey, where the anti-racetrack revolt and its aftermath had their greatest influence on the elections of 1893–95, Bryan suffered a sharp defeat, losing support in every town and ward. McKinley, gaining strength in nearly every political unit, more than wiped out the modest Democratic recovery of 1895 in Atlantic County, and exceeded the slight Republican gain of the previous year in Cape May County.[107] Atlantic County's Germans and evangelical Protestants had shifted together toward the Democrats in 1893; now they shifted together toward the Republicans. Egg Harbor City, a German community, reacted sharply to the campaign of 1896; McKinley received 64.1 per cent of the vote there, a gain of 17.1 points, to Bryan's 31.7 per cent, a loss of 20.6 points; Palmer polled 3.6 per cent, exceeding his countywide average of 1.6 per cent. During the campaign an anti-Bryan Democratic newspaper had suggested that if McKinley lost ground anywhere in Atlantic County, it would be in Hammonton, where the "people are prone to take up with new and 'advanced' notions." The newspaper may have had in mind the fact that the Prohibitionists had outpolled the Republicans in Hammonton in 1893 and that the Prohibitionists and Populists together had polled over one-fifth of the vote there in 1894. Whatever the case, McKinley gained 6.1 percentage points and Bryan lost 3.6 in below-average percentage shifts in Hammonton. The Republicans' gain was also limited in Buena Vista, another dry town, but McKinley routed Bryan in Weymouth, where the Democrats had been victorious during 1892–95 and the Prohibitionists had equaled the Republicans' vote in 1893.[108] The Democratic vote fell from 63.0 to 29.7 per cent in Weymouth; the Republican vote rose from 31.5 to 58.6 per cent; and the Prohibition vote climbed from 5.5 to 9.0 per cent. One dry town went its own way in 1896, Joshua Levering of the Prohibition party actually carrying Brigantine Borough with 47.2 per cent of the vote while McKinley received 38.9 per cent and Bryan 13.9 per cent. The Prohibitionists gained 28.0 percentage points as the Republicans and Democrats lost 14.9 and 13.0 points, respectively. Galloway (District 2) and Somers Point, which had been strongly Democratic during 1892–95, were the only Atlantic County towns carried by Bryan, but in both Democratic support fell off sharply.[109]

To the south of Atlantic, Cape May County's major Methodist, dry communities—Ocean City, Sea Isle City, and West Cape May—contributed more than their share to McKinley's decisive victory. (Still, these percentage shifts were not as great as those of 1893.) Sea Isle City alone of the three had voted Democratic in 1892 and 1895; the Democratic defeat there was not as decisive as that of 1893. In the other two towns, the Bryan-McKinley election marked the low point of Democratic fortunes during the period. Two other units in which McKinley scored major gains—Middle (District 1) and Upper—were traditionally Republican; a third, South Cape May, which was also Republican, had been created in 1894. Bryan's weakness among old-stock American voters was further revealed in Dennis, where he gained marginally in Precinct 1, which contained an East European Jewish settlement, while losing ground in Precinct 2, whose population was native American.[110] Newspapers had reported agrarian unrest in Burlington County and support for the National Silver party, whose ticket Bryan headed in New Jersey, in the towns of Pemberton, Palmyra, and Cinnaminson. Pemberton and one other Burlington town did register Democratic percentage gains, but Cinnaminson and Palmyra were among the Republican and Democratic units that shifted toward the G.O.P.[111] Among the Democratic towns doing so was Riverside, a German community. The regularity with which German districts moved toward McKinley suggested that New Jersey Republicans had succeeded in reducing the saliency of cultural issues that had hurt the G.O.P. among Germans in that state before 1893, issues that continued to do so in New York in 1896. Certainly campaign predictions regarding the negative response of Germans to Bryan's candidacy and free silver were confirmed in New Jersey on election day.[112]

Democratic losses were not confined to Atlantic, Cape May, and Burlington counties. They occurred in most southern New Jersey towns where the Republican party had been traditionally dominant and the Prohibition party strong. Like western New York, where the same could be said of the Republican and Prohibition parties, the area was largely populated by old-stock evangelical Protestants, particularly Methodists. But southern New Jersey had not necessarily shared the historical experiences of western New York. Though Republicanism, prohibitionism, and anti-Catholicism had influenced both regions, Populism had never gained widespread support in southern New Jersey. Southern New Jersey agriculture faced problems, but it was oriented toward the cultivation of vegetables and fruits for nearby urban markets—e.g., Philadelphia, Camden, and other cities along the Delaware River.[113] It did not face the locational and transportation problems of western and northern New York agriculture. Bryan's weakness in southern New Jersey involved more than a lack of Populists to recruit to his cause. As in eastern New York and rural Connecticut, he failed both to attract Republicans and Prohibitionists and to retain the support of Democrats, who were already in the minority.

Bryan did gain percentage strength in three contiguous counties—Hunterdon, Sussex, and Warren—setting them apart from New Jersey's eighteen other counties. A number of observers had suggested that the Bryanite Democracy stood its best chance for success in the largely rural northwestern corner of the state. Economically, the region appeared the most likely in New Jersey to respond favorably to Bryan's appeal. Though Hunterdon grew peaches in large quantity, the three counties remained heavy producers of grains. Farmers were disadvantageously located relative to the growing urban markets in the Philadelphia–Camden and New York City–Brooklyn–northeastern New Jersey areas. At the same time, the local iron industry languished in the face of competition from larger and better located works. All three counties had lost population during the 1880s; Hunterdon continued to decline during the 1890s. Politically, the three counties presented an unusual background. All had voted Democratic in every presidential election from 1836 through 1892; Hunterdon had also done so during 1893–95, while Warren had gone Republican in 1894 and Sussex had voted Republican in all three years. At the same time, the Prohibitionists had received considerable support in Hunterdon and Warren counties, including towns where the Democrats were dominant. Populist strength had been limited in the three counties—only in Hunterdon had it ever reached 1.0 per cent. Now Bryan gained all of 2.8 percentage points in Warren, 1.0 in Hunterdon, and 0.2 in Sussex. Not only was the Democratic recovery weak, but McKinley gained 0.9, 1.9, and 0.7 points in the respective counties. (The mean percentage point shifts in these three counties were Democratic, +1.3; Republican, +1.2. In New York counties where Bryan gained strength the shifts were +3.9 and −0.5, respectively.) Thus McKinley outgained Bryan in Hunterdon and Sussex counties, and he carried the latter to boot.[114]

The near standoffs in Hunterdon, Sussex, and Warren counties were reflected on the town level, where shifts in opposite directions took place in units of all descriptions in each county. Patterns were less clear than in counties that shifted sharply, but even though exceptions to the following generalizations should not be ignored, Bryan did gain more often than not in towns that had leaned toward the Democratic party before 1896 and McKinley did likewise in towns that had supported the Republican party. Among the towns where Bryan picked up support were four of six old Dutch, Democratic banner towns. The Democrats gained slightly more often than the Republicans in Democratic and Republican towns where the Prohibition party had polled 5.0 per cent or more of the vote in 1895.[115] Bryan lost ground in four Sussex County towns where the local iron industry was concentrated; he clearly gained in the fifth. The only two cities in the area shifted in opposite directions in 1896, Phillipsburg increasing its Democratic orientation and Lambertville moving into the Republican column. In each of these small cities Bryan fared best in the ward ranking highest in Irish population.[116] Percentage shifts in the three New Jersey counties hardly constituted a Democratic upswing, but they did represent Bryan's best showing in any Democratic area in the three states under study.

The presidential election of 1896 marked the nadir of Democratic fortunes during the 1890s in Connecticut, New York, and New Jersey—indeed, in the Northeast as a whole. Bryan Democrats could salvage only one small consolation from their defeat in the Northeast: unlike the Cleveland Democrats, they did not need the region. They had written off the Northeast in planning the campaign of 1896; it would not figure in their plans to retain control of the national Democratic party. All the same, Bryanites could not escape the fact that their hero had suffered a resounding defeat in the Northeast, even by the standards of earlier Democratic setbacks during the depression of 1893.

Within the cities of Connecticut, New York, and New Jersey, wherein resided a majority of the electorate and an even larger share of those groups upon which pre-1893 Democratic successes had been based, Bryan lost ground among all elements. The intensity of this shift of urban voters varied among and within the three states, but its direction and strength were clear. Bryan's decline in silk-stocking and middle class districts, where old-stock Democrats were numerous, was to be expected, for contemporary accounts unanimously agreed that "respectable" northeasterners had been deeply frightened and angered by the Bryan Democratic-Populist campaign. The ballots cast for Palmer and lesser National Democratic candidates, as well as the sharp increase in the Republican vote, revealed such districts to be strongholds of the Democracy of Grover Cleveland. At the same time, urban election returns did not reveal a pitting of the masses against the classes. Bryan failed to create a working class constituency; indeed, he lost strength in working class districts, albeit less than in upper class ones. Within working class areas, Bryan generally lost less support and polled higher percentages in Irish Catholic districts than in German, East European Jewish, Scandinavian, and other districts, but this reflected the loyalty of Irish Catholics to the Democratic party that had nominated Bryan, not Bryan's personal appeal to Irish Catholics. (In 1894, state and local Democratic leaders had sought to reinforce the party loyalty of Irish Catholic voters by denouncing Republican involvement with anti-Catholic groups. In 1896, the disorganization of Democratic parties in the Northeast, the decline of organized anti-Catholicism, and the rival national parties' emphasis on economic issues rendered impossible such a reinforcing campaign.) Bryan never appeared to understand ethnic and religious divisions within the electorate, but he failed in the urban Northeast not so much because he did not address himself to these realities as because northeastern workers regardless of background, rejected the economic arguments he did advance—just as they had those of the Cleveland Democrats earlier in the depression. Instead, these workers favored Republican arguments that a G.O.P. victory would restore prosperity by contributing to business confidence, maintaining the value of the currency, and safeguarding businessmen, laborers, and farmers alike through the protective tariff.

If Bryan did not overcome defections among the urban rich by gaining among the urban poor, neither did he compensate for his urban losses by gaining among rural voters. The Democracy fared worst in Connecticut's rural towns, where alone among the three states its losses exceeded those in the cities, but the party's over-all position deteriorated in rural New York and New Jersey as well. At the same time, Bryan did gain modest strength across a broad area of western and northern New York. Nothing of this sort occurred in the urban Northeast. Bryan did not build on the traditional Democratic rural base. Rather he gained the support of Populists and won over some Prohibitionists and Republicans in areas traditionally hostile to the Democracy. Bryan fared best in areas where the People's party had been relatively strong, not only because they contained large numbers of Populists but also because their political culture was such that he gained Prohibition and Republican votes therein. The combination of economic and cultural factors that contributed to limited Democratic gains in western and northern New York appear to have been confined to those areas, for Bryan lost strength in all other rural areas where New Englanders and other old-stock evangelicals predominated and where Republicanism and (sometimes) prohibitionism, though not Populism, had flourished—i.e., Connecticut, eastern New York, and southern New Jersey.[117] At the same time, Bryan's weakness among Democrats in the rural Northeast was manifest in election returns from what few Democratic towns there were in rural Connecticut and New

York. Only in three counties in the economically stagnant northwestern corner of New Jersey was Bryan able to hold his own in a rural area that had traditionally supported the Democrats. Of such stuff agrarian crusades were hardly made.

During the campaign of 1896, William McKinley and other Republicans increased their chances of gaining an audience for their economic arguments among Democrats by avoiding involvement in the cultural conflicts that had led many (e.g., Catholics and German Lutherans) to become and remain Democrats. Further, Democratic newspapers, politicians, and public figures who bolted their national party following its nomination of Bryan carried the attack on Bryan to Democratic audiences that might otherwise have avoided exposure to Republican campaign arguments. Republicans and, more particularly, dissident Democrats, hammered at the Bryanites as Populists in disguise, as usurpers of the proud Democratic name. Republicans portrayed Bryanism as a revival of southern sectionalism. Southerners had threatened the North before the Civil War; now they menaced both the economy and the social order of the Northeast by advocating free silver and a low tariff and by denouncing in the name of state's rights federal intervention in class conflicts such as that which erupted at Pullman, Illinois, in 1894. In the years before 1893, the Republican party had suffered from its identification with governmental intervention on behalf of temperance, Sabbatarianism, and the Negro. The depression and social unrest of 1893–96 created a political climate in which the Republican party could profit from its self-proclaimed willingness to employ the powers of government to assure prosperity and social order. By cloaking themselves in the mantle of nationalism the Republicans hoped to win over Democrats irrespective of their socioeconomic or ethno-cultural background; by attacking Bryanites as Populists, usurpers, and southerners, the Republicans and anti-Bryan Democrats hoped to loosen the traditional bonds between Democratic voters and their party's nominees. Election returns from Connecticut, New York, and New Jersey attested to the potency of this strategy—and to the inability of the Bryanites to piece together a campaign strategy and organization to counter the Republicans: large numbers of Democrats of diverse backgrounds voted straight Republican tickets, while others cast National Democratic ballots, abstained, or split their tickets by voting Republican in the presidential contest and Democratic or National Democratic in lesser races. These losses heavily outweighed Democratic gains among Populists, Prohibitionists, and Republicans. Before setting out for New York City for the first time during the campaign, William Jennings Bryan had referred to the Northeast as "the enemy's country." Election day, 1896, confirmed that Bryan knew whereof he spoke.

VII

Conclusions

TAKEN as a period, the years from 1893 through 1896 produced major changes in the fortunes of the Democratic and Republican parties in Connecticut, New York, and New Jersey, to say nothing of the Northeast and the nation as a whole. In 1892, the Democracy had carried all three states in the presidential election, captured the governorship of Connecticut and retained that of New Jersey, and maintained its dominant position in the legislatures of New York and New Jersey. (It had again won the governorship of New York the previous year.) Between 1893 and 1895, the Democratic party lost the governorships of all three states and was reduced to a helpless minority position in the legislature of each. Finally, in the presidential election of 1896, the Democracy suffered defeats more complete than any it had experienced during the previous three years in the three northeastern states. Voting shifts within the electorate were impressive in magnitude: between 1892 and 1896, the Democratic party lost between 10.3 and 17.6 percentage points—a defection ratio of from 21.0 to 35.1—in Connecticut, New York, and New Jersey. The major beneficiary of this decline was the Republican party. Between 1892 and 1896, the People's and Prohibition parties lost strength; the Socialist Labor party gained support. The minor parties' vote was larger in 1896 than in 1892 in Connecticut and New Jersey only because of the support received by the National Democratic party in the later year. (See Table 14.)

TABLE 14 *Republican, Democratic, and Other Parties' Percentages, Presidential Elections of 1892 and 1896, Percentage Shifts, 1892–1896, and Democratic Defection Ratio, 1892–1896, Connecticut, New York, and New Jersey*

	CONNECTICUT			NEW YORK			NEW JERSEY		
	REP.	DEM.	OTHER	REP.	DEM.	OTHER	REP.	DEM.	OTHER
1892 %	46.8	50.1	3.1	45.6	49.0	5.4	46.2	50.7	3.1
1896 %	63.2	32.5	4.2	57.6	38.7	3.6	59.7	36.0	4.3
±, 1892–1896	+16.4	−17.6	+1.1	+12.0	−10.3	−1.8	+13.5	−14.7	+1.2
Dem. defection ratio, 1892–1896		35.1			21.0			29.0	

Source: Svend Petersen, *A Statistical History of the American Presidential Elections* (New York: Frederick Ungar, 1963), 61–65.

The voting shifts of 1893–96 testified to the political impact of the depression of 1893 and to the skill with which the Republican party exploited the economic issues created by that depression. Still, examination of election returns indicates that the politics of depression did not obliterate the cultural lines that had divided the major parties before 1893. Though the Republicans gained among all segments of the electorate in the midterm elections of 1894, they were more successful with groups that already leaned toward their party than with those that did not. Among the former, depression issues reinforced the cultural appeal of the G.O.P.; among the latter, depression issues cut one way, the cultural appeal of the Democracy the other. Though the national leadership of the Democratic party proclaimed the virtue of tariff reduction during 1894, grass-roots Democratic politicians felt that they could not afford the luxury of going to the electorate on this economic issue. Rather they sought to reinforce the cultural bonds that linked many groups—Irish Catholics and German Lutherans, in particular—to the Democratic party, by identifying the Republican party with anti-Catholicism and prohibitionism. For their part, Republican politicians parried Democratic thrusts on cultural issues and maintained relentless pressure on depression issues. The Republicans also sought to win over Democrats of all backgrounds during the presidential campaign of 1896 by depicting their own party as the party of prosperity and portraying the Bryanite Democracy as a threat to the economy and social order, all the while avoiding involvement in cultural conflicts that would increase Democratic cohesion. In the urban Northeast, Irish Catholics again proved to be the group most loyal to the Democratic party, but so strong did the regional anti-Bryan tide flow that even among the Irish voters Democratic losses were high.

Voting patterns of 1896 differed from those of 1894 in two important respects. First, middle and upper class Democrats who had not abandoned the Democracy of Grover Cleveland in large numbers in the midterm election deserted the Democracy of William Jennings Bryan wholesale in the presidential election. The capture of the national Democratic party by a coalition of southerners and westerners, rather than the economic depression *per se,* led them to defect. Second, Bryan actually gained percentage strength in western and northern New York, but he did so by picking up support among groups that normally voted Populist, Prohibitionist, and Republican, not by raising his level of support among groups that already leaned toward the Democratic party. This pattern was repeated nowhere else in Connecticut, New York, or New Jersey; and for the second time during the depression of the 1890s, voters in all three states gave increased support to the Republican party.

In both the midterm campaign of 1894 and the presidential campaign of 1896, Republican leaders sought to increase their party's chances of winning over Democrats discontented with hard times and/or their own party by dissociating the G.O.P. from the cultural conflicts that had defined politics before the depression. Though they stood to gain from this strategy, Republican leaders such as William McKinley were not simply calculating in terms of short-term advantages. They had long sought to broaden their party's (and their own) popular base; the depression provided them with a rich opportunity to create a Republican majority by cutting across cultural lines with appeals relating to economic issues.

At the same time, a close examination of politics at the state and local levels reveals the persistence of cultural conflict during the depression. In New York State Republican leaders were willing, during an election year, to tolerate constitutional sanction for continued public spending in support of sectarian charitable institutions, but under no circumstances would their party permit the continuation of such assistance to parochial educational institutions. Further, the G.O.P. moved to protect the public schools of New York City from Catholic-Tammany influences by centralizing the administration of the city's school system. (The New York City Fusion administration that pressed for this safeguard had won office after a campaign marked by anti-Catholic agitation, as had a Citizens' administration in New Britain earlier in 1894.) A constitutional amendment in Connecticut requiring that prospective voters be able to read English and a law in New Jersey prohibiting naturalizations during the thirty days before general elections provided additional evidence of continued

Republican concern with cultural issues on the state level. Indeed, its depression victories enabled the Republican party to resolve a number of these disputes to the satisfaction of groups that supported the G.O.P.

In one instance, renewed cultural strife temporarily and partially reversed the Republican tide: the Sunday closing controversy, which divided German and evangelical Protestant supporters of the Fusion administration of New York City and pitted Democrats against Republicans in New York State, New York City, and Brooklyn during the off-year campaign of 1895, contributed to Democratic gains in the metropolitan area and Republican gains upstate. In New Jersey, on the other hand, Germans and evangelical Protestants moved in the same direction—toward the Democrats in Atlantic County, toward the Republicans elsewhere—in the anti-racetrack legislative election of 1893. The racetrack controversy produced dramatic shifts in voting behavior (to the net benefit of the G.O.P.), but the patterns of 1893 were not lasting; counties that moved sharply that year were to be found in more normal percentage ranges during 1894 and thereafter. Differences between the positions taken by politicians concerned with building broad-based national coalitions and those taken by state and local politicians, particularly by politicians whose constituencies were relatively homogeneous, toward cultural issues suggest the necessity of studying political behavior on various levels (e.g., national, state, and local) in order to understand politics in all its complexity.

Analysis of voting patterns in New York State reveals the existence of Democratic factionalism in the elections of 1893, 1894, and 1896, as well as in municipal elections in New York City (1894, 1895) and Brooklyn (1893, 1895). This conflict, which pitted supporters of U.S. Senator Hill and Democratic organizations in New York City and Brooklyn against followers of President Cleveland, contributed significantly to the defeat of Democratic organization candidates in municipal elections in New York City and Brooklyn. But analysis of the crucial gubernatorial election of 1894 and the presidential election of 1896 indicates that Republican gains at the expense of the regular Democratic party were more broadly based than were those of the Cleveland Democrats. Democratic factionalism did not forge a majority coalition for the Republicans during 1893–96. The politics of depression did that.

The significance of the political upheaval of 1893–96 lay not only in its destroying a political stalemate of long duration, but also in its giving rise to a Republican majority that would dominate politics for years thereafter. To be sure, the fading of memories of the depression and fears of social conflict, the decline of animosity toward the Bryanites, and the papering over of differences among Democratic politicians contributed to a stronger Democratic showing in the Northeast in 1900, when Bryan challenged McKinley for a second time, than in 1896, when they first contested for the presidency. Still, in 1900, McKinley, during whose administration the nation had triumphed in war, experienced economic recovery, and reduced its fear of imminent social crisis, soundly trounced Bryan in Connecticut, New York, and New Jersey—indeed, in the nation as a whole.[1] The Republican and Democratic percentages of 1900 were much closer to those of 1896 than the percentages of 1892 had been. Further, the vote of 1900 foreshadowed the votes in a series of presidential elections in each of the three states, just as the vote of 1892 had been similar to the votes in earlier elections, during the political stalemate. (See Table 15.)

TABLE 15 *Republican and Democratic Percentages, Presidential Elections, 1876–1892, 1896, and 1900–1916, Connecticut, New York, and New Jersey*

	CONNECTICUT		NEW YORK		NEW JERSEY	
ELECTIONS	REP.	DEM.	REP.	DEM.	REP.	DEM.
$\bar{M}$ %, 1876–88	48.8	49.2	48.9	49.0	47.7	50.3
%, 1892	46.8	50.1	45.6	49.0	46.2	50.7
%, 1896	63.2	32.5	57.6	38.7	59.7	36.0
%, 1900	56.9	41.1	53.1	43.8	55.3	41.1
$\bar{M}$ %, 1904–16[a]	55.3	40.0	52.8	42.2	55.5	40.3

Source: Svend Petersen, *A Statistical History of the American Presidential Elections* (New York: Frederick Ungar, 1963), 123, 144, 146.

[a]Progressive party vote included with Republican party vote, 1912, all three states.

In Connecticut and New Jersey, the return to the Democratic fold, in almost every county, of some of the voters who had deserted to the Republicans or National Democrats narrowed the percentage gap between the Republican and Democratic parties, but it did not disrupt voting patterns that had emerged in the election of 1896. Correlations between the elections of 1892, 1894, 1895 (New Jersey only), and 1896 and the election of 1900 reveal that the election of 1896 was more strongly correlated with the election of 1900 than were any of the others.[2] (See Appendix F.) New York did not fit into the same pattern. There the Democrats regained more percentage strength in 1900 in New York City, Brooklyn, and the metropolitan counties than in other regions of the state. Upstate, the Democrats registered small gains in most counties, but lost ground in some; the Republicans lost slightly in most, but gained in some.[3] The marked Democratic recovery in the New York City–Brooklyn metropolitan area supports the hypothesis that the unusually heavy shift of Democrats to the Republican and Gold Democratic parties there in 1896 did not involve their abandoning their identification with the Democratic party. Indeed, in 1900, many Democrats demonstrated their willingness to vote for William Jennings Bryan—under circumstances other than those of 1896. The impact of forces unique to the campaign of 1896 upon voting patterns in New York, alone of the three states, is further suggested by the fact that both the election of 1892 and that of 1894 correlated more strongly with the election of 1900 than did the election of 1896. (See Appendix F.)

Still, in none of the three states was the correlation between any state-wide election during 1892–96 and the election of 1900 weaker than +.775—and most such correlations were considerably stronger. In short, the primary significance of net shifts in voting behavior from 1892 through 1900 lay not in any dramatic re-shuffling of the bases of support for the rival parties—in most respects, the voting coalitions of 1900 resembled those of 1892—but rather in the decisive enlargement of the Republican coalition and the reduction of the Democratic one so that a new party balance was achieved.

The political situation that favored the Republican party

was not upset in a presidential election until 1912, when Woodrow Wilson carried all three states. But Wilson's success was based on the division of the Republican vote between William Howard Taft and Theodore Roosevelt, not on the creation of any new Democratic majority. In winning, Wilson fell short of Bryan's losing percentage of 1900 in Connecticut and New York and exceeded it by the narrowest of margins in New Jersey. The three states returned to the Republican column in 1916 and remained there through the 1920s. Even in the presidential election of 1932, held during the depths of the depression, Herbert Hoover retained Connecticut for the G.O.P. and Franklin Delano Roosevelt, who carried the other two states for the Democrats, fell short of Grover Cleveland's 1892 percentage strength in New Jersey. Not until the presidential election of 1936 did the Democrats capture all three states and surpass their showing of 1892 in each. That it required the Great Depression, the New Deal, and the emergence of "the Roosevelt coalition" to effect this Democratic recovery offers final testimony to the durability of the Republican majority created by the politics of depression, 1893–96.

Appendix A

Sources of Election Data: Connecticut, New York, and New Jersey

CONNECTICUT

The State of Connecticut, Secretary of State, *Register and Manual of the State of Connecticut,* provided official town-level returns from presidential, gubernatorial, and other state-wide elections, as well as from elections to the state legislature and for sheriff. The votes of all minor parties were usually reported. Registration figures were also provided.

The *Register and Manual* did not provide returns from boroughs and cities within towns, or from wards within cities. Various Connecticut newspapers contained generally reliable tallies that filled many, but not all, of these gaps.

NEW YORK

The State of New York, Secretary of State, *Manual for the Use of the Legislature,* provided official returns from rural and urban election districts for all parties from the following elections: 1892, president; 1893, secretary of state; 1894, governor; 1895, secretary of state; and 1896, governor.

The [New York] *Tribune Almanac and Political Register* and *The Brooklyn Daily Eagle Almanac* proved quite useful, providing detailed returns from municipal elections and a number of lesser state-wide elections in the state's two largest cities. The *Eagle Almanac* also reported the 1894 vote on the revised state constitution and the 1895 vote on improvement of the state canals. The *Tribune Almanac* reported returns from assembly districts only, the *Eagle Almanac* from election districts as well as wards. In some instances, the almanacs reported the vote for all parties; in others, they did not. The *Tribune Almanac* provided state-wide Republican, Democratic, and National Democratic returns from towns, assembly districts, and wards for the presidential election of 1896; the *Eagle Almanac* contained the same information from election districts within Brooklyn.

NEW JERSEY

The State of New Jersey, State Legislature, *Manual of the Legislature of New Jersey,* contained official returns from presidential, gubernatorial, and legislative elections. These were broken down to the election district or precinct level within cities and rural towns. The *Manual* did not always provide returns for all minor parties below the county level. In some instances, only the vote of the two major parties was reported.

* * *

The manuals of the three states provided all-party, county-level returns from state-wide elections. New York manuals also contained county-level returns from the 1894 vote on the revised state constitution and the following year's vote on canals improvement. The *Tribune Almanac* offered a wide range of county-level election returns from all three states.

U.S., Bureau of Labor, *The Slums of Baltimore, Chicago, New York, and Philadelphia,* Seventh Special Report of the Commissioner of Labor (Washington, D.C.: Government Printing Office, 1894), 126–27 (Tables VI, VII), attempted to provide information on voting among foreign-born interviewees in selected slum districts. (In New York City, these selected districts were predominantly Italian in population.) Unfortunately, information on the interviewees' length of residence in the United States and the districts was not compiled. As a consequence, there is no way of knowing whether differing rates of participation among samples of various nationalities were a function of ethnic background or length of residence. Other potentially relevant variables were not examined in the study.

Appendix B

Sources of Data on the Electorates of Connecticut, New York, and New Jersey

Various volumes of the federal censuses of 1890, 1900, 1910, and 1920 contained valuable information on the ethnic, religious, and racial composition of the population. In addition to volumes on population in each of these censuses, volumes devoted to New York City and Brooklyn, cities of over 100,000 population, and religious membership by county, all in the census of 1890, and a special report on religious membership (1906) were consulted. The "Federal Population Schedules, Tenth Census of the United States, 1880" (microfilm) provided information not found in published federal censuses. The census of 1880 was the first to solicit information on the birthplaces of parents of respondents; it is the most recent manuscript census available to researchers. Among other things, the population schedules provided data on lightly populated towns that were left unreported in published censuses.

State censuses contained essential data on the populations of New York and New Jersey. (Connecticut did not conduct a census.) Among published ones, the New York censuses of 1855 and 1875 and the New Jersey censuses of 1885, 1895, and 1905 were consulted. The manuscript population schedules of the New Jersey censuses of 1895 and 1905 (New Jersey State Library, Trenton) proved informative. The New Jersey censuses of 1885 and 1895 identified the foreign-born as Irish, German, and "all other Nationalities"; the census of 1905 added the Italians and English to the identified nationalities. The manuscript population schedules of 1905 listed the birthplace of all respondents and their parents and provided information on length of residence in the United States and citizenship. The New Jersey census presented data on race and nationality by sex, an important service to those studying eras prior to woman suffrage.

Sources other than censuses shed light on important questions relating to population characteristics. Though valuable, federal census data on religion are related only to counties, but gazetteers and city, county, and town histories frequently identify churches within minor civil divisions and sometimes discuss the religious and ethnic composition thereof. The gazetteers on New York that were compiled by J. H. French and Franklin B. Hough are particularly informative. Together with pre-Civil War state census data, they shed light on patterns of migration within New York and into the state from New England, New Jersey, and Pennsylvania. In all three states, local histories enable one to identify various old-stock American groups that federal censuses simply lumped together as native-born of native parentage. D. C. Hurd, *Town and City Atlas of the State of Connecticut,* not only locates by town or ward most of Connecticut's churches, but frequently indicates the nationality of particular church memberships (e.g., Swedish Lutheran, German Methodist.) Town boundaries were rarely altered in Connecticut, New York, and New Jersey during the late nineteenth century, but ward and assembly district boundaries within cities were frequently modified. Many sources were consulted, not always successfully, in an attempt to identify and characterize urban districts. Next to censuses and atlases, magazines and newspapers proved most useful in this effort: e.g., *Harper's Weekly* offered ethnic maps of New York City; the New York *Times* ran a series of articles on New York City assembly districts. Information of this sort is important because censuses dealt with New York City's wards, while election returns were reported by assembly districts. (In Brooklyn, wards were the basic political units as well as the basic census units.)

Federal census data on agriculture (1890) and manufacturing (1900) contribute to an understanding of economic activity on the county and city levels. The New York State Census of 1875 provides town-level information on the number and size of farms, on the value of farms, dwellings, farm buildings, stock, tools and implements, and on the value of gross farm sales. Volumes in the "Economic Study of Land Utilization" series, published by the Cornell University Agricultural Experiment Station (later published by the New York State College of Agriculture), update information on town-level land values in twenty-two New York counties. (For a listing of these volumes, see below, p. 238, State of New York . . . *Annotated Bibliography on Low Incomes in Rural New York State.*) Comparable quantitative data are not available for Connecticut and New Jersey. County and town histories of the three states often contain information and judgments on the prosperity of rural towns. Such accounts allow us to make cautious observations about the relative prosperity of units within the scope of particular studies at particular points in time, but not about the ranking of units across broader areas or in other periods. Censuses, other official reports, and unofficial sources (e.g., atlases and newspapers) yield information on economic activity, population density, housing, sanitation, and health within the political subdivisions of many cities. The nature of the evidence does not permit an economic ranking of wards or assembly districts, but it does allow us to characterize many such units (e.g., upper, middle, and working class, etc.).

Taken together, official and unofficial sources of voting data yield all-party or at least major-party election returns from virtually every political unit in Connecticut, New York, and New Jersey during the 1890s. Unfortunately, sources of data on the population and economy do not similarly illuminate every political unit in the three states. Rich though their yield is, these sources simply fail to provide basic information on many rural towns and urban districts (e.g., wards and assembly districts). In other cases, boundary differences between units reporting election returns and those reporting population and economic data limit the utility of, or render useless, the latter information. So does the fact that there was periodic redistricting of political units within cities. (To illustrate: the federal census of 1890 provides information on six aldermanic districts in Jersey City and fifteen wards in Newark. But Jersey City reported election returns from eight assembly districts in 1892 and 1893, while Newark did so from nine wards. In 1894, when New Jersey assembly candidates ran at large in each county, Jersey City did report election returns from its six aldermanic districts, but Newark reported its vote from fifteen newly formed wards, and their boundaries differed in important respects from those of 1890. The New Jersey State Census of 1895 provides information on the population of twelve wards in Jersey City and fifteen in Newark. Jersey City reported election returns from these wards in 1895 and 1896; Newark did so in 1894, 1895, and 1896.) Finally, in some instances, election returns were reported from units smaller than those for which population and economic data are available—e.g., from election districts within urban wards or assembly districts as well as from election districts within some rural towns, particularly in New York State. In such cases, the smallest units for which both election returns and population and economic data are available were utilized in this study. In cases where voting data, but not population and economic data, are available, continuities and discontinuities in political behavior were sometimes analyzed—but they were not related to the ethno-cultural and socio-economic characteristics of the electorate.

Among the most useful published volumes consulted in the preparation of this study were:

State of New Jersey, Department of State. *Census of 1885, with a Recapitulation of the Census of 1875*. Trenton: J. L. Murphy, 1886.

——. *Census of 1895, with a Recapitulation of the Census of 1885*. Somerville: The Unionist-Gazette Printing House, 1896.

——. *Census of 1905, with a Recapitulation of the Census of New Jersey Since 1790*. Trenton: J. L. Murphy, 1905.

——. *Compendium of Censuses, 1726–1905, Together with the Tabulated Returns of 1905*. Trenton: J. L. Murphy, 1906.

State of New York, Interdepartmental Committee on Low Incomes. *Annotated Bibliography on Low Incomes in Rural New York State: Supplement to Analytical Report.* Compiled by Howard E. Conklin and Irving R. Starbird. n. p. [New York]: Interdepartmental Committee on Low Incomes, 1958.

State of New York, Secretary of State. *Census of the State of New York, for 1855. . . .* Compiled by Franklin B. Hough, Superintendent of the Census. Albany: Charles Van Benthuysen, 1857.

——. *Census of the State of New York for 1875. . . .* Compiled by C. W. Seaton, Superintendent of the Census. Albany: Weed, Parsons and Co., 1877.

U.S. Census Office. *Eleventh Census: 1890,* Vol. I, Part 1: *Report on the Population of the United States.* Washington, D.C.: U.S. Government Printing Office, 1895.

——. *Report on Vital and Social Statistics in the United States at the Eleventh Census: 1890,* Vol. IV, Part 2—*Vital Statistics. Cities of 100,000 Population and Upward.* Washington, D.C.: U.S. Government Printing Office, 1896.

——. *Eleventh Census, 1890,* Vol. V: *Report on the Statistics of Agriculture in the United States.* Washington, D.C.: U.S. Government Printing Office, 1895.

——. *Eleventh Census, 1890,* Vol. IX: *Report on Statistics of Churches in the United States at the Eleventh Census: 1890.* Washington, D.C.: U.S. Government Printing Office, 1894.

——. *Eleventh Census of the United States, 1890,* Vol. XXVII: *Vital Statistics of New York City and Brooklyn Covering a Period of Six Years Ending May 31, 1890.* Washington, D.C.: U.S. Government Printing Office, 1894.

——. *Compendium of the Eleventh Census: 1890.* Part I—*Population.* Part II—*Vital and Social Statistics. . . .* Washington, D.C.: U.S. Government Printing Office, 1892, 1894.

——. *Twelfth Census of the United States, Taken in the Year 1900.* Vol. I: *Population,* Part 1. Vol. II: *Population,* Part 2. Washington, D.C.: U.S. Census Office, 1901, 1902.

——. *Twelfth Census of the United States, Taken in the Year 1900*. Vol. VIII: *Manufactures,* Part 2. Washington, D.C.: U.S. Census Office, 1902.

U.S. Bureau of the Census. *Thirteenth Census of the United States, Taken in the Year 1910*. Vol. II: *Population, 1910 . . . , Alabama-Montana*. Vol. III: *Population, 1910 . . . , Nebraska-Wyoming*. Washington, D.C.: U.S. Government Printing Office, 1913.

——. *Fourteenth Census of the United States Taken in the Year 1920: Population 1920: Number and Distribution of Inhabitants,* Vol. I. Washington, D.C.: U.S. Government Printing Office, 1921.

——. *Special Reports: Religious Bodies: 1906,* Vol. I: *Summary and General Tables*. Vol. II: *Separate Denominations: History, Description and Statistics.* Washington, D.C.: U.S. Government Printing Office, 1910.

U.S. Industrial Commission. *Reports of the Industrial Commission*. Vol. X: *Report on Agriculture and Agricultural Labor*. Vol. XV: *Report on Immigration . . . And on Education, . . .* Washington, D.C.: U.S. Government Printing Office, 1901.

U.S. Library of Congress. *State Censuses; an Annotated Bibliography of Censuses of Population Taken After the Year 1790 by States and Territories of the United States.* Prepared by Harry J. Dubester. Washington, D.C.: U.S. Government Printing Office, 1948.

——. *United States Atlases: A Catalogue of National, State, County, City, and Regional Atlases in the Library of Congress and Cooperating Libraries.* Vol. II. Compiled by Clara Egli Le Gear. Washington, D.C.: U.S. Government Printing Office, 1953.

French, J. H. (comp.) *Gazetteer of the State of New York. . . .* Syracuse: R. Pearsall Smith, 1860.

Greater New York Federation of Churches [The Federation of Churches and Christian Workers in New York City]. *Second Sociological Canvass (Report B), The Nineteenth Assembly District.* New York: G. F. Nesbitt & Co., 1897.

Harper's Weekly, XXXIX (January 19, 1895), 60–62.

Hough, Franklin B. (comp.) *Gazetteer of the State of New York, Embracing a Comprehensive Account of the History and Statistics of the State*. Albany: Andrew Boyd, 1872.

Town and City Atlas of the State of Connecticut. Compiled from Government Surveys, County Records, and Personal Interviews. Boston: D. C. Hurd & Co., 1893.

Appendix C

Pearsonian Correlations, County-level Democratic and Republican Percentages of the Total Vote, Presidential Elections, 1860–1892, Connecticut, New York, and New Jersey

	1860[a]		1864		1868		1872	
	DEM.	REP.	DEM.	REP.	DEM.	REP.	DEM.	REP.
					CONNECTICUT			
1860[a]	—	—	+.567	+.663	+.468	+.568	+.231	+.3
1864	+.567	+.663	—	—	+.920	+.920	+.849	+.8
1868	+.468	+.568	+.920	+.920	—	—	+.927	+.9
1872	+.231	+.314	+.849	+.850	+.927	+.927	—	—
1876	+.333	+.478	+.885	+.880	+.979	+.988	+.958	+.9
1880	+.370	+.538	+.894	+.904	+.981	+.984	+.914	+.8
1884	+.304	+.486	+.833	+.848	+.977	+.980	+.931	+.9
1888	+.185	+.359	+.750	+.720	+.881	+.857	+.845	+.8
1892	−.004	+.279	+.692	+.730	+.758	+.803	+.804	+.8
					NEW YORK			
1860	—	—	+.965	+.965	+.961	+.961	+.851	+.8
1864	+.965	+.965	—	—	+.978	+.978	+.864	+.8
1868	+.961	+.961	+.978	+.978	—	—	+.892	+.8
1872	+.851	+.851	+.864	+.864	+.892	+.892	—	—
1876	+.948	+.947	+.959	+.956	+.976	+.973	+.897	+.9
1880	+.911	+.868	+.933	+.889	+.941	+.901	+.874	+.8
1884	+.901	+.828	+.921	+.824	+.916	+.836	+.855	+.8
1888	+.932	+.877	+.936	+.863	+.944	+.881	+.874	+.8
1892	+.920	+.884	+.930	+.867	+.931	+.884	+.818	+.8
					NEW JERSEY			
1860	—	—	+.920	+.920	+.943	+.943	+.733	+.7
1864	+.920	+.920	—	—	+.944	+.944	+.896	+.8
1868	+.943	+.943	+.944	+.944	—	—	+.853	+.8
1872	+.733	+.733	+.896	+.896	+.853	+.853	—	—
1876	+.829	+.811	+.928	+.915	+.925	+.902	+.939	+.9
1880	+.792	+.729	+.873	+.831	+.900	+.841	+.897	+.8
1884	+.873	+.798	+.922	+.892	+.940	+.868	+.907	+.8
1888	+.913	+.850	+.939	+.926	+.942	+.900	+.883	+.8
1892	+.917	+.831	+.902	+.883	+.929	+.869	+.783	+.7

Source: Data made available by the Inter-university Consortium for Political Re search. The Consortium bears no responsibility for either the accuracy of the dat or interpretations presented here.

1876		1880		1884		1888		1892	
EM.	REP.	DEM.	REP.	DEM.	REP.	DEM.	REP.	DEM.	REP.
.333	+.478	+.370	+.538	+.304	+.486	+.185	+.359	−.004	+.279
.885	+.880	+.894	+.904	+.833	+.848	+.750	+.720	+.692	+.730
.979	+.988	+.981	+.984	+.977	+.980	+.881	+.857	+.758	+.803
.958	+.944	+.914	+.899	+.931	+.909	+.845	+.840	+.804	+.809
—	—	+.968	+.979	+.977	+.991	+.844	+.827	+.737	+.760
.968	+.979	—	—	+.981	+.988	+.892	+.856	+.798	+.808
.977	+.991	+.981	+.988	—	—	+.908	+.848	+.793	+.772
.844	+.827	+.892	+.856	+.908	+.848	—	—	+.947	+.970
.737	+.760	+.798	+.808	+.793	+.772	+.947	+.970	—	—
.948	+.947	+.911	+.868	+.901	+.828	+.932	+.877	+.920	+.884
.959	+.956	+.933	+.889	+.921	+.824	+.936	+.863	+.930	+.867
.976	+.973	+.941	+.901	+.916	+.836	+.944	+.881	+.931	+.884
.897	+.901	+.874	+.850	+.855	+.805	+.874	+.840	+.818	+.813
—	—	+.961	+.942	+.943	+.907	+.963	+.927	+.917	+.905
.961	+.942	—	—	+.959	+.931	+.962	+.932	+.909	+.856
.943	+.907	+.959	+.931	—	—	+.958	+.952	+.936	+.904
.963	+.927	+.962	+.932	+.958	+.952	—	—	+.950	+.945
.917	+.905	+.909	+.856	+.936	+.904	+.950	+.945	—	—
.829	+.811	+.792	+.729	+.873	+.798	+.913	+.850	+.917	+.831
.928	+.915	+.873	+.831	+.922	+.892	+.939	+.926	+.902	+.883
.925	+.902	+.900	+.841	+.940	+.868	+.942	+.900	+.929	+.869
.939	+.937	+.897	+.882	+.907	+.879	+.883	+.880	+.783	+.776
—	—	+.956	+.939	+.963	+.940	+.919	+.924	+.849	+.851
.956	+.939	—	—	+.965	+.934	+.891	+.898	+.830	+.834
.963	+.940	+.965	+.934	—	—	+.945	+.964	+.882	+.925
.919	+.924	+.891	+.898	+.945	+.964	—	—	+.952	+.966
.849	+.851	+.830	+.834	+.882	+.925	+.952	+.966	—	—

[a]Democratic and Southern Democratic votes combined to yield one Democratic
te in Connecticut (1860).

Appendix D

Democratic and Republican Percentage Strength in Six Northern States Holding Annual Elections, 1892–1896

STATE	1892[a]		1893[a]		1894[a]		1895[a]		1896[a]	
	DEM.	REP.	DEM.	REP.	DEM.	REP.	DEM.	REP.	DEM.	REP.
Iowa	44.4	49.6 (P)	42.1	49.8 (G)	35.6	54.4 (SS)	38.1	53.3 (G)	42.9	55.5 (P)
Ohio	47.5	47.7 (P)	42.8	52.6 (G)	36.2	54.2 (SS)	39.9	51.0 (G)	46.8	51.9 (P)
Pennsylvania	45.1	51.5 (P)	39.5	56.9 (ST)	35.0	60.3 (G)	36.7	59.4 (ST)	36.3	61.0 (P)
Massachusetts	49.0	48.4 (G)	43.0	52.8 (G)	37.0	56.5 (G)	37.1	56.8 (G)	26.1	67.1 (G)
	45.2	51.9 (P)							26.3	69.5 (P)
New York	49.0	45.6 (P)	45.8	47.9 (SS)	40.8	53.1 (G)	43.8	51.6 (SS)	38.7	57.6 (P)
									40.3	55.3 (G)
New Jersey	48.9	48.5 (L)	43.7	51.8 (L)	38.9	55.3 (C)	43.6	52.3 (G)	36.0	59.7 (P)
	50.7	46.2 (P)								

Sources: *Tribune Almanacs, 1893–1897.*

[a] P=Presidential Vote; G=Gubernatorial Vote; SS=Vote for Secretary of State; ST=Vote for State Treasurer; L=Vote for Legislature (lower house); C=Vote for Congress.

Appendix E

Percentages, All Parties, 1892–1896, Connecticut, New York, and New Jersey

YEAR (Office)[a]	REP.	DEM.	OTHER	POP.	PRO.	SLP
		CONNECTICUT				
1892 (P)	46.8	50.1	X	0.5	2.4	0.2
1892 (G)	46.6	50.3	X	0.5	2.4	0.2
1894 (G)	54.2	42.8	X	1.0	1.5	0.5
1896 (P)	63.2	32.5	2.5[b]	X	1.0	0.7
1896 (G)	62.5	32.5	3.2[b]	X	1.1	0.7
		NEW YORK				
1892 (P)	45.6	49.0	X	1.2	2.9	1.3
1893 (SS)	47.9	45.8	X	1.6	3.0	1.8
1893 (J)	51.4	42.5	X	1.5	2.9	1.7
1894 (G)	53.1	40.8	2.1[c]	0.9	1.9	1.3
1894 (L-G)	53.0	43.0	X	0.9	1.9	1.2
1895 (SS)	51.6	43.8	X	0.6	2.2	1.8
1896 (P)	57.6	38.7	1.3[b]	X	1.1	1.2
1896 (G)	55.3	40.3	1.9[b]	X	1.2	1.3
		NEW JERSEY				
1892 (P)	46.2	50.7	X	0.3	2.4	0.4
1892 (G)	47.4	49.7	X	0.3	2.3	0.4
1892 (L)	48.5	48.9	X	0.1	2.4	0.1
1893 (L)	51.8	43.7	0.9[d]	0.1	2.9	0.7
1894 (C)	55.3	38.9	0.4[e]	1.4	2.4	1.5
1895 (G)	52.3	43.6	X	0.6	2.1	1.3
1896 (P)	59.7	36.0	1.7[b]	X	1.5	1.1

Sources: *Tribune Almanacs, 1893–1897*.

[a] P=President; G=Governor; SS=Secretary of State; J=Judge, State Court of Appeals; L-G=Lieutenant-Governor; L=State Legislature (lower house); C=United States House of Representatives.

[b] National Democratic party.

[c] Democratic Party Reform Organization.

[d] Independents.

[e] People's party–Socialist Labor party coalition.

Appendix F

Pearsonian Correlations, County-level Democratic and Republican Percentages of the Total Vote, Selected Elections, 1892–1900, Connecticut, New York, and New Jersey

CONNECTICUT

	1892[a]		1894[a]		1896[b]		1900[b]	
	DEM.	REP.	DEM.	REP.	DEM.	REP.	DEM.	REP.
1892[a]	—	—	+.892	+.911	+.724	+.831	+.814	+.882
1894[a]	+.892	+.911	—	—	+.786	+.818	+.775	+.803
1896[b]	+.724	+.831	+.786	+.818	—	—	+.913	+.890
1900[b]	+.814	+.882	+.775	+.803	+.913	+.890	—	—

NEW YORK[c]

	1892[b]		1894[a]		1896[b]		1900[b]	
	DEM.	REP.	DEM.	REP.	DEM.	REP.	DEM.	REP.
1892[b]	—	—	+.836	+.874	+.647	+.779	+.858	+.892
1894[a]	+.836	+.874	—	—	+.749	+.857	+.841	+.901
1896[b]	+.647	+.779	+.749	+.857	—	—	+.836	+.878
1900[b]	+.858	+.892	+.841	+.901	+.836	+.878	—	—

NEW JERSEY

	1892[a]		1894[d]		1895[a]		1896[b]		1900[b]	
	DEM.	REP.	DEM.	REP.	DEM.	REP.	DEM.	REP.	DEM.	REP.
1892[a]	—	—	+.826	+.838	+.924	+.915	+.798	+.893	+.812	+.840
1894[d]	+.826	+.838	—	—	+.921	+.922	+.784	+.914	+.815	+.892
1895[a]	+.924	+.915	+.921	+.922	—	—	+.831	+.928	+.869	+.919
1896[b]	+.798	+.893	+.784	+.914	+.831	+.928	—	—	+.951	+.968
1900[b]	+.812	+.840	+.815	+.892	+.869	+.919	+.951	+.968	—	—

Source: Data made available by the Inter-university Consortium for Political Research. The Consortium bears no responsibility for either the accuracy of the data or interpretations presented here.

[a] Gubernatorial Vote.

[b] Presidential Vote.

[c] Fulton and Hamilton counties treated as one unit in all elections. Nassau County (created out of Queens County in 1899) and Queens County recombined to form one unit in 1900.

[d] Vote for Congress.

Notes

The notes to this volume provide full references to the primary and secondary sources on which the study rests. For that reason I have given no formal Bibliography here.

PREFACE

1. V. O. Key, Jr., "A Theory of Critical Elections," *The Journal of Politics,* XVII (Feb. 1955), 3–4. (Emphasis added.)
2. Duncan MacRae, Jr., and James A. Meldrum, "Critical Elections in Illinois: 1888–1958," *The American Political Science Review,* LIV (Sept. 1960), 669–83. Key, *loc. cit.,* 12–13, did take note of political shifts in the midterm elections of 1894.
3. See, for example, John D. Hicks, *The Populist Revolt: A History of the Farmers' Alliance and the People's Party* (Minneapolis: University of Minnesota Press, 1931), and Stanley L. Jones, *The Presidential Election of 1896* (Madison: The University of Wisconsin Press, 1964).
4. Samuel P. Hays, "New Possibilities for American Political History: The Social Analysis of Political Life" (lithoprinted; Ann Arbor: The Inter-university Consortium for Political Research, 1964), 20.
5. See, however, Roger E. Wyman, "Wisconsin Ethnic Groups and the Election of 1890," *Wisconsin Magazine of History,* LI (Summer 1968), 269–93, and the books cited below, Note 6.
6. For recent analyses of the Midwest, see Paul Kleppner, *The Cross of Culture: A Social Analysis of Midwestern Politics, 1850–1900* (New York: The Free Press, 1970), which contributed to my thinking; and Richard J. Jensen, *The Winning of the Midwest: Social and Political Conflict, 1888–1896* (Chicago: University of Chicago Press, 1971), which appeared after the writing of this book.

   Sources of election returns for the present study will be found in Appendix A, sources of data on the electorate in Appendix B. On methodology, see Hubert M. Blalock, Jr., *Social Statistics* (New York: McGraw-Hill, 1960).
7. Samuel P. Hays, "Political Parties and the Community-Society

Continuum," *The American Party Systems: Stages of Political Development,* eds. William N. Chambers and Walter Dean Burnham (New York: Oxford University Press, 1967), 152–81, esp. 153, has contributed much to my thinking regarding this problem.

H. Wayne Morgan, *From Hayes to McKinley: National Party Politics, 1877–1896* (Syracuse: Syracuse University Press, 1969), is the most recent and detailed traditional account of the period.

Robert D. Marcus, *Grand Old Party: Political Structure in the Gilded Age, 1880–1896* (New York: Oxford University Press, 1971), appeared too late for me to consult during the writing of this book.

I. THE ANATOMY OF STALEMATE: POLITICS, 1874–1892

1. W. Dean Burnham, *Presidential Ballots, 1836–1892* (Baltimore: Johns Hopkins University Press, 1955), *passim;* Vincent P. De Santis, *Republicans Face the Southern Question—The New Departure Years, 1877–1897* (The Johns Hopkins University Studies in Historical and Political Science, Series LXXVII, No. 1; Baltimore: Johns Hopkins University Press, 1959), 21–22.
2. De Santis, *ibid., passim;* Stanley P. Hirshson, *Farewell to the Bloody Shirt: Northern Republicans & the Southern Negro, 1877–1893* (Bloomington: University of Indiana Press, 1962), *passim,* esp. chap. xii and David Donald's Introduction.
3. On campaigning, see Hirshson, *ibid.,* 299–301; Matthew Josephson, *The Politicos: 1865–1896* (New York: Harcourt, Brace, 1938), 372–73, 428–33; Harry J. Sievers, *Benjamin Harrison,* Vol. II: *Benjamin Harrison: Hoosier Statesman, From the Civil War to the White House, 1865–1888* (New York: University Publishers, 1959), 254–57, 262–64, 416–21; and Allan Nevins, *Grover Cleveland: A Study in Courage* (New York: Dodd, Mead, 1932), 172, 180–81, 186–87, 435–39. In particular, political biographers, who tend to identify with their subjects, seem prone to make such interpretations.

   On raising and spending campaign funds, see Edward A. White, The Republican Party in National Politics, 1888–1891 (unpublished Ph.D. dissertation, Dept. of History, University of Wisconsin, 1941), *passim;* Josephson, *ibid., passim,* esp. chaps. ii, iii, vii–ix, xi, xii.

   Of the three Democratic presidential candidates from 1876 through 1892, Samuel Tilden and Grover Cleveland had proven themselves by winning the governorship of New York, which state was virtually essential to Democratic victory in a national election. Among four Republican presidential candidates during the same period, only Rutherford Hayes of Ohio had won election to state-wide office.
4. Josephson, *ibid.,* 287. (Emphasis added.) The authors of American history textbooks have expressed similar views. See, for example, texts by John D. Hicks, Harold U. Faulkner, and Samuel Eliot Morison and Henry Steele Commager. Cf. Morgan, *From Hayes to McKinley, op. cit., passim.*
5. W. Dean Burnham, "The Changing Shape of the American Political Universe," *The American Political Science Review,* LIX (March 1965), 7–28.

6. Mean Republican and Democratic percentages in the three states in four presidential elections from 1860 through 1872 and five from 1876 through 1892 were:

PRESIDENTIAL	NEW YORK		CONNECTICUT		NEW JERSEY	
ELECTIONS	R ($\overline{M}$%)	D ($\overline{M}$%)	R ($\overline{M}$%)	D ($\overline{M}$%)	R ($\overline{M}$%)	D ($\overline{M}$%)
1860–1872	51.7	48.3	52.3	46.6	49.7	50.3
1876–1892	48.3	49.0	48.4	49.4	47.4	50.4

7. In New York, Democratic victories during the first period occurred in 1862, 1868, and 1870; the sole Republican triumph during the second period took place in 1879. The only post-Civil War Republican victory in New Jersey came in 1865. Democrats won the Connecticut governorship in 1867, 1868, 1870, 1873, 1874, 1875, and 1876. During the period covered by this study, New York State elected governors for two-year terms until 1876, for three-year terms until 1894, then for two-year terms; New Jersey elected governors for three-year terms; and Connecticut elected governors for one-year terms until 1876, then for two-year terms.

   Mean Republican and Democratic percentages in the three states in gubernatorial elections from 1860 through 1872 and from 1873 through 1892 were:

GUBERNATORIAL	NEW YORK		CONNECTICUT		NEW JERSEY	
ELECTIONS	R ($\overline{M}$%)	D ($\overline{M}$%)	R ($\overline{M}$%)	D ($\overline{M}$%)	R ($\overline{M}$%)	D ($\overline{M}$%)
1860–1872	50.5	49.5	51.5	48.3	47.8	52.3
1873–1892	45.8	51.6	46.8	49.8	46.4	50.5

8. Indeed, there were no major shifts in county-level voting patterns after the political realignment of the 1850s had run its course. Inter-election correlations of the county-level vote in all presidential elections from 1860 through 1892 reveal remarkably strong and positive correlations among elections in New York and New Jersey throughout the period and somewhat less strong positive correlations among elections in Connecticut during 1864–92. See Appendix C.

   The measure of correlation employed in Appendixes C and F is the Pearsonian product-moment correlation. See Blalock, *Social Statistics, op. cit.,* chaps. xvii, xviii. On the measures of rank-order correlation employed in the main body of the study, see below, Chap. II (Note 47).

9. Paul Wallace Gates, *The Farmer's Age: Agriculture, 1815–1860,* Vol. III of *The Economic History of the United States,* eds. Henry David and Others (10 vols.; New York: Holt, Rinehart and Winston, 1945–), 159–69, 400–403, 416–17; Fred A. Shannon, *The Farmer's Last Frontier: Agriculture, 1860–1897,* Vol. V of *The Economic History of the United States, op. cit.,* chap. xi; also New England, New York, and New Jersey county and town histories.

10. According to federal census definitions, Rhode Island and Massachusetts, alone of nine New England and Middle Atlantic states, were predominantly urban in 1850. Fifty years later, only Maine, Vermont, and New Hampshire remained predominantly rural.

	% RURAL			% RURAL			% RURAL	
STATE	1850	1900	STATE	1850	1900	STATE	1850	1900
Me.	86.5	66.5	Mass.	49.3	14.0	N.Y.	71.8	27.1
N.H.	82.9	53.3	R.I.	44.4	11.7	N.J.	82.4	29.4
Vt.	98.1	77.9	Conn.	84.1	40.1	Pa.	76.4	45.3

Source: U.S., Bureau of the Census, *U.S. Census of Population: 1960,* Vol. I: *Characteristics of the Population,* Part A: *Number of Inhabitants* (Washington, D.C.: Government Printing Office, 1961), 8:5, 21:8, 23:6, 31:5, 32:7, 34:7, 40:14, 41:5, 47:4.

11. These counties were: Chenango, Clinton, Columbia, Essex, Greene, Jefferson, Lewis, Livingston, Madison, Ontario, Oswego, Otsego, Putnam, St. Lawrence, Schoharie, Schuyler, Seneca, Sullivan, Tioga, Tompkins, Washington, Wayne, Wyoming, and Yates in New York State; and Hunterdon, Sussex, and Warren in New Jersey.

A number of counties—Allegany, Cortland, Orleans, and Rensselaer (New York); Burlington (New Jersey); and Tolland (Connecticut)—lost population for the first time during the 1890s, while others—Clinton, Jefferson, Ontario, St. Lawrence, Sullivan, and Tompkins (New York); and Sussex and Warren (New Jersey)—reversed their declines, if only temporarily.

U.S., Bureau of the Census, *Fourteenth Census of the United States Taken in the Year 1920: Population 1920: Number and Distribution of Inhabitants* (Washington, D.C.: Government Printing Office, 1921), I, 97, 118–20.

12. Of the counties listed in Note 11 above, the Democrats carried only the following in one or more of nine presidential elections from 1860 through 1892 (figure in parentheses indicates number of times each voted Democratic): Schoharie (9); Greene and Seneca (7); Sullivan (6); Columbia and Otsego (5); Putnam (3); Clinton and Lewis (1).

13. In presidential elections from 1860 through 1892 the Democrats carried New York counties which exceeded the state-wide rate of population growth 52.8% of the time; they carried lagging counties only 18.6% of the time. In Connecticut, the percentages were 59.3 and 6.7, respectively; in New Jersey, 46.0 and 42.5; in the three states combined, 51.5 and 23.3.

14. By 1890, the aforementioned groups of cities contained 43.5% of the population in New York State, 23.9% in New Jersey, and 25.1% in Connecticut. In 1860, the respective percentages had been 30.3, 15.0, and 16.9.

Carl Degler, "American Political Parties and the Rise of the City: An

Interpretation," *The Journal of American History,* LI (June 1964), 41–59, contends that most major non-southern cities were Republican, rather than Democratic during the 1880s. Erroneously equating county with city election data, he incorrectly assigns a number of cities to one or the other party in various elections. He fails to analyze percentage shifts during the period, neglects to compare urban and rural election returns, misses the point that immigrant groups were to be found in both major parties, and slights the role played by ethnic factors in the politics of the period.

15. Duane Lockard, *New England State Politics* (Princeton: Princeton University Press, 1959), 229–30, relates the impotence of the Democratic party in rural Connecticut during the twentieth century to the demoralizing effect of Bryan's presidential campaign. Bryan's candidacy was disastrous for the Democracy, but (as Lockard notes) the party had last controlled the legislature in 1876. That the Republicans were dominant between 1876 and 1896 cannot be attributed to Bryan.
16. Lee Benson, *The Concept of Jacksonian Democracy: New York as a Test Case* (paperbound edition; New York: Atheneum, 1966), 130, 139–40, 290. See also Edward J. Miles, "New York Politics," *Richards Atlas of New York State,* ed. Joseph J. Rayback (Phoenix, New York: Frank E. Richards, 1959), 37–44, 66. Professor Miles's maps offer a vivid picture of the decline of Democratic areal strength from 1860 through 1954. We lack comparable studies of the 1850s in Connecticut and New Jersey politics.
17. Connecticut's Democratic senators were retired in 1879 and 1881, New York's only Democrat in 1881. The two states' Republican senators gave the G.O.P. control of the 47th, 48th, 50th, and 51st senates.

    Southern Republicans elected to the Senate late in the Reconstruction aided the Republicans until the last one was retired in 1883. Six western states admitted to the Union in 1889–90 later contributed to Republican senatorial strength.
18. The previous paragraphs are based on Nevins, *op. cit., passim;* and Herbert J. Bass, *"I Am A Democrat": The Political Career of David Bennett Hill* (Syracuse: Syracuse University Press, 1961), *passim.*
19. Robert P. Kerker, The Democratic Party in Albany County: A Study in Intraparty Politics from 1870 to 1889, with Emphasis upon the Relationship of State and Local Party Organization (unpublished M.A. thesis, Dept. of History, Columbia University, 1954), 185.
20. On Connecticut, see letter of Albert H. Walker to Simeon E. Baldwin, Sept. 14, 1892, in Baldwin Family Papers (Yale University Library, New Haven, Conn.), cited hereafter as Baldwin Family Papers; New York *Tribune,* Dec. 28, 1892.

    On another state, see Lewis W. Rathgeber, The Democratic Party in Pennsylvania, 1880–1896 (unpublished Ph.D. dissertation, Dept. of History, University of Pittsburgh, 1956), 299–300.
21. Ray Billington, *The Protestant Crusade: 1800–1860* (New York: Macmillan, 1938); Michael F. Holt, *Forging a Majority: The Formation of the*

Republican Party in Pittsburgh, 1848–1860 (New Haven: Yale University Press, 1969).

22. Benson, *op. cit.*, 114–22, 137, 208, 213–15, 291; Holt, *ibid.*, *passim.*
23. Charles Garrett, *The La Guardia Years, Machine and Reform Politics in New York City* (New Brunswick: Rutgers University Press, 1961), chap. i. In 1880, the Democratic national ticket carried New York City by 42,283 votes; Grace's plurality was only 3045.
24. William J. Niven, Jr., The Time of the Whirlwind: A Study in the Political, Social and Economic History of Connecticut from 1861 to 1875 (unpublished Ph.D. dissertation, Dept. of History, Columbia University, 1954), 395–96; Robert A. Dahl, *Who Governs? Democracy and Power in an American City* (paperbound edition; New Haven: Yale University Press, 1963), 25–31, 36.
25. Mary Cobb Nelson, The Influence of Immigration on Rhode Island Politics, 1865–1910 (unpublished Ph.D. dissertation, Dept. of History, Radcliffe College, 1954), 50, 62–63, 65, 319–30; Elmer E. Cornwell, Jr., "Party Absorption of Ethnic Groups: The Case of Providence, Rhode Island," *Social Forces,* XXXVIII (March 1960), 205–10; and Thomas N. Brown, *Irish-American Nationalism, 1870–1890, Critical Periods of History,* ed. Robert D. Cross (Philadelphia & New York: Lippincott, 1966), 54–55.
26. Nevins, *op. cit.*, chaps. vii, viii, esp. 134–36; Leonard Dinnerstein, "The Impact of Tammany Hall on State Politics in the Eighteen-Eighties," *New York History,* XLII (July 1961), 237–52. Civil service reformers admired Cleveland, but the Irish felt that this reform would deny them the appointments to which they claimed their political activity entitled them. Brown, *op. cit.*, 140. On Maynard's defeat, compare returns for various offices in 1883 and Maynard's vote with that for Purcell, who had run for Secretary of State against the same Republican in 1881. *The* [New York] *Tribune Almanac and Political Register for 1882,* 76, 83–89; *1884,* 83–84, 90–96, cited hereafter as *Tribune Almanac.*
27. Lee Benson, *Merchants, Farmers, & Railroads: Railroad Regulation and New York Politics, 1850–1887* (Cambridge: Harvard University Press, 1955), chap. ix, esp. 200–201. Cf. Nevins, *op. cit.*, 115–18.
28. Nevins, *ibid.*, 146–55; Gordon S. Wood, "The Massachusetts Mugwumps," *New England Quarterly,* XXXIII (Dec. 1960), 438–39.
29. Wood, *ibid.*, 439–40; Dinnerstein, *loc. cit.*, 245–46.
30. Brown, *op. cit.*, 141, 187 (notes 4 and 5); Nelson, *op. cit.*, 87; Wood, *loc. cit.*, 440; Nevins, *op. cit.*, 184–85.
31. This paragraph is based on Lee Benson, "Research Problems in American Political Historiography," *Common Frontiers of the Social Sciences,* ed. Mirra Komarovsky (Glencoe, Ill.: The Free Press, 1957), 123–46, esp. 129–31, 141–42, 145, 168 (table IX). (Italics in original, p. 131.)
32. Compare Nevins, *op. cit.*, 428–30, with Brown, *op. cit.*, 142–46, 187 (notes 4, 5, and 6).
33. Bass, *op. cit.*, 23–25, 65–68. George received 31.0% of the mayoralty vote. In the same year, labor candidates in New Jersey polled 16.7% of the

vote in an Essex County congressional district and won two races for the assembly in Passaic County. Labor's gubernatorial candidate secured 2.3% of the vote in Connecticut, contributing to the Democrats' failure to receive a majority. *Tribune Almanac, 1887,* 53, 69–71, 84. Labor candidates appear to have run best in districts where Germans were numerous.

34. Bass, *op. cit.,* 19, 21–24, 46–47, 60, 177; New York *Tribune,* Feb. 19, April 2, 15, 1892.
35. Bass, *op. cit.,* 28–33; Kerker, *op. cit.,* 203; Brown, *op. cit.,* 144–45; statement of Frank White, in George S. Bixby Papers (New York State Library, Albany), cited hereafter as Bixby Papers. For years, the Bixby Papers were the major source on David B. Hill. The New York State Library now possesses a large collection of Hill's papers. Cited hereafter as Hill Papers.
36. See, for example, letter of Frank P. Demarest to David B. Hill, Sept. 24, 1890; letter of Henry Bacon to David B. Hill, Oct. 7, 1890, both in Bixby Papers. The correspondents opposed the nomination of Thomas Finnigan, an Irish Catholic, for an upstate assembly seat; Bacon felt that the local Irish were pressing for too many offices. See also letter of Thomas A. Fulton to William C. Whitney, Nov. 14, 1892, in William C. Whitney Papers (Library of Congress, Washington, D.C.), cited hereafter as Whitney Papers. Fulton bitterly opposed the nomination of Edward Murphy or any other Catholic for the U.S. Senate.

    Fully one-third of the nineteenth-century Irish immigration had taken place in a seven-year period (1847–54); the Irish-born population reached its peak in New York State in 1870, and in Connecticut and New Jersey twenty years later. But the American-born children of these immigrants attained maturity during the final three decades of the century. As a consequence, the political strength of the Irish community increased. On Irish immigration, see Arnold Schrier, *Ireland and the American Emigration, 1850–1900* (Minneapolis: University of Minnesota Press, 1958), 4–5, 159 (table 5), 161 (table 8).
37. Benson, *The Concept of Jacksonian Democracy, op. cit.,* 187–91, 322; John Webb Pratt, *Religion, Politics, and Diversity: The Church-State Theme in New York History* (Ithaca: Cornell University Press, 1967), chap. vii, esp. 171–90.
38. See, in particular, the long and perceptive letter of James S. Clarkson to Welker Given, Sept. 18, 1894, in James S. Clarkson Papers (Library of Congress, Washington, D.C.), cited hereafter as Clarkson Papers.
39. Brown, *op. cit.,* chap. viii; Nelson, *op. cit.,* 87. See also correspondence in the Wharton Barker Papers (Library of Congress, Washington, D.C.), cited hereafter as Barker Papers. Barker contributed to the Republican effort among Irish Americans.
40. Letters of Whitelaw Reid to Charles W. Hackett, Chairman of the Executive Committee, New York State Republican Committee, Sept. 2, 1892; to Patrick Egan, U.S. Minister to Chile, Sept. 1, 1892; to Secretary of State John W. Foster, Sept. 21, 26, 1892; and to Mrs. Richard Crowley, Sept.

23, 1892, all in Whitelaw Reid Papers (Library of Congress, Washington, D.C.), cited hereafter as Reid Papers. Richard Crowley was a former U.S. Representative from western New York State; New York *Tribune*, Oct. 23, 25, 1890, July 17, Oct. 4, 26, 1892.

Letters of Donald Nicholson to George W. Smalley, Feb. 4, 9, July 5, 1892; and to Whitelaw Reid, n.d. [1892]; letters of George W. Smalley to Donald Nicholson, Feb. 15, 1892; and to Whitelaw Reid, March 6, 14, 1892; letter of Whitelaw Reid to Donald Nicholson, Jan. 4, 1891 [1892], all in Reid Papers.

41. This paragraph is based closely on the thoughtful analysis in Brown, *op. cit., passim.*
42. Letter of Samuel F. Barr to William McKinley, Sept. 13, 1896, in William McKinley Papers (Library of Congress, Washington, D.C.), cited hereafter as McKinley Papers. Barr was an Irish-born Protestant.
43. New York *Tribune*, Aug. 21, 24, 28, 1892; New York *Times*, Sept. 2, 1892; letters of Whitelaw Reid to P. Hall Packer, Aug. 29, 1892; to S. Manning Wykoff, Sept. 2, 1892; and to A. E. S. Bush, Sept. 30, 1892, all in Reid Papers.
44. Benson, *The Concept of Jacksonian Democracy, op. cit.*, chap. ix; Seymour Martin Lipset, "Religion and Politics in the American Past and Present," *Religion and Social Conflict*, eds. Robert Lee and Martin Marty (New York: Oxford University Press, 1964), 76–82.
45. D. Leigh Colvin, *Prohibition in the United States: A History of the Prohibition Party and of the Prohibition Movement* (New York: George H. Doran Company, 1926), 101, 107–8; Niven, *op. cit.*, 475–78; William E. Sackett, *Modern Battles of Trenton, being a History of New Jersey's Politics and Legislation from the Year 1868 to the Year 1894* (Trenton: John L. Murphy, 1895), 285.
46. *Tribune Almanac, 1887*, 70–73.
47. Sackett, *op. cit.*, 285–87. The measure passed the assembly 31 to 26, with only 2 Democrats (from Cumberland County) favoring it and 5 Republicans (3 from Essex, 1 each from Hudson and Mercer counties) opposing it. The affirmative senate vote was 12 to 6, with a Democrat from Hunterdon County voting with the majority. One Democratic absentee (from Cumberland) later announced support for the bill, another (from Bergen) indicated opposition. The law further provided severe penalties for selling without a license or on Sundays.
48. *Ibid.*, 288–89; *Manual of the Legislature of New Jersey . . . 1889*, 281–316.
49. S. H. Popper, "New Tensions in Old Newark: Germanic Influence and the Sabbath Observance Controversy, 1870–1910," *Proceedings*, The New Jersey Historical Society, LXX (April 1952), 124–26; Rudolph J. Vecoli, *The People of New Jersey, The New Jersey Historical Series*, eds. Richard M. Huber and Wheaton J. Lane (Princeton: Van Nostrand, 1964–), 88–98 (esp. 93–94), 116–26, 153–54, 167, 280–81; Newark *Daily Advertiser*, Oct. 7, 1893.

50. *Manual of the Legislature of New Jersey . . . 1890,* 155–61, 180–86; Sackett, *op. cit.,* 291–93; *Tribune Almanac, 1890,* 112. The Werts bill passed the assembly, 32 to 27, and the senate, 11 to 10, with one Republican assemblyman the only man to cross party lines.
51. Lee Benson, *The Concept of Jacksonian Democracy, op. cit.,* 131, 138, observes that each major party lost strength in its strong counties while gaining in its weak ones during stable phases of voting cycles in nineteenth-century New York State. Analyses of county-level presidential returns from Connecticut, New York, and New Jersey confirm this for 1860–92. The following coefficients of variability indicate that on the county level, the dispersion of Republican and Democratic percentage strength about their respective mean percentage strengths was greater in 1860 than 1892 in all three states:

	1860		1892	
	REP.	DEM.	REP.	DEM.
Connecticut	.112	.095	.059	.079
New York	.157	.220	.121	.157
New Jersey	.157	.117	.118	.112

The Prohibition party contributed particularly to the narrowing dispersion of Republican percentages by drawing off G.O.P. support in strongly Republican counties.

On the coefficient of variability see Blalock, *Social Statistics, op. cit.,* 67–74.

52. Bass, *op. cit.,* 61–65, chap. v; Nevins, *op. cit.,* 174–75, 187–88, 427, 439; De Alva S. Alexander, *Four Famous New Yorkers: The Political Careers of Cleveland, Platt, Hill and Roosevelt Forming Volume Four of "The Political History of the State of New York" 1882–1905* (New York: Henry Holt, 1923), 134–35. It should be noted that Harrison carried New York State in the face of a Prohibition vote larger than that which had allegedly contributed to the defeat of Blaine four years earlier. For the best brief analysis of the Prohibition vote in New York, see Benson, "Research Problems in American Political Historiography," *loc. cit.,* 128–30. My Table 3 owes much to his Table I, p. 129.
53. For reports on various states, see *Tribune Almanac, 1882,* 29; *1883,* 95; *1884,* 80–81, 99–100; *1885,* 60, 107; *1886,* 97–98; *1887,* 56, 79, 99; *1888,* 76–79, 103–5; *1889,* 93, 96, 118; *1890,* 65, 73, 81–82, 86–87, 111–12; *1891,* 344–45. Many reports include the legislative and/or popular votes involved.

Frederick C. Luebke, *Immigrants and Politics: The Germans of Nebraska, 1880–1900* (Lincoln: University of Nebraska Press, 1969), analyzes intensively the response of Germans of diverse religious backgrounds to the cultural conflict of the period.

54. Donald L. Kinzer, *An Episode in Anti-Catholicism: The American Protective Association* (Seattle: University of Washington Press, 1964), 64–67; Kleppner, *op. cit.,* chap. iv; Wyman, *loc. cit., passim.*

55. Kinzer, *op. cit.*, 25–28; *Tribune Almanac, 1883*, 63; *1884*, 100; *1885*, 107; *1886*, 97–98; *1887*, 82, 99; *1888*, 104–5; *1889*, 88, 96, 118; *1890*, 73, 86–87, 111; *1891*, 311, 344.
56. J. Rogers Hollingsworth, *The Whirligig of Politics: The Democracy of Cleveland and Bryan* (Chicago: University of Chicago Press, 1963), 3–4; Hicks, *op. cit.*, 153–85; Nevins, *op. cit.*, 463–64.
57. *Tribune Almanac, 1890*, 65, 69, 73, 81–82; Gerald W. McFarland, "The Breakdown of Deadlock: The Cleveland Democracy in Connecticut, 1884–1894," *The Historian*, XXXI (May 1969), 391–92.
58. *Tribune Almanac, 1890*, 66–67, 69, 73–82, 89–110. Cf. Horace S. Merrill, *Bourbon Democracy of the Middle West, 1865–1896* (Baton Rouge: Louisiana State University Press, 1953), 203–9, 220–37.
59. *Tribune Almanac, 1891*, 271–347; Kleppner, *op. cit.*, chap. iv; Wyman, *loc. cit.*, *passim*. The Democrats captured the more representative house of the Connecticut legislature, but suffered a disputed defeat in the gubernatorial contest. *The* [New York] *World Almanac, 1892*, 329.
60. *Tribune Almanac, 1893*, 311.
61. Mark D. Hirsch, *William C. Whitney, Modern Warwick* (New York: Dodd, Mead, 1948), 401–7; Nevins, *op. cit.*, 493–98; Merrill, *op. cit.*, 227–30; letter of Grover Cleveland to William C. Whitney, Aug. 23, 1892; letter of William C. Whitney to Grover Cleveland, Aug. 30, 1892; letters of Douglas A. Levian to William C. Whitney, Oct. 3, 5, 1892; letter of Douglas A. Levian to Col. George B. M. Harvey, Sept. 25, 1892; letter of C. S. S. Miller to William C. Whitney, Sept. 28, 1892, all in Whitney Papers.
62. The parties gained (+) or lost (−) percentage strength in counties in the three states as follows:

PARTY	NEW JERSEY		CONNECTICUT		NEW YORK	
Democratic	+15	−6	+8	0	+20	−37
Republican	+5	−16	+1	−7	+5	−53

In New York, Democratic percentage strength did not fluctuate in two counties; Republican percentage strength remained unchanged in one county. Fulton and Hamilton counties have been counted as one unit (as they had been in 1888).

The pattern of Democratic gains in the Northeast suggests that the party had reaped the benefit of shifts in the composition of the population and electorate as well as having won over some Republicans: i.e., normally Democratic groups were growing faster than their Republican counterparts. (Rhode Island provided a special case: widening of the suffrage had worked to the Democrats' advantage there. New York *Times*, May 18, 19, 1893.)

On long-term shifts, see Benson, *The Concept of Jacksonian Democracy*, *op. cit.*, 131; V. O. Key, Jr., "Secular Realignment and the Party

System," *Journal of Politics,* XXI (May 1959), 198–210. Everett S. Lee and Others, *Population Redistribution and Economic Growth: United States, 1870–1950,* Vol. I: *Methodological Considerations and Reference Tables* (Philadelphia: The American Philosophical Society, 1957), 107–231, contains a wealth of information on net intercensal migration, rates of net migration, and average population by nativity, but unfortunately sheds no light on trends in the second-generation population.

63. Compare percentage point shifts, 1888–92, in the three most populous counties with state-wide shifts in turnout (T) and Democratic (D) and Republican (R) gain or loss:

	T	D	R		T	D	R
New York State	+ 1.3	+0.8	−3.7	Kings County	+11.5	+3.2	−5.6
Erie County	+10.5	−0.3	−3.7	New York County	+ 4.5	+1.8	−4.5

Kings County more than accounted for the state-wide increase in turnout; the Democrats' plurality in New York County more than offset the Republicans' upstate plurality.

64. Letter of Theodore Roosevelt to Henry Cabot Lodge, Oct. 11, 1892, quoted in Elting Morison (ed.), *The Letters of Theodore Roosevelt,* Vol. I: *The Years of Preparation, 1868–1898* (8 vols.; Cambridge: Harvard University Press, 1951), 292; letter of Walter Thorn to Benjamin F. Tracy, Oct. 17, 1892, in Benjamin F. Tracy Papers (Library of Congress, Washington, D.C.), cited hereafter as Tracy Papers; letter of Benjamin S. Pardee to William E. Chandler, Nov. 14, 1892, in William E. Chandler Papers (Library of Congress, Washington, D.C.), cited hereafter as Chandler Papers; Wanamaker statement reported in the New York *Herald,* Nov. 10, 1892, quoted in George Harmon Knoles, *The Presidential Campaign and Election of 1892* (Stanford University Publications. University Series. History, Economics, and Political Science, Vol. V, No. 1; Stanford: Stanford University Press, 1942), 233.

65. Letter of Andrew Powell to Henry Baldwin, Oct. 27, 1891; letter of Charles L. Hoyt to Henry Baldwin, May 4, 1891, both in Henry Baldwin Papers (New York Public Library), cited hereafter as Henry Baldwin Papers. The Henry Baldwin Papers include letters and other materials relating to nativistic, anti-Catholic, and patriotic organizations during this period; New York *Tribune,* Sept. 5, 1892.

66. See the Chandler Papers, Nov. 1892–Jan. 1893. Despite the importance of Chandler in the immigration restriction movement, his papers have not been worked by students of nativism.

67. Letter of Max Hasselbach to William E. Chandler, Dec. 7, 1892, in Chandler Papers.

68. On the nativist temper of the 1880s and 1890s, see John Higham, *Strangers in the Land: Patterns of American Nativism, 1860–1925* (New Brunswick: Rutgers University Press, 1955) chaps. iii–iv. The writer has been

deeply influenced by Professor Higham's writings on nativism, anti-Catholicism, and anti-Semitism.

It should be borne in mind that Democratic popular support reached its peak in the midterm elections of 1890. Still, the Democratic capture of the presidency two years later did bring home to many the altered political situation.

For the only restrictionist sentiments discovered in the papers of Democrats consulted during the course of the present research, see letter of John L. Martin to David B. Hill, Dec. 21, 1892, in Hill Papers.

69. U.S., Bureau of the Census, *Historical Statistics of the United States, Colonial Times to 1957* (Washington, D.C.: Government Printing Office, 1960), 56–59, 66.

70. On New York City, see *Tribune Almanac, 1893,* 316; map, *Harper's Weekly,* XXXIX (Jan. 19, 1895), 60–61; on Chicago, see Bessie Louise Pierce, *A History of Chicago,* Vol. III: *The Rise of the Modern City, 1871–1893* (New York: Knopf, 1957), 515–16, 520–21, 542. The Republicans were understandably stunned by the increased turnout and Democratic strength in Chicago, which provided Cleveland's margin of victory in Illinois. But Poles, Russians, and Italians constituted only 2.2%, 0.7%, and 0.5% of Chicago's population (1890) and 1.9%, 1.1%, and 0.4% of its registered voters (1892).

71. Still, politicians were not about to miss a trick: the Republican national platform of 1892 not only proclaimed for Irish home rule but denounced the persecution of Jews in Russia.

II. 1893: THE FIRST SHOCK

1. New York *Times,* March 22, April 6, 26, May 15–19, 30, 31, June 2, 1893; New York *Tribune,* April 10, 1893; *Tribune Almanac, 1894,* 282, 343–44; Nelson, The Influence of Immigration, *op. cit.,* 185, 187.

2. Rendigs Fels, *American Business Cycles, 1865–1897* (Chapel Hill: University of North Carolina Press, 1959), chaps. x–xii; and Charles Hoffmann, *The Depression of the Nineties: An Economic History* (Westport, Conn.: Greenwood, 1970) are basic to an understanding of the depression.

3. Samuel Rezneck, "Unemployment, Unrest, and Relief in the United States During the Depression of 1893–1897," *Journal of Political Economy,* LXI (Aug. 1953), 329–31; Charles O. Burgess, "The Newspaper as Charity Worker: Poor Relief in New York City, 1893–1894," *New York History,* XLIII (July 1962), 249–53.

4. Rezneck, *loc. cit.,* 329–31; Burgess, *loc. cit.,* 251–52; New York *Tribune,* Dec. 21, 24, 27, 28, 1893; "Letters to Mayor Gilroy, 1894. Relief for the Unemployed," box in Thomas F. Gilroy Papers (Municipal Archives and Records Center, New York City), cited hereafter as Gilroy Papers. The largest contribution listed was that made by the Lager Beer Brewers Board of Trade of New York and Vicinity.

5. New York *Tribune,* Aug. 11, 28, 1893, Jan. 4, 1894; letters of Roswell P.

Flower to Timothy S. Williams, n.d. [Sept. 12, 1893], Sept. 12, 1893, both in Timothy S. Williams Papers (New York Public Library), cited hereafter as Timothy S. Williams Papers; speeches of Governor Roswell P. Flower, Cortland County Agricultural Society's Annual Fair, Cortland, Sept. 14, 1893; New York State Fair, Syracuse, Sept. 16, 1893; Palmyra, Sept. 29, 1893; Ontario County Fair, Canandaigua, Sept. 27, 1893, copies in Bixby Papers. Both quotations are from the Syracuse speech. For the inspiring words of Grover Cleveland, see Nevins, *Grover Cleveland, op. cit.*, 331–32.

6. New York *Times,* Aug. 25, 1893; New York *Tribune,* Aug. 25, 1893; Newark *Daily Advertiser,* July 8, Sept. 15, 30, Oct. 17, 1893; letter of Michael T. Barrett to James Smith, Jr., Oct. 2, 1893, in Daniel Lamont Papers (Library of Congress, Washington, D.C.), cited hereafter as Lamont Papers; Higham, *Strangers in the Land, op. cit.*, 72.
7. Moses Rischin, *The Promised City: New York's Jews, 1870–1914* (Cambridge: Harvard University Press, 1962), chap. iv, 178, 272 (table 3); New York *Times,* July 17, 18, Aug. 17–29, 1893; New York *Tribune,* July 5, Aug. 17–28, 1893. For similar difficulties in Newark, see Newark *Daily Advertiser,* July 11, Aug. 21, 22, Sept. 4, 1893; New York *Tribune,* Aug. 19, 20, 1893.

   The New York *Times* was ambivalent toward Jews during the early 1890s. It denounced anti-Semitism in the United States, Russia, and Germany. See New York *Times,* April 19, 26, Sept. 2, 1893. But referring to the dissemination of radical literature in the Lower East Side, the New York *Times,* Aug. 23, 1893, concluded that "on this base and poisonous diet the hatchet-faced, pimply, sallow-cheeked, rat-eyed young men of the Russian-Jew colony feed full. . . . [O]n these depraved, diseased, diabolical natures the appalling nonsense of creatures like [Emma] Goldman falls like alcohol on a kindling flame." The youthful immigrants, the *Times* warned, are "atrociously hideous, atrociously ignorant, atrociously cruel"; their faces are not those of "wild beasts, but of malignant reptiles."
8. Harold U. Faulkner, *Politics, Reform, and Expansion, 1890–1900, The New American Nation Series,* eds. Henry Steele Commager and Richard B. Morris (New York: Harper & Row, 1954–   ), 102–5, 125, 147.
9. Nevins, *op. cit.*, 523–27, 541–42. For weak dissent from the regional orthodoxy, see New York *Tribune,* July 7, Aug. 7, 1893.
10. Festus P. Summers, *William L. Wilson and Tariff Reform* (New Brunswick: Rutgers University Press, 1953), 157–60; Nevins, *op. cit.*, 533–48.
11. New York *Times,* Oct. 31, Nov. 1, 1893; New York *Tribune,* Nov. 1, 2, 1893.
12. Letters of Representative John DeWitt Warner to Charles S. Fairchild, March 9, 1892, March 30, April 1, 1893; letter of Representative William L. Wilson to Charles S. Fairchild, May 7, 1892, all in Charles S. Fairchild Papers (New-York Historical Society, New York City), cited hereafter as Fairchild Papers; letter of Senator David B. Hill to Manton Marble, Aug. 14, 1893, in Manton Marble Papers (Library of Congress, Washington,

D.C.), cited hereafter as Marble Papers; Hollingsworth, *The Whirligig of Politics, op. cit.*, 14–15; Nevins, *op. cit.*, 547 (note 2).

13. Nevins, *ibid.*, 540; *Tribune Almanac, 1894,* 114–16.
14. Nevins, *ibid.*, 533–34.
15. Hartford *Courant,* July 10, 1893; Newark *Daily Advertiser,* July 25, Aug. 7, 1893; New York *Tribune,* July 12, 21, 22, Aug. 1, 7, 21, 1893; letters of Benjamin Harrison to E. A. Angen, July 27, 1893; and to W. H. H. Miller, July 28, 1893; letter of Louis T. Michener to Benjamin Harrison, Aug. 26, 1893, all in Benjamin Harrison Papers (Library of Congress, Washington, D.C.), cited hereafter as Harrison Papers.
    For sharp Democratic replies, see New York *Times,* July 22, 24, 1893.
16. Nevins, *op. cit.*, chaps. xxi, xxii, xxiv, xxvi, xxvii.
17. Samuel P. Hays, *The Response to Industrialism, 1885–1914, The Chicago History of American Civilization,* ed. Daniel J. Boorstin (Chicago: University of Chicago Press, 1957–), 132–37.
18. Summers, *op. cit.*, 72–77; Geoffrey Blodgett, *The Gentle Reformers: Massachusetts Democrats in the Cleveland Era* (Cambridge: Harvard University Press, 1966), chap. iv; Harold F. Williamson, *Edward Atkinson: The Biography of an American Liberal, 1827–1905* (Boston: Old Corner Book Store, 1934), chaps. iii, v.
19. Edward C. Kirkland, *Industry Comes of Age: Business, Labor, and Public Policy, 1860–1897,* Vol. VI of *The Economic History of the United States, op. cit.*, 188.
20. Summers, *op. cit.*, 154–56, 164–72; Williamson, *op. cit.*, 178–86.
21. Nevins, *op. cit.*, 288, 292–93, 375–77, 415–16; Bass, *"I Am a Democrat," op. cit.*, 88–89; *Tribune Almanac, 1893,* 36, 45; *1895,* 124–26; letter of I. Tomlinson to Simeon E. Baldwin, Sept. 14, 1892, in Baldwin Family Papers; Hanna G. Roach, "Sectionalism in Congress (1870–1890)," *The American Political Science Review,* XIX (Aug. 1925), 500–526, esp. 523–24.
22. New York *Tribune,* July 17, 28, Aug. 7, Sept. 5, 9, 13, 16, 19, Nov. 5, 1893; New York *Times,* July 17, 1893; Hartford *Courant,* Sept. 19, 1893; Newark *Daily Advertiser,* July 28, Aug. 3, 4, Sept. 9, 1893; Trenton *Daily True American,* Sept. 9, 12, 1893; Summers, *op. cit.*, 163–67.
    Steel operators on the East Coast were among the minority favoring tariff reductions. Abram S. Hewitt, the venerable New Jersey ironmaster, prepared the iron and steel schedules for the committee. But New England manufacturers were by this time thoroughly frightened of tariff reform. See New York *Times,* Dec. 11, 1893; letters of Abram S. Hewitt to James M. Swank, July 8, 12, 1893; to William L. Wilson, Oct. 4, 27, 31, Nov. 15, 1893, all in Abram S. Hewitt Papers (Cooper Union Library, New York City), cited hereafter as Hewitt Papers; Williamson, *op. cit.*, 180–81.
    Summers contends that the time was ripe for tariff reform because the Democracy was united and revision "would be less painful if performed while business slept." (p. 164). These judgments reflect Professor Sum-

mers's sympathy with the proponents of tariff reform rather than an accurate assessment of the political realities of 1893.

23. States other than those analyzed here also held elections in the fall of 1893. In Kansas and South Dakota, the Republicans won county and local elections. In Michigan, the Democrats won by a reduced margin in a special congressional election. Detailed returns were not available to the writer, but see *Tribune Almanac, 1894,* 321, 326, 345.
24. *Tribune Almanac, 1886,* 66; *1894,* 54–70, 318–19, 324–25, 338–43; New York *Times,* Aug. 11, 16, 17, Sept. 14, Oct. 8, 11, 13, Nov. 6, 8, 1893, Jan. 19, 1894; New York *Tribune,* Aug. 17, 19, Nov. 9, 1893; Newark *Daily Advertiser,* June 14, Aug. 11, Sept. 13, Nov. 16, 1893; Trenton *Daily True American,* Sept. 2, 16, 1893; Rathgeber, The Democratic Party in Pennsylvania, *op. cit.,* 302–5; Thomas A. Flinn, "Continuity and Change in Ohio Politics," *Journal of Politics,* XXIV (Aug. 1962), 529–32; I. Ridgeway Davis, "A Century of Voting in Three Ohio Counties," *The Ohio Historical Quarterly,* LXIX (April 1960), 121–56.
25. *Tribune Almanac, 1894,* 65–66; New York *Times,* Feb. 7, Oct. 5, 7, 30, 1893; New York *Tribune,* Sept. 1, 21, Oct. 30, Nov. 3, 7, 1893; Newark *Daily Advertiser,* Sept. 13, 20, 21, 25, 1893.
26. Alexander, *Four Famous New Yorkers, op. cit.,* 158–63, 198–99.
27. New York *Times,* Sept. 23, Oct. 3, 5–7, 10, 11, 15, 18–20, 24, 27, Nov. 1, 3, 6, 1893; New York *Tribune,* Oct. 7, 8, 10, 12, 16, 17, 20, 22, 23, 28, 30, Nov. 1–3, 1893.
28. New York *Times,* May 3, Oct. 1, 14, 15, 24, 26, 29, 30, 1893; New York *Tribune,* Sept. 27, 29, Oct. 3, 4, 8, 27, 30, Nov. 1, 1893; Brooklyn *Daily Eagle,* March 20, 21, April 17–21, May 15, June 5, 16, July 8, 9, Sept. 6-Nov. 12, 1893; letter of Edward M. Shepard to Daniel S. Lamont, Sept. 22, 1893, in Lamont Papers; Harold F. Gosnell, *Boss Platt and His New York Machine* (Chicago: University of Chicago Press, 1924), 45–47; Harold C. Syrett, *The City of Brooklyn, 1865–1898: A Political History* (New York: Columbia University Press, 1944), chap. xiii.
29. Letter of Timothy S. Williams to Delos McCurdy, Oct. 17, 1893, in Timothy S. Williams Papers; New York *Tribune,* Oct. 24, Nov. 5, 1893.
30. Bass, *op. cit.,* chaps. ii–v, vii–viii; Nevins, *op. cit.,* chaps. xiv–xxiv, xxvi–xxvii; letter of Nathan D. Bates to Charles S. Fairchild, March 18, 1892, in Fairchild Papers; letter of Francis Lynde Stetson to William C. Whitney, May 5, 1892, in Whitney Papers; letter of R. Hover to Manton Marble, Feb. 27, 1892; letter of George P. Irish to Manton Marble, March 1, 1892, both in Marble Papers.
31. Bass, *op. cit.,* 236–39; Hirsch, *William C. Whitney, op. cit.,* 400–407; Nevins, *op. cit.,* 463, 496–98; Knoles, *The Presidential Campaign and Election of 1892, op. cit.,* 163–67; letters of Charles S. Fairchild to William L. Wilson, March 26, 1892; to C. F. Kingsley, July 5, 1892; to George R. Crawford, July 5, 1892; and to [George Cary] Eggleston, July 13, 1892, all in Fairchild Papers.

   Whitney and Croker maintained mutually profitable relations: Whitney's urban transit interests involved him in extensive dealings with the municipal government of which Croker was master.

32. Nevins, *op. cit.*, 568–69; above, Chap. I, Note 36; New York *Times,* Jan. 21, 22, 1893. On patronage, see the Fairchild Papers, Nov.-Dec., 1893.
33. Nevins, *op. cit.*, 516, 569–72; Bass, *op. cit.*, 241; New York *Tribune,* July 1, Sept. 20, 30, Oct. 4, 1893; New York *Times,* Sept. 19–24, Oct. 1–3, 1893; also the Hill Papers, Sept. 1893.
34. Letter of W. Caryl Ely to Daniel S. Lamont, Oct. 25, 1893, in Lamont Papers; New York *Times,* Oct. 24, 27, Nov. 1, 6, 1893; letter of Timothy S. Williams to Isaac H. Maynard, Nov. 2, 1893; letter of Isaac H. Maynard to Timothy S. Williams, Nov. 5, 1893, both in Timothy S. Williams Papers.
35. Sackett, *Modern Battles of Trenton, op. cit.*, 383–88, 442–43.
36. *Ibid.*, 440–49; New York *Times,* Feb. 21–28, March 3–7, 1893. The Assembly passed the bills, 33 to 22, with 2 Republicans voting yea and 6 Democrats nay; the Senate concurred, 12 to 9, with 1 Republican voting yea and 5 Democrats nay. The Assembly overrode the governor's veto, 33 to 25, with 3 Republicans voting with the majority and 8 Democrats voting with the minority; the Senate followed suit, 11 to 9, with 1 Republican and 6 Democrats similarly shifting sides. Majority votes sufficed to override the veto.
37. New York *Times,* Feb. 24, 26, 27, March 1, 2, 6–10, May 15, 1893; New York *Tribune,* Feb. 25–27, March 1–3, 5–7, 11, 20, June 24, 1893; Sackett, *op. cit.*, 448–53.

    Newark *Daily Advertiser,* Sept. 15, Oct. 5, 16, 21, 23, 1893; Trenton *Daily True American,* Oct. 17–19, Nov. 4, 1893; New York *Tribune,* Sept. 24, 30, Oct. 4, 8, 9, 16, 18, 23, 25, 29, 30, Nov. 2, 6, 1893.
38. For references to Protestant clergymen and denominations, see above, Note 37. For references of one kind or another to Catholics and/or Jews, see New York *Tribune,* March 2, Oct. 9, 11, 25, 1893.

    My thinking on this subject has been greatly stimulated by Gerhard Lenski, *The Religious Factor: A Sociological Study of Religion's Impact on Politics, Economics, and Family Life* (Garden City, N.Y.: Doubleday, 1961), *passim,* esp. 174–79; Lipset, "Religion and Politics," *loc. cit., passim,* esp. 72–83; Benson, *The Concept of Jacksonian Democracy, op. cit.*, 192–207; Samuel P. Hays, "History as Human Behavior," *Iowa Journal of History,* LVIII (July 1960), 196–97.
39. New York *Times,* March 2, 1893; New York *Tribune,* March 2, 1893. Father Dean McNulty of Paterson, the only priest prominent in the anti-racetrack movement, spoke at this meeting.
40. Newark *Daily Advertiser,* Feb. 25, 28, March 7, 1893; New York *Times,* Feb. 25–28, March 7, 10, 1893, June 11, 1894; New York *Tribune,* Feb. 25, March 20, 27, 1893; Sackett, *op. cit.*, 112–22, 386; Carl D. Hinrichsen, The History of the Diocese of Newark, 1873–1901 (unpublished Ph.D. dissertation, Dept. of History, Catholic University of America, 1963), 62–78, 272–75.

41. Trenton *Daily True American,* Oct. 11, 16, 19, 21, 23, 28, 30, Nov. 2, 6, 1893; Newark *Daily Advertiser,* Nov. 3, 1893; New York *Times,* Jan. 14, Sept. 15, 24, 26, Oct. 2, 9, 11, 16, 27, 1893; New York *Tribune,* Sept. 9, 19, 24–30, Oct. 1, 4, 6, 8–11, 16–18, 23, 25, 30, Nov. 2, 5, 6, 10, 11, 1893; also Sackett, *op. cit.,* chap. xxxiv.
42. The Republicans gained 4 senate and 17 assembly seats. Ironically, Isaac Maynard, who ran for Secretary of State in 1883 as the personal choice of Governor Cleveland against the wishes of Irish politicians, had been the last Democrat to fail of election to state office. See above, Chap. I.

    For the sources of election data and information relating to the electorate, see Appendixes A and B. Local returns from the election for judge of the court of appeals are available only for units in New York and Kings counties.
43. On Maynard's defeat, see Nevins, *op. cit.,* 569; Hirsch, *op. cit.,* 471; Bass, *op. cit.,* 242.

    In 1894, Niagara County ranked fifth in support for the Democratic Party Reform Organization, but Queens and Westchester tied for seventh, so no metropolitan county fell below that rank.
44. Socialist Labor strength ranged from 3.8 to 10.3% in A.D.s 3, 4, 5, 6, 7, and 10 in the Lower East Side (south of 17th Street) and from 3.7 to 8.2% in A.D.s 16, 20, 22, 24, and 25 in the East Side (between 44th and 105th streets); the party also received 3.5% in A.D. 29 in the southern Bronx. No other assembly district reported an above-average vote for the SLP. (The party's improved showing in New York City contributed greatly to state-wide percentage gains, which exceeded those of the People's and Prohibition parties.)

    Mean Republican (R) and Democratic (D) percentage point shifts in the election for Secretary of State; percentage points by which Maynard trailed Meyer (M); and Socialist Labor party (SLP) percentage strength in these A.D.s were:

A.D.S	R	D	M	SLP
1, 2	−7.9	+7.8	− 1.9	1.4
3–7, 10	−8.0	+5.1	− 5.6	6.2
7 (only)	−0.4	−2.7	−11.7	6.4

    On alleged election irregularities in the 2nd A.D., see below, Chap. IV. On factionalism in the 7th A.D., see New York *Times,* Jan. 21, 22, 1893; New York *Tribune,* May 25, 1893. For a description of the 10th A.D., see New York *Times,* July 18, 1893. See also New York *Sun,* Jan. 20, 1895 (New York Public Library Scrapbooks).
45. Mean Republican (R) and Democratic (D) percentage point shifts in the election for Secretary of State; percentage points by which Maynard trailed Meyer (M); and Socialist Labor party (SLP) percentage strength in east and west side A.D.s were:

A.D.S	R	D	M	SLP	A.D.S	R	D	M	SLP
12, 14	−2.9	+1.6	− 5.9	2.0	8, 9	−0.9	+0.4	−4.8	1.3
16, 20, 22, 24, 25	−1.1	−4.1	−10.2	5.5	13, 15, 17, 18, 19	−1.4	+0.8	−5.1	2.5

The New York *Times,* July 24, Aug. 7, 14, 21, 28, Sept. 7, 11, 25, Oct. 2, 1893, describe A.D.s 13, 20, 19, 9, 8, 16, 15, 12, and 17, respectively; Caroline F. Ware, *Greenwich Village, 1920–1930: A Comment on American Civilization in the Post-War Years* (Boston: Houghton Mifflin, 1935), 9–15, treats the 8th A.D.

46. Mean Republican (R) and Democratic (D) percentage point shifts in the election for Secretary of State; percentage points by which Maynard trailed Meyer (M); and Socialist Labor party (SLP) percentage strength in these A.D.s were:

A.D.S	R	D	M	SLP
11, 21, 23, 26–28	+6.5	−7.7	−11.2	1.6
29, 30	−1.2	+0.4	−10.6	2.8

The 29th and 30th A.D.s, where Meyer gained, were located in the Bronx. On the 23rd and 27th A.D.s, see New York *Times,* July 10, Sept. 18, 1893. The James R. Sheffield Papers (Yale University, New Haven), cited hereafter as Sheffield Papers, shed some light on the 11th A.D., where Sheffield, a Republican who received support from Good Government clubs and independent Democrats, defeated Tammany's assembly candidate.

Even in the harmony election of 1892, Cleveland had run ahead of Tammany's mayoralty candidate in the 21st A.D. Cleveland had received 54.8% of the vote in 1892, Maynard only 26.5% one year later—a defection ratio of 51.6. The defection ratio, a measure developed by V. O. Key, Jr., here indicates a party's percentage loss between elections as a percentage of that party's percentage strength in the earlier election.

47. Contemporary observers noted the ethnic dimensions of the vote. See New York *Times,* Nov. 8, 9, 1893; New York *Tribune,* Nov. 9, 1893.

Blalock, Jr., *Social Statistics, op. cit.,* 317–24, treats two measures of rank-order correlation, Spearman's r_s and Kendall's tau, employed in the main body of this study. Unless otherwise noted, Spearman's measure has been utilized.

48. Meyer's percentage point loss (1) and the percentage points by which Maynard trailed Meyer (2) in these counties were:

COUNTY	(1)	(2)	COUNTY	(1)	(2)	COUNTY	(1)	(2)
Queens	−3.5	−11.1	Rockland	−5.1	−8.7	Westchester	−4.6	−5.0
Richmond	−4.8	− 5.7	Suffolk	−3.9	−4.6	Mean	−4.4	−7.0

49. In Kings County, Meyer fell 10.5 percentage points short of Cleveland's mark. Maynard trailed Meyer by 3.7 points.

    Brooklyn's foreign-born population was proportionally smaller than that of New York City, and a larger proportion of Brooklyn's foreign-born population was English or Canadian, while a smaller proportion was Russian, Hungarian, or Italian. Most of these groups cannot be geographically isolated for political analysis. East European Jews did predominate in Election District 2 of Ward 26. There the Democrats received 33.4%, the Republicans 34.4%, and the Socialist Labor party 26.6% in 1893. The E.D. was Socialist Labor's ranking unit in Brooklyn. On this district, see Alter F. Landesman, *Brownsville: The Birth, Development and Passing of a Jewish Community in New York* (New York: Bloch, 1969), 43ff.
50. Meyer lost percentage strength in 53 of 59 counties, as follows: −0.01 to −2.4 (15); −2.5 to −4.9 (19); −5.0 to −7.4 (14); −7.5 to −9.9 (2); −10.0 to −12.4 (2); and −12.5 or more (1); Maynard trailed the ticket in 57 counties, as follows: −0.01 to −0.9 (17); −1.0 to −1.9 (21); −2.0 to −2.9 (9); −3.0 to −3.9 (4); −4.0 to −4.9 (1); and −5.0 or more (5).
51. O. H. White, *An Economic Study of Land Utilization in Clinton County, New York* (Bulletin 689, April 1938; Ithaca: Cornell University Agricultural Experiment Station, 1938), treats the agricultural economy of Clinton County. On Democratic factionalism, see New York *Times*, Oct. 3, 1893; New York *Sun*, Sept. 17, 1893 (New York Public Library Scrapbooks). The town of Clinton, a French Canadian and Irish settlement, had been the Democrats' banner town for half a century. Buffalo and Rochester contained large German and relatively small Irish populations. Britons and British Canadians, numerous in both cities, gave the Republicans important immigrant support. Correlations between 1892 Democratic percentage strength in Clinton County's towns and the wards of Rochester and Buffalo and Democratic percentage declines therein in 1893 (+.622, +.305, and −.830, respectively) highlight the differences among the three.

    For a perceptive contemporary reading of New York State election returns, see letter of De Alva S. Alexander to Benjamin Harrison, Dec. 4, 1893, in Harrison Papers.
52. For the titles of studies of the agricultural economies of Chemung, Rensselaer, and Schuyler counties, see Howard E. Conklin and Irving R. Starbird, *Annotated Bibliography on Low Incomes in Rural New York State: Supplement to Analytical Report* (n.p. [New York City]: State of New York, Interdepartmental Committee on Low Incomes, 1958), 26–29.

    Meyer gained 2.8 percentage points in Schuyler, 10.5 in Chemung, 8.2 in Rensselaer, 6.8 in Albany, 2.1 in Greene, and 1.2 in Schoharie counties.
53. For Cleveland Democrats' charges of betrayal in 1892 see letter of F. H. Williams to Charles S. Fairchild, Nov. 14, 1892; letter of Israel Lawton to Charles S. Fairchild, Dec. 23, 1892; letter of Charles S. Fairchild to Israel Lawton, Dec. 23, 1892, all in Fairchild Papers; letter of John H. Farley to

William C. Whitney, Sept. 28, 1892; letter of David C. Robinson to William C. Whitney, Nov. 8, 1892, both in Whitney Papers. The writer uncovered no charges involving other counties. Chemung, Schuyler, Greene, and Albany ranked high (1, 2, 7, 8) among counties in which the Democrats lost percentage strength in 1892. Also compare the percentage margin by which Maynard trailed Meyer in Albany, Chemung, Greene, Rensselaer, Schoharie, and Schuyler counties ($\overline{M}$=0.4 points) with the margin in the seven metropolitan area counties ($\overline{M}$=6.6 points).

54. For the sources of election data and information relating to the electorate, see Appendixes A and B.

55. In Cape May County the Democratic assembly candidate fell 14.4 percentage points from 1892, the Republican rose 12.7, and the Prohibitionist rose 1.8. On the county, see Lewis T. Stevens, *The History of Cape May County, New Jersey, from the Aboriginal Times to the Present Day* . . . (Cape May City: Lewis T. Stevens, 1897), 445, 448–49. Anglesea, Avalon, Cape May City, and Cape May Point were the units in which Democratic losses were lighter than in Methodist towns. Anglesea contained a Swedish settlement; 40.7% of the male population of Cape May Point was Negro. Both were Republican towns.

In Cumberland, the Democrats lost 19.0 percentage points, the Republicans gaining 2.1, the Prohibitionists 1.1, and an Independent 15.8. See Sackett, *op. cit.*, 289.

56. In Atlantic County, the Democrats and Prohibitionists gained 7.5 and 3.4 percentage points, respectively, as the Republicans declined by 11.0. On a famous German settlement, see Dieter Cunz, "Egg Harbor City: New Germany in New Jersey," *Proceedings,* The New Jersey Historical Society, LXXIII (April 1955), 89–123.

57. County-wide percentage shifts in assembly elections in Warren, Sussex, and Hunterdon were: Democrats, +6.5, −7.5, −6.0; Republicans, −6.7, +8.4, −1.2; Prohibitionists, +2.3, −0.9, +7.9. In the Warren senatorial election, the respective shifts were: −8.1, +9.3, −1.2. In Hunterdon, the Democrats lost 11.1 points in the district in which they had renominated a racetrack assemblyman and gained 0.3 points in the district in which they had not.

On these counties, see James P. Snell (comp.), *History of Sussex and Warren Counties, New Jersey* . . . (Philadelphia: Everts & Peck, 1881); ——, *History of Hunterdon and Somerset Counties, New Jersey,* . . . (Philadelphia: Everts & Peck, 1881). E. M. Woodward and John F. Hageman, *History of Burlington and Mercer Counties, New Jersey* . . . (Philadelphia: Everts & Peck, 1883), deals with an area in which most Presbyterians appear not to have been of old Dutch origin. Also see New York *Sun,* Dec. 27, 1894 (New York Public Library Scrapbooks).

58. Sackett, *op. cit.*, 451; New York *Tribune,* Feb. 27, 1893; New York *Times,* March 1, 1893, June 11, 1894; Newark *Daily Advertiser,* April 12, 1893; Trenton *Daily True American,* Nov. 2, 6, 1893.

59. Newark *Daily Advertiser,* Nov. 3, 1893; *Manual of the Legislature of New*

Jersey . . . 1894, 224–29. See Appendix B for an explanation of the absence of detailed returns from Newark and Jersey City.

60. In Union, the Democrats lost 6.2 percentage points, the Prohibitionists, 0.8; the Republicans gained 5.5, and the Socialist Labor party, 1.5. The SLP received 2.6% of the county vote and 8.7, 9.0, and 10.2% in Wards 3, 5, and 7 of Elizabeth.
61. In Passaic County, the Democrats lost 7.8 percentage points, the Republican, Socialist Labor, and Prohibition parties gaining 5.2, 2.2, and 0.3, respectively. In Paterson, Wards 5, 6, 7, and 8 had given Democratic assembly candidates 80.4, 82.6, 70.0, and 70.7% of the two-party vote in 1892, Wards 1, 2, 3, and 4, 33.3, 42.5, 42.9, and 32.0%.
62. Correlations among the elections of 1892, 1893, 1894, 1895, 1896, and 1900 in New Jersey reveal the election of 1893 to have been more weakly correlated with each of the others than any other election. Indeed, the strongest correlation between the election of 1893 and another election was weaker than the weakest correlation between any other pair of elections. This held true for both the Republican and Democratic parties.
63. For partisan reactions, see Trenton *Daily True American*, Nov. 9, 11, 1893; Newark *Daily Advertiser*, Nov. 9, 11, 1893; New York *Times*, Nov. 8, 9, 12, 19, 1893; New York *Tribune*, Nov. 9, 10, 1893; Alexander, *op. cit.*, 202–3; letter of David B. Hill to Alton B. Parker, Dec. 7, 1893, in Alton B. Parker Papers (Library of Congress, Washington, D.C.), cited hereafter as Parker Papers.

    For comments by ministers, see New York *Tribune*, Nov. 13, Dec. 1, 1893; New York *Times*, Nov. 13, Dec. 1, 1893. In his Thanksgiving sermon before the Calvary Baptist Church in New York City, the Reverend Robert S. MacArthur praised the elections as a victory of "Protestantism over Romanism," "patriotism over bossism," "Americanism over foreignism," and "religionism . . . over ruffianism."

III. THE POLITICS OF CONSTITUTIONAL REVISION

1. *Tribune Almanac, 1887*, 83; New York *Times*, April 17, May 7, 1887; *Messages from the Governors . . .* , ed. Charles Z. Lincoln (11 vols.; Albany: J. B. Lyon, 1909), VIII: *1885–1891*, 308–11, 397, 470–74.
2. *Messages from the Governors . . . , ibid.*, IX: *1892–1898*, 13, 154–55, 194–96; New York *Times*, Nov. 30, 1892, Jan. 3, 5, 17, 21, 25–28, Oct. 4, 8, 24, 1893; New York *Tribune*, May 14, Nov. 23, 1892, Jan. 5, 8, 17, 26, July 9, Oct. 5, 1893; Alexander, *Four Famous New Yorkers, op. cit.*, 197–98; *Revised Record of the Constitutional Convention of the State of New York, May 8, 1894, to September 29, 1894*, rev. William H. Steele (5 vols.; Albany: The Argus Co., 1900), IV, 86 (remarks of Edward J. Lauterbach), cited hereafter as *R.R.C.C.*; Pratt, *Religion, Politics, and Diversity, op. cit.*, 240.
3. *R.R.C.C.*, I, 9, 22, 171, 244–46, 334–35, 399–433, 498–99, 547–82, 1153–73.

4. *R.R.C.C.,* V, 708–19, Document No. 65. "Report of the Committee on Legislative Organization on Reapportionment of Senate and Assembly Districts." For debates, see *R.R.C.C.,* II, 225; III, 343–56, 632, 765, 921–32, 987–1242; IV, 6–96, 348–76, 460, 644–94.
5. Ruth C. Silva, "Apportionment in New York. Part Two: Apportionment of the New York Senate," *Fordham Law Review,* XXX (April 1962), 604–10, 628–32; *R.R.C.C.,* III, 1213–15, 1223–34; IV, 374 (remarks of John I. Gilbert).
6. Silva, *op. cit.,* 616–28, 633–38.
7. Ruth C. Silva, "Apportionment of the New York Assembly," *Fordham Law Review,* XXXI (Oct. 1962), 13–24. For exchanges over the issue, see *R.R.C.C.,* III, 1002–21, 1031–32, 1046–54, 1064–77, 1083–96, 1128–44, 1149, 1206, 1230–31; IV, 10–11, 31–37, 65–96, 658–62, 691. Henry J. Cookinham, who drew the sharpest contrast between rural virtue and urban vice, pledged to urban delegates the assistance of ruralites when anarchists and socialists threatened life and property.
8. *R.R.C.C.,* IV, 80, 92–93, 96, 644–47, 667–77, 694; New York *Tribune,* Sept. 14, 1894; New York *Times,* Aug. 18, 20, 24, 25, 27–29, Sept. 5–7, 11, 12, 14, 1894.
9. Ruth C. Silva, "The Population Base for Apportionment of the New York Legislature," *Fordham Law Review,* XXXII (Oct. 1963), 9–10, 17; *R.R.C.C.,* V, 525–31, Document No. 30. "Statement Showing the Population of the State of New York, According to the Enumeration of 1892." Aliens accounted for 11.1% of the state's population. Only in New York (21.0%), Richmond (12.8%), Kings (12.7%), Queens (12.6%), and Erie (12.3%) counties did they exceed this proportion. Had aliens been included in the population base in 1894, New York City would have gained 1 senator and 6 assemblymen.
10. *R.R.C.C.,* III, 933–41; IV, 456–58, 460–78; V, 532, Document No. 32. "Statistics of Naturalization in Certain Counties of the State in Response to the Resolution of Mr. Roche"; New York *Tribune,* Sept. 13, 1894. On the final vote, 98 Republicans and 4 Democrats opposed 54 Democrats.
11. *R.R.C.C.,* I, 26, 194–95, 277, 287–88, 618–37; II, 147, 165–66; III, 633; V, 1049; New York *Times,* June 6, July 6, 1894; New York *Tribune,* July 6, 1894. The vote to sustain the committee (and Republican leadership) was 64 to 48, 34 Democrats and 30 Republicans forming the majority, 6 Democrats and 42 Republicans the minority (in support of the Lincoln resolution). During the floor debate, William J. Roche, a Democrat, condemned the proposal as "part of the platform of the American Protective Association" while John A. Barhite, a Republican, denounced alien radicals.

    Kinzer, *An Episode in Anti-Catholicism, op. cit.,* 134, errs in stating that the convention approved Lincoln's resolution.
12. *R.R.C.C.,* I, 500; II, 148; III, 632; IV, 942–50; V, 99–123, 499, 716–24, 736. The vote was 105 to 46, with 6 Democrats voting in the majority. On earlier Democratic efforts in the legislature, see *Messages from the*

Governor . . . , op. cit., IX: *1892–1898,* 180; New York *Tribune,* April 15, 1892, Jan. 27, March 11, 24, 27, April 11, 12, 1893; New York *Times,* March 1, 5, 1893.

In cities covered by the proposal, voters would have to register for each election. Elsewhere, only those who had moved into a district since the previous registration or whose names were not on the list of voters were required to register.

13. For these rambling debates, see *R.R.C.C.,* I, 3, 22, 113, 127, 139, 265, 295, 312, 355, 1053–54; II, 32–34, 102–31, 167–92, 225–64, 334–45, 348–405, 447–50, 1158; III, 68, 272, 275–343, 357–93, 418–19, 424–48, 457–92, 531–98, 600–631, 638–58, 677–79, 686; IV, 380–93, 452–54, 458–60, 547, 727–39, 814–23, 979–1005; V, 768–69, 775–76; New York *Times,* May 18, Aug. 28, 31, Sept. 21, 1894; New York *Tribune,* Aug. 15, 23, 1894. Also see *R.R.C.C.,* II, 104–6, 617–18; V, 533–42.
14. Resolutions of the City Club of New York City, the Union League Club, and the Manufacturers' Association of Kings County, New York *Times,* Nov. 9, 1893, Jan. 12, June 20, 1894; New York *Times,* May 31, June 7, 13, 14, 27, July 28, 1894; *R.R.C.C.,* II, 108–12, 167–70; III, 276–77, 291–92, 561, 563.

   Samuel P. Hays, "The Politics of Reform in Municipal Government in the Progressive Era," *Pacific Northwest Quarterly,* LV (Oct. 1964), 157–69; and James Weinstein, "Organized Business and the City Commission and Manager Movements," *Journal of Southern History,* XXVIII (May 1962), 166–82, treat a later period, but have influenced my thinking.
15. *R.R.C.C.,* III, 278–80, 630; IV, 730–31, 736; letter of Mayor Thomas F. Gilroy of New York City to William McM. Speer, July 24, 1894, in Andrew H. Green Papers (New York Public Library), cited hereafter as Green Papers. Ralph A. Straetz and Frank J. Munger, *New York Politics* (New York: New York University Press, 1960), 48–49, allude to one unforeseen consequence of the reform: in some upstate cities, partisan competition gave way to ethnic competition for office.
16. The foregoing is based on Kinzer, *op. cit.,* chap. i; Robert D. Cross, *The Emergence of Liberal Catholicism in America* (Cambridge: Harvard University Press, 1958), chaps. ii, vii, esp. 26–27, 38–40, 135–42; Edward M. Connors, *Church-State Relationships in Education in the State of New York* (The Catholic University of America, Educational Research Monographs, Vol. XVI [March 1, 1951], No. 2; Washington, D.C.: Catholic University of America, 1951), 106–17, 125–27; and Pratt, *op. cit.,* 199–201, 234–36, 250–51.
17. Kinzer, *ibid.,* 56–57; James M. King, *Facing the Twentieth Century; Our Country: Its Power and Peril* (New York: American Union League Society, 1899), 518–30; New York *Tribune,* Feb. 19, 1892; New York *Times,* Nov. 11, 15, 1892. King's book clearly reveals the depth of its author's animus toward Roman Catholicism.

18. New York *Times,* Sept. 20, Nov. 27, Dec. 1, 4, 6–8, 11, 13, 19, 1893; New York *Tribune,* Nov. 19, 27, Dec. 3, 5, 6, 8, 13, 19, 1893; King, *ibid.,* 331–32; Connors, *op. cit.,* 130. Connors's account is misleading.

    The New York *Tribune,* Dec. 6, 1893, rejected Father Alfred Young's protest against the newspaper's distinguishing between the "American" and "Catholic" positions relative to the issue. Rabbi Joseph Silverman, of Temple Emanu-El, joined ministers in attacking the proposal, but pointed out that Jews, like Catholics, felt public school readings of the Bible to be Protestant in orientation. New York *Times,* Dec. 18, 1893.

    For attacks on Catholic and Tammany influence on public schools, see New York *Times,* Nov. 16, Dec. 1, 7, 8, 1893. "An American," whose letter (Brooklyn, Dec. 5, 1893) appeared in the New York *Times,* Dec. 7, 1893, called for the removal of Catholic and Jewish teachers from "our Protestant schools."

19. New York *Tribune,* Oct. 22, Dec. 5, 1893; letter of James M. King to James R. Sheffield, Jan. 6, 1894, in Sheffield Papers; King, *op. cit.,* 531–33; letter of Joseph H. Choate to Frederick W. Holls, May 19, 1894; letter of Frederick W. Holls to Melvil Dewey, May 17, 1894; letter of Frederick W. Holls to Joseph H. Choate, May 18, 1894, all in [George] Frederick William Holls Papers (Columbia University), cited hereafter as Holls Papers; *R.R.C.C.,* I, 25. For other proposals, see *R.R.C.C.,* I, 349, 499, 526, 537, 712.

    I am grateful to Professor John W. Pratt of the State University of New York at Stony Brook for clarifying my thinking at an early stage of my research and for directing my attention to the Holls Papers. I subsequently utilized a number of sources to which Pratt did not have access. Pratt, *op. cit.,* chap. ix, deals with the sectarian spending issue in the constitutional convention.

20. Committee on Catholic Interests of the Catholic Club [of the City of New York], *Catholic Charities and the Constitutional Convention of 1894 of the State of New York* (New York: J. J. O'Brien and Son, n.d. [1894]), "Arguments June 6th," *passim,* esp. 24, 26–27, cited hereafter as *C.C.C.C.*

21. *Ibid.,* "Arguments June 20th," 1–20, esp. 11–13.

22. Connors, *op. cit.,* 131–32. On financing the campaign in one locality, see letter of Robert B. ——, Treasurer of the Catholic Club, to Thomas M. A. Burke, May 29, 1894; letter of Thomas M. A. Burke to n.n., June 5, 1894, both in the Archives of the Diocese of Albany (Chancery, Diocese of Albany, Albany, New York), cited hereafter as A.D.A. Six orphanages in the vicinity of Albany were assessed $874.39.

23. Letters of John E. Robinson to Archbishop Michael Corrigan, March 7, 25, April 6, 23, 30, 1894; letters of George Parsons Lathrop to Archbishop Michael Corrigan, April 14, 23, 27, May 14, 1894; letter of W. Bourke Cockran to Archbishop Michael Corrigan, May 15, 1894, all in Michael Corrigan Papers (Archives of the Archdiocese of New York, St. Joseph's Seminary, Dunwoodie, New York), cited hereafter as Corrigan Papers. The Committee on Catholic Interests finally called on Lathrop to pre-

pare a lecture for fall delivery in the event the convention approved Holls's amendment.

New York *Times,* April 29, May 15, 16, 20, June 4, 1894; "Hostility to Roman Catholics," *North American Review,* CLVIII (May 1894), 563–82, contains a debate between Lathrop and Bishop Doane that was undoubtedly prepared before Lathrop's final exchange with Archbishhop Corrigan.

24. Typed memoranda in the Papers of Bishop Bernard McQuaid (St. Bernard's Seminary Library, Rochester, New York), cited hereafter as McQuaid Papers.
25. Pratt, *op. cit.,* 247–49. In a sermon before the Eighteenth Street Methodist Church in New York City, the Reverend Dr. John A. B. Wilson denounced the Roman Catholic Church as "everywhere and always the enemy of civil liberty" and charged that "in Albany . . . attorneys, Protestant bred, hired themselves out as paid prostitutes to this political libertine and enemy of civil liberty throughout the ages." New York *Tribune,* July 16, 1894.
26. *C.C.C.C.,* "Arguments June 20th," Remarks of Frederic Coudert, 3–16, esp. 5–7; Remarks of George Bliss, 1–42, esp. 1–2; letter of Paul Fuller to Archbishop Michael Corrigan, June 16, 1894, in Corrigan Papers. Also see the undated memorandum on points justifying public assistance to private charities in the McQuaid Papers. This lengthy memorandum, written in the hand of Bishop McQuaid on the stationery of the New York Archdiocese, includes language almost identical to that quoted by Bliss during his reading of a prelate's letter. Bishop McQuaid may very well have been the dignitary who wrote to Bliss.
27. For an index to petitions and memorials, see *R.R.C.C.,* V, 1077–78; New York *Tribune,* April 11, May 7, 1894; New York *Times,* April 7, 1894. Cf. Pratt, *op. cit.,* 250–51.
28. New York *Times,* June 1, 1894; Kinzer, *op. cit.,* 124–25; *C.C.C.C.,* "Arguments June 20th," Remarks of Frederic Coudert, 8–9; Remarks of Joseph Choate, *R.R.C.C.,* IV, 762; *Irish World and American Industrial Liberator* (New York), Nov. 4, 1893; New York *Tribune,* March 18, April 1, 1893.

The Reverend Dr. George S. Baker of the N.L.P.A.I. pointedly denied an association between his organization and the A.P.A. See *C.C.C.C.,* "Arguments, June 6th," 38–39. The New York *Times,* June 2, 24, 1894, distinguished between the two groups, as did Edward Lauterbach, New York *Times,* June 10, 1894.

29. William E. Akin, "The War of the Bishops: Catholic Controversy on the School Question in New York State in 1894," *The New-York Historical Society Quarterly,* L (January 1966), 41–61; Frederick J. Zwierlein, *Letters of Archbishop Corrigan to Bishop McQuaid and Allied Documents* (Rochester: Art Print Shop, 1946), 166–71.

Kinzer, *op. cit.,* 145–46; and Cross, *op. cit.,* 102–3, mistakenly refer to Malone's victory as occurring in the midterm elections of November,

1894. For a report that Pope Leo XIII later praised the New York State Republican party as "liberal" for having elected a Roman Catholic priest to the Board of Regents, see New York *Times,* March 11, 1895. The Pope failed to touch upon the struggle that had preceded Malone's election.

30. New York *Tribune,* March 30, 1894; *C.C.C.C.,* "Arguments June 20th," Remarks of George Bliss, 1.
31. Letter of Frederick W. Holls to James M. King, July 23, 1894; letter of James M. King to Frederick W. Holls, n.d., both in Holls Papers; *C.C.C.C.,* "Address of Rev. James M. King" [July 11, 1894], 15, 17.
32. New York *Times,* June 15, July 16, 20, Aug. 16, 1894; New York *Tribune,* Aug. 16, 1894; *R.R.C.C.,* II, 948–57; III, 753–54. (The New York *Times,* August 14, 1894, had reported that Holls and others were attempting to gain jurisdiction over the charities article for the education committee, which was hostile to sectarian spending. The attempt, if made, was unsuccessful.)
33. *R.R.C.C.,* III, 686–762, esp. Remarks of Joseph Choate, 739–43; letter of Frederick W. Holls to Melvil Dewey, Sept. 1, 1894, in Holls Papers.
34. *R.R.C.C.,* III, 743–53. The Reverend Dr. King had earlier denounced the very proposal Cassidy made, warning that it "may emanate from an unfriendly source"; General Thomas J. Morgan, who had also testified in Albany for the N.L.P.A.I., protested Cassidy's amendment in a letter to the New York *Tribune.* See *C.C.C.C.,* "Address of Rev. James M. King" [July 11, 1894], 1–2; New York *Tribune,* Sept. 4, 1894.
35. *R.R.C.C.,* III, 754–807, esp. 758–62, 766–71, 795–96, 803–6; King, *op. cit.,* 384–86. The *Jewish Messenger* (New York), Sept. 29, 1893, Sept. 21, 1894, favored a ban on public assistance to sectarian institutions.
    The Louis Marshall Papers (American Jewish Archives, Cincinnati, Ohio) contain no correspondence bearing on the education and charities questions. Cited hereafter as Marshall Papers.
36. The Lauterbach-Marshall amendment failed by a rising vote of 51 to 55; Root turned the tide against Cassidy, 71 to 68, 71 Republicans voting against 16 Republicans and 52 Democrats; the education article was moved to a third reading by a vote of 77 to 60, 76 Republicans and 1 Democrat opposing 9 Republicans and 51 Democrats. See *R.R.C.C.,* III, 955–86; also letter of Frederick W. Holls to Melvil Dewey, Sept. 4, 1894, in Holls Papers; letter of Henry J. Sayers to Archbishop Michael Corrigan, September 8, 1894, in Corrigan Papers. Sayers, Secretary of the Committee on Catholic Interests and its observer in Albany, now expressed confidence that the Catholic campaign to defeat a ban on public aid to sectarian charities would succeed.
37. *R.R.C.C.,* IV, 740–72, 776–814. Gilbert's amendment lost by a vote of 29 to 91, 50 Republicans and 41 Democrats defeating 27 Republicans and 2 Democrats. Compare letter of Frederick W. Holls to James M. King, July 23, 1894, with letters of Frederick W. Holls to Melvil Dewey, September 1, 4, 1894, all in Holls Papers, and Holls's actions on September 14.
38. *R.R.C.C.,* IV, 857–87. The education article passed by a vote of 108 to 37,

79 Republicans and 29 Democrats defeating 15 Republicans and 22 Democrats; the charities article carried, 113 to 16, 71 Republicans and 42 Democrats defeating 11 Republicans and 5 Democrats. Though both majorities were overwhelming and bipartisan, Republicans supported the education article, which banned public aid to parochial schools, more strongly than did Democrats, while Democrats supported the charities article, which permitted public aid to sectarian charities, more strongly than did Republicans.

Kinzer, *op. cit.*, 134–35, erroneously states that both amendments were favored by the N.L.P.A.I. and opposed by the Catholic Church.

39. *R.R.C.C.*, IV, 1278–79; Connors, *op. cit.*, 136–37; Frederick J. Zwierlein, *The Life and Letters of Bishop McQuaid* (3 vols.; Rochester: Art Print Shop, 1925–1927), III, 323–24; New York *Times*, Oct. 12, 13, 23, 24, 1894; New York *Tribune*, Sept. 10, 17, Oct. 20, 28, 29, 31 (letter from Joseph Choate), Nov. 4, 5, 10, 1894; letter of Frederick W. Holls to James M. King, Sept. 26, 1894, in Holls Papers.
40. Zwierlein, *ibid.*, 219.
41. New York *Tribune*, June 17, 1895, March 17, 1896. King, *op. cit.*, 386–88, reacted bitterly to these honors.
42. Benson, *Merchants, Farmers, & Railroads*, *op. cit.*, *passim*, esp. 9–16, chap. ii; ———, *The Concept of Jacksonian Democracy*, *op. cit.*, 299–301; New York *Times*, Jan. 4, 5, 1893; New York *Tribune*, Jan. 12, 1893.
43. New York *Tribune*, June 23, 1892, May 26, Dec. 6, 1893, Feb. 25, June 21, Aug. 19, 21, 22, Sept. 3, 10, 1894; New York *Times*, Jan. 9, Dec. 7, 1893, June 16, 21, Sept. 3, 20, 1894; Utica *Daily Press*, Oct. 8, 1892, scrapbook in Bixby Papers; Roswell P. Flower speech before the Lewis County Agricultural Society's Annual Fair, Lowville, New York, Sept. 13, 1893, copy in Bixby Papers.
44. *R.R.C.C.*, I, 67; V, 729–31, Document 69. "Memorial of the Various Farmers' Associations of the State of New York Asking the Incorporation into the Constitution of Proposed Amendments as to Taxation, Railroads, Transfer of Canals"; New York *Tribune*, June 11, 21, 1894; New York *Times*, July 12, 1894.

    At the 1893 convention of the New York State People's party, Populists from Buffalo and New York City championed the canals as competitors of the rapacious railroads, but delegates from interior counties opposed cheap through traffic, whether by water or rail. New York *Times*, Aug. 20, 1893.
45. *R.R.C.C.*, IV, 227–350, 355–57, 923–69; V, 725–26, Document 67. "Minority Report of the Committee on Canals"; New York *Tribune*, Sept. 11–13, 1894; New York *Times*, Sept. 20, 1894; letter of Jacob Amos to Louis Marshall, Aug. 27, 1894, in Marshall Papers.
46. *R.R.C.C.*, I, 454, 512, 638, 678; II, 946; III, 163–239; IV, 512–33; New York *Times*, July 30, Aug. 26, Nov. 5, 1894; New York *Tribune*, Sept. 13, Nov. 1, 1894; letter of Manufacturers of Plumbing Materials to Members of the Constitutional Convention, n.d. [1894], copy in Green Papers; Re-

port, Bureau of Statistics of Labor to Governor Roswell P. Flower, July 18, 1894, copy in Timothy S. Williams Papers.

47. Letter of Sam Kaufman to Andrew H. Green, n.d. [1894], in Green Papers; New York *Times,* May 31, June 28, July 19, 21, Sept. 4, 5, 21, 26, 1894; New York *Tribune,* Sept. 26, 1894; *R.R.C.C.,* I, 877, 881.

48. "Report of the Committee on Address," *R.R.C.C.,* V, 1251–58; New York *Times,* Sept. 22, 29, 30, Oct. 3, 4, 7, 12–14, 16, 18, 23, 24, Nov. 1, 4, 5, 8, 1894; New York *Tribune,* Sept. 10, 17, Oct. 3, 14, 20, 22, 28, 29, 31, Nov. 5, 1894; letter of William M. Irish to Charles S. Fairchild, Nov. 3, 1894, in Fairchild Papers; letter of Richard Watson Gilder to Joseph H. Choate, Dec. 12, 1894, in Richard Watson Gilder Papers (New York Public Library), cited hereafter as Gilder Papers.

49. The Republican gubernatorial candidate polled 53.0% of the total (and 56.6% of the two-party) vote; the main section of the constitution, the reapportionment article, and the canals article received 52.7%, 53.6%, and 57.5% of the vote, respectively.

For the sources of voting data on the constitutional questions, see Appendix A. Returns on all questions are available for all counties and Brooklyn wards; unofficial returns on the reapportionment question are also available for New York City assembly districts.

50. In Brooklyn's wards, rank-order correlations among the amendments were: main section with reapportionment, +.916; main section with canals, +.910; reapportionment with canals, +.964. The canals amendment ran first and the reapportionment amendment last in 10 counties containing major cities along the Erie Canal–Hudson River route and in 27 of 31 Brooklyn wards.

51. New York *Tribune,* Dec. 3, 21, 1894; New York *Times,* Jan. 3, 5, 8, June 1, 6, 1895; letter of Executive Committee to Levi P. Morton, Dec. 28, 1894, in Levi P. Morton Papers (New York Public Library), cited hereafter as Morton Papers.

The George W. Aldridge Papers (Rochester Public Library, Rochester, New York) are disappointing, but make abundantly clear the political role played by the superintendent. Cited hereafter as Aldridge Papers.

52. New York *Tribune,* Feb. 1, 20, 1895; *Journal of the Assembly of the State of New York . . .* [118th Sess., 1895], I, 624–25; *Journal of the Senate of the State of New York . . .* [118th Sess., 1895], I, 379–81. Assemblymen from New York, Kings, Erie, Albany, Rensselaer, and Monroe counties cast a bipartisan bloc vote for the measure; they accounted for 61 of 83 affirmative votes. One rural Democrat joined 30 Republicans in opposition; the only other rural Democratic assemblyman did not vote.

53. Between 1894 and 1895, the dispersion of county-level percentage support for the successive canals proposals increased markedly—from a coefficient of variability of .148 to one of .428. Even the compromise canals proposal of 1894 had produced a dispersion of percentage support greater than those on reapportionment and the main section of the constitution, and

that for the Republican gubernatorial candidate, .105, .111, and .101, respectively. In Brooklyn, on the other hand, the dispersion of ward-level support for the canals proposals decreased from .227 in 1894 to a remarkably low .040 in 1895. It should also be noted that the 1894 vote on the canals had been larger than the votes on reapportionment and the main body of the revised constitution.

54. On the campaign to win the electorate's approval of the canals proposal, see New York *Times,* Aug. 29, 31, Sept. 9, 13, 14, 16, 20, 21, Nov. 2, 5, 1895; New York *Tribune,* June 6, Oct. 4, 29, 30, 1895.

Obviously, not all voters in even those counties most involved in the canals controversy had a direct or indirect economic stake in the struggle, but one cannot but be impressed by the consensus regarding the issue that formed in many counties. In Erie and St. Lawrence counties (to take the extreme cases), approximately eight of nine voters in each opposed the stand taken by a like proportion in the other. The size of percentage shifts between 1894 and 1895 provides further testimony to the intense feelings generated by the controversy.

On the other hand, turnout on the canals question still fell 20.9% short of that for state office in 1895, suggesting that the controversy simply did not motivate a sizable minority of the electorate to vote on the canals. It may well be that only partisan contests in which the rival political parties mobilized voters were likely to achieve relatively full turnouts.

55. Letter of George Bliss to Elihu Root, Jan. 26, 1895; letter of John W. O'Brien to Elihu Root, n.d.; letter of G. Be Adams [?] to Elihu Root, Nov. 10, 1894, all in Elihu Root Papers (Library of Congress, Washington, D.C.), cited hereafter as Root Papers; also telegram of John F. Parkhurst to Joseph H. Choate, Nov. 7, 1894, in Joseph H. Choate Papers (Library of Congress, Washington, D.C.), cited hereafter as Choate Papers.

IV. THE MIDTERM UPHEAVAL OF 1894

1. Samuel P. Hays, "Political Parties and the Community-Society Continuum," *op. cit.,* 161–63; Benson, *The Concept of Jacksonian Democracy, op. cit.,* chaps. v, xi; Degler, "American Political Parties," *loc. cit.,* 44–45.
2. New York *Tribune,* Feb. 14, April 11, 1894; *The Nation,* LVIII (Feb. 22, 1894), 131; letter of Benjamin Harrison to Louis T. Michener, Feb. 17, 1894, in Louis T. Michener Papers (Library of Congress, Washington, D.C.), cited hereafter as Michener Papers; letter of A. B. Farquhar to Grover Cleveland, November 13, 1893, quoted in Morgan, *From Hayes to McKinley, op. cit.,* 449.
3. Unpublished Papers of the Committee on Ways and Means, 53d Cong., 2d sess., in House of Representatives Papers (National Archives, Washington, D.C.), cited hereafter as Committee on Ways and Means Papers; New York *Tribune,* Nov. 30, Dec. 8, 16, 20, 26, 29, 1893, Jan. 1, 11, 18,

19, 27, 1894; New York *Times,* Dec. 16, 1893, Jan. 11, 1894; Newark *Daily Advertiser,* Dec. 7, 8, 27, 1893, Jan. 18, 1894; Hartford *Courant,* Jan. 2, 4, 1894; letter of C. S. Merrill to Daniel S. Lamont, Nov. 28, 1893; letter of [David D.] Kirby and [Charles H.] Burckett to Grover Cleveland, Dec. 12, 1893; and letter of L. J. Salomon to William L. Wilson, Dec. 2, 1893, all in Grover Cleveland Papers (Library of Congress, Washington, D.C.), cited hereafter as Cleveland Papers.

4. Committee on Ways and Means Papers; New York *Times,* July 17, 1893, Jan. 20, 1894; New York *Tribune,* July 17, Sept. 5, Nov. 25, 1893, Jan. 4, 1894; New Haven *Register,* Jan. 9, 10, 13, 25, Feb. 1, 1894; Hartford *Courant,* July 19, 1893, Jan. 1, 4, 1894.
5. John R. Lambert, *Arthur Pue Gorman* (Baton Rouge: Louisiana State University Press, 1953), 212–13; letter of Andrew Carnegie to Whitelaw Reid, Jan. 3, 1894, marked "confidential," in Reid Papers; New York *Tribune,* Jan. 8, 1894.
6. On coordination and coercion in the campaign against the Wilson bill, see New York *Times,* Dec. 5, 10, 1893, Jan. 2, 1894; Summers, *William L. Wilson and Tariff Reform, op. cit.,* 179–81.

For scattered support for the Wilson bill, see Committee on Ways and Means Papers; New York *Times,* Dec. 10, 1893; Hartford *Courant,* Jan. 19, 1894; letter of Bennett, Day & Co. to Grover Cleveland, Jan. 25, 1894, in Cleveland Papers.

Letter of Simeon E. Baldwin to James P. Pigott, Jan. 12, 1894; letter of James P. Pigott to Simeon E. Baldwin, Jan. 13, 1894, both in Baldwin Family Papers; New York *Times,* Dec. 3, 1893, Jan. 26, 1894.

Summers, *op. cit., passim,* esp. 179–81, 219, and Nevins, *Grover Cleveland, op. cit., passim,* esp. 293, 766, are clearly committed to tariff reform. They accept at face value the arguments of tariff reformers and heap scorn on protectionists.

7. Letter of Wharton Barker to George Murray, Jan. 17, 1894; letter of Tom O'Reilly to Wharton Barker, Jan. 18, 1894; letter of Wilbur F. Wakeman to Wharton Barker, Jan. 22, 1894, all in Barker Papers.
8. On the tariff bill in Congress, see Summers, *op. cit.,* chaps. xi, xii; Nevins, *op. cit.,* chap. xxxi; and Lambert, *op. cit.,* chap. x; on Tammany, see New York *Tribune,* Jan. 28, Feb. 12, 1894; New York *Times,* Feb. 14, March 3, 4, April 9, May 8, 12, 1894.

For petitions, memorials, and correspondence relating to the tariff bill as it made its way through the Senate, see *Journal of the Senate of the United States of America . . .* [53d Cong., 2d sess.], 35–161, *passim;* Hill Papers; Lamont Papers; and Lemuel E. Quigg Papers (New York Public Library), cited hereafter as Quigg Papers. *Replies of Importers, Manufacturers, and Others to Tariff Inquiries . . .* [53d Cong., 2d sess.], Bulletins 2–51 (Washington, D.C.: Government Printing Office, 1894), is even more detailed.

The New York *Times,* April 7, 1894, contended that Democratic defeats in spring elections reflected the anger of the electorate toward Democrats who were obstructing tariff reform. The *Times* did not point out that the victorious Republican party was pledged to thwart tariff reform.

9. New York *Tribune,* Dec. 22, 31, 1893, Jan. 5–30, 1894; New York *Times,* Nov. 18, Dec. 27, 29, 1893, Jan. 10–Feb. 1, 1894; letter of Oswald Ottendorfer to Grover Cleveland, Jan. 13, 1894; letter of Isidor Straus to Grover Cleveland, Jan. 14, 1894, both in Cleveland Papers; letter of John P. Peters to Isidor Straus, Feb. 3, 1894, in Isidor Straus Papers (R. H. Macy & Co., New York City), cited hereafter as Isidor Straus Papers; letters of Whitelaw Reid to Representative Thomas B. Reed, Jan. 5, 1894; to Senator William P. Frye, Jan. 5, 1894; and to Frank P. Stearns, Jan. 26, 1894, all in Reid Papers; copies of letters of Lemuel E. Quigg to George W. Wanmaker, June 11, 1894; to George W. Winterburn, June 13, 1894; and to J. P. Miller, June 25, 1894, all in Quigg Papers; Naomi Wiener Cohen, The Public Career of Oscar S. Straus (unpublished Ph. D. dissertation, Dept. of History, Columbia University, 1959), 109–11.

   The New York *Tribune,* Jan. 31, 1894, provides detailed returns from both congressional districts.

10. New York *Times,* Jan. 31, 1894. Compare this (and New York *Times,* Nov. 12, 1893) with the interpretation of Lemuel E. Quigg in New York *Times,* April 19, 1894.

11. Nevins, *op. cit.,* 600–603; Summers, *op. cit.,* 216.

12. Donald L. McMurry, *Coxey's Army: A Study of the Industrial Army Movement of 1894* (Boston: Little, Brown, 1929), *passim,* esp. 107–8; New York *Tribune,* March 25, April 26, 27, May 13, 23, 1894; New York *Times,* April 8, May 5, 10, 1894; Hartford *Courant,* April 6, 1894; New Haven *Register,* April 23, May 3, 5, 1894.

   Almont Lindsey, *The Pullman Strike: The Story of a Unique Experiment and of a Great Labor Upheaval* (Chicago: The University of Chicago Press, 1942), *passim,* esp, chap. xiii; New York *Times,* July 7–11, 1894; New Haven *Register,* July 9, 1894; Newark *Daily Advertiser,* July 11, 1894.

13. New York *Times,* May 23–June 1, June 5–29, 1894.

14. Kinzer, *An Episode in Anti-Catholicism, op. cit.,* chap. i, 35–41; John Higham, "Origins of Immigration Restriction, 1882–1897: A Social Analysis," *Mississippi Valley Historical Review,* XXXIX (June 1952), 83–84; Blodgett, *The Gentle Reformers, op. cit.,* 148–55; Schrier, *Ireland and the American Emigration, op. cit.,* 33–34; New York *Tribune,* Jan. 1, 1894; New York *Times,* May 23, 27, 1894.

15. New York *Times,* Nov. 8, Dec. 1, 5, 18, 1893; New York *Tribune,* Nov. 12–14, 1893; New Haven *Register,* Sept. 28, Oct. 3, 7, 23, 24, Nov. 16, Dec. 1, 4, 11, 1893; Newark *Daily Advertiser,* Aug. 15, 1893; Kinzer, *op. cit.,* 34; Nelson, The Influence of Immigration, *op. cit.,* 198–200.

16. Rowland T. Berthoff, *British Immigrants in Industrial America, 1790–1950* (Cambridge: Harvard University Press, 1953), chap. xii; Kinzer, *op. cit., passim;* New York *Times,* June 8, July 4, 6, 13, 15, 26, 1894.

   The definition of "nativism" derives from Higham, *op. cit.,* 4.

Irish Americans, many of whom were native-born, objected to being categorized as "foreigners" by "nativists," many of whom were immigrants. See New York *Times,* July 13, 1894; speech of Father Edward McGlynn, in New York *Tribune,* Oct. 8, 1894; and resolution of Irish National Federation of America condemning a sermon of the Reverend Robert S. MacArthur, in New York *Times,* Dec. 5, 1894. MacArthur had termed the Irish flag "the little green rag that represents no nation," adding that ". . . the green flag represents bigotry on one side, national disloyalty on the other." New York *Times,* Nov. 30, Dec. 1, 1894.

17. Benson, *The Concept of Jacksonian Democracy, op. cit.,* 166, 185 (table 11), 321–27; New York *Tribune,* Aug. 21, 1892; Hartford *Courant,* Sept. 9, 1895, Sept. 29, Oct. 13, 17, 23, 27, 28, 1896; letter of George D. Scott to Governor O. Vincent Coffin, July 26, 1895, in O. Vincent Coffin Papers (Connecticut Historical Society, Hartford), cited hereafter as Coffin Papers; New York *Times,* May 27, June 5, 6, 9, 12, 22, 29, 1894.
18. This analysis of the Democratic campaign is based on accounts in the Connecticut, New York, and New Jersey press and the Democratic state platforms, for which see *Tribune Almanac, 1895,* 47–83. Also see New York *Times,* May 7, Aug. 23, 26, 1894; New Haven *Register,* Aug. 22, 1894; Newark *Daily Advertiser,* Oct. 8, 1894; letter of Charles S. Commerford to Daniel S. Lamont, July 31, 1894, in Lamont Papers; Hirsch, *William C. Whitney, op. cit.,* 471–72; Bass, *"I Am a Democrat," op. cit.,* 243.
19. Letter of O. Vincent Coffin to George W. Daw, Feb. 17, 1894, in Coffin Papers; New York *Times,* May 6, 7, Oct. 15, 25, 26, 28, 1894; also press cited above, Note 18.
20. New York *Times,* Jan. 27, May 15, 21, 26, 31, June 5, 6, 10, 16, 19–21, 23, 26, 1893, April 2, Sept. 10, 12, 17, 20, 22, 24–29, Oct. 1, 3, 5, 6, 8, 29, 1894; New Haven *Register,* June 20, 23, 1893, Sept. 11, 26, 1894; Hartford *Courant,* June 19, Sept. 20, Nov. 12, 1894; New York *Tribune,* Sept. 26, 1894.
21. New Haven *Register,* Sept. 28, Oct. 23, 24, 1893, April 6, 10, Aug. 31, Sept. 6, 8, 12, 29, Oct. 1, 3, 8, 13, 16, 19, 23, 27, Nov. 2, 1894; Hartford *Courant,* April 5, 7, 9, Sept. 25, Oct. 2, 4, 5, 8, 16, 20, 24–26, Nov. 5, 6, 1894; New York *Times,* May 7, Sept. 26, Oct. 1–3, 16–19, 1894; also Hartford *Post,* Sept. 18, 1894; Bridgeport *Farmer,* Oct. 1, 1894; New Haven *Union,* Oct. 2, 1894; New Haven *News,* Oct. 17, 19, 1894; Bridgeport *Standard,* Oct. 19, 23, 24, 1894, all in scrapbooks in Coffin Papers; letter of O. Vincent Coffin to Charles R. Spiegel, Oct. 17, 1894; letter of O. Vincent Coffin to George W. Corbin, Oct. 16, 1894, both in Coffin Papers; Frederick M. Heath, Politics and Steady Habits: Issues and Elections in Connecticut, 1894–1914 (unpublished Ph.D. dissertation, Dept. of History, Columbia University, 1965), 23–27.
22. Letter of Charles S. Cary to Daniel S. Lamont, Nov. 24, 1893; letter of Daniel S. Lamont to Charles S. Cary, Nov. 29, 1893, both in Lamont Papers; letter of Charles S. Cary to Grover Cleveland, Dec. 5, 1893, in

Cleveland Papers; letter of Charles S. Fairchild to Grover Cleveland, March 6, 1894, in Fairchild Papers; letters of Richard Watson Gilder to Oscar Straus, March 6, 1894; to William E. Russell, March 10, 1894; and to Grover Cleveland, March 14, 1894, all in Gilder Papers.

23. New York *Times,* July 29, Aug. 1, 17, 21, Sept. 26–30, Oct. 1, 3, 8–10, 16, 17, 1894; New York *Tribune,* July 31, Sept. 18, 26–30, Oct. 3, 6, 8, 10, 11, 1894; letter of David B. Hill to Daniel S. Lamont, Aug. 23, 1894, in Lamont Papers; letter of Timothy S. Williams to David B. Hill, Dec. 12, 1893; letter of Timothy S. Williams to John Kelley, May 24, 1894, both in Timothy S. Williams Papers; Alexander, *Four Famous New Yorkers, op. cit.,* 218–22; *Tribune Almanac, 1895,* 69–70.

24. On Hill on the tariff and income tax, see New York *Times,* April 7, 10, May 4, June 22, Oct. 12, 18–20, 23–28, 30, Nov. 1–4, 1894; on Tammany and the tariff, see letter of George W. Green to George B. McClellan, Oct. 22, 1894; letter of George B. McClellan to George W. Green, n.d. [October 1894], both in George B. McClellan Papers (microfilm copy, Columbia University), cited hereafter as McClellan Papers.

    On Cleveland and Hill, see numerous letters to the President; also letters of Grover Cleveland to Daniel S. Lamont, Sept. 28, Oct. 2, 12, 1894, all in Cleveland Papers.

25. New York *Times,* Jan. 5, 1893, Jan. 26, 1894; New York *Tribune,* Jan. 7, Dec. 10, 1893; above, Chap. III, Note 14; Edwin L. Godkin, "The Problems of Municipal Government," *Annals of the American Academy of Political and Social Science,* IV (May 1894), 857–82, esp. 858, 872.

26. New York *Times,* Dec. 22, 1893, Jan. 26, Feb. 10, May 23, July 21, Aug. 15, 1894; New York *Tribune,* Dec. 10, 1893, May 21, Sept. 18, 1894; letter of Anson Phelps Stokes to Charles S. Fairchild, Nov. 9, 1893, in Fairchild Papers; Everett P. Wheeler, *Sixty Years of American Life, Taylor to Roosevelt, 1850 to 1910* (New York: E. P. Dutton, 1917), 339–40.

    Friends of fusion referred to the promise it held for a "business administration" of New York City. See letter of Benjamin Harrison to William L. Strong, Nov. 7, 1894, in Harrison Papers; also New York *Tribune,* Oct. 7, 11, 1894. Cf. letter of Lemuel E. Quigg to the Reverend George R. Van DeWater, Aug. 7, 1894, in Quigg Papers.

27. New York *Times,* Nov. 10, Dec. 10, 1893, March 22, 28, April 27, Sept. 7, Oct. 9, 10, 1894; New York *Tribune,* April 26, May 17, June 14, Oct. 12, 13, 28, Nov. 1, 6, 1894; New Haven *Register,* Oct. 9, 1893; letter of John DeWitt Warner to Grover Cleveland, Jan. 3, 1894, in Cleveland Papers.

    On ethnic and religious factors in mobility, see Oscar Handlin, *The Newcomers: Negroes and Puerto Ricans in a Changing Metropolis,* Vol. III of *New York Metropolitan Region Study,* ed. Max Hall (9 vols.; Cambridge: Harvard University Press, 1959), 17–33, *passim;* Nathan Glazer and Daniel Patrick Moynihan, *Beyond the Melting Pot: The Negroes, Puerto Ricans, Jews, Italians, and Irish of New York City* (Cambridge: M.I.T. Press and Harvard University Press, 1963), 254–62, 310–13; Dahl,

Who Governs?, op. cit., 32–36; Lenski, *The Religious Factor, op. cit.*, 76–87, 91–93. Cf. John Higham, "Another Look at Nativism," *American Catholic Historical Review*, XLIV (July 1958), 157–58.

On the relationship between Irish politics and Irish economic activities, see Daniel Bell, *The End of Ideology: On the Exhaustion of Political Ideas in the Fifties* (Glencoe, Ill.: The Free Press, 1960), 128; Dahl, *op. cit.*, 42. *Tribune Almanacs* listed New York city and county officials and Tammany officers, clearly revealing the Irish dominance of Democratic politics.

Carl F. Wittke, *The Irish in America* (Baton Rouge: Louisiana State University Press, 1956), 184–87, treats Irish-German relations. Also see the fascinating letter of James Coughlan to Archbishop Michael Corrigan, Nov. 30, 1893, in Corrigan Papers. Coughlan noted that Protestants, Jews, and "Infidels" meekly submitted to robbery by an Irish Catholic minority in the cities of the United States. He added that Tammany could be overthrown by a coalition of Germans and Americans, concluding that at some point Corrigan would have to decide whether Tammany helped or hurt the Church in New York City. E[dwin] L. Godkin, "Criminal Politics," *North American Review*, CL (June 1890), 706–23, compared the Irish unfavorably with the Germans in his analysis of the sad state of municipal politics. Emil Karg was later to note the underrepresentation of Germans in Tammany's administrations, which, he observed, were of, by, and for the Irish. Letter of Emil C. Karg to Mayor William Strong, April 3, 1895, in William L. Strong Papers (New York Municipal Archives, New York City), cited hereafter as Strong Papers.

28. New York *Times*, Jan. 20, Sept. 20, 1893, March 7, 14–17, 28, May 25, 1894; New York *Tribune*, March 6, 12, 14, 16, 17, April 23, 1894.

29. On Parkhurst, see Gosnell, *Boss Platt and His New York Machine, op. cit.*, 47–49; for anti-Irish Catholic sermons, see New York *Tribune*, March 5, 12, 14, April 2, 9, 24, 1894 (Rev. Madison C. Peters); New York *Times*, Dec. 1, 1893 (Rev. Robert S. MacArthur). Also see the Reverend William S. Rainsford, *The Story of a Varied Life: An Autobiography* (London: George Allen & Unwin, Ltd., 1922), chap. xxiv, esp. 360.

MacArthur was later to sermonize that Tammany's recipe for success had been "intellectual ignorance, social vulgarity, political fever, religious bigotry, typical thuggism, political venality, variegated murder, and sprinkle the whole with holy water." New York *Times*, Nov. 30, 1894. Numerous letters written during 1895 reflect the animus against Irish Catholics that pervaded the campaign of 1894. See the Strong Papers and the Theodore Roosevelt Papers (microfilm copy, Harvard University, Cambridge), cited hereafter as Roosevelt Papers.

30. Alexander, *op. cit.*, 214–15; Garrett, *The La Guardia Years, op. cit.*, chap. ii. E[dwin] L. Godkin, ed., *The Triumph of Reform; A History of the Great Political Revolution, November Sixth, Eighteen Hundred and Ninety-Four* (New York: Souvenir Publishing Co., 1895), 372–97, provides biographical sketches of persons prominent in the reform movement, a

valuable contribution to an understanding of its socio-economic composition.

31. Letter of Isidor Straus to William L. Wilson, Oct. 12, 1894, in Isidor Straus Papers (copy loaned to author by Professor Festus P. Summers); telegram of Nathan Straus to Grover Cleveland, Oct. 17, 1894; letter of Grover Cleveland to Nathan Straus, Oct. 18, 1894, both in Cleveland Papers; letter of Nathan Straus to David B. Hill, Oct. 17, 1894, in Hill Papers; letter of Oscar Straus to Montefiore Levy, Nov. 6, 1894, in Oscar Straus Papers (Library of Congress, Washington, D.C.), cited hereafter as Oscar Straus Papers; New York *Times,* Oct. 17–19, 1894; New York *Tribune,* Oct. 18–20, 1894.

    Prominent anti-Tammany Jews felt that Tammany had nominated Straus to capture the Jewish vote; M. D. Rothschild asked Richard Watson Gilder to counsel the President against endorsing Straus. Gilder declined to do so. See letter of M. D. Rothschild to Richard Watson Gilder, Oct. 15, 1894; letter of Richard Watson Gilder to William E. Russell, Oct. 17, 1894, both in Gilder Papers.

32. New York *Times,* April 15, 20–26, May 12, Nov. 5, 1893, Oct. 17, 1894, Jan. 7, 8, 10, 1895; New York *Tribune,* April 14–17, 20–24, 1893, April 24, 30, May 3, 11, July 19, Oct. 1, 14, 23, 26, 30, 31, Nov. 3, 6, 1894, Jan. 6, 1895; letters of Jesse Seligman to Elihu Root, May 26, June 20, 1893, in Root Papers; letter of Richard Watson Gilder to Trustees of the City Club, Jan. 24, 1894, in Gilder Papers; *R.R.C.C.,* III, 1094.

33. On the Republican state convention and the New York campaign, see Zwierlein, *Letters of Archbishop Corrigan, op. cit.,* 175–76; letter of Patrick Ford to Levi P. Morton, Nov. 22, 1894, in Morton Papers; letter of J. W. Hendrick to Daniel S. Lamont, Sept. 28, 1894, in Lamont Papers; Kinzer, *op. cit.,* 144–45; New York *Times,* Sept. 7, 19–21, Oct. 3, 11, 12, 20, 21, 23, 27, 30, Nov. 1, 1894; New York *Tribune,* Sept. 12, Oct. 12, 13, 24, 25, 27, 30, Nov. 1, 4, 1894.

    On the preparation of Democratic literature to exploit the religious issue, see letter of Timothy S. Williams to John Boyd Thacher, Oct. 13, 1894; letter of John Boyd Thacher to Timothy S. Williams, Oct. 19, 1894, both in Timothy S. Williams Papers.

34. Zwierlein, *ibid.,* 176–88; Cross, *The Emergence of Liberal Catholicism, op. cit.,* 101–3; King, *Facing the Twentieth Century, op. cit.,* 431–35; New York *Times,* Oct. 22, 29, Nov. 5, 6, 11, 12, 24, 26, 27, 30, Dec. 2, 3, 1894; New York *Tribune,* June 18, Oct. 8, 15, 22, 28, 29, Nov. 3, 5, 6, 11, 12, 15, 20, 21, 28, Dec. 2, 3, 8, 10–12, 18, 24, 1894; letter of Mrs. Josephine Lowell to Archbishop Michael Corrigan, Oct. 14, 1894; letter of Lawrence P. Mingey to Archbishop Michael Corrigan, Nov. 22, 1894, both in Corrigan Papers. Mrs. Lowell privately protested Tammany's equating the reform movement with anti-Catholicism; Mingey, a State Democratic candidate for the assembly, publicly protested the priests' intervention in the campaign.

35. New York *Times,* Sept. 30, Oct. 3, 4, 12, 15, 24–31, Nov. 1, 2, 5, 6, 1894;

Trenton *Daily True American,* Sept. 13, 19, Oct. 5, 22, Nov. 6, 1894; Newark *Daily Advertiser,* March 9, July 31, Sept. 22, Oct. 4, 6, 11, 23, 1894; letter of Preston Stevenson to Grover Cleveland, Oct. 30, 1894, in Cleveland Papers.

36. Trenton *Daily True American,* Sept. 29, Oct. 2, 8, 22, Nov. 6, 1894; New York *Times,* Oct. 11, 24, 25, 28–31, Nov. 1, 2, 5, 6, 1894; Newark *Daily Advertiser,* Oct. 11, 23, Nov. 3, 1894.

37. Newark *Daily Advertiser,* May 12, June 7, Sept. 13, 15, 17, 25, Oct. 11, 19, 27, 29, Nov. 26, 1894; Trenton *Daily True American,* Sept. 27, 1894; New York *Tribune,* March 8, June 8, 1894; New York *Times,* Oct. 24, 25, 1894.

38. Election returns can be found in *Tribune Almanac, 1895,* 276–352. For the shift in congressional seats in the New England, Middle Atlantic, and East North Central states, see above, Table 1, Preface; for percentage shifts in selected northern states and in Connecticut, New York, and New Jersey, see Appendixes D and E.

In the West North Central, Mountain, and Pacific states, the Republicans gained 18 congressional seats, the Democrats losing 10 and the Populists 8; in the Border States, the Republicans captured 23 Democratic seats. On the politics of depression in the Midwest, see Kleppner, *The Cross of Culture, op. cit.,* chaps. v, vi.

39. This section is based on Nevins, *op. cit.,* 651–52; letters of A. B. Farquhar to Henry T. Thurber, Nov. 8, 14, 1894, both in Cleveland Papers; New Haven *Register,* Nov. 7, 8, 12, 1894; New York *Times,* July 15, Oct. 17, Nov. 7, 8, 12, 1894; New York *Tribune,* Oct. 29, Nov. 6, 1894.

40. City-wide, the Democrats received 47.0% of the vote, a decline of 14.3 percentage points, the Republicans 46.0%, an increase of 12.8 points. The Reform Democrats polled 3.3%, the Socialist Labor party 2.8%, a decline of 0.5 points. The measure of correlation is Kendall's tau.

Mean Republican (R) and Democratic (D) percentage point shifts; Reform Democratic (RD) and Socialist Labor (SLP) percentage strength in the gubernatorial election; and percentage points by which the Fusion mayoralty candidate (F) led the Republican gubernatorial candidate in Lower East Side (3, 4, 5, 6, 7, 10), lower Manhattan (1, 2), and Lower West Side (8, 9) A.D.s were:

A.D.S	R	D	RD	SLP	F
1, 2	+17.8	−18.9	1.8	1.7	9.1
3–7, 10	+17.1	−20.3	2.4	7.6	9.8
8, 9	+10.2	−10.2	2.5	0.8	9.3

41. *Report and Proceedings of the Senate Committee Appointed to Investigate the Police Department of the City of New York* (5 vols.; Albany: J. B. Lyon, 1895), I, *passim,* esp. 16–17, 63–66. Turnout increased 11.4% city-wide and in every district except A.D.'s 1, 2, 3, and 4, where it declined by 1.4%, 29.5%, 22.3%, and 4.0%, respectively.

42. Mean Republican (R) and Democratic (D) percentage point shifts; Reform Democratic (RD) and Socialist Labor (SLP) percentage strength in the gubernatorial election; and percentage points by which the Fusion mayoralty candidate (F) led the Republican gubernatorial candidate in mid-East Side (12, 14), Upper East Side (16, 20, 22, 24, 25), and West Side (13, 15, 17, 18, 19) A.D.s were:

A.D.S	R	D	RD	SLP	F
12, 14	+11.7	−12.4	3.1	1.2	10.7
16, 20, 22, 24, 25	+10.7	−11.6	4.0	4.2	12.1
13, 15, 17, 18, 19	+ 8.7	− 9.3	2.5	1.5	9.4

43. Mean Republican (R) and Democratic (D) percentage point shifts; Reform Democratic (RD) and Socialist Labor (SLP) percentage strength in the gubernatorial election; and percentage points by which the Fusion mayoralty candidate (F) led the Republican gubernatorial candidate in central and uptown Manhattan (11, 21, 23, 26, 27, 28) and Bronx (29, 30) A.D.s were:

A.D.S	R	D	RD	SLP	F
11, 21, 23, 26, 27, 28	+ 7.2	− 9.7	4.8	0.8	11.7
29, 30	+14.0	−16.1	3.6	2.3	10.8

44. In correlations between the 1893 anti-Maynard vote and the 1894 Reform Democratic vote and between the latter vote and Republican percentage gains, 1893–94, the measure is Kendall's tau.
45. On Fusion's mayoralty vote relative to the Republican gubernatorial vote, see above, Notes 40, 42, 43. Strong led Morton by above-average margins in 12 of 13 assembly districts in the Upper East Side, central and upper Manhattan, and the Bronx—but in only 5 of 17 districts to the south of these. (The measure of correlation is Kendall's tau.)
46. Compare above, Chap. II, Notes 44, 45, 46, with Chap. IV, Notes 40, 42, 43.
47. The Democrats lost 14.9 percentage points in Troy and 18.7 points ($\overline{M}$) in Wards 1, 7, 8, 9, 11, and 12, where they had polled 75% or more of the 1893 vote. They declined by 12.8 percentage points in Rensselaer County. In the city of Albany, the Democrats lost 11.3 percentage points. They gained 0.1 points in Ward 11 and held firm in Ward 14. County-wide, they lost 8.2 points.
48. County-wide, Hill lost 5.2 percentage points and Morton 0.2; Wheeler polled 5.6% of the vote. To maintain continuity through the period, I have limited correlations to the 28 wards of old Brooklyn. In 1894, Flatbush, New Utrecht, and Gravesend became Wards 29, 30, and 31. Flatlands later became Ward 32.
49. Brooklyn *Daily Eagle,* Feb. 21, March 1, April 1, 4, 9, 23, 28, 30, May 1,

22, 1894; New York *Times,* Dec. 3, 1893, Feb. 4, 7, 8, 1894; New York *Tribune,* May 5, June 11, 1894.

50. The Democrats gained 0.3 percentage points in Erie County, the Republicans 0.2 points. Shifts in Buffalo were D +1.1, R −0.5; in outlying towns, D −2.6, R +2.8. In Monroe County the Democrats gained 7.1 percentage points and the Republicans lost 1.9. Shifts in Rochester were D +9.1, R −4.4; in outlying towns, D +2.0, R +3.7.

    Democratic percentage point gains in Buffalo and Rochester wards correlated at +.259 and +.502 with 1893 percentage point losses.

51. County-level percentage gains and losses, the figures in parentheses indicating counties in which the Republican shift exceeded the Democratic, were:

	REP. GAIN	REP. LOSS
Dem. Gain	19 (14)	5
Dem. Loss	34	1 (0)

    See Appendix E for minor parties' state-wide percentage shifts.

52. Whitney R. Cross, *The Burned-Over District: The Social and Intellectual History of Enthusiastic Religion in Western New York, 1800–1850* (Ithaca: Cornell University Press, 1950), *passim;* Benson, *The Concept of Jacksonian Democracy, op. cit., passim,* esp. chaps. i, ii, and xiv; also New York *Sun,* Dec. 24, 1894 (New York Public Library Scrapbooks).

53. Lee Benson and Joel Silbey are currently analyzing the realignment of the 1850s in New York State. Their study is tentatively entitled *New York Public Opinion and the Coming of the Civil War.*

54. Five cities (Ansonia, Bridgeport, Hartford, New Haven, and New London) were coterminous with towns of the same name; six cities (Danbury, Meriden, New Britain, Norwich, Stamford, and Waterbury) were not. Official election returns from the latter cities do not exist; unofficial returns are not always available. Town returns have been employed. In 1890, 93.2% of the population of the eleven towns lived within the eleven cities.

    In New Haven, Bridgeport, and Waterbury, the Democrats lost 10.8, 9.2, and 10.1 percentage points and the Republicans gained 9.5, 8.0, and 9.1 points. The cities ranked first, third, and fourth in population, and first, second, and third in manufacturing among the state's cities.

    For the sources of election data and information relating to the electorate, see Appendixes A and B.

55. Election returns derive from New Haven *Register,* Nov. 9, 1892; New Haven *Journal-Courier,* Nov. 7, 1894, both in scrapbooks in Coffin Papers. Dahl, *op. cit.,* 32–47, deals with Democratic districts. On Louis Ullman and his brother, Isaac, see New Haven *Register,* Oct. 18, 1894, Nov. 3, 1896; also Dahl, *op. cit.,* 38–40. On street attacks on Russian Jews and A.P.A. charges, see New Haven *Register,* April 24, 1894; Hartford *Courant,* June 15, 1894; and New Haven *Union,* Oct. 2, 1894, scrapbook in Coffin Papers.

Mean percentage point shifts were: in Wards 4, 7, and 12, Rep. +6.7, Dem. −8.4; in Wards 3, 5, and 6, Rep. +10.9, Dem. −13.6. Ward-level Democratic percentage losses and the Democratic defection ratio were correlated negatively (−.154 and −.690) with 1892 Democratic percentage.

56. New Haven *Register,* Sept. 18, 1894. Mean Democratic percentage losses and Republican gains in Wards 9, 10, and 15 were −15.6 and +14.9. Correlations between the percentage strength of the A.P.A.-backed school board slate and Democratic percentage strength (1892), Democratic percentage losses (1892–94), and Democratic defection ratios (1892–94) were −.714, +.424, and +.744, respectively.
57. Dahl, *op. cit.,* 32. The Democrats lost 8.7 percentage points in Ward 1; the Republicans gained 7.7 points. The ward-level correlation between 1892–94 Democratic percentage losses and 1896 National (Gold) Democratic percentage strength, a measure of Clevelandite support, was weak—+.160.
58. The correlation between Democratic percentage strength, 1892, and percentage loss, 1892–94, was −.800 in Waterbury and −.086 in Bridgeport. In Waterbury, the Democrats lost 5.4 percentage points in Ward 4 and 11.6 points ($\bar{M}$) in Wards 1, 2, and 3. In Bridgeport, the Democrats lost 9.1 and 5.5 points in Wards 3 and 4 and 15.4 points in Ward 6. In Ward 2, where they lost 9.5 points, they received 39.7% of the vote.

    Election data derive from Waterbury *American,* Nov. 9, 1892, Nov. 8, 1894; Bridgeport *Farmer,* Nov. 9, 1892, Nov. 7, 1894. Copies of the 1892 issues were provided by Fred Heath; those of 1894 are in scrapbooks in Coffin Papers. On Bridgeport's Swedish population, see *Town and City Atlas of the State of Connecticut.*
59. Ward-level Democratic percentage shifts ranged from −7.1 to 0.0 points, Republican from +6.9 to −0.8; city-wide shifts were −3.7 and +3.6 points. Democratic percentage losses correlated +.280 with 1892 Democratic percentage strength. In no other Connecticut city was this association positive.

    On Republican factionalism, consult Health, *op. cit.,* 30. For election returns, see Hartford *Courant,* Nov. 9, 1892 (copy provided by Fred Heath); Hartford *Courant,* Nov. 7, 1894.

    Hartford ranked second among Connecticut's cities in population and fourth in manufacturing.
60. Hartford *Courant,* April 5, 7, 9, Sept. 18, Oct. 2–5, 1894; New Haven *Register,* April 6, 10, 1894; Bridgeport *Standard,* Oct. 2, 1894, scrapbook in Coffin Papers. George W. Corbin, who had been elected mayor on the Citizens' ticket, figured in Democratic attacks on Republican involvement with A.P.A. during the state-wide campaign of 1894. The *Town and City Atlas of the State of Connecticut* provides information on the religious and ethnic composition of New Britain's wards.
61. New Britain *Record,* Nov. 9, 1894 (copy provided by Fred Heath); Hartford *Post,* Nov. 7, 1894, scrapbook in Coffin Papers.

City-wide, the Democrats fell from 53.9% in the gubernatorial election of 1892 to 43.8% in 1894; the Republicans rose from 41.7 to 51.3%. Ward-by-ward Democratic percentages, percentage point losses, and defection ratios were: (1) 27.8%, −10.9, 28.2; (2) 22.9%, −13.8, 37.6; (3) 61.5%, −8.9, 12.6; (4) 63.2%, −5.9, 8.5. The correlation between Democratic losses and 1892 strength was −.800; the coefficient of variability of ward-level Democratic strength rose from .300 in 1892 to .421 in 1894.

62. The Democratic defection ratio in towns containing the eleven most populous cities was 15.1; elsewhere it was 15.0.
63. The Democrats lost 6.0 percentage points in Hartford County, and 12.4, 4.6, 3.5, 6.3, 7.5, and 4.3 points in the towns of Suffield, East Hartford, East Windsor, Glastonbury, South Windsor, and Windsor.
64. Thus in Hartford County, Democratic percentage shifts ranged from +10.5 in Hartland (their best showing) to −12.6 in Burlington (their next-to-worst showing). In New London County, the Democrats fared best (Salem, +4.7 points) and worst (Franklin, −13.9 points) in agricultural towns. The same held true in Litchfield County and, to a lesser degree, in Tolland, Windham, and Fairfield counties, where other economic activities were carried on in the agricultural towns in question.

    Shannon, *The Farmer's Last Frontier, op. cit.*, chap. xi, treats Connecticut agriculture during this period.
65. The Democrats lost 13.1 percentage points in Manchester. In Litchfield County, where they lost 7.3 percentage points, they declined by 19.4 points in Warren and by 3.4, 2.5, and 1.4 points in the agricultural towns of Goshen, Litchfield, and New Hartford. In the manufacturing towns of Torrington, Winchester, Thomaston, Watertown, and New Milford, they lost 7.5, 9.0, 7.1, 4.7, and 6.8 percentage points; in Salisbury, North Canaan, Sharon, Roxbury, and Kent, where quarrying or mining and smelting were carried on, they declined by 11.8, 10.8, 10.4, 9.3, and 6.0 points.
66. *Twelfth Census of the United States . . . 1900,* Vol. VIII: *Manufactures,* Part II, 75–77, 80, 85. Between 1890 and 1900, manufactures increased 42.1% by value in Connecticut. They decreased by 15.7% and 14.5% by value in Tolland and Windham counties during the same period.
67. In Windham County the Democrats declined by 7.8 percentage points, losing 15.4 points in Plainfield, 15.0 in Thompson, 11.6 in Killingly, 8.1 in Putnam, and 2.3 in Windham (town). Plainfield, Thompson, and Killingly ranked second, third, and fourth in percentage decline. Only the small town of Chaplin, in which agriculture and paper making were important, ranked higher (D, −16.7). The Democrats fared best (+0.5) in Pomfret, an agricultural town.

    In Tolland County the two major mill towns, Stafford (−11.9) and Vernon (−10.8), ranked somewhat above average (−9.9) in Democratic percentage point loss. Willington (−19.4) and Coventry (−0.1), towns in which agriculture and manufacturing took place, ranked highest and lowest in Democratic percentage point loss.
68. Brookfield, Newtown, New Fairfield (Fairfield County); Hartland, Marl-

borough (Hartford County); Middlebury (New Haven County); Griswold, Lisbon, Salem (New London County); Pomfret (Windham County).

69. Democratic percentage point gains in Lisbon, Griswold, and Salem were 1.8, 1.2, and 4.7. On Newtown, see D. Hamilton Hurd (comp.), *History of Fairfield County, Connecticut* . . . (Philadelphia: J. W. Lewis, 1881), 459–81, esp. 470. On Chaplin, see Ellen D. Larned, *History of Windham County, Connecticut,* Vol. II: *1760–1880* (Worcester, Mass.: Charles Hamilton, 1880), 563.

70. Larned, *ibid., passim,* esp. 551–55, 563–64, 576–77; *A Memorial Volume of the Bi-Centennial Celebration of the Town of Windham, Connecticut* (Hartford: New England Home Printing Co., 1893), *passim,* esp. 55–56, 92; Richard M. Bayles (ed.), *History of Windham County, Connecticut* (New York: W. W. Preston, 1889), *passim,* esp. 335, 357, 691–94, 778–79, 786 ff., 921 ff., and 990 ff; Hartford *Courant,* Nov. 6, 1894. Also see Leon E. Truesdell, *The Canadian Born in the United States: An Analysis of the Statistics of the Canadian Element in the Population of the United States, 1850 to 1930* (New Haven: Yale University Press, 1943), 111, 113, 117.

    Even before the depression, Windham had been the only manufacturing town in Windham County carried by the Democrats. According to the federal census, Catholics outnumbered Protestants by a greater margin in Windham County than in any other Connecticut county. But the county remained solidly Republican because a disproportionate share of those Catholics were non-voting French Canadians.

71. The Democrats received 82,787 votes in 1892, the Republicans 83,975 votes in 1894. Midterm election declines in turnout were: 1886, 11.0%; 1890, 12.6%; 1894, 5.8%; 1898, 14.3%. Turnouts as a percentage of registration were 82.1, 82.8, 85.7, and 79.2, respectively.

72. Letters of Charles C. Commerford to Daniel S. Lamont, Nov. 16, 28, 1894, both in Lamont Papers; letter of Thomas H. Sullivan to Grover Cleveland, Nov. 12, 1894, in Cleveland Papers; also New York *Tribune,* Aug. 28, Oct. 16, 31, 1892; letter of James P. Pigott to Simeon E. Baldwin, Sept. 9, 1893, in Baldwin Family Papers.

    New York *Times,* Nov. 30, 1894.

73. In Cape May County, 1894 percentage point shifts in towns that had been marked by sharp Democratic declines in 1893 were:

TOWN	DEM.	REP.	PRO.
Sea Isle City	+24.2	−21.1	− 3.2
West Cape May	+ 7.9	+ 3.6	−11.4
Ocean City	+ 5.0	+ 2.2	− 7.2

    Democratic percentage point shifts in Sussex County towns associated with the iron industry were: Andover, +0.3; Byram, +0.9; Hardyston, +3.5; Sparta, −0.7; and Vernon, −17.7.

    Hunterdon County percentage point shifts were:

PARTY	1892–1893	1893–1894	1892–1894
Democratic	−6.0	+3.0	−3.0
Republican	−1.2	+4.3	+3.1
Prohibition	+7.9	−9.3	−1.4

74. Percentage returns from these towns were:

	1893				1894			
TOWN	DEM.	REP.	PRO.	POP.	DEM.	REP.	PRO.	POP.
Buena Vista	82.3	7.7	9.9	—	32.8	57.3	1.7	8.3
Hammonton	76.2	8.4	15.3	—	23.5	55.7	13.1	7.7
Egg Harbor City	58.5	40.9	0.6	—	34.2	62.1	0.3	3.3
Linwood	59.2	34.2	6.6	—	34.3	63.7	2.0	0.0

On Democratic gains, 1892–93, see above, p. 57.

75. Percentage point shifts in Camden and Mercer counties were:

	1893		1894	
	REP.	DEM.	REP.	DEM.
Camden County	+1.8	−3.8	+17.3	−17.6
Mercer County	+5.2	−6.3	+ 3.8	− 4.1

The New York *Tribune,* Nov. 8, 1894, perceived the relationship between the closing of the Gloucester City racetrack and the decline of Democratic fortunes there.

Camden and Trenton were the state's fourth and fifth most populous cities.

76. Percentage point shifts in these counties were:

	ESSEX	HUDSON	PASSAIC	UNION
Democrats	−7.2	+2.2	−12.1	−4.5
Republicans	+4.6	−0.2	+ 2.6	+3.7

77. Paterson *Labor Standard,* April 14, 1894. Maguire was to be his party's vice-presidential candidate in 1896. Paterson's textiles, its silk industry in particular, attracted large numbers of English, Scottish, Dutch, French, and Swiss workers. See Berthoff, *op. cit.,* 41–46; Vecoli, *The People of New Jersey, op. cit.,* 73–77, 97–98.

78. The two-party percentage point shifts in Elizabeth, 1893 and 1894, were ±4.8 and ±3.5, respectively.

79. See Appendix B for an explanation of the absence of detailed returns from Newark and Jersey City.

The vote of Irish Catholics clearly contributed to the Democrats' strength in their banner ward (Ward 12, 55.0% Democratic) in Newark, as the following breakdown of Ward 12 districts reveals:

DISTRICT	% IRISH-BORN	% GERMAN-BORN	DEM. %	REP. %	SLP %
1	2.8	31.7	36.9	57.5	2.0
2	21.6	9.2	69.9	27.3	0.1
3	25.6	13.2	65.0	32.7	1.3
4	22.1	7.9	66.0	33.1	0.0
5	1.3	38.2	30.8	60.9	4.7

In Jersey City, the Democrats received 54.1%, 62.3%, 51.6%, 38.7%, 44.3%, and 34.7% in Aldermanic Districts 1–6.

80. The coalition congressional candidate received 2.5% of the vote; he polled 3.6%, 10.7%, 7.6%, and 9.1% in Aldermanic District 4 of Jersey City, Guttenburg, Union (Town), and West Hoboken, where Germans were numerous.

On Populist activity in northeastern New Jersey, see Newark *Daily Advertiser,* Sept. 14, Oct. 3, 16, 22, 23, 29, 30, Nov. 27, 1894.

81. On socialism during the 1890s, see Chester McArthur Destler, *American Radicalism, 1865–1901: Essays and Sources* (Connecticut College Monograph No. 3; New London: Connecticut College, 1946); Howard Quint, *The Forging of American Socialism: Origins of the Modern Movement* (Columbia: University of South Carolina Press, 1953); Philip S. Foner, *History of the Labor Movement in the United States,* Vol. II: *From the Founding of the American Federation of Labor to the Emergence of American Imperialism* (New York: International Publishers, 1955); and Norman Pollack, *The Populist Response to Industrial America: Midwestern Populist Thought* (Cambridge: Harvard University Press, 1962).

82. On SLP recruiting among various ethnic groups, see *The People* (New York), Nov. 5, 1893, June 10, 1894, May 19, June 2, 1895; letter of Bernard [?] Katz to Daniel DeLeon, Dec. 18, 1895, in Daniel DeLeon Papers (State Historical Society of Wisconsin, Madison), cited hereafter as DeLeon Papers.

On Prohibitionists and Populists, see letter of Frances E. Willard to Henry Demarest Lloyd, Oct. 23, 1894, in Henry Demarest Lloyd Papers (State Historical Society of Wisconsin, Madison), cited hereafter as Lloyd Papers; *Tribune Almanacs, 1895,* 43–83; *1896,* 34–64; *1897,* 29–70; Jones, *Presidential Election of 1896, op. cit.,* 204–6; Newark *Daily Advertiser,* Sept. 10, 13, 1894; New York *Times,* Aug. 20, 1894.

For comments on the narrow ethnic base of the SLP, see letter of Friedrich Engels to Friedrich A. Sorge, Dec. 2, 1893, in Karl Marx and Friedrich Engels, *Letters to Americans, 1848–1895: A Selection* (New York: International Publishers, 1953), 257–58; letter of Florence Kelley to Henry Demarest Lloyd, June 18, 1896, in Lloyd Papers; letter of Joseph B. Keim to New Jersey State Committee of the Socialist Labor Party, Aug. 25, 1896, in DeLeon Papers. On opposition to recruiting among

Americans, see *The People* (New York), Dec. 1, 1895; letter of Charles A. Baustian to Henry Kuhn, Oct. 16, 1896, in Socialist Labor Party Papers (State Historical Society of Wisconsin, Madison), cited hereafter as SLP Papers.

83. For a contemporary appreciation of popular voting shifts in Baltimore that coincides with my own reading of the Northeast, see letter of Frederick J. Brown, in New York *Times*, Nov. 21, 1894.
84. Close analysis of late-nineteenth-century election data eliminates two other possibilities: (1) that Republicans were more likely than Democrats to vote in midterm elections; and (2) that in 1892 Grover Cleveland had activated non-voters and first voters, who then failed to vote Democratic in 1894.
85. Summers, *op. cit.*, 195.

V. 1895: OFF-YEAR POLITICAL PATTERNS

1. Paul W. Glad, *McKinley, Bryan, and the People, Critical Periods of History,* ed. Robert D. Cross (Philadelphia and New York: Lippincott, 1964), chap. v; Jones, *Presidential Election of 1896, op. cit.,* chaps. viii–xi.
2. Marian Silveus, The Antecedents of the Campaign of 1896 (unpublished Ph.D. dissertation, Dept. of History, University of Wisconsin, 1932), 21–25, 72–73; *Tribune Almanac, 1896,* 34–64.
3. Nevins, *Grover Cleveland, op. cit.,* chaps. xxxv, xxxvi, esp. 689; Glad, *op. cit.,* chap. vi; Jones, *op. cit.,* chaps. iv, v.
4. New York *Times,* Nov. 11, 1894.
5. New York *Times,* July 19, 1894; New York *Tribune,* Aug. 28, 1892, Feb. 19, May 28, 29, Aug. 3, 9, 23, 1894, Sept. 1, 1895; New Haven *Register,* July 31, 1895, March 25, 1896; Hartford *Courant,* Aug. 1, Nov. 7, Dec. 11, 1895, April 24, May 4, 22, 1896; Newark *Daily Advertiser,* Aug. 16, 1895, Feb. 24, 1896; George Frisbie Hoar, *Autobiography of Seventy Years* (2 vols.; New York: Scribner's, 1903), II, 282–93, esp. 291; Blodgett, *The Gentle Reformers, op. cit.,* 151–52; Nelson, The Influence of Immigration, *op. cit.,* 24; Wittke, *The Irish in America, op. cit.,* 188–90.
6. New Haven *Register,* March 19, April 2, 1895, March 21, 1896; Hartford *Courant,* March 26, April 1, 2, 1895; New York *Tribune,* April 1, 2, 1895; Heath, Politics and Steady Habits, *op. cit.,* 51–55. An astute observer of Massachusetts politics reported early in 1896: "The A.P.A.s are in a clearly declining condition in the state." See "Templeton," Hartford *Courant,* Feb. 29, 1896.
7. Newark *Daily Advertiser,* March 4, 7, 13, June 25, Aug. 7, 17, Sept. 5, 1895; New York *Times,* Feb. 13, March 8, June 29, Aug. 16, 1895; William E. Sackett, *Modern Battles of Trenton,* Vol. II: *From Werts to Wilson* (New York: Neale Publishing Co., 1914), 32–33; see also below, pp. 148–49.

   Rogers's bill was supported by 4 Republicans and 1 Democrat and opposed by 12 Republicans and 4 Democrats. On a similar proposal in Pennsylvania and a second round in New Jersey, see New York *Times,* March 7, 1895, Jan. 29, Feb. 12, 1896.

8. New York *Tribune,* March 21, April 23, July 5, 1895; Newark *Daily Advertiser,* June 17, July 15, 1895, Feb. 24, 1896; Trenton *Daily True American,* Oct. 11, 1895, June 3, 1896; Hartford *Courant,* July 5, Oct. 18, Dec. 13, 1895, Jan. 9, April 14, 1896.
9. Letter of Thomas F. Tracy to Governor O. Vincent Coffin, March 15, 1895, in Coffin Papers; letters of Governor Levi P. Morton to Thomas C. Platt, Jan. 27, 1896, and Jan. 27, 1896, both in Morton Papers; New York *Times,* Jan. 23, 1895. Also letter of M. D. Gallagher to Mayor William Strong, April 5, 1895, in Strong Papers. The Morton and Strong papers, as well as those of George W. Aldridge, Superintendent of the State Department of Public Works, contain a number of letters relating to the patronage.
10. New York *Times,* Feb. 7, 1895; New York *Tribune,* Oct. 1, 1895; letters of George Bliss to Archbishop Michael Corrigan, Oct. 26, 1894, Dec. 11, 1895, both in Corrigan Papers; Connors, *Church-State Relationships, op. cit.,* 118–25; King, *Facing the Twentieth Century, op. cit.,* 346–49; Zwierlein, *Letters of Archbishop Corrigan, op. cit.,* 188–89.
11. This discussion closely follows Sol Cohen, *Progressives and Urban School Reform: The Public Education Association of New York City, 1895–1954* (New York: Bureau of Publications, Teachers College, Columbia University, 1964), chaps. i, ii, esp. 40–42; also letter of Jacob H. Schiff to Mayor William Strong, Feb. 26, 1895; letter of Jacob W. Mack, Commissioner of Common Schools, to Mayor William Strong, April 16, 1896; letter of Theodore Bourne to Mayor William Strong, April 13, 1896, all in Strong Papers; and New York *Times,* April 1, 8, 1896.
12. Newark *Daily Advertiser,* March 12, 20, 22, 25, 1895; Hartford *Courant,* March 20, April 5, June 15, 21, 1895; New York *Tribune,* Jan. 23, June 18, 26, Aug. 8, 14, 25, 1895; New York *Times,* Feb. 22, June 18, 1895; *Connecticut State Register and Manual, 1899,* 60, 65.

    The Connecticut legislature tabled a resolution denouncing by name the American Protective Association. Heath, *op. cit.,* 50–51.
13. Newark *Daily Advertiser,* Dec. 12, 1893, Feb. 29, 1896; New York *Times,* Dec. 3, 24, 1893, Feb. 22, Oct. 5, 1894, May 1, 19, 22, 31, June 23, 24, 1895; Hartford *Courant,* Feb. 21, March 15, April 26, May 15, 22, 23, 30, June 5–7, 19, 20, 1895; New Haven *Register,* Feb. 7, May 3, 16, June 5, 6, 1895, July 2, 20, 1896; New York *Tribune,* Sept. 3, 1896; *Journal of the House of Representatives of the State of Connecticut, January Session, 1895, passim,* esp. 983–88, 1005–9; *Journal of the Senate of the State of Connecticut, January Session, 1895, passim,* esp. 990–91, 1014–15.

    During the debate over plurality elections, a Republican state senator warned that "with plurality elections a man might be elected by the growing foreign vote who as governor would imperil the safety of the state." Hartford *Courant,* June 19, 1895.

14. New York *Tribune,* Jan. 30, 1892, Oct. 13, 1894; New York *Times,* Nov. 24, 27, Dec. 5, 10, 11, 1894, July 11, 1895.
15. New York *Times,* Jan. 14–17, 22, 29, 30, March 15, 17, 18, 21, June 21, 27, July 5, 6, 11, Aug. 7, 9, 29, Sept. 7, 8, 12, 19, 1895; New York *Tribune,* Jan. 16, 17, 22, Feb. 7, March 1, 11, 18, 21, April 23, May 9, June 30, July 1, 7, 13, 19, 23, Aug. 6, 7, 9, 14, 28, Sept. 7, 1895; letters of Theodore Roosevelt to Anna Roosevelt, June 30, 1895, and to Henry Cabot Lodge, July 14, 1895, both quoted in Morison (ed.), *Letters of Theodore Roosevelt, op. cit.,* I, 464, 466; letter of Arthur von Briesen to Carl Schurz, July 3, 1895; letter of Theodore Roosevelt to Carl Schurz, July 13, 1895, both in Carl Schurz Papers (Library of Congress, Washington, D.C.), cited hereafter as Schurz Papers; Henry F. Pringle, *Theodore Roosevelt: A Biography* (Harvest Books edition; New York: Harcourt, Brace, 1956), 98–102; William H. Harbaugh, *Power and Responsibility: The Life and Times of Theodore Roosevelt* (New York: Farrar, Straus and Cudahy, 1961), 85. Also see letter of Theodore Roosevelt to Alphonse Major, Jan. 29, 1896, in Roosevelt Papers.
16. New York *Times,* July 12, 15, 17, Sept. 8, 12, 1895; New York *Tribune,* July 12, 13, Sept. 8, 9, 16, 1895; letter of Theodore Roosevelt to Henry Cabot Lodge, July 20, 1895, quoted in Morison (ed.), *op. cit.,* I, 469.
17. New York *Tribune,* June 2, 8, 9, 11, 16, Sept. 16–19, 1895; New York *Times,* Sept. 5, 6, 16–18, 1895; Trenton *Daily True American,* Sept. 6, 1895; Alexander, *Four Famous New Yorkers, op. cit.,* 235–38.

    On legislation requiring temperance instruction in public schools and German opposition thereto, see New York *Times,* May 28, June 7, 8, 10, 11, 15, 1895; letter of Frederick W. Holls to Charles R. Skinner, June 17, 1895, in Holls Papers.
18. Letter of George Cary Eggleston to David B. Hill, Sept. 20, 1895; telegram of Joseph B. Pulitzer to David B. Hill, Sept. 23, 1895; letter of C. R. Miller to George F. Spinnery, Sept. 21, 1895, all in Hill Papers; New York *Times,* Sept. 9, 25, 26, 1895; New York *Tribune,* Sept. 24, 26, 27, 1895; *Tribune Almanac, 1896,* 54.
19. New York *Tribune,* Sept. 27, 29, 30, Oct. 10, 11, 14, 16, 17, Nov. 2, 3, 1895; New York *Times,* Oct. 8, Nov. 1, 2, 1895; letters of Theodore Roosevelt to Henry Cabot Lodge, Oct. 3, 11, 18, 29, 1895, all quoted in Morison (ed.), *op. cit.,* I, 482–93; letter of Warner Miller to Whitelaw Reid, Oct. 8, 1895, in Reid Papers.
20. Rischin, *The Promised City, op. cit.,* 88, 222–23; New York *Times,* Feb. 10, 18, 19, 28, May 9, 17, 1895; New York *Tribune,* March 11, April 21, 22, 1895. The Strong Papers include considerable correspondence on both subjects.
21. Letter of Frederick W. Holls to Gustav Schwab, July 23, 1895, in Schurz Papers; letters of Richard Watson Gilder to the Reverend Charles H. Parkhurst, Oct. 22, Nov. 8, 1895, both in Gilder Papers.

    On differences between "reform" and "machine" politicians and their relations with the public, see Garrett, *The La Guardia Years, op. cit.,* 15–17, 20–21, 34–35. Theodore J. Lowi, *At the Pleasure of the Mayor: Patronage and Power in New York City, 1898–1958* (Glencoe, Ill.: The Free Press, 1964), *passim,* esp. 34–54, 175–214, is invaluable on the ethnic composition of "reform" and "machine" administrations. No comparable analysis of the Strong administration has been made, but its essential similarity to later "reform" governments is clear.

22. New York *Times,* Oct. 1, 1895; New York *Tribune,* Oct. 1, 2, 12, 15, 29, 1895; letter of Richard Watson Gilder to John H. C. Nevins, Oct. 16, 1895, in Gilder Papers; letter of Theodore Roosevelt to Henry Cabot Lodge, Oct. 3, 1895, quoted in Morison (ed.), *op. cit.,* I, 483. Roosevelt referred to the Good Government clubs as "those prize idiots, the Goo-Goos."

23. Alexander, *op. cit.,* 239–45; New York *Times,* Jan. 13, April 16, Aug. 19, 26, 27, Sept. 4, 7, 26, 27, Oct. 1, Nov. 1, 3, 1895; New York *Tribune,* June 12, Aug. 16, 22, Sept. 2, 22, 24, 26, Oct. 8, 1895; *Tribune Almanac, 1896,* 53–54; letters and telegram of David B. Hill to Daniel S. Lamont, Aug. 7, Sept. 18, Oct. 15, 1895; letter of Daniel S. Lamont to John B. Howe, Aug. 2, 1895; letter of Daniel S. Lamont to Charles Tracey, Sept. 26, 1895; letter of E. I. Wagee [?] to Daniel S. Lamont, Oct. 4, 1895, all in Lamont Papers; letter of Norman E. Mack to David B. Hill, Sept. 20, 1895, in Hill Papers.

24. Newark *Daily Advertiser,* June 26, July 2, 17, Oct. 18, 1895; Trenton *Daily True American,* Sept. 13, 20, 23–27, 1895; New York *Times,* March 11, 25, April 1, Sept. 18, 19, 23, 26, 1895; New York *Tribune,* Sept. 6, 11, 15, 27, Oct. 7, 1895; *Manual of the Legislature of New Jersey . . . 1896,* 157–58.

25. Newark *Daily Advertiser,* Aug. 27, 29, Sept. 27, Oct. 19, 1895; New York *Times,* Sept. 26, 27, Oct. 1, 1895; New York *Tribune,* Sept. 27, 1895; *Manual of the Legislature of New Jersey . . . 1896,* 158–61.

   The Trenton *Daily True American,* Oct. 26, 1895, reported the circulation in southern New Jersey of a leaflet that attacked McGill for supporting the Catholic Protectory. The newspaper linked the leaflet to Griggs's campaign appearances in the area and contended that McGill had favored chartering the Protectory only after public funds were withdrawn from the project.

26. The Democrats carried all six A.D.s (4, 8, 10, 12, 14, and 16) in the Lower East Side and all eight (22, 24, 26, 28, 30, 32, 33, and 34) in the Upper East Side, all but A.D. 8 by majorities. The SLP received 17.8 % of the vote in A.D. 12, its best showing in the city. Mean party strengths in the aforementioned districts were:

DISTRICTS	DEM. %	REP. %	SLP %
A.D.s, Lower East Side	54.9	31.6	13.1
A.D.s, Upper East Side	58.9	35.0	5.5

27. In 1894, Tammany, −7.0; Fusion, +10.6; in 1895, −5.1 and +2.9, respectively. Tammany had trailed the regular and independent Democratic state tickets combined by 10.3 percentage points in 1894.
28. Letter of Frederick W. Holls to John E. Milholland, Nov. 6, 1895, in Holls Papers; New York *Tribune,* Nov. 4, 12, 18, 1895.
29. Brooklyn *Daily Eagle,* Nov. 23–30, Dec. 12, 1894, Jan. 8, 10, 14, 15, 25, Feb. 21, March 24, 31, Oct. 1, 2, 5, 6–31, Nov. 7, 15, 20, 26, 1895; New York *Times,* March 4, July 17, Aug. 5, 9, 19, 21, 25, Sept. 4–12, Oct. 6–31, Nov. 11, 17, 1895; New York *Tribune,* Nov. 25, 1895.
30. The correlation between Republican percentage losses and Reform Democratic percentage strength was −.437; that between Republican and Reform Democratic percentage shifts, +.380. The correlation between Republican losses and Socialist Labor party strength (a rough indicator of German strength in the wards of Brooklyn, where East European Jews were not yet numerous or widely dispersed) was +.773. As in New York County, SLP strength reached its peak in Kings (2.9%) in 1895.

    Compare mean Republican percentage point declines, 1894–95, with the Reform Democratic vote, 1894, and Democratic percentage point gains, 1894–95; also the SLP vote, 1895, in the following wards:

WARDS	REP.−	REF. DEM. %	DEM.+	SLP %
German (16, 18, 21, 26, 27, 28)	7.2	4.9	9.4	8.2
Old-stock (1, 3, 7, 20, 23, 25)	3.5	7.2	10.5	0.9

31. Percentage point shifts were:

UNIT	DEM.	REP.	UNIT	DEM.	REP.
Rensselaer Co.	+2.0	−1.0	Albany Co.	+0.5	+0.4
Troy	+3.7	−2.6	Albany	+0.9	+0.2
Outlying towns	+0.4	+0.5	Outlying towns	+0.2	+0.8

    The Democrats gained most heavily in Ward 11 of Troy (+13.8 percentage points), a party stronghold where they had suffered major losses in 1894. Albany's redistricting prevents a ward-by-ward comparison of 1894 and 1895 returns there.
32. On Buffalo, see New York *Times,* Nov. 1, 1895. Percentage point shifts were:

UNIT	DEM.	REP.	UNIT	DEM.	REP.
Erie Co.	−2.1	+3.3	Monroe Co.	−1.2	+2.0
Buffalo	−2.2	+3.3	Rochester	−1.4	+2.7
Outlying towns	−2.1	+2.9	Outlying towns	−1.9	+0.7

    In Buffalo Wards 7, 21, 23, and 24, the Democrats gained 1.3, 4.6, 2.2, and 3.3 percentage points, the Republicans losing 0.6, 1.0, 0.1, and 1.1

points. In Wards 1, 2, and 19, the Republicans gained 10.2, 13.3, and 9.1 percentage points, the Democrats losing 7.8, 13.8, and 8.5 points. The Prohibition party gained 0.3 percentage points in Erie County, 0.4 in Monroe.

33. Republican and Democratic percentage strength and percentage point shifts in seven German towns and in the five counties in which they were located were:

UNIT	REP.	DEM.
Fulton Co.	57.9% (+0.2)	36.9% (−0.2)
Bleecker	30.2% (+9.4)	66.2% (−8.0)
Lewis Co.	57.9% (+2.4)	38.8% (−1.2)
Croghan	52.6% (+6.5)	46.3% (−3.9)
Lewis	27.6% (−2.1)	68.7% (+3.6)
New Bremen	50.1% (−0.5)	48.8% (+4.0)
Monroe Co.	58.9% (+2.0)	37.4% (−1.2)
Irondequoit	56.0% (+3.5)	37.7% (−6.7)
Niagara Co.	54.4% (−0.5)	40.3% (+2.9)
Wheatfield	49.4% (−4.5)	42.8% (+6.4)
Steuben Co.	59.4% (+3.3)	31.7% (−4.7)
Wayland	50.1% (+5.2)	45.8% (−5.1)

34. In the one New Jersey county where the Democrats lost percentage strength, the Republicans lost even more. Republican gains exceeded Democratic gains in two counties; in three other counties, Republican strength remained constant as Democratic strength increased. Republican losses accompanied Democratic gains in fifteen counties.

35. Percentages and percentage shifts in these counties were:

COUNTY	DEM. %	REP. %	PRO. %	POP. %	SLP %
Cumberland	33.9 (+10.1)	55.6 (——)	5.2 (−2.0)	5.1 (−7.9)	0.3 (−0.2)
Gloucester	40.3 (+ 5.7)	55.9 (−2.8)	3.1 (−0.8)	0.6 (−2.1)	0.2 (——)
Camden	33.2 (+ 7.6)	63.4 (−6.1)	2.4 (−1.0)	0.4 (−0.4)	0.6 (−0.2)

The Democrats gained 8.4 percentage points in Camden city.

36. In Cape May County, the Democrats gained 0.7 percentage points, the Republicans 0.9 points. Sea Isle City recorded a Democratic gain of 18.5 points. During 1892–95, the Democratic vote in that city fell from 72.8 to 18.8%, then rose to 42.1 and 60.6%.

37. In Atlantic County, the Democrats (+3.2) and Socialist Laborites (+0.3) gained percentage points at the expense of the Republicans (−0.8), Prohibitionists (−1.5), and Populists (−1.2). Democratic percentage shifts in

Egg Harbor City, Buena Vista, Hammonton, and Linwood were +16.9, +3.8, +4.9, and −5.6.

38. Democratic percentage gains in Mercer and Warren were 6.4 and 4.0 percentage points, Republican losses 4.3 and 5.9 points. Pre-depression Democratic ward-level percentage strength and Democratic percentage gains in Trenton correlated at +.636.

In Hunterdon, the Democrats gained 1.0 percentage points and the Republicans lost 0.6; in Sussex, the shifts were −0.3 and −0.4, respectively.

39. Maior party percentages and percentage shifts in these counties were:

COUNTY	DEM.	REP.	COUNTY	DEM.	REP.
Essex	42.0% (+5.1)	54.6% (−3.7)	Passaic	39.6% (+8.4)	53.7% (−1.6)
Hudson	54.5% (+6.5)	42.5% (−6.4)	Union	42.9% (+5.2)	52.4% (−5.0)

40. In Wards 12, 13, and 14, the Democratic mean gain was 10.3 percentage points. Percentages and percentage shifts in Ward 12 districts were:

DIST.	DEM.	REP.	DIST.	DEM.	REP.
1	50.0% (+13.1)	46.6% (−10.9)	4	64.8% (− 1.2)	34.6% (+ 1.5)
2	80.4% (+10.5)	19.3% (− 8.0)	5	49.1% (+18.3)	48.6% (−12.3)
3	74.7% (+ 9.7)	23.2% (− 9.5)			

It should be noted that the Republican defection ratio was greater in Districts 2 and 3 (29.3, 29.1) than in Districts 1 and 5 (19.0, 20.2).

City-wide, ward-level Democratic percentage strength correlated more strongly with percentage Irish male (+.733) than percentage German male (+.278), but the correlation between Democratic percentage gain and percentage German male (+.642) was stronger than correlations between percentage gain and percentage Irish male (+.030) and percentage gain and Democratic percentage strength, 1894 (+.219).

The SLP received 1.8% of the total vote in Newark; 7.8, 5.0, and 4.7% in Wards 3, 13, and 14; and 18.5 and 11.9% in Ward 3, Districts 4 and 5.

41. In Wards 2, 8, and 9, the Democrats gained 2.9, 1.3, and 3.5 percentage points; the Republicans polled 58.6, 69.9, and 74.6% of the total vote. City-wide, ward-level correlations between percentage native-born white male and (1) Democratic percentage strength, 1895, and (2) percentage gains, 1894–95, were −.332 and −.738.

42. Newark *Daily Advertiser,* Nov. 5, 1895; New York *Tribune,* Oct. 18, 1895.

43. In Elizabeth, the Democrats gained 1.6, 8.7, 8.4, 6.1, 5.1, and 4.2 percentage points in the two-party vote in Wards 3, 5, 7, 10, 11, and 12; city-wide they gained 4.9 points.

Democratic percentage gains in Paterson's wards correlated positively with Democratic percentage strength in 1894 (+.690) and Republican percentage losses (+.452), but most strongly with Socialist Labor percentage losses (+.815).

Democratic, Republican, and Socialist Labor percentage point shifts in the city of Passaic were +4.8, −5.5, and +0.6; in Ward 3, −0.2, +0.9, and −0.6.

44. The relevant coefficients of variability are:

	NEW YORK		NEW JERSEY	
	DEM.	REP.	DEM.	REP.
1894	.151	.101	.175	.114
1895	.215	.123	.144	.086

45. See Appendix D.

VI. "THE ENEMY'S COUNTRY": THE PRESIDENTIAL CAMPAIGN AND ELECTION OF 1896

1. Jones, *Presidential Election of 1896, op. cit.*, chaps. vii–xii; Glad, *McKinley, Bryan, and the People, op. cit.*, chap. v, esp. 107–8; *Tribune Almanac, 1897*, 20–23.
2. Jones, *ibid.*, chaps, v, xiii, xiv, covers the Democratic preconvention fight in various areas; also see *Tribune Almanac, 1897*, 34–70, esp. 56–57. On the New York State Democratic convention, see Alexander, *Four Famous New Yorkers, op. cit.*, 261–65; Nevins, *Grover Cleveland, op. cit.*, 691; Hollingsworth, *The Whirligig of Politics, op. cit.*, 44; Jones, *ibid.*, 200–202; letter of Calvin Tompkins to Charles S. Fairchild, June 26, 1896, in Fairchild Papers.

   On the Democratic national convention, see Jones, *ibid.*, chaps. xvi, xvii; William Jennings Bryan, *The First Battle: A Story of the Campaign of 1896* (Chicago: W. B. Conkey Co., 1896), 207–9, 214–18, 223–27, 406–9; Perry Belmont, *An American Democrat: The Recollections of Perry Belmont* (New York: Columbia University Press, 1940), 422–23; letter of L. E. Sexton to Charles S. Fairchild, July 14, 1896, in Fairchild Papers; New York *Times*, July 9, 1896.

   Nevins, *op. cit.*, 703–4, reports Cleveland's personal reactions to the stunning news from Chicago and laments that with acceptance of the Democratic national platform of 1896, "the old Democratic party, the party of Tilden and Cleveland, passed out of existence."
3. Jones, *ibid.*, chaps. xv, xviii, xxii; Robert F. Durden, *The Climax of Populism: The Election of 1896* (Lexington: University of Kentucky Press, 1965).
4. Jones, *ibid.*, 100, 141, 293–94.
5. Jones, *ibid.*, chap. xix; *Tribune Almanac, 1897*, 28–29.
6. Jones, *ibid.*, 264–71, 274–75; Glad, *op. cit.*, 163–64. Letter of William C.

P. Breckinridge to Charles S. Fairchild, July 13, 1896; letter of Calvin Tompkins to William C. P. Breckinridge, July 17, 1896, both in Fairchild Papers; letter of Calvin Tompkins to William D. Bynum, July 17, 1896, in William D. Bynum Papers (Library of Congress, Washington, D.C.), cited hereafter as Bynum Papers; letter of George Gray to William C. Whitney, July 29, 1896, in Whitney Papers; letters of B. B. Smalley to Daniel S. Lamont, June 9, Aug. 14, 20, 1896, all in Lamont Papers.

7. Letter of Clinton B. Davis to Grover Cleveland, June 15, 1896, in Cleveland Papers; letters of Lynde Harrison to William C. Whitney, June 20, July 30, 1896; letters of Clinton B. Davis to William C. Whitney, July 11, 27, 1896, all in Whitney Papers; Hartford *Courant,* June 6, 10, 1896; New Haven *Register,* June 10, 11, July 10, 11, 14, 15, 23, 25, 28, 30, Aug. 3, 4, 9, 1896; *Tribune Almanac, 1897,* 37.

8. New Haven *Register,* Aug. 12–14, 20, Sept. 10, 16, 20, 21, Oct. 8, 1896; Hartford *Courant,* Aug. 14, Sept. 11, 1896; New York *Times,* Aug. 20, 21, Sept. 14, 17, 18, 1896; New York *Tribune,* Aug. 30, 1896; *Tribune Almanac, 1897,* 37–38; letter of Clinton B. Davis to William C. Whitney, Aug. 1, 1896, in Whitney Papers; letter of Lynde Harrison to David B. Hill, Sept. 3, 1896, in Hill Papers.

Harrison's letter to Hill made clear the role played by party workers in carrying the day for the Bryanites.

9. New York *Times,* July 13–Aug. 4, 1896; letter of David B. Hill to William E. Chandler, Aug. 1, 1896, in Chandler Papers; Festus P. Summers (ed.), *The Cabinet Diary of William L. Wilson, 1896–1897* (Chapel Hill: University of North Carolina Press, 1957), 118–19, 148–49.

For suggestions to Hill that he support Bryan, see the letters of William L. Calkins, July 15, 1896; Charles A. Burke, July 22, 1896; and C. Boyd Barrett, July 23, 1896, all in Hill Papers. For suggestions to Hill that he oppose Bryan, see the letters of Timothy S. Williams, Aug. 25, 1896; Roswell P. Flower, Aug. 27, 1896; and Daniel S. Lamont, n.d., all in Bixby Papers.

On the Bryan-Hill episode, see New York *Times,* Aug. 22–26, 1896; Bryan, *op. cit.,* 349–50; letter of William Jennings Bryan to George S. Bixby, May 16, 1920, in Bixby Papers.

Among Democrats breaking with their national party during this period were William C. Whitney, Frederic R. Coudert, former Governor Roswell P. Flower, and two former mayors of New York City, William R. Grace and Hugh J. Grant.

10. New York *Times,* July 15, 16, 17, 22, 23, 24, 26, 30, 31, Aug. 2, 6, 12, 13, 14, 15, 20, 25, Sept. 1, 4, 1896; Alexander, *op. cit.,* 272–74; letter of Maurice J. Power to Daniel S. Lamont, n.d.; letter of David B. Hill to Daniel S. Lamont, Sept. 14, 1896, both in Lamont Papers; *Tribune Almanac, 1897,* 28–29, 58–59.

11. On the political situation in upstate New York during the summer of 1896, see the following letters to Hill: J. P. Merrill, July 14, Aug. 3, 1896; Robert C. Titus, July 12, 1896; P. J. Quinn, July 13, 1896; Thomas Car-

mody, July 13, 1896; William M. Cameron, July 20, 1896; B. G. Foss, July 21, 1896; C. A. Lux, Aug. 1, 1896; Edson Potter, Aug. 3, 1896; Luke McHenry, Aug. 5, 1896; James C. Stout, Aug. 21, 1896; Edwin J. Brown, Aug. 24, 1896; and Charles A. Burke, July 22, 1896 (enclosing letters of Charles A. Burke to "Dear Sir," July 20, 1896, and M. B. Ramsdell to Charles A. Burke, July 21, 1896), all in Hill Papers.

Some free silver sentiment had been reported at the time of the first Democratic state convention. See letter of Calvin Tompkins to William D. Bynum, June 19, 1896, in Bynum Papers; New York *Tribune,* June 23, 1896.

12. Alexander, *op. cit.,* 274; letter of Warren S. (?) to David B. Hill, Aug. 3, 1896; letter of Calvin J. Huson to David B. Hill, Aug. 31, 1896, both in Hill Papers.
13. See the following letters to Hill: J. P. Merrill, Aug. 3, 1896; Hosea Rockwell, Sept. 21, 1896; Luke McHenry, Sept. 10, 1896; H. D. Brewster, Aug. 24, 1896; De Forest Van Fleet, Aug. 24, 1896; and John Flannigan, Sept. 4, 1896, all in Hill Papers; also Bernard J. York, Aug. 26, 1896; and John B. Stanchfield, Sept. 18, 1896, both in Bixby Papers; letter of David B. Hill to Daniel S. Lamont, Sept. 14, 1896; letter of John Courtney, Jr., to Daniel S. Lamont, Sept. 22, 1896, both in Lamont Papers; New York *Times,* Aug. 21, 22, Sept. 10–16, 1896; Alexander, *ibid.,* 274.
14. New York *Tribune,* Sept. 7, 13, 14, 1896; letter of W. Caryl Ely to David B. Hill, Sept. 8, 1896, in Bixby Papers; letter of David B. Hill to Daniel S. Lamont, Sept. 14, 1896, in Lamont Papers. Among the bolting Democrats were Perry Belmont; U.S. Representative Franklin Bartlett; W. Caryl Ely, Treasurer of the Democratic State Committee; and William F. Sheehan, a member of the Democratic National Committee, former lieutenant-governor, and brother of John C. Sheehan of Tammany Hall.

    Two days before his comment to Lamont, Hill confided to an old associate: "I am a Democrat still—very still." Letter of David B. Hill to Judge Hamilton Ward, Sept. 12, 1896, copy in Bixby Papers.
15. New York *Times,* Sept. 16–21, 1896; *Tribune Almanac, 1897,* 57–58; Alexander, *op. cit.,* 274–77. The convention went so far as to declare "as its deliberate judgment that never in the history of the Democratic party has a platform been written which embodied more completely the interests of the whole people, as distinguished from those who seek legislation for private benefit, than that given to the country by the National Democratic Convention of 1896."
16. New York *Times,* Sept. 21–Oct. 1, 1896; letter of Hosea Rockwell to David B. Hill, Sept. 21, 1896; letter of Robert C. Titus to David B. Hill, Sept. 23, 1896; letter of Luke McHenry to David B. Hill, Sept. 26, 1896, all in Hill Papers; Alexander, *ibid.,* 277–80.

    The evidence does not permit a final judgment as to whether Thacher gave up the fight or was forced to withdraw from the race.
17. New York *Times,* Sept. 1, 19, 22, 24, 25, 1896. Also see the following letters to David B. Hill: W. R. Hopkins, Sept. 3, 1896; Hosea Rockwell,

Sept. 21, 1896; Robert C. Titus, Sept. 23, 1896; and Louis M. Antisdale, Sept. 24, 1896 (enclosing letter of (?) Burrill to Louis M. Antisdale, Sept. 24, 1896), all in Hill Papers; letter of E. Ellery Anderson to Daniel S. Lamont, Sept. 19, 1896; letter of Maurice J. Power to Daniel S. Lamont, n.d., both in Lamont Papers.

18. Josephus Daniels, *Editor in Politics* (Chapel Hill: University of North Carolina Press, 1941), 194; New York *Times*, Sept. 19, 23, 24, 26, 27, 1896. Cf. Glad, *op. cit.*, 184; Jones, *op. cit.*, 312–13.

19. New York *Times*, Feb. 9, 11, 13–15, July 13–28, 31, Aug. 1, 2, 5, 22, Sept. 24, Oct. 8, 13–17, 1896; New York *Tribune*, July 14, 17, 19, Aug. 1, Sept. 30, Oct. 4, 14, 1896.

On Tammany's financial problems, see New York *Times*, Aug. 21, Sept. 9, 1896; letter of George B. McClellan, Jr., to Richard Croker, Sept. 8, 1896, in McClellan Papers; letter of Edward M. Caffell to William Jennings Bryan, Nov. 6, 1896, in William Jennings Bryan Papers (Library of Congress, Washington, D.C.), cited hereafter as Bryan Papers.

20. New York *Tribune*, Sept. 21, 1896; New York *Times*, Oct. 4, 6, 7, 9, 23, 1896; New York *Journal*, Oct. 13, 1896; letter of Maurice J. Power to Daniel S. Lamont, n.d.; letter of George B. McClellan, Jr., to Daniel S. Lamont, Sept. 26, 1896, both in Lamont Papers; letters of George B. McClellan, Jr., to Richard Croker, Sept. 8, 1896, and n.d.; letter of George B. McClellan, Jr., to Charles F. Murphy, Oct. 5, 1896, all in McClellan Papers; Harold C. Syrett (ed.), *The Gentleman and the Tiger: The Autobiography of George B. McClellan, Jr.* (Philadelphia and New York: Lippincott, 1956), 114–17.

21. New York *Tribune*, July 15, 1896.

22. Newark *Daily Advertiser*, July 8, 15, Sept. 1, 29, 1896; Trenton *Daily True American*, June 27, Aug. 7, 20, Sept. 10, 16, 18, 21, 1896; New York *Tribune*, July 16, Aug. 7, Sept. 3, 19, 20, 25, 1896; New York *Times*, Sept. 10, 1896; *Tribune Almanac, 1897*, 54; letter of Louis T. Michener to E. F. Tibbott, June 5, 1896, in Harrison Papers; letter of William A. Cotter to William C. Whitney, June 22, 1896, in Whitney Papers; letter of Garret Hobart to William McKinley, Aug. 20, 1896, in McKinley Papers; Sackett, *Modern Battles of Trenton*, Vol. II: *From Werts to Wilson*, *op. cit.*, 54–55.

Clarence Atkinson and James E. Martine were foremost among the Democratic "radicals" who gained prominence during the summer. Martine later served in the U.S. Senate (1911–17) after defeating James Smith, Jr., in the Democratic primary.

23. New York *Tribune*, July 2, 7, 10, Aug. 26, 27, Oct. 20, 1896; New York *Times*, Aug. 3, 15, 18, 27, Sept. 9, 1896; Newark *Daily Advertiser*, Sept. 19, 26, Oct. 20, 27, 1896; Trenton *Daily True American*, Aug. 8, 18, 27, Sept. 7, 28, Oct. 9, 26, 1896; letter of William J. Curtis to Grover Cleveland, June 4, 1896 (enclosing letter of William J. Curtis to James Smith, Jr., June 3, 1896), in Cleveland Papers; letter of Asa W. Dickinson to Daniel S. Lamont, Sept. 23, 1896, in Lamont Papers.

Among the more prominent bolters were William McAdoo, a former congressman and Cleveland's Assistant Secretary of the Navy; E. F. C. Young, former Democratic state committeeman, president of the First National Bank in Jersey City, and financial backer of "Bob" Davis's Hudson County machine; and George L. Record, a young reformer who had battled the machine. Davis's organization neither bolted nor went all-out for the national ticket. Record joined the Republican party, where, with Mark Fagan, he led reform forces. On Young and Davis, see John Morton Blum, *Joe Tumulty and the Wilson Era* (Boston: Houghton Mifflin, 1951), 7; on Record and Fagan, see Ransom E. Noble, Jr., *New Jersey Progressivism Before Wilson* (Princeton: Princeton University Press, 1946), 12–13, 15.

24. Troup, a former Greenbacker, became chairman of Bryan's campaign in Connecticut and the state's Democratic committeeman. Among young recruits to Bryan's cause in Connecticut, Homer S. Cummings became the most famous. He ran for Connecticut Secretary of State in 1896 and later served as Chairman of the Democratic National Committee and Attorney General of the United States. Heath, Politics and Steady Habits, *op. cit.*, 79–80.

    On the post-1896 activities of Cleveland Democrats, some of whom returned to their party, others of whom became Republicans or retired from politics, see Hollingsworth, *op. cit.*, 109, 117–20.

25. New York *Times*, July 15, 1896; letter of Maurice J. Power to Daniel S. Lamont, n.d., in Lamont Papers; letter of Elliot Danforth to David B. Hill, Nov. 10, 1896, in Hill Papers.

26. Alexander, *op. cit.*, chaps xxviii–xxxvi. For the picturesque and contemptuous remarks of George Washington Plunkitt on the inability of Hill and the upstate Democracy to deliver the vote, see William L. Riordon (recorder), *Plunkitt of Tammany Hall: A Series of Very Plain Talks on Very Practical Politics* (New York: E. P. Dutton, 1963), 43–44.

27. Letter of Lynde Harrison to David B. Hill, Sept. 3, 1896, in Hill Papers; Heath, *op. cit.*, 81; *Connecticut State Register and Manual, 1897*, 350–51.

    Hartford *Courant*, Aug. 29, 1896; letter of F. A. Hobart to George Fred Williams, July 15, 1896, in William E. Russell Papers (Massachusetts Historical Society, Boston), cited hereafter as Russell Papers. Hobart cautioned Williams, the Democratic gubernatorial candidate in Massachusetts, that overrepresentation of the Irish on the ticket would increase defections among other groups.

28. Dahl, *Who Governs?*, *op. cit.*, chap. i, esp. 11–14, 25–38; Kerker, The Democratic Party in Albany County, *op. cit.*, 260–61; Blodgett, *The Gentle Reformers*, *op. cit.*, chaps. viii, ix; Cornwell, "Party Absorption of Ethnic Groups," *loc. cit.*, 207–8.

29. Glad, *op. cit.*, 166–72; Jones, *op. cit.*, chap. xx; Josephson, *The Politicos*, *op. cit.* 693–99.

30. Bryan, *op. cit.*, 392–97; *Tribune Almanac, 1897*, 34–70; New York *Tribune*, July 21, 29, Aug. 23, Sept. 10, 11, Oct. 25, Nov. 1, 1896; New York

Times, Sept. 23, 1896; Hartford *Courant,* Aug. 8, 21, Sept. 3, 14, 30, 1896; New Haven *Register,* Sept. 2, 1896; Trenton *Daily True American,* Aug. 28, Sept. 4, 24, 1896; Newark *Daily Advertiser,* July 27, 1896.

31. New York *Times,* July 17, 20, 23, 25, 27, Aug. 26, 28, Sept. 8, 1896; New York *Tribune,* July 29, 1896; letter of Charles W. Hackett to Benjamin Harrison, Aug. 7, 1896; letter of Stephen B. Elkins to Benjamin Harrison, Aug. 8, 1896; letter of W. H. H. Miller to Benjamin Harrison, Aug. 13, 1896, all in Harrison Papers; letter of Whitelaw Reid to Donald Nicholson, Sept. 9, 1896, in Reid Papers; letter of William M. Osborne to William McKinley, Sept. 1, 1896, in McKinley Papers.

32. *Tribune Almanac, 1897,* 25; New York *Tribune,* Sept. 17, 1896; New York *Journal,* Oct. 4, 11 1896; *The People* (New York), March 15, Aug. 23, Oct. 4, 1896; *Irish World and American Industrial Liberator* (New York), Oct. 10, 1896; Trenton *Daily True American,* Aug. 3, Sept. 8, 1896; Newark *Daily Advertiser,* July 25, Oct. 1, 1896; also see Eugene V. Debs in the *Railway Times,* Sept. 15, 1896, reported in letter of George H. Baker to William McKinley, Oct. 3, 1896, in McKinley Papers; and the perceptive analysis of the impact of Bryan's campaign on workers in New York City in letter of Henry White to William Jennings Bryan, Nov. 8, 1896, in Bryan Papers. Also see Bryan, *op. cit.,* 199–206, 315–37, 375–83, 412, 589; Hollingsworth, *op. cit.,* 92; Blodgett, *op. cit.,* 237.

33. New York *Tribune,* Sept. 3, Oct. 25, 1896; Newark *Daily Advertiser,* July 18, Aug. 6, Sept. 5, 23, 1896. Cf. Trenton *Daily True American,* July 21, Oct. 3, 1896.

34. Bryan, *op. cit.,* 351, 353; Lee Benson, The New York Farmers' Rejection of Populism: The Background (unpublished Master's thesis, Dept. of History, Columbia University, 1948), 62; ———, *Merchants, Farmers, & Railroads, op. cit.,* 10–16, 80–93; also *The People* (New York), May 19, 1895, for a fascinating editorial on New York agriculture and railroad rates. The Hill Papers contain numerous letters relating to the oleomargarine question.

35. Benson, *Merchants, Farmers, & Railroads, op. cit.,* 81, 86, 271–72 (note 7), 273 (note 27); New York *Times,* June 18, 1895; New York *Tribune,* Nov. 18, 1895; Hartford *Courant,* July 19, 1893, Jan. 10, Feb. 13, July 10, Sept. 13, 1894, March 11, May 11, 25, 1895, March 13, Oct. 15, 1896; New Haven *Register,* Jan. 13, Aug. 14, 1896; Newark *Daily Advertiser,* Aug. 13, 14, 1896; Trenton *Daily True American,* Jan. 15, June 16, 1896.

36. Jones, *op. cit.,* chap. xx, esp. 291–93. William C. Beer was forced to admit to his wife that the anti-southern campaign had its trying moments, declaring that "above all I hope & pray that when this cruel war is over I may never-never hear again the tune of 'Marching through Georgia.'" Letter of William C. Beer to Mrs. William C. Beer, Oct. 9, 1896, in Beer Family Papers (Yale University Library, New Haven), cited hereafter as Beer Papers.

37. New York *Tribune,* July 28, Aug. 28, Oct. 28, Nov. 4, 1896; New York

Times, Aug. 19, 1896; Hartford *Courant,* July 13, 15, 16, Sept. 12, 1896; Newark *Daily Advertiser,* July 13, 1896; C. Vann Woodward, "The Populist Heritage and the Intellectual," *The American Scholar,* XXIX (Winter 1959–60), 67–69.

Letter of William C. Beer to Mrs. William C. Beer, Oct. 19, 1896, in Beer Papers; letter of John Byrne to Charles S. Fairchild, Sept. 11, 1896, in Fairchild Papers; letter of Abram S. Hewitt to Edward M. Shepard, July 15, 1896, in Hewitt Papers; letters of John Hay to Whitelaw Reid, Aug. 31, Nov. 7, 1896, both in Reid Papers.

See Pollack, *The Populist Response to Industrial America, op. cit.,* 127–30, for similar expression in the Midwest.

38. New York *Times,* July 20, Aug. 3, 10, 17, 24, Sept. 7, 14, 21, 28, Oct. 5, 19, 1896; New York *Tribune,* July 6, 14, Oct. 18, 26, Nov. 1, 2, 1896; Brooklyn *Daily Eagle,* Oct. 5, 8, 26, 29, Nov. 2, 1896; New Haven *Register,* July 27, Aug. 24, Sept. 28, 1896; Hartford *Courant,* Aug. 31, 1896; Trenton *Daily True American,* Sept. 22, 28, 1896; Newark *Daily Advertiser,* Nov. 2, 1896; Bryan, *op. cit.,* chap. xxxv. Rev. Dr. Charles H. Parkhurst; Rev. Dr. Robert S. MacArthur; Rev. Thomas Dixon, Jr.; Rev. Cortland Myers; and Rev. Everhard Kempshall were among the clergymen who opposed Bryan.

On the stand of the Protestant ministry for sound money during the 1870s, see Irwin Unger, *The Greenback Era: A Social and Political History of American Finance, 1865–1879* (Princeton: Princeton University Press, 1964), *passim,* esp. 27–28, 120–26, 237–38, 362–63.

39. New York *Times,* June 21, Oct. 14, 1896; New York *Tribune,* Oct. 29, 1896; Bryan, *ibid.,* 469–71, 475; and the following letters to Bryan: from John W. Cochran, Nov. 4, 1896; from James W. Meers, Nov. 8, 1896; from Charles Henry, Nov. 5, 1896; from Alba Satterthwaite, Nov. 8, 1896; from James L. Tibbetts, Nov. 5, 1896, all in Bryan Papers.

40. New York *Times,* May 18, 23, June 5, 16, Aug. 22, Oct. 1, 16, 18, 24, 1896; New York *Tribune,* Aug. 2, 4, 1896; New York *Journal,* Oct. 19, Nov. 1, 1896; Newark *Daily Advertiser,* Aug. 31, Oct. 26, 1896; letter of Gilbert Gardner to William Jennings Bryan, Nov. 9, 1896, in Bryan Papers.

William Steinway, Carl Schurz, Oswald Ottendorfer, Jacob H. Schiff, Theodore Sutro, and Gustav H. Schwab were among the founders of the German-American Sound-Money League. The German-American Reform Union, declaring itself to be a civic reform organization, did not take a stand on the presidential campaign.

On German opposition to inflation during the currency controversy of the 1870s, see Unger, *op. cit.,* 134–35 (note 72), 276, 282–83; New York *Times,* May 14, 1896.

41. See, for example, letter of John Berwald to Grover Cleveland, July 18, 1896; letter of T. J. Mead to Grover Cleveland, Aug. 1, 1896, both in Cleveland Papers; letter of Washington Hesing to William McKinley,

July 25, 1896; letter of N. B. Scott to William McKinley, Sept. 7, 1896; letter of Joe J. Irwin to Moses P. Handy, July 25, 1896, all in McKinley Papers; New York *Tribune,* Aug. 1, Sept. 3, Oct. 15, 1896.

The Republican National Committee chose Julius Goldschmidt of Milwaukee to coordinate campaigns among ethnic groups largely because he was prominent in the German community. Letter of Frederick W. Holls to Mark Hanna, June 27, 1896, in Holls Papers; Hartford *Courant,* Nov. 2, 1896.

42. Bryan, *op. cit.,* 362–65, 380–83, 485–86, 571, 596–97, 617–18; New York *Journal,* Oct. 13, 31, 1896; New York *Times,* Oct. 20, 22, 24, 28, Nov. 6, 1896; New York *Tribune,* Oct. 3, 17, 20, 22, 24, 28, 31, Nov. 6, 14, 1896; also numerous letters in the Bryan Papers.

   On fraud and vote buying, see New York *Times,* Nov. 6, 1896; also numerous letters in the Bryan Papers.

43. Josephson, *op. cit.,* 701–06; Foner, *History of the Labor Movement, op. cit.,* II, 339–41; James A. Barnes, "Myths of the Bryan Campaign," *Mississippi Valley Historical Review,* XXXIV (December 1947), 399–402.

   Recent accounts have been more judicious. See Glad, *op. cit.,* 172–73; Jones, *op. cit.,* 339.

44. New York *Journal,* Oct. 11, Nov. 2, 1896; New York *Tribune,* Aug. 4, 5, 14, 17, 22, Nov. 5, 16, 1896; New Haven *Register,* Aug. 10, 14, 20, 21, Oct. 26, 30, 1896; Hartford *Courant,* Aug. 22, Nov. 5, 1896; also numerous letters in the Beer Papers.

   A poll of Brooklyn factory employees reported the office force dividing 86.3% for McKinley, 7.8% for Bryan, and 5.9% for Palmer, and the laborers dividing 41.3%, 58.7%, and 0.0% for the respective candidates. Though differences between the two groups were striking, the poll did not indicate the religious, ethnic, or political identifications of respondents. As a consequence, one cannot identify factors contributing to those differences. New York *Times,* Oct. 29, 1896.

45. New York *Tribune,* Nov. 1, 1896; Hartford *Courant,* July 18, 1896; New York *Times,* July 20, 1896.

46. See above, p. 7 (esp. Note 3); Degler, "American Political Parties," *loc. cit.,* 48 (note 22).

47. For Bryan's speeches, see Bryan, *op. cit., passim,* esp. 350. Kleppner, *The Cross of Culture, op. cit.,* 347–51, offers a thoughtful analysis of McKinley.

48. Jones, *op. cit.,* 169–70; Kinzer, *An Episode in Anti-Catholicism, op. cit.,* chap. vii, esp. 222–24; King, *Facing the Twentieth Century, op. cit.,* 263–68.

49. Bryan, *op. cit.,* 592–93; Kinzer, *ibid.,* 214–17, 224–29; King, *ibid.,* 245.

50. Compare the Republican national platform temperance planks of 1888, 1892, and 1896. *Tribune Almanacs, 1889,* 22; *1893,* 33; *1897,* 22.

   On the Populists and Prohibitionists, see Jones, *op. cit.,* chaps. xv, xviii, xxii; also the New York *Times,* July 24, 1896, for an exchange over

German views on prohibition and free silver at the convention of the National Silver party, which supported Bryan. For reports of drys supporting Bryan in the Northeast, see letter of P. J. Quinn to David B. Hill, Aug. 31, 1896, in Hill Papers; letter of R. E. Bisbee to George Fred Williams, July 27, 1896, in Russell Papers.

51. On the Raines Act, see New York *Times,* Jan.-April, 1896; New York *Tribune,* Jan.-April, 1896; *Tribune Almanac, 1897,* 79–80; letters of Frederick W. Holls to Charles Z. Lincoln, Feb. 21, March 16, 1896; and to William Cary Sanger, March 11, 18, 1896, all in Holls Papers; letter of Otto Kempner to David B. Hill, March 31, 1896, in Hill Papers; letter of Ashley W. Cole to Thomas C. Platt, March 9, 1896; letter of Levi P. Morton to Thomas C. Platt, March 20, 1896, both in Morton Papers.
52. Edward Flower, Anti-Semitism in the Free Silver and Populist Movements and the Election of 1896 (unpublished Master's thesis, Dept. of History, Columbia University, 1952). For divergent views of and references to the secondary literature on the subjects treated in this section, see Norman Pollack, Oscar Handlin, Irwin Unger, and J. Rogers Hollingsworth, "Papers on Populism," *Agricultural History,* XXXIX (April 1965), 59–85.
53. New York *Tribune,* Aug. 4, 1896; New York *Sun,* July 23, 1896, quoted in *Menorah* (New York), XXI (August 1896), 102; *Menorah,* XXI (November 1896), 357; *Jewish Messenger* (New York), Aug. 21, 1896; New York *Times,* Aug. 11, Oct. 28, 1896; Bryan, *op. cit.,* 580–82; letter of S. J. Klauber to William Jennings Bryan, Oct. 29, 1896, in Bryan Papers.

    For an earlier criticism of Jews by Mrs. Lease, see Hartford *Courant,* March 2, 1894.
54. New York *Times,* Sept. 15, 1896; New York *Sun,* Sept. 16, 1896; Flower, *op. cit.,* 31–33. On Europe, see P. G. J. Pulzer, *The Rise of Political Anti-Semitism in Germany and Austria* (New York: John Wiley, 1964). Unger, *op. cit.,* 210–12, 339–40, reports anti-Semitism in the earlier Greenback movement.
55. C. Vann Woodward, *loc. cit.,* 64–66; also numerous letters in the Bryan Papers.

    Letter of Sigourney Butler to Richard Olney, Jan. 29, 1896, in Richard Olney Papers (Library of Congress, Washington, D.C.), cited hereafter as Olney Papers; New York *World,* n.d., referred to in Nevins, *op. cit.,* 665; Newark *Daily Advertiser,* March 17, 1893.

    Arthur F. Beringause, *Brooks Adams: A Biography* (New York: Knopf, 1955), 146–53; letter of Theodore Roosevelt to Anna Roosevelt Cowles, Nov. 13, 1896, quoted in Morison (ed.), *Letters of Theodore Roosevelt, op. cit.,* I, 566.
56. See above, Chap. IV; John Higham, "Anti-Semitism in the Gilded Age: A Reinterpretation," *Mississippi Valley Historical Review,* XLIII (March 1957), *passim;* Newark *Daily Advertiser,* Jan. 19, May 4, 1895; Brooklyn *Daily Eagle,* March 18, 1896.
57. Svend Petersen, *A Statistical History of the American Presidential Elec-*

tions (New York: Frederick Ungar, 1963), 62–65. On the Midwest, see Kleppner, *op. cit.*, chaps. vii, viii.

Bryan received one electoral vote each in Kentucky and California.

58. Petersen, *ibid.*, 65; Jones, *op. cit.*, 273; also see Appendix D.
59. Burnham, *Presidential Ballots, op. cit.*, 156; also see Appendix E. Percentage point shifts in the three states were:

STATE	REP. + POINTS	DEM. — POINTS	DEM. DEFECTION RATIO
Connecticut	16.4	17.6	35.1
New York	12.0	10.3	21.0
New Jersey	13.5	14.7	29.0

60. In 1894, New Haven percentage point shifts had been: Dem. −10.8; Rep. +9.5. In 1896, mean percentage point shifts in Wards 3–7, 9, 10, and 12 were: Dem. −3.0; Rep. +3.0.

    Sources of ward-level election returns do not report the SLP vote (1.7%) in the presidential election. Given the narrow range of (a) percentage shifts; and (b) differences between percentages in the presidential and gubernatorial elections in New Haven, reliance on the incomplete returns would be ill-advised. My analysis is based on the gubernatorial vote, but I have also studied the presidential vote.
61. Percentage shifts in Wards 8, 13, and 15 were: ($\overline{M}$) Dem. −8.8; ($\overline{M}$) Rep. +4.8; in Ward 1 they were −16.4 and +7.2, respectively.

    On the Yale incident, see Bryan, *op. cit.*, 484–88; New York *Times*, Sept. 25, 26, 27, 28, Oct. 3, 1896. Many Yale students had won the right to vote in New Haven. See New York *Herald*, Nov. 1, 1896 (copy provided by Fred Heath). Yale was not the only northeastern upper class school whose students rejected Bryan. At St. Paul's School, Concord, New Hampshire, a poll gave Bryan 4.9% of the vote to 81.0% for McKinley and 14.2% for Palmer. Polls taken there in 1884, 1888, and 1892 had given Grover Cleveland 42.6, 34.9, and 36.7% support. See Arthur S. Pier, *St. Paul's School: 1855–1934* (New York: Scribner's, 1934), 180–81.
62. Correlations among (A) Democratic and (B) Republican percentage point shifts and (C) Gold Democratic percentage strength were: A-B, +.772; A-C, +.518; and B-C, −.007.
63. Percentage point shifts and percentage strengths in the two cities were:

WATERBURY	1894	1896	1896	BRIDGEPORT	1894	1896	1896
Rep.	+ 9.1	+5.9	55.8%	Rep.	+8.0	+7.9	57.9%
Dem.	−10.1	−5.7	41.0%	Dem.	−9.2	−8.0	39.7%

Ward-level correlations between percentage foreign-born plus native-born of foreign parentage and Democratic, Socialist Labor, Republican, and National Democratic percentage strengths in Bridgeport were: +.601, +.399, −.601, and −.685. The redistricting of both cities prevents correlations between 1894 and 1896 returns; the lack of census data on Waterbury precludes correlations with 1896 returns. Election data derive from Waterbury *American,* Nov. 4, 1896, and Bridgeport *Farmer,* Nov. 4, 1896 (copies provided by Fred Heath).

64. Bryan, *op. cit.,* 488–89; New York *Tribune,* July 19, 1896; Hartford *Courant,* Nov. 4, 1896.

    Ward-level correlations between first- and second-generation Americans and Democratic, Socialist Labor, Republican, and National Democratic percentage strengths were: +.809, +.667, −.806, and +.006.

65. Mean party strengths in Wards 1, 2, 3, and 4 were: Rep. 79.3%, Dem. 16.2%; in Wards 5 and 6, they were 39.6% and 57.2%, respectively. Election data from New Britain *Record,* Nov. 4, 1896 (copy provided by Fred Heath).

66. Seymour M. Lipset, "Religion and Politics," *loc. cit.,* 86–87, refines V. O. Key's data on Massachusetts to establish that the severity of Democratic percentage losses, 1892–96, varied inversely with the population of towns in that state.

67. Bryan received 50.9% in Naugatuck, 61.1% in Newtown, and 51.0% in New Fairfield, losing 4.4, 13.9, and 10.1 percentage points in the three towns. Naugatuck and Newtown had large immigrant populations; the Irish were particularly numerous in Newtown; New Fairfield was an old-stock American town.

    Compare Democratic percentage point shifts in the following towns:

TOWN	1894	1896	TOWN	1894	1896	TOWN	1894	1896
Manchester	−13.1	+1.3	Thompson	−15.0	− 5.1	Stafford	−11.9	−18.1
Killingly	−11.6	−2.9	Windham	− 2.3	− 9.4	Vernon	−10.8	−15.7
Plainfield	−15.4	−5.6	Putnam	− 8.1	−13.3			

    McKinley gained 2.3 percentage points in Manchester.

68. Letter of Lynde Harrison to David B. Hill, Sept. 3, 1896, in Hill Papers. Compare, for example, percentage point shifts in the following Connecticut towns:

TOWN	REP.	DEM.	TOWN	REP.	DEM.	TOWN	REP.	DEM.
Franklin	− 0.9	+ 4.1	Monroe	+17.6	−24.1	E. Granby	+18.7	−29.8
Bethlehem	− 7.2	+ 3.8	Oxford	+21.1	−30.7	Granby	+12.9	−27.0
Warren	− 7.4	+ 3.1	Prospect	+16.7	−24.9	Ashford	+23.2	−26.9
Andover	− 4.0	+ 2.7	Woodbridge	+16.9	−24.2	Eastford	+16.2	−24.6
Sterling	− 8.9	+ 7.5	Bridgewater	+24.9	−39.0	Pomfret	+20.7	−27.4
Easton	+15.7	−26.3	Canton	+17.6	−32.3	Union	+29.5	−26.9

69. Palmer received 10% of the vote or more in Avon, Bolton, Bridgewater, Granby, Kent, Mansfield, Morris, Newington, Old Saybrook, Oxford, Salisbury, Somers, Union, and Wolcott, outpolling Bryan in Granby, Ox-

ford, Somers, and Union, as well as West Hartford, where he did not poll 10% of the vote. Mean Democratic strength in these towns was 15.8%, National Democratic strength 12.6%. Bryan received no votes in Union, where Palmer polled 15.8% of the vote.

70. In Bolton, Bridgewater, Chaplin, Mansfield, Newington, and Watertown, the mean strength of National Democratic legislative candidates was 46.0%; the mean strengths of Bryan (20.3%) and Palmer (11.7%) combined, only 32.0%.

71. Of registered voters, 92.2% voted in 1892, 86.6% in 1896, and 86.7% in 1900. Registration rose less between 1894 and 1896—7.4%—than between 1890 and 1892 or between 1898 and 1900, 9.1% and 8.6%, respectively.

On New England, see Key, "A Theory of Critical Elections," *loc. cit.*, 16–17 (note 14). Burnham, "Changing Shape of the American Political Universe," *loc. cit.*, 16 (note 26) provides data on Indiana, Iowa, and Kentucky.

72. Mean major party percentage point shifts, party percentages, and the Democratic defection ratio (Dem. DR) in A.D.s 1, 2, 3, 6, 7, 9, 11, 13, 15, and 17 were:

REP. +	REP. %	DEM. −	DEM. DR	DEM. %	NAT. DEM. %	SLP %
8.4	42.3	8.2	13.0	54.8	1.1	1.5

Bryan carried these A.D.s, receiving majorities in all but the 9th, which he carried by three votes.

73. Mean major party percentage point shifts, party percentages, and the Democratic defection ratio (Dem. DR) in A.D.s 4, 8, 10, 12, 14, and 16 were:

REP. +	REP. %	DEM. −	DEM. DR	DEM. %	NAT. DEM. %	SLP %
11.7	43.2	9.9	18.1	45.1	1.0	10.6

Bryan received majorities in A.D.s 4 and 14; he also carried A.D. 12. He lost A.D. 16 by 0.3 percentage points.

74. Mean major party percentage point shifts, party percentages, and the Democratic defection ratio (Dem. DR) in A.D.s 22, 24, 26, 28, 30, and 32–34 were:

REP. +	REP. %	DEM. −	DEM. DR	DEM. %	NAT. DEM. %	SLP %
11.5	46.5	11.5	19.5	47.4	1.6	4.4

Bryan carried A.D.s 22, 24, 26, 28, and 32, all but A.D. 22 by pluralities.

75. Mean major party percentage point shifts, party percentages, and the Democratic defection ratio (Dem. DR) in A.D.s 5, 19, 21, 23, 25, 27, 29, and 31 were:

REP. +	REP. %	DEM. −	DEM. DR	DEM. %	NAT. DEM. %	SLP %
15.7	68.4	17.9	39.5	27.8	3.0	0.6

The silk-stocking 29th A.D. ranked first in Republican strength (78.9%), National Democratic strength (3.7%), Republican percentage point gain (27.6), Democratic percentage point loss (30.7), and Democratic defection ratio (64.6); and last in Democratic strength (16.8%). The Republicans easily carried all eight A.D.s.

76. Cf. above, pp. 198–200, and Benson, "Research Problems in American Political Historiography," *loc. cit.*, 171, with Foner, *op. cit.*, II, 341–42, and Jones, *op. cit.*, 344–45, which base their analyses on William Diamond, "Urban and Rural Voting in 1896," *American Historical Review*, XLVI (January 1941), 281–305.

    The measure of correlation in all correlations except that between 1893 Republican shifts and the anti-Maynard vote is Kendall's tau.

77. Compare Democratic percentage losses, defection ratios, and percentage strengths in such wards:

WARD	D. −	DEM. DR	D. %	WARD	D. −	DEM. DR	D. %	WARD	D. −	DEM. DR	D. %
2	9.8	12.2	70.5	9	16.6	28.4	41.9	14	3.5	5.0	66.5
5	6.9	9.3	67.4	10	12.1	17.5	56.9	17	2.8	5.5	47.9
6	13.5	19.7	55.2	12	4.2	5.7	70.1	$\overline{M}$	8.7	12.9	59.6

Bryan lost Ward 17 by 0.5 points. The National Democrats' mean vote in these wards was 1.4%, while the Socialist Laborites' vote was 1.0%.

78. Mean major party percentage point shifts, party percentages, and the Democratic defection ratio in Wards 16, 18, 21, 26, 27, and 28 were:

REP. +	REP. %	DEM. −	DEM. DR	DEM. %	NAT. DEM. %	SLP %
8.8	55.3	6.5	14.9	38.4	1.2	5.0

Bryan carried only Ward 18. It will be noted that the Democrats were weaker to begin with in Brooklyn's German wards than they were in New York City's German A.D.s. Bryan may have suffered comparatively light losses in Brooklyn's German wards because weak Democratic identifiers had already abandoned the party.

In Ward 26, E.D. 2, an East European Jewish enclave, the Republican state ticket won 57.5% of the vote, the Democrats 24.8%, and Socialist Labor 17.8%. Respective percentage point shifts were: +4.0, +5.4, −8.9. No all-party breakdown of the presidential vote is available for E.D.s in Brooklyn.

79. Mean major party percentage point shifts, party percentages, and the Democratic defection ratio in Wards 1, 3, 7, 20, 23, 25, 30, and 32 were:

REP. +	REP. %	DEM. −	DEM. DR	DEM. %	NAT. DEM. %	SLP %
13.3	66.7	15.2	34.3	29.6	3.0	0.5

The Republicans easily carried all eight wards.

80. Democratic percentage point losses, defection ratios, and percentages; and National Democratic percentages were:

COUNTY	D. −	DEM. DR	D. %	ND %	COUNTY	D. −	DEM. DR	D. %	ND %
Queens	13.1	26.1	37.2	2.0	Suffolk	9.5	25.7	27.5	2.6
Richmond	13.6	25.5	39.8	2.6	Westchester	8.5	19.0	36.2	2.0
Rockland	7.9	16.7	39.4	2.0					

81. Benson, *The Concept of Jacksonian Democracy, op. cit.*, chap. viii, treats Democratic-Whig differences during the 1840s. Also see New York *Sun*, Dec. 27, 1894 (New York Public Library Scrapbooks).

Eastern New York towns in which Baptists were numerous among the New Englanders were often not as strongly Republican as those in which Congregationalists, Presbyterians, and Methodists predominated. Baptists had supported the party of Jefferson against the Federalist party and the established Congregational Church in early-nineteenth-century Connecticut and Massachusetts. Their later support for the Democratic party had diminished as Catholics became identified with the Democracy, but many still voted Democratic.

82. Democratic percentages and Democratic and Republican percentage point shifts in these cities and towns were:

CITY	DEM. %	DEM. ±	REP. ±	TOWNS	DEM. %	DEM. ±	REP. ±
Albany	45.7	− 7.1	+6.0	Albany Co.	39.2	+2.7	−3.5
Troy	53.2	− 4.7	+4.0	Rensselaer Co.	33.6	−5.6	+5.0
Syracuse	36.3	−10.3	+9.6	Onondaga Co.	33.0	−2.6	+1.8

Town-level, all-party presidential election returns from New York State were unavailable to the writer. Unless otherwise noted, comparisons were drawn between a three-party 1895 vote (Democrat, Republican, Populist) and a four-party, three-candidate 1896 vote (Democrat-Populist, Republican, National Democrat). For purposes of analysis, the all-party 1895 vote was also compared with the all-party 1896 gubernatorial vote.

83. Bryan trailed the Democratic state ticket by 5.4 percentage points in Syracuse and by 1.3 percentage points in Onondaga County towns.

84. Percentage point shifts, 1895–96, and 1896 percentages in these towns were:

TOWN	REP. ± (%)	DEM.-POP. ± (%)	PRO. ± (%)	NAT. DEM. %
Clermont	+10.0 (45.4)	−13.3 (50.7)	−0.1 (0.5)	3.4
Kinderhook	+14.1 (55.9)	−16.8 (41.0)	— (0.5)	2.6
Stuyvesant	+12.2 (57.7)	−14.3 (39.4)	−0.6 (0.2)	2.6
Germantown	− 8.3 (51.7)	+ 9.9 (42.9)	−2.3 (4.6)	0.7

Percentage point shifts and percentages in towns that had received large numbers of German immigrants during the nineteenth century ranged from slightly below average to well above average:

UNIT	REP. ± (%)	DEM.-POP. ± (%)	PRO. ± (%)	NAT. DEM. %
Fulton County	+ 4.0 (61.9)	− 4.2 (32.7)	−0.9 (3.3)	1.4
Bleecker	+ 4.4 (34.6)	− 2.5 (63.7)	−2.4 (0.5)	1.1
Sullivan County	+ 3.6 (57.9)	− 3.1 (39.6)	−1.3 (1.3)	1.0
Callicoon	+ 7.9 (43.5)	−10.5 (53.5)	— (0.0)	2.5
Cohecton	+ 0.7 (42.7)	− 2.3 (52.1)	−0.9 (1.9)	2.2
Delaware	+ 1.8 (36.0)	− 2.4 (62.0)	−0.7 (0.7)	1.2
Fremont	+ 3.5 (53.0)	− 4.4 (44.0)	−1.0 (0.8)	1.8
Tusten	+18.7 (47.6)	−21.8 (48.9)	−0.4 (0.0)	3.5

The 1896 gubernatorial vote has been presented above to permit an all-party comparison of returns. The 1895 People's and Democratic parties' votes have been combined to facilitate comparison with 1896 returns. Bleecker was the only town in which Bryan did not trail the Democratic state ticket.

85. Compare, for example, voting patterns in towns where the Prohibition party had received over 10% of the vote in 1895:

TOWN (COUNTY)	REP. ± (%)	DEM. ± (%)	PRO. ± (%)	POP. ± (%)
Pawling (Dutchess)	+ 7.2 (60.1)	− 3.3 (31.0)	−6.5 (6.3)	+0.7 (0.7)
Stanford (Dutchess)	+ 3.7 (52.0)	− 2.5 (38.3)	−2.8 (7.9)	+0.2 (0.2)
Windham (Greene)	+ 5.0 (50.6)	+ 0.3 (43.4)	−5.1 (5.6)	−0.3 (0.2)
Georgetown (Madison)	+ 0.4 (76.1)	+ 8.1 (20.2)	−7.8 (2.9)	−1.0 (0.4)
Remsen (Oneida)	+ 4.0 (73.6)	− 1.8 (17.4)	−4.4 (6.4)	+0.6 (1.0)
Spafford (Onondaga)	− 0.8 (66.9)	+10.9 (31.9)	−9.1 (1.2)	−1.0 (0.0)
Corinth (Saratoga)	+ 7.2 (70.1)	− 3.9 (19.7)	−4.3 (8.7)	−0.4 (0.0)
Luzerne (Warren)	+ 9.6 (72.9)	− 1.4 (19.6)	−7.3 (7.0)	−1.3 (0.0)
Putnam (Washington)	+ 5.8 (79.4)	− 3.5 (7.2)	−2.7 (11.3)	+0.3 (2.0)
Scarsdale (Westchester)	+19.7 (78.2)	−16.1 (14.8)	−8.5 (2.1)	— (0.0)

Remsen was a Welsh town, Putnam an old Scots town; New Englanders predominated in most of the other towns. Pawling, Stanford, and Scarsdale contained settlements of Friends. The Democratic and Populist columns have not been combined above.

86. Cross, *The Burned-Over District, op. cit., passim;* Benson, The New York Farmers' Rejection of Populism, *op. cit., passim;* various volumes in the "Economic Study of Land Utilization" series.

Among eastern New York counties, Washington had ranked highest (16th) in the state in Prohibitionist-Populist strength (1892), but even there Bryan lost (−0.8) and McKinley gained (+0.9) fractionally.

87. The Prohibitionists polled over 5% of the vote in 22 counties in 1893, in 3 in 1894, and in 11 in 1895; the Populists polled over 5% in 5, 2, and 2 counties in those years. State-wide percentages (see Appendix E), which include the two parties' weak showing in populous urban counties, conceal their strength in lightly populated rural counties. The Democrats' over-all rural loss in 1894 should not be permitted to obscure their slight gains in many rural counties.

88. Percentage point shifts, 1895–96, in the six ranking counties were:

COUNTY	DEM.	REP.	PRO.	POP.	COUNTY	DEM.	REP.	PRO.	POP.
Cattaraugus	+12.2	−4.8	−3.0	−4.6	Chautauqua	+8.4	−2.4	−3.4	−2.9
Yates	+10.4	−3.2	−2.2	−5.2	Livingston	+7.8	−3.8	−2.2	−2.0
Allegany	+ 9.8	+1.4	−5.0	−6.8	Wyoming	+7.5	−3.7	−1.9	−2.7

89. Note, for example, voting patterns in selected towns:

TOWN (COUNTY)	REP. ± (%)	DEM. ± (%)	POP. ± (%)	PRO. ± (%)
Ward (Allegany)	+ 2.7 (30.0)	+17.1 (49.3)	−13.9 (16.7)	−6.6 (3.3)
Cold Spring (Cattaraugus)	− 7.7 (42.6)	+30.6 (56.7)	−20.4 (0.0)	−2.4 (0.8)
Elko (Cattaraugus)	— (54.4)	+28.1 (45.6)	−24.6 (0.0)	−3.5 (0.0)
Lyndon (Cattaraugus)	−11.5 (58.0)	+32.8 (40.4)	−21.9 (0.0)	— (1.0)
Bristol (Ontario)	− 8.4 (53.0)	+21.0 (42.5)	−13.9 (0.0)	−0.8 (2.2)
Bennington (Wyoming)	− 4.1 (38.7)	+24.7 (60.3)	−19.8 (0.0)	−1.2 (0.2)

Some Populists supported fusion by voting the Democratic line, others (as in the town of Ward, above) the Populist line. In Caneadea (Allegany County), however, Democrats moved into the Populist camp. The Democracy polled 0.8%, a loss of 25.6 percentage points; the People's party 32.1%, a gain of 28.1 points.

90. Compare, for example, voting patterns in selected towns:

TOWN (COUNTY)	REP. ± (%)	DEM. ± (%)	PRO. ± (%)	POP. ± (%)
Bolivar (Allegany)	+ 3.8 (46.5)	+ 5.1 (35.8)	− 4.7 (7.9)	− 4.6 (9.1)
New Hudson (Allegany)	− 9.7 (60.8)	+23.6 (33.0)	− 9.2 (5.5)	− 4.7 (0.7)
French Creek (Chautauqua)	− 9.2 (60.6)	+27.6 (36.5)	− 5.2 (2.5)	−12.4 (0.0)
Hanover (Chautauqua)	+10.9 (61.1)	+ 1.2 (33.2)	−10.2 (3.5)	− 3.6 (0.3)
Rush (Monroe)	− 3.3 (49.3)	+19.9 (47.5)	− 8.4 (2.8)	− 8.6 (0.0)
Farmersville (Cattaraugus)	+ 4.6 (63.2)	+15.8 (33.0)	− 7.6 (3.9)	−11.5 (0.0)

91. Compare, for example, voting patterns in selected towns:

TOWN (COUNTY)	REP. ± (%)	DEM. ± (%)	PRO. ± (%)	POP. ± (%)
Grove (Allegany)	− 9.3 (63.3)	+10.7 (34.4)	−0.5 (0.0)	−0.4 (2.3)
West Almond (Allegany)	+21.1 (51.5)	−11.0 (28.1)	−8.5 (11.1)	−2.7 (8.2)
Livonia (Livingston)	− 8.3 (52.3)	+13.2 (43.8)	−3.7 (3.1)	−1.5 (0.5)
Portage (Livingston)	+ 5.3 (65.4)	− 1.3 (30.8)	−4.3 (3.2)	−0.1 (0.3)
Clarkson (Monroe)	− 7.7 (52.2)	+12.8 (46.0)	−2.0 (1.6)	−3.3 (0.0)
Caton (Steuben)	+ 7.7 (76.9)	− 0.2 (16.8)	−7.7 (5.7)	−0.4 (0.0)

92. Returns from Busti and Carroll, Swedish-Yankee farming towns in Chautauqua County, illustrate differences in voting shifts between towns in which 1895 Democratic strength was comparable but in which the strength of other parties was not. The Democrats were more successful in Busti, where the Populists and Prohibitionists had had considerable support, than in Carroll, where the Republicans had accounted for a larger share of the opposition vote.

TOWN		REP. % (±)	DEM. % (±)	POP. % (±)	PRO. % (±)
Busti	1895	69.1	11.3	10.4	8.9
	1896	64.2 (−4.9)	23.0 (+11.7)	8.8 (−1.6)	1.9 (−7.0)
Carroll	1895	84.7	9.2	1.3	4.7
	1896	86.3 (+1.6)	11.6 (+ 2.4)	0.2 (−1.1)	1.6 (−3.1)

93. Percentage point shifts in these counties were:

COUNTY	D, '92–'95	D, '95–'96	D, '92–'96	R, '92–'95	R, '95–'96	R, '92–'96
Allegany	− 4.7	+ 9.8	+5.1	+ 8.0	+1.4	+9.4
Cattaraugus	−12.0	+12.2	+0.2	+10.8	−4.8	+6.0
Livingston	− 5.6	+ 7.8	+2.2	+ 6.9	−3.8	+3.1
Schuyler	+ 0.3	+ 1.5	+1.8	+ 1.8	+2.7	+4.5
Yates	− 4.6	+10.4	+5.8	+ 7.9	−3.2	+4.7

In many towns 1896 Democratic percentages exceeded 1892 marks, but in some of these Republican percentages also did. There were also many towns in which marked Democratic recoveries could not erase the losses of 1893–95.

94. Percentage point shifts, 1895–96, in these six counties were:

COUNTY	REP.	DEM.	PRO.	POP.	COUNTY	REP.	DEM.	PRO.	POP.
Clinton	−2.8	+2.8	−0.4	−0.1	Lewis	+0.5	+1.0	−1.8	−0.1
Franklin	−0.9	+1.8	−1.2	−0.5	Oswego	+0.3	+1.7	−2.0	−0.4
Jefferson	+1.6	−0.2	−1.7	−0.2	St. Lawrence	−2.0	+4.2	−1.9	−0.6

Jefferson had ranked 26th in Prohibitionist strength among the state's counties in 1892 and 19th in 1895; Oswego 10th in Populist strength in 1892; and St. Lawrence 22nd (a six-way tie) in 1895. Clinton County did rank 5th in Republican percentage point loss in 1896, but no higher than 16th in Democratic gain.

95. Percentage point shifts, 1895–96, were:

CITY	REP. ±	DEM. ±	TOWNS	REP. ±	DEM. ±
Binghamton	+7.2	− 7.6	Broome Co.	−1.8	+1.9
Watertown	+4.5	− 5.5	Jefferson Co.	−1.2	+0.6
Elmira	+9.8	−10.3	Chemung Co.	+6.0	−5.7

96. Percentage point shifts, 1895–96, were:

CITY	REP. ±	DEM. ±	TOWNS	REP. ±	DEM. ±
Buffalo	−0.3	−0.7	Erie Co.	−3.1	+3.6
Rochester	+0.2	−1.0	Monroe Co.	−3.2	+4.2

The Democratic state ticket ran ahead of Bryan by 4.4 percentage points in Erie, by 2.1 in Monroe, and by 5.3 in Buffalo. The National Democrats polled 1.6% of the presidential vote in Buffalo and 2.8% of the gubernatorial vote. (Buffalo percentages are of the three-party vote.)

97. The Republican gain in Seneca County was based on comparable advances in four Democratic (1895: $\overline{M}$ Dem. 52.5%, $\overline{M}$ Rep. 44.2%) and six Republican (1895: $\overline{M}$ Rep. 53.1%, $\overline{M}$ Dem. 43.9%) towns. The Democrats' defection ratio was 3.6 in the former and 3.4 in the latter.
98. Percentage point shifts, 1895–96, and 1896 percentages were:

TOWN	REP. ± (%)	DEM. ± (%)	N.D. %	PRO. ± (%)	POP. ± (%)	SLP ± (%)
High Market	−8.1 (20.8)	+8.4 (78.6)	0.6	−0.9 (0.0)	− (0.0)	− (0.0)
Clinton	−0.7 (37.4)	+2.4 (60.9)	0.6	−0.6 (1.1)	− (0.0)	−1.7 (0.0)
Cape Vincent	−0.7 (43.1)	− (53.1)	2.2	−1.3 (1.6)	− (0.0)	−0.2 (0.0)
Cape Vincent (E.D.3)	−3.7 (13.8)	+3.7 (86.2)	0.0	− (0.0)	− (0.0)	− (0.0)

In 1892, Grover Cleveland had polled 68.1, 73.4, and 61.2% in the respective towns and 92.6% in E.D. 3 of Cape Vincent.

99. Percentage point shifts, 1895–96, and 1896 percentages were:

TOWN	REP. ± (%)	DEM. ± (%)	N.D. %	PRO. ± (%)	POP. ± (%)	SLP ± (%)
Lewis	− 5.7 (21.9)	+ 8.6 (77.3)	0.0	−2.9 (0.8)	− (0.0)	− (0.0)
Croghan	− 1.3 (51.3)	+ 1.7 (48.0)	0.3	−0.1 (0.3)	−0.5 (0.0)	−0.1 (0.1)
New Bremen	+ 0.4 (50.5)	− 0.4 (48.4)	0.6	−0.7 (0.4)	− (0.0)	− (0.0)
Wayland	− 7.9 (42.2)	+ 8.4 (54.2)	0.4	−0.5 (1.7)	−0.4 (1.4)	+0.1 (0.1)
Wayland (E.D.2)	−16.7 (36.1)	+14.5 (60.5)	0.3	+0.3 (0.3)	+1.6 (2.7)	− (0.0)
Wheat-field	+ 3.7 (53.1)	− 0.4 (42.4)	1.6	−2.1 (2.3)	−0.6 (0.0)	−2.3 (0.6)

In 1892, the Democracy had received 73.1, 53.8, 54.3, 50.0, and 53.4% in the respective towns.

100. Compare voting patterns in the following towns:

TOWN (COUNTY)	REP. ± (%)	DEM. ± (%)	PRO. ± (%)	POP. ± (%)
Maryland (Otsego)	+ 0.7 (48.2)	— (48.2)	−1.7 (2.3)	−0.3 (0.0)
Cayuta (Schuyler)	+ 1.9 (40.4)	+ 1.2 (56.8)	−3.0 (0.7)	−2.2 (0.0)
Middlefield (Otsego)	− 2.3 (44.2)	+ 3.9 (55.5)	−0.8 (0.2)	−0.4 (0.0)
Pinckney (Lewis)	+ 1.1 (45.2)	+ 2.6 (54.1)	−4.1 (0.4)	— (0.0)
Springfield (Otsego)	+ 6.5 (42.7)	−10.0 (53.1)	−0.1 (0.4)	−0.2 (0.0)
Baldwin (Chemung)	+10.5 (53.7)	−10.2 (41.3)	−1.3 (4.0)	+0.5 (0.5)

101. Percentage point shifts and percentages in these counties were:

	ESSEX	HUDSON	PASSAIC	UNION
Rep.	+10.4 (65.0%)	+10.0 (52.5%)	+5.1 (58.8%)	+ 9.2 (61.6%)
Dem.	−10.7 (31.3%)	−10.6 (43.9%)	−4.2 (35.4%)	−11.0 (31.9%)

102. Democratic percentages, percentage point shifts, and defection ratios were:

WARD	D. %	D. ±	DEM. DR	WARD	D. %	D. ±	DEM. DR	WARD	D. %	D. ±	DEM. DR
1	59.9	+2.4	X	5	56.4	− 6.9	10.9	8	26.1	−11.0	29.6
2	71.7	−7.0	8.9	7	33.8	−12.5	27.0	12	35.1	−15.4	30.5

City-wide, the Democrats received 45.2% of the vote, a loss of 8.1 percentage points. Their defection ratio was 15.2.

103. Democratic percentages, percentage point losses, and defection ratios (all two-party vote) in Ward 12 and its five districts were:

UNIT	DEM. %	DEM. −	DEM. DR	UNIT	DEM. %	DEM. −	DEM. DR
Ward 12	52.4	−13.2	20.1	Dist. 3	66.2	−10.1	13.2
Dist. 1	34.3	−17.5	33.8	Dist. 4	58.7	− 6.5	10.0
Dist. 2	69.3	−11.3	14.0	Dist. 5	35.7	−14.6	29.0

Districts 2, 3, and 4 were Irish, 1 and 5 German. City-wide, the Democrats received 34.6% of the vote, a loss of 11.4 percentage points. Their defection ratio was 24.8. On the campaign, see Newark *Daily Advertiser,* Oct. 10, 1896.

104. Democratic percentages and percentage point losses (both two-party vote) in five such communities in Essex County, and in Leonia in Bergen, were:

UNIT	DEM.	UNIT	DEM.	UNIT	DEM.
Bloomfield	22.4% (−10.4)	Glen Ridge	11.1% (−15.6)	Verona	25.8% (−20.5)
Caldwell	27.8% (− 7.2)	Montclair	18.5% (−18.5)	Leonia	20.0% (−13.6)

On politics in businessmen's communities, see Trenton *Daily True American,* Oct. 26, 1896.

105. Ward-level correlations between % Irish, % German, and % native-born males and Democratic percentage losses (1) and defection ratios (2) were:

GROUPS	JERSEY CITY (1)	JERSEY CITY (2)	NEWARK (1)	NEWARK (2)	ELIZABETH (1)	ELIZABETH (2)
Irish	−.538	−.573	−.044	−.626	−.573	−.713
German	+.238	+.245	+.008	−.485	−.259	−.455
Native-born	+.448	+.559	−.550	+.118	+.273	+.608

The second column is the more accurate barometer of shifts, particularly in the case of Newark where Democratic percentage point losses were heavier in Irish and German wards, in which the party had considerable support, than in old-stock American wards, in which it did not. The defection ratio was highest in old-stock American wards.

106. The coefficient of variability of Republican percentage strength in Camden's wards was unusually low (.029).

McKinley received 56.8% of the three-party vote in Paterson to Bryan's 38.8% and Matchett's 4.4%; the respective percentage point shifts were +5.3, −3.8, and −1.5. Republican ward-level gains correlated at +.905 with Democratic losses and −.190 with Socialist Labor losses. The Republicans received 69.0% of the vote in Passaic, the Democrats 30.2%, and Socialist Labor 0.8%; percentage point shifts were +8.1, −5.9, and −2.2. In Ward 3, an old-stock American district, McKinley polled 87.0% of the vote, Bryan only 13.0%; Matchett was shut out. Passaic County ranked highest in SLP percentage strength.

107. Percentage point shifts and percentages were:

COUNTY	REP.	DEM.
Atlantic	+8.0 (66.1%)	−7.9 (29.5%)
Cape May	+8.6 (65.5%)	−8.9 (28.5%)

108. On Hammonton, see Trenton *Daily True American,* Aug. 25, 1896.

Percentages and percentage point shifts in Hammonton and Buena Vista were:

TOWN	REP.	DEM.	NAT. DEM.	PRO.
Hammonton	67.0% (+6.1)	26.8% (−3.6)	1.5%	4.7% (−4.0)
Buena Vista	62.2% (+2.4)	35.6% (−3.9)	0.6%	1.6% (+0.8)

109. Percentages and percentage point shifts in the two towns were:

TOWN	REP.	DEM.	NAT. DEM.	PRO.
Galloway (Dist. 2)	47.7% (+12.7)	49.7% (−15.3)	2.6%	0.0% (—)
Somers Point	42.9% (+23.9)	50.0% (−31.0)	5.7%	1.4% (+1.4)

110. Percentages and percentage point shifts in the aforementioned towns were:

TOWN	REP. %	DEM. %	N.D. %	PRO. %	POP.	SLP %
Ocean City	71.8 (+12.0)	18.6 (− 6.9)	1.3	8.0 (−5.7)	(−1.0)	0.3 (+0.3)
Sea Isle City	56.7 (+18.2)	40.2 (−20.4)	1.6	1.6 (+0.6)	(—)	0.0 (—)
West Cape May	70.5 (+10.9)	21.5 (−12.0)	1.0	7.0 (+0.2)	(—)	0.0 (—)
Middle (1)	71.1 (+12.8)	24.9 (−14.6)	2.4	1.4 (−0.3)	(−0.3)	0.3 (—)
Upper	78.5 (+11.0)	13.3 (− 9.9)	1.1	6.8 (−0.5)	(−1.9)	0.3 (+0.3)
S. Cape May	100.0 (+25.0)	0.0 (−18.8)	0.0	0.0 (—)	(—)	0.0 (−6.3)
Dennis (1)	47.9 (− 1.5)	46.1 (+ 0.1)	1.1	2.1 (+0.8)	(−0.4)	2.8 (−0.1)
Dennis (2)	61.0 (+ 9.7)	31.8 (− 6.7)	0.5	6.3 (−1.7)	(−2.2)	0.5 (+0.5)

111. Percentages and percentage point shifts in these units were:

UNIT	REP. %	DEM. %	N.D. %	PRO. %	POP.
Pemberton (East)	51.2 (− 4.5)	45.4 (+ 6.3)	2.4	1.0 (−2.6)	(−1.6)
Pemberton (West)	51.7 (+ 0.4)	45.8 (+ 2.3)	0.5	2.0 (−2.7)	(−0.5)
Cinnaminson (1)	74.6 (+ 8.5)	22.6 (− 9.3)	0.7	2.1 (+0.9)	(−0.8)
Cinnaminson (2)	49.0 (+10.9)	45.9 (−13.1)	2.8	2.4 (−0.1)	(−0.4)
Palmyra	74.6 (+12.5)	18.2 (−14.6)	2.5	4.7 (—)	(−0.4)

A number of the units shifting toward the Republicans had given more support to the Populists than had Pemberton in 1895. On politics in Burlington County, see New York *Tribune,* Aug. 23, 1896; Newark *Daily Advertiser,* Oct. 22, 1896; and New York *Times,* Nov. 1, 1896.

112. In Riverside, the G.O.P. polled 57.3%, a gain of 14.9 percentage points; the Democrats 40.6%, a loss of 15.9; the Prohibitionists 1.2%, a gain of 0.1; and the National Democrats 0.9%. The Populists had received no votes in Riverside in 1895. Also see Newark *Daily Advertiser,* Oct. 26, 1896.

The great majority of towns and boroughs in Bergen and Hudson counties, where Germans were numerous, shifted, generally sharply, toward the G.O.P. in 1896.

113. For a general treatment of the subject, see George W. Luke, New Jersey Agriculture from 1850 to 1950: An Economic Analysis (unpublished Ph.D. dissertation, Dept. of Economics, New York University, 1956).

It should be noted that the Democrats fared relatively best in southern New Jersey in Cumberland County, the only New Jersey county in which the Populists ever polled 5.0% of the vote or more. Even there, they lost 0.2 percentage points as the G.O.P. gained 5.5 points.

114. Percentages and percentage point shifts in the three counties were:

COUNTY	REP. %	DEM. %	N.D. %	PRO. %	POP.	SLP %
Hunterdon	44.2 (+1.9)	51.8 (+1.0)	1.0	3.0 (−2.4)	(−1.2)	0.1 (−0.2)
Sussex	49.1 (+0.7)	48.0 (+0.2)	0.8	2.0 (−0.8)	(−0.7)	0.2 (−0.1)
Warren	42.8 (+0.9)	52.8 (+2.8)	0.7	3.6 (−3.4)	(−0.9)	0.2 (−0.1)

On the political outlook in the aforementioned counties, see Newark *Daily Advertiser,* Aug. 17, Sept. 24, 1896; Trenton *Daily True American,* July 14, Oct. 6, 26, 1896; New York *Tribune,* Nov. 2, 1896.

Bergen County shared with Hunterdon, Sussex, and Warren the distinction of having voted Democratic in every presidential election from 1836 through 1892. But unlike the other three counties, whose populations remained stable in their composition during the late nineteenth century, Bergen was transformed by the arrival of large numbers of German, Dutch, and other immigrants, and of businessmen and professionals from New York City and nearby New Jersey cities. Bergen voted Republican during 1893–96 and ranked second (a tie) in Republican percentage gain, first in Democratic percentage loss, and first in National Democratic percentage in 1896. The Gold Democrats received above-average support in diverse counties; their strength was not concentrated in one area, as in New York, or in rural towns, as in Connecticut.

115. Shifts favorable to the rival parties in towns in the three counties occurred as follows:

TOWNS/SHIFTS			HUNTERDON	SUSSEX	WARREN	TOTAL
Dem.	town:	Dem. +	11	6	10	27
Dem.	town:	Rep. +	8	2	7	17
Rep.	town:	Rep. +	3	6	3	12
Rep.	town:	Dem. +	2	3	2	7
Pro.	5%:	Dem. +	8	0	7	15
Pro.	5%:	Rep. +	6	1	5	12

In cases where both parties gained or lost, the town was assigned to the party faring better. The cities of Phillipsburg (Warren Co.) and Lambertville (Hunterdon Co.) were omitted from the tally, as was Newton, District 2, which fluctuated from 1892 through 1895 and witnessed virtually identical shifts by the major parties in 1896. In old Dutch towns. Bryan gained in Pahaquarry and Washington (Warren Co.), Sandyston (Sussex Co.), and Union (Hunterdon Co.); he lost in Walpack and Montague (Sussex Co.).

116. Bryan lost strength in Byram, Hardyston, Sparta, and Vernon; he gained strength in Andover.

Bryan gained 3.3 percentage points (two-party vote) in Phillipsburg and 5.4 points in Ward 4; he lost 5.7 percentage points in Lambertville and 1.7 points in Ward 1.

117. Differences between voting patterns in New York and in Connecticut and New Jersey can be seen in various county-level indicators. As already noted, correlations between 1894–95 and 1895–96 Republican and Democratic percentage point shifts in New York differed from those in Connecticut (1892–94 and 1894–96) and New Jersey (1894–95 and 1895–96). Further, the correlation between Democratic percentage shifts and Populist-Prohibitionist declines was stronger in New York (+.805, 1895–96) than in Connecticut (+.206, 1894–96) and New Jersey (+.441, 1895–96). Finally, Democratic percentage shifts in New York, involving as they did declines in Democratic counties and increases in some Republican ones, narrowed the dispersion of the Democratic vote. In the two other states, the reverse occurred. The relevant coefficients of variability were:

	CONNECTICUT		NEW YORK		NEW JERSEY	
	DEM.	REP.	DEM.	REP.	DEM.	REP.
1895*	.075	.075	.215	.123	.144	.086
1896	.200	.067	.133	.086	.214	.129

* Connecticut, 1894.

VII. CONCLUSIONS

1. If McKinley's strength sagged in the Northeast in 1900, Bryan's ebbed on the Plains and in the Rocky Mountains. Over-all, Bryan lost 1.2 percentage points; McKinley gained 0.7 points. See Petersen, *Statistical History of the American Presidential Elections, op. cit.*, 65–68.
2. In Connecticut, the Democrats gained and the Republicans lost percentage strength in all 8 counties. In New Jersey, the Democrats gained in 19 of 21 counties, and the Republicans lost in all 21.
3. In 1900, New York City and Brooklyn accounted for 42.5% of the Democrats' state-wide vote, a mark closer to the levels of 1892, 1893, and 1895 ($\overline{M}$=43.5%) than to those of 1894 and 1896 ($\overline{M}$=38.4%). State-wide, the Democrats gained in 50 of 59 counties; the Republicans lost in 48 counties and experienced no percentage shift in 1 county.

Index